OUR
ENDANGERED
RIGHTS

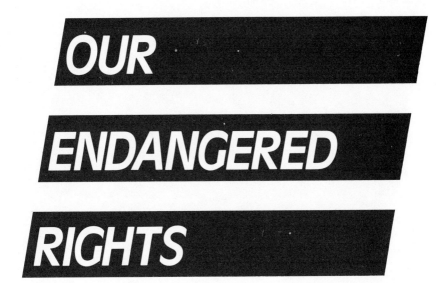

OUR

ENDANGERED

RIGHTS

*THE ACLU REPORT ON
CIVIL LIBERTIES TODAY*

*EDITED BY
NORMAN DORSEN*

*PANTHEON BOOKS
NEW YORK*

Copyright © 1984 by the American Civil Liberties Union

All rights reserved under International and Pan-American Copyright Conventions. Published in the United States by Pantheon Books, a division of Random House, Inc., New York, and simultaneously in Canada by Random House of Canada Limited, Toronto.

Library of Congress Cataloging in Publication Data
Main Entry under title:

Our endangered rights.

Includes index.
1. Civil rights—United States—Addresses, essays, lectures. I. Dorsen, Norman.
KF4749.A2093   1984   342.73'085   83–43146
ISBN 0–394–53261–9   347.30285
ISBN 0–394–72229–9 (pbk.)

Manufactured in the United States of America

First Edition

Book design by Iris Weinstein

This book is dedicated to the memory of Roger N. Baldwin, principal organizer and guiding spirit of the American Civil Liberties Union, on the 100th anniversary of his birth.

ACKNOWLEDGMENTS

I thank André Schiffrin for conceiving the idea of this volume, and for making Pantheon Books its natural publisher.

I thank Wendy Wolf for her insightful, efficient, and good-humored editing on a tight deadline.

I thank Betty Kranzdorf for her administrative and secretarial skills, which contributed so much to the final product.

—Norman Dorsen

CONTENTS

PART THREE: CHANGING CONCEPTS IN THE STRUGGLE FOR RIGHTS

INTRODUCTION

Orwell's symbolic year—1984—is an appropriate occasion to assess the state of individual freedom in the United States, and to provide informed perspectives on how we have come to this point and where we seem to be heading. Readers will soon appreciate that this does not involve a simple audit—one up or one down for civil liberty. The roots of our present state are tangled, and assessing the prospects for the future is a complex and subtle enterprise: a formidable task even for the acknowledged experts who have contributed to this volume.

"Endangered rights" well sums up the current situation. In this book's predecessor, *The Rights of Americans*,* another group of authors reviewed the state of American rights on the fiftieth anniversary of the American Civil Liberties Union in 1970. At that time the sweeping progress of the previous fifty years, spearheaded by the Supreme Court under Earl Warren, had come to a jarring halt. Our confident march seemed suddenly on the verge of disorderly retreat. Today we have lived through an era in which there have been some gains for civil liberties, but more losses. The Supreme Court has been unpredictable in the face of new, and in some ways unprecedented, pressures on civil liberties.

The good news is that in 1984 Americans, far more than most peoples, on the whole enjoy "rights": the liberty to express oneself, to guard one's privacy, and to receive fair and equal treatment at the hands of government as a matter of law and not at the whim and sufferance of officials high or low. Given the United States's size, cultural and ethnic variety, and stormy history at home and abroad, the fact that such guarantees have survived two hundred years is no small feat. Our national treasury of individual rights is a tribute to the sturdiness of the institutions created by the framers of the Constitution, and to the courage and common sense of the people and their leaders—particularly federal judges—over two centuries.

But there is a darker side. What we think of as the birthright of freedom for all Americans is continually under siege. And for many others the situation is even bleaker. Despite much progress in recent decades, it would be ingenuous to assert that racial minorities, homosexuals, and aliens share fully in the bounty of liberty that the rest of us enjoy. Women

*Norman Dorsen, ed. (New York: Pantheon Books, 1971).

and radical dissenters are also constrained, although perhaps less flagrantly. These are groups readily identifiable by common characteristics or circumstances. But there is another large group of people of diverse backgrounds for whom traditional constitutional rights are remote from daily problems of survival. These are the poor. In a society whose legal processes can befuddle even the most educated, poor people are frequently deprived of the minimal resources needed to exercise their rights in a free, democratic country. One must not exaggerate. Sensitivity to the special problems of ensuring justice has resulted in some institutional compensations for the disfavored. Nor do they live in a totalitarian society; the right to protest brings with it a degree of hope for change. But until economic status no longer plays such a dominant role in securing access to justice, the very poor will remain second-class Americans.

Even for the rest of us, the landscape is uneven, uncertain, and sometimes treacherous. Three traditional hazards imperil the rights of all Americans, joined now by a fourth and especially ominous development.

The first problem is the curse that has accompanied the rich diversity of America's racial, religious, and cultural heritages: bigotry. Not only racial minorities, but Irish, Scandinavians, Jews, Slavs, Italians and others, at one time or another, have felt the lash of prejudice. Today we have outlawed the obvious forms of preference and exclusion, but we have surely not eliminated them or seriously weakened the subtler techniques of discrimination. Since communal loyalties are still so prevalent in the United States, politicians with an eye to votes and glory are often tempted to appeal to some ethnic groups at the expense of others. These days it is usually a wink and a codeword rather than a more blatant message. The practice is recognizable in Washington and in our large polyglot cities. As Drew Days's essay explains, such attitudes perpetuate a stratification in our population that is inherently at odds with the security of equal status —and equal liberties—for all citizens.

Ethnic rivalry and discrimination heat up in times of economic stringency. This is our second problem as we confront 1984. The instability caused by high inflation, followed by mass unemployment, has strained the social order. Competition rises for jobs; venom is loosed; violence occasionally follows. Minorities pay the heaviest price. Other victims, once again, are the dependent poor, whose government benefits are increasingly resented. Entitlements to the powerless are among the first casualties in belt-tightening administrations. Throughout American history this has been the pattern in bad times.

The link between economics and civil liberties is complex. Economic independence obviously encourages the exercise of rights by providing a margin of safety in risk or protest. Indeed, it is now universally conceded that a degree of control over resources is a precondition to the exercise of civil liberties. One may also analyze the effect on liberties of such government policies as are reflected in the tax structure and in the allocation of scarce resources. Sylvia Law's essay widens our understanding of these relationships.

A third sure source of trouble for civil liberties is international tension. Hot and cold war alike strain the Bill of Rights, for a state threatened from without is rarely the best guardian of civil liberties within. Even liberal governments can feel pressed to mobilize the entire society in face of perceived danger, and they are usually not finicky about how to do it. That the process is familiar does not render it acceptable. As Morton Halperin shows, the deterioration of détente in the 1980s has led to unjustified draft registration, interference with peaceful demonstrations, widespread surveillance of Americans, travel bans, visa denials, secrecy orders, and censorship of former government officials. The peril is deepened by the apparent lack of limits to what a government may define as "national security." Most recently, the government's exclusion of the press from the Grenada invasion in October 1983, and its arrest and detention of several reporters who reached Grenada on their own, ran directly against the American tradition of a free press.

These three historic sources of constitutional instability are today compounded by the resurgence of a fourth—the excesses of religious fundamentalism. The issue is of course not Christianity, which is rooted in the humanitarianism and altruism of the Sermon on the Mount. It is rather the zealotry and insensitivity evinced by some of its modern leaders. Thus, the Moral Majority and its allies not only want their children to pray in school; they want everyone's to do so. They not only want to prevent fundamentalist women from choosing to seek an abortion; they want to keep every woman from this choice. They not only want their children to learn "scientific creationism" as an alternative to science; they want every child to learn it. They not only want to decide which books their children cannot read; they want to decide for the children of all. They not only want to spend their own money on church schools; they want everyone to be taxed for this purpose. It is sadly ironic, as Norman Redlich's essay explains, that such anti–civil libertarian attitudes are presented in the name of religion.

Unfortunately, it is not only fundamentalists who seem insensitive to the linking of religious belief to patriotism. When President Reagan was asked at a recent press conference to differentiate the United States from Communist regimes, he did not emphasize our belief in the Constitution and our tradition of individual liberty; he replied, "We believe in God." But the Supreme Court has long recognized that those who drafted our Constitution intended to protect unbelievers as well as believers. Arthur Schlesinger has correctly observed that "it is quite possible to detest communism without worshiping Mr. Reagan's God or indeed without worshiping any God at all." During the McCarthy period there was much talk of "atheistic communism," which effectively equated Americans who were atheists or agnostics with disloyalty. It is disturbing that President Reagan has revived this divisive formula.

The Reagan administration has also used the vast presidential power to promote the fundamentalist agenda at the expense of the Bill of Rights. Walter Lippmann noted in 1961 that "this is a most presidential country. The tone and example set by the president have a tremendous effect on the quality of life in America." If, as the *Federalist Papers* predicted, the courts were destined to be the "least dangerous branch" of the federal government, the presidency has turned out to be the most dangerous because it controls the apparatus of government and can use it to hurt people in so many ways. This is a principle theme of the essays by Paul Bender, Ira Glasser, and John Shattuck.

Let us be clear: Though we sharply criticize the Reagan administration's anti–civil liberties policies, this book is not a political tract directed at this president or at the Republican party. The ACLU is non-partisan, and it has never endorsed a candidate for elective office. Its task is to smite all officials, of whatever rank and party, who are faithless to their oath to uphold the Constitution. The ACLU has vigorously attacked every chief executive since Woodrow Wilson for policies that have infringed on civil liberties, and no doubt we shall oppose policies of future administrations. But it would be idle to deny that Ronald Reagan has led an especially widespread assault on American civil liberties. He has espoused an ostensibly conservative philosophy—dedicated to limited government, but curiously he has selected as a target the Bill of Rights, which was expressly designed to keep government off the backs of people.

In principle, "rights" or "civil liberties" are personal privileges that cannot be taken away, that do not rest on anyone's discretion, but rather are ours free and clear under the law, like title to a house with no mortgage and all taxes paid. Supreme Court Justice Robert Jackson, in classic cadences, expressed this conception in a 1943 decision that denied government power to coerce schoolchildren to salute the American flag:

> The very purpose of a Bill of Rights was to withdraw certain subjects from the vicissitudes of political controversy, to place them beyond the reach of majorities and officials and to establish them as legal principles to be applied by the courts. One's right to life, liberty, and property, to free speech, a free press, freedom of worship and assembly, and other fundamental rights may not be submitted to vote; they depend on the outcome of no elections.

But exercising these rights is not quite so simple. Justice Jackson leaves out a key factor in the calculus—that courts, staffed by independent judges dedicated to the Constitution, will be open and available to all people to protect their "rights." And in practice, whether or not they are open depends at least in part on elections and majorities. For majorities can elect presidents and senators with authority to appoint judges who lack dedication to the Bill of Rights, and large majorities can even amend the Constitution to weaken our liberties or erase them. Thus, despite the quip of Chief Justice Hughes that "the Constitution is what the judges say it is," in the long run the Constitution is what the people want it to be.

Judge Learned Hand made a similar point some years ago. He said:

> Liberty lies in the hearts of men and women; when it dies there, no constitution, no law, no court can save it; no constitution, no law, no court can even do much to help it.

But even that is an overstatement. Courts can indeed "help" liberty, as the Supreme Court proved so gloriously under Chief Justice Earl Warren and, more sporadically, throughout our history. But as Burt Neuborne demonstrates, courts cannot play their vital constitutional role if judges are timid. Timid judges betray the constitutional plan; they make a charade of the Bill of Rights; they threaten our heritage.

This means that judges must stand firmly on the principles that underlie the Constitution and Bill of Rights. These principles—free expression, equality, due process, and privacy—have their roots in the English charters of liberty, in the philosophy of the Enlightenment, and in the words of the wise Athenians who first gave them coherent expression.

At the center of these principles is an idea, stark in its simplicity but almost universally ignored throughout human history: the idea of consistency in the protection of human rights. Shortly before his death, Roger Baldwin reminded us of this truth:

> The test of the loyalty of the ACLU to its principles lies in the impartiality with which they are applied—there can be no favorites in defense of rights for all. This is a hard test to impose against natural sympathies and prejudices: [It is] even harder to defend the "thought we hate."

True to its traditions, the ACLU adhered to principle a few years ago when it defended the right of self-styled American "Nazis" to march peaceably in Skokie, Illinois. The ACLU had participated in hundreds of similar cases, including several on behalf of "Nazis." But the climate of the country had altered in a way that caused many to assail us. The fact that the demonstration was planned for a town populated by many survivors of Hitler's death camps partly explains this response. In the months following Skokie, the ACLU lost thousands of members and hundreds of thousands of dollars; at one stage the organization seemed in jeopardy.

But over time the Skokie case became a long-term asset for the ACLU. Americans who did not understand or care about the fine points of civil liberties could still respect a decision based on principle. The entire country—including to their credit some who initially opposed us—recognized that the ACLU was undergoing financial hardship because it would not sacrifice the first amendment even for the most despised and unpopular. Eventually, financial stability returned, and the Union's credibility was higher than before.

The centrality of courts to the constitutional plan must not obscure the equally important role of legislatures. They can enhance or weaken civil liberty and, absent a declaration of unconstitutionality, their actions are final. During the period of the Warren Court, it was widely assumed that courts alone would take care of our rights. Even then that was an exaggeration. During the 1960s Congress prohibited discrimination in employment, access to public accommodations and voting. It passed the Freedom of Information Act, and it created legal services for the poor. A few years later it enacted a privacy law. Astute civil libertarians recognized that Congress was a reservoir of civil liberties protection; it could authorize expenditures, create and dismantle agencies, and legislate across broad subject areas—powers almost always beyond the institutional capacity of courts.

By the same token, Congress can reduce civil liberties—not only indirectly by exercising its general powers insensitively, but directly by cutting back on previous grants of rights. Thus, within the past few years battles have raged within the Congress over the Legal Services Corporation, the Freedom of Information Act, the Voting Rights Act, school prayer, tuition tax credit, the United States Commission on Civil Rights, the powers of the CIA and FBI, and scores of other legislative issues. This agenda reflects an intense national public debate over the meaning and scope of civil rights in the 1980s. While Congress has severely impaired the right of access by poor women to abortion, it has rejected a wide variety of legislative assaults on the Constitution, the most dramatic and far-reaching of which was an effort to strip the federal courts of jurisdiction to hear civil liberties claims. In recognizing this legislative power, our book underscores the importance of persuading Congress to uphold civil liberties.

To understand our rights, we need to analyze them in a variety of contexts and from different angles. Since abstract rights can work only in a process, in the first section of this book three officials of the ACLU examine the institutions and their interplay that, in the end, determine whether our liberties will be secured. The next group of essays examines the rights of particular groups—racial minorities, women and homosexuals, teachers, those accused of crime and those incarcerated for it, and aliens. But there are constitutional concepts that go beyond the interests of defined groups; the book's last section analyzes developing doctrines that underlie the rights of all citizens: privacy, religious liberty, and national security. The last two essays step back from the battles raging around us to consider civil liberties from the broader perspectives of history and the relatively new field of international human rights.

These varied approaches will from time to time cover overlapping territories. For example, one can view restraints on the right to an abortion as a problem of discrimination against women or poor people, as an invasion of privacy, as an abridgement of religious liberty, or in terms of institutional tension between courts and legislatures. These perspectives are not redundant; they are rather alternative vectors with which to enter a complex reality.

The contributors to this book have deep affection for the United States, for its many gifts to its people, for its leadership in creating the first Constitution that is both written and judicially enforceable, and for its record in advancing liberty in so many ways. We are therefore all the more persistent in our efforts to help our country meet its full promise. We are saddened when it resorts to unworthy means to achieve its ends, when it betrays the faith of the founders that a great people can live freely in all its parts. *Our Endangered Rights* is a homage to the best of our national heritage, and a regretful criticism of the worst. But in the end it points us to the future: to aid in the difficult, often frustrating, but ultimately rewarding task of the defense of liberty for everyone in our vast land.

—Norman Dorsen
November 1983

PART ONE

THE PROCESSES

OF RIGHTS

MAKING CONSTITUTIONAL RIGHTS WORK

IRA GLASSER

Ira Glasser is executive director of the American Civil Liber-
ties Union. He is the author of many articles on civil liberties
and a coauthor of Doing Good: The Limits of Benevolence.

LIBERTY AS A LIMIT ON DEMOCRACY

The American political system is built upon two fundamental ideas. The first is the idea of majority rule through electoral democracy. This idea is well rooted and firmly established in our political culture. Nearly everyone believes in it, and is prepared to abide by it. To overturn the principle of democratic majority rule would, in our country, require nothing less than an armed revolution.

The second idea upon which the American political system is built is less well established, less understood, less rooted in popular culture, and much more fragile. This is the idea that *even in a democracy* the majority must be limited in order to guarantee individual liberty and personal autonomy.

Just because one group outvotes another, it cannot be allowed to gain unlimited power. If whites have more votes than blacks, they cannot be allowed to deny blacks their constitutional rights. If Christians have more votes than Jews, or Christians and Jews together outvote followers of Krishna Consciousness, they cannot deny those they outvote the right to practice their religion freely. If men have more political power than women, that cannot permit them to deny women certain individual rights. Winning an election should not permit the victors to assemble their votes and enact laws or govern in a way that strips those who lost of their liberty.

Thus, from the very beginning of American history, rights have been defined as limits on democratic power. To say that a citizen had the "right" to distribute a leaflet or worship freely meant that the government —even a democratically elected government—was without the legal authority to stop him.

Similarly, the right to be secure in one's own home from unreasonable government intrusion meant that not even the highest government official possessed the legal power to enter:

> The poorest man may in his cottage bid defiance to the crown. It may be frail—its roof may shake—the wind may enter—the rain may enter—but the King of England cannot enter—all his force dares not cross the threshold of the ruined tenement![1]

"Over himself," wrote John Stuart Mill, "over his own body and mind, the individual is sovereign,"[2] and it was precisely to define and construct legal protections for personal sovereignty that the Bill of Rights was added to the fledgling United States Constitution in 1789.

The early American colonists had ample reason to be wary of unlimited power. The Fourth Amendment to the Constitution, which sharply limited the power of government officials to conduct searches and seizures, was no abstract ideal invented by law professors in academic ivory towers, but rather the direct product of searing experience. During the fifteen years before the American Revolution, homes were frequently invaded by British soldiers conducting unrestricted, house-to-house searches in order to enforce harsh tax laws and seize literature hostile to the Crown. Those searches—feared then as burglars are feared today—created the political climate in which the Fourth Amendment, and indeed the entire Bill of Rights, was adopted.[3]

Similarly, the strict separation of church and state, which was written into the First Amendment, was not the product of theoretical analysis, but rather was based on hard, political experience, both in Europe and in colonial America, which convinced those who wrote the Constitution that the only way to protect religious liberty was to keep government out of religion and religion out of government.

The Bill of Rights was therefore a list of substantive legal limits on democratic power, largely posed in the negative: "Congress shall make no law . . . abridging the freedom of speech," says the First Amendment; "No person . . . shall be compelled in any criminal case to be a witness against himself," says the Fifth Amendment; "Nor shall any State deprive any person of life, liberty or property without due process of law," says the Fourteenth Amendment.[4] While most of the Constitution grants power to the government, these amendments say what government may *not* do. For those early Americans who believed that "governments are instituted" in part "to secure [individual] rights,"[5] it was not enough merely to enumerate the powers of government and assume that government officials would not exceed those powers as long as they were democratically elected. It was crucial, they believed, also to enumerate those powers that government officials should never be allowed to exercise—even if they were democratically elected.

Several constitutional methods of limiting governmental power were adopted. The prohibition of standing armies was one method (now fallen into disuse). A second method was the Bill of Rights itself, which established specific limits on democratic government. A third method was procedural: the distribution and fragmentation of power—horizontally between the states and the federal government, and vertically within the federal government among the three branches—legislative, executive, and judicial. Traditional political analysis, at least since Montesquieu, had divided the operations of government into three distinct exercises of power:

1. The *enunciation* of policy, rules, or law;

2. The *implementation* of such policy, rules, or law; and

3. The *resolution of disputes* over how a particular rule, law, or policy applied in a specific situation.

The structure of Articles 1, 2, and 3 of the United States Constitution maps those three operations and provides the legal basis for the tripartite separation of powers that is an essential feature of our political system. The legislature is the branch that enunciates rules; the executive is the branch that implements those rules; and the judiciary is the branch that resolves particular disputes over what the rules mean and how they apply to specific situations. In practice, of course, these functions overlap; the constitutional separation of powers is intended not to establish a rigid and simplistic exclusivity of function, but rather to resist the tendency of the three functions to merge and thereby become concentrated in a way that threatens liberty.[6]

Of course, anything in the Constitution, including the limits contained in the Bill of Rights, can be amended if a large enough majority wants to do it. Two-thirds of both houses of Congress may propose a change in the Constitution, and if that change is ratified by three-quarters of the states it becomes part of the Constitution. Thus, the separation of powers and the Bill of Rights were not designed to be completely impervious to democratic change. But they were designed to create an inertia in favor of liberty that no momentary majority could overcome during troubled times, or when the appetite for power grew too strong.

HOW CONSTITUTIONAL LIMITS
ARE ENFORCED

Independent Federal Courts. Although the Constitution established legal limits on democratic power, these limits were not self-enforcing. For example, the right of free speech is substantively established by the First Amendment, which prohibits Congress from making any law that abridges free speech. But this prohibition does not operate automatically, nor is its meaning clear in every situation. What happens if, despite the First Amendment, Congress enacts a law abridging, or appearing to abridge, free speech?

Curiously, neither the original Constitution nor the Bill of Rights mentions any remedy for people whose liberties have been violated. This crucial element of civil liberties defense was missing until 1803, when the Supreme Court, in *Marbury v. Madison*,[7] ruled that courts had the power to nullify laws that exceeded the government's limited authority.[8] Thus, if Congress should pass a law prohibiting citizens from distributing leaflets, any citizens affected by such a law could challenge it in court, and the court is constitutionally empowered to strike down that law. Similarly, courts are empowered to enjoin the executive branch when it violates individual rights or exercises powers exclusively reserved for Congress.

Over time, courts emerged as the institution best designed to enforce constitutional limits. Of the three branches, the judiciary is the most insulated from day-to-day politics, precisely because it is intended to act as a check upon day-to-day politics. Its judges are not elected. Although subject to the prevailing political winds through the appointment process, federal judges once appointed preside for life, subject only to the impeachment process. This independence renders them peculiarly fit to exercise a checking role.

Citizen Action. But courts alone cannot safeguard civil liberties. The president and Congress do not need judicial approval before acting, and the courts cannot move on their own initiative to strike down unconstitutional government actions. To invoke the power of judicial review, an individual or group must challenge a particular government action, and the suit must generally be brought by those who are directly harmed by the government's action.

Thus, even with the Bill of Rights' written declaration of civil liberties and even with an independent judicial mechanism to invalidate offending laws, a third element is needed to secure civil liberties: *the action of citizens to assert their rights.*

Few individuals, however, are able singlehandedly to test the constitutionality of a law or other government action. Even for the affluent, the cost of constitutional litigation is usually prohibitive, and many of those whose rights are pervasively violated are far from affluent.

For these reasons, a mechanism outside of government must exist through which individuals can join together to invoke the power of the courts in defense of civil liberties. To be effective, such a mechanism must be politically and financially independent of the government. What is required, in effect, is a fourth branch of the system outside the government. In 1920, one element of such a mechanism was established under the name of the American Civil Liberties Union (ACLU), the first private organization to undertake the nonpartisan defense of the entire Bill of Rights. By that time, however, civil liberties were in a sorry state.

In 1920, intolerance bred of war and fear was riding high; citizens sat in jails for holding antiwar views, some for criticizing the Red Cross in their own homes. A man was sentenced to prison for reading sections of the Declaration of Independence in public. A minister was sentenced to fifteen years for saying that war was un-Christian. During the war years, more than nineteen hundred legal actions were brought against speeches, newspaper articles, pamphlets, and books. At the crest of a fierce anti-foreigner sentiment rode the attorney general, A. Mitchell Palmer, who conducted a series of nationwide raids upon aliens suspected of holding unorthodox opinions. Four thousand were pulled out of their homes. Palmer had one thousand of them deported.

That wasn't all. Racial segregation was the law of the land, and racial violence against blacks was frequent and irremediable. Sex discrimination was firmly institutionalized. No legal remedy existed to prevent employers from using violence to break up labor organizations. Constitutional rights for homosexuals, the poor, children, prisoners, mental patients, American Indians, or the physically handicapped were, literally, unthinkable. And the Supreme Court had yet to uphold a single claim of free speech under the First Amendment.

From the beginning, two things distinguished the ACLU from ad hoc groups of citizens that had banded together around specific issues. First, the ACLU was conceived as permanent. The ACLU would not disband after fighting a particular battle but would maintain a continuing vigil against civil liberties abuses. Second, the ACLU was not formed to advance the interests or protect the rights of any particular group or class, like the NAACP or the American Jewish Committee, founded some years previously. Rather, the ACLU was founded on a principle that was embedded in the Constitution itself, although it remained—and remains today—elusive to many. It is the principle that *any* infraction of liberties, any breach of the limits imposed by the Constitution, weakens all liberties, regardless of who the particular victim happens to be.

Application of this principle often results in actions that many Americans see as contradictory. Thus, although the ACLU was a leading defender of the legal rights of labor during the 1920s and 1930s, it also defended the right of Henry Ford to distribute antiunion leaflets to his employees. Similarly, although the ACLU throughout its history has brought thousands of cases challenging police misconduct, it has also defended police officers when their rights were violated. And just as the ACLU has defended the right of blacks to march and speak out against racial segregation, so it has also defended the right of free speech for the Ku Klux Klan and neo-Nazi groups, when government attempted to inhibit the peaceful expression of their views.

For those who understand exactly how constitutional rights work, of course, none of this is surprising. The key is to prevent government from exceeding the constitutional limits upon its power, for those limits are what protect everyone's rights. Once government gains the power to exceed those limits at its own discretion—to decide, for example, who should speak and which speech is acceptable—no one's rights are safe. No matter who is the *first* target of illegitimate power, the exercise of that power threatens everyone. If permitted, it will establish a precedent and will be used again, against different targets of the government's choosing.

But organizations alone cannot protect constitutional rights against illegitimate power. What is also required is the assertion of rights by citizens and the vigorous resistance to violations of rights by its victims.

Two examples illustrate the point. Shortly after the ACLU was founded, one of the most famous trials in American history took place: the Scopes "Monkey Trial." The case began when Tennessee passed a law forbidding schools to teach the theory of evolution. John Thomas Scopes, a young biology teacher, placed himself in jeopardy of the law by violating it. He continued to teach the theory of evolution, and was soon indicted. The ACLU retained Clarence Darrow as a volunteer lawyer and defended Scopes by challenging the constitutionality of the law. Without the ACLU, Scopes probably couldn't have adequately defended himself. But without Scopes and his willingness to place himself in jeopardy, the ACLU could not have challenged the law in court.

A quarter-century later, Oliver Brown—a railroad welder and part-time minister from Topeka, Kansas—walked his seven-year-old daughter Linda to school. Ordinarily, Linda, who was black, attended a school for "colored" children that was far from her home. On that day, however, Oliver Brown took his daughter to the nearby Sumner school, which was reserved for white children.

He and Linda were turned away, but the NAACP challenged the rejection in federal court, and with it the entire system of racial segregation in public schools. Nearly four years later, in a unanimous and historic decision, the Supreme Court ruled that the separation of school children on the basis of race violated the constitutional guarantee of equal treatment under the law. Without the NAACP, the case could not have been successfully brought. But without the willingness of Oliver Brown to assert his rights and challenge the system, the NAACP could not have invoked the court's authority.

These two examples illustrate something else too: civil liberties victories never stay won, but must be fought for over and over again. In 1979, twenty-five years after the Supreme Court declared school segregation illegal, Linda Brown's own children—Oliver Brown's grandchildren—still attended segregated schools in Topeka, Kansas. Most black children in Topeka still attend predominantly black schools, with black teachers and black staff. And most white children attend predominantly white schools. The reasons for this persistent segregation are more complicated today, but the effect upon children is just as suffocating. And now Linda Brown has gone to court again, represented by ACLU and NAACP lawyers, to try to win again the victory she thought was won a generation ago.

Similarly, in 1981, fifty-seven years after John Scopes was indicted, the state of Arkansas passed a law that once again attempted to blot out the teaching of evolution. This time, instead of prohibiting the teaching of evolution, the law required the teaching of the Biblical story of divine creation in every class where the scientific theory of evolution was taught. At the same time, similar laws were introduced in over fifteen other states. Represented by ACLU lawyers, more than a dozen ministers, priests, rabbis, and teachers challenged the law. After months of expensive litigation, the law was struck down by a federal judge, and that decision also appeared to stop the legislation pending in other states. The struggle of citizens to protect their constitutional rights over a half-century ago did not protect citizens today. Each generation must be prepared to assert its rights, or lose them.

The defense of liberty is therefore a continuing task. Moreover, although some public officials are more threatening than others, even the friends of liberty have abused their power when the circumstances seemed compelling. Franklin Roosevelt interned Japanese-Americans; Abraham Lincoln suspended the right of habeas corpus; and even so fervent an apostle of liberty as Thomas Jefferson was far more of a libertarian as a private citizen than he was as a president.[9] This timeless tendency for government to overstep its constitutional bounds demands a permanent counterforce of citizens. For liberty is fragile, and forever vulnerable to the encroachments of illegitimate power.

COMPLETING THE CONSTITUTION

Making the Constitution work is not limited to assuring mechanisms for enforcement, however important these are. Painstaking attention to the substance of individual rights is also required. Although the Constitution is one of history's most remarkable documents, the fact that it was intended to endure inevitably meant that it had to be adapted to new circumstances and new crises. In particular, it meant that the Constitution must evolve: to secure for new groups the benefits of traditional rights, to develop new remedies to thwart persistent violations, and above all to adapt old rights to new circumstances.

Extending Traditional Rights. The vision of the framers of the Constitution was astonishing, but they nonetheless were trapped in the culture of their time. The original Bill of Rights left a lot out.

To begin with, it didn't apply to state and local governments. So although Congress couldn't make a law abridging freedom of speech, press, or religion, state and local governments could. If a state legislature passed a law establishing an official state religion, the First Amendment didn't prohibit it. If a local police officer broke up a peaceful meeting, the First Amendment couldn't prevent it. It was not until the Civil War amendments were ratified and enforced that the Bill of Rights was applied to state and local officials.

The original Bill of Rights also left out whole classes of people. It left out racial minorities, and to a large extent it left out women. To this day, the laws of the land are stained with the residue of those original exclusions.

The Bill of Rights left out others too, not explicitly but in effect— homosexuals, children, welfare recipients, mental patients, prisoners and other institutionalized people, military personnel, American Indians, and the physically handicapped. It was not until the mid-1960s that many of those groups began systematically to organize and challenge the power of government officials whose decisions affected their lives and diminished their rights. A dozen different civil rights movements arose. In case after case, rulings were issued that brought these groups within the general protection of the Bill of Rights.

This phenomenon was particularly clear within institutions designed to provide services. Enmeshed in these institutions, often against their will but ostensibly for their own good, people were often forced to waive their rights as a condition of receiving benefits. All lived under the jurisdiction of government institutions whose managers claimed to be exempt from the limits imposed by the Bill of Rights.

For people who needed shelter, the government provided public housing. But admission was denied for reasons such as poor housekeeping, irregular work history, frequent separations of husband and wife, single-parent families, common-law marriages, lack of furniture, apparent mental retardation, dishonorable military discharges, or the arrest of one's child. Regulations of public housing authorities embodied these conditions, which established unprecedented dominion over other people's lives.

For people who needed money, welfare was provided. But eligibility depended on government standards of morality. Every detail of a recipient's life was subject to scrutiny. Women were allowed different numbers of sanitary napkins each month, depending on whether they were employed. There were no allowances for newspapers, and telephones were considered a luxury even for the blind. A single woman with preschool dependent children could have her children's benefits revoked if she was found sleeping with a man, and midnight raids by caseworkers became a common method of surveillance. The surrender of privacy became a condition of survival.

For children in trouble whose families did not have resources to help, the government provided a system of family courts. Punishment was not a purpose of these courts. But in fact children were removed from their families and incarcerated—like criminals and often together with criminals—for truancy, for running away from home, for staying out too late, for obscene language, for promiscuity, or for vague reasons like disobedience or incorrigibility. If their families had started to break up under the pressure of poverty, government intervention often accelerated the breakup and made it permanent.

One by one during the 1960s these groups and others went to court to limit the power of officials to govern their lives. Although progress was uneven, the provisions of the Bill of Rights were substantially extended during these years to whole classes of people not previously protected.[10]

Finding Remedies for Persistent Problems The process of completing the Constitution is sometimes excruciatingly slow. Often the nature of the problem changes, and remedies that once worked seem not to work anymore. Coalitions shift; patterns of support change; frustration grows. Nothing illustrates this better than the effort to dismantle the structure of racial separation and discrimination. Thirty years ago, when the modern civil rights movement began, the facts concerning racial discrimination were relatively clear and uncomplicated; the law required separation of the races, and no one denied it. The moral issue was unmistakable, and starkly visible to the rest of the country.

In the courts and in the Congress, the facts were equally clear and undisputed: blacks and whites were kept apart by law and custom, in schools, on buses, in theaters; at luncheonettes, restaurants, hotels, and toilets; at drinking fountains, swimming pools, parks, and baseball games; at the ballot box and in the jury box (where blacks were effectively excluded altogether); and in the workplace, where blacks were pervasively denied equal opportunity.

The question for the courts and for the nation was purely one of law and right: were such separation and exclusion consistent with the Constitution and with American ideals? The answer—after more than a decade of struggle during which many lives were risked, and more than a few were lost—was no. The courts consistently struck down legislation that required or permitted racial separation, and the Congress passed a series of laws prohibiting racial discrimination in voting, housing, public accommodations, and employment. By 1968, most of the important legal principles initially sought by the civil rights movement had been established.

But the residual effects of centuries of slavery and legal discrimination were not easily erased, and the removal of legal barriers to equal opportunity proved to be only the first stage in a longer, more painfully redemptive, struggle.

For most of the past decade, the problem has been exactly the reverse of what it was thirty years ago. We are faced now not with clear moral or constitutional issues, but rather with hotly disputed assertions of fact, difficult problems of proof, and even more difficult problems of remedy:

• In many counties of the old South, for example, blacks are still effectively excluded from the political system, even though the blunter instruments of intimidation and formal legal barriers to voting no longer exist.

• In many school systems, both North and South, racially separate attendance patterns and exclusionary practices still exist, even though there are no laws on the books mandating racial segregation.

• In most metropolitan areas, there is still a firm division of the races between city and suburb—what a presidential study commission once called "two separate Americas"—that cannot be traced to a law that is explicitly racist.[11]

• Unemployment rates for blacks are still disproportionately and explosively higher than corresponding rates for whites, and racial stratification in employment, including public employment, is still widespread, especially in the South.

• In social services, blacks are disproportionately channeled into lower-ability tracks in school, disproportionately suspended or otherwise excluded from their right to a public education, disproportionately referred to family or juvenile courts, disproportionately taken into foster-care custody by the state, and disproportionately committed to reform schools and mental hospitals.

Are such starkly unequal results caused by racially discriminatory acts? Many people do not think so, and virtually all defendants in contemporary race discrimination lawsuits vigorously deny their complicity. School segregation, they claim, is the result of housing patterns and cannot be blamed on the actions and patterns of school boards. Housing segregation, they claim, is the result of economic differences, not racial discrimination. And economic differences, we are told, cannot be traced to employment discrimination or the acts of government, but to lack of education and qualifications. Are racial differentials in education somehow connected to racial discrimination in schools? No, such differentials are mainly the consequences of broken families.

At first glance, each of these arguments has just enough merit to blur the moral clarity of the results, and it requires detailed, painstaking scrutiny to reveal discrimination. Facts need to be uncovered, proven, and linked to the discriminatory result. The adjudication of claims of racial discrimination is therefore radically more complicated now than it was thirty years ago, and requires considerable expenditures of time, effort, and money. Moreover, the kinds of questions that arise in race discrimination cases today inevitably lead to determinations of motive. Proof of motive is very difficult, partly because defendants have learned to cover their tracks, and partly because contemporary acts of racial discrimination are less obvious than they were thirty years ago.

For these reasons, the moral urgency of this problem has faded badly. The public is often at a total loss to discern the moral issue that lies beneath complex factual disputes, and blame is often shifted back onto the victims themselves. Today, race discrimination does not require racists. No George Wallace stands in the schoolhouse door; no Jim Clark bars the Selma bridge; no Bull Connor moves blacks away from the courthouse with cattle prods. The effects of race discrimination today cannot easily be shown on television, or encapsulated in a dramatic image. Yet exclusionary suburban zoning, school segregation, employment discrimination, political gerrymandering, foster-care practices, school suspension practices, and juvenile courts must be seen together in order to measure adequately the extent and impact of institutionalized racism today.

The cumulative effect is suffocating: it stifles the hopes and limits the opportunities of many, perhaps most, black Americans. Yet we are in the midst of a period when both Congress and the executive branch are decidedly less sympathetic to civil rights and to the efforts to find remedies for the effects of past and current race discrimination. There will not likely be any direct assault on the established legal principles. But there will be less vigorous enforcement of those principles, as well as attempts to abandon certain remedies as unnecessary or too extreme. This is a relatively new problem, though it has been with us increasingly for over a decade, and it complicates enormously the task of enforcing constitutional rights.

Old Rights Under New Circumstances. New circumstances create new problems and new frontiers for civil liberties. Many of today's threats to traditional rights occur under conditions that were unimaginable during the eighteenth century when the Bill of Rights was adopted.

Under modern conditions of mass communication, for example, the function of free speech may be effectively diminished if no one can hear what the speaker says. If speech is inaudible, what matters that it is free? Effective communication requires access to the mass media, but unpopular views often cannot gain access. Some have therefore suggested that in order to fulfill the purposes of the First Amendment under modern conditions, we should establish a right of access to newspapers and television. But should government have the power to force a policy of access on privately owned newspapers or even on publicly owned airwaves? And how will the advent of cable television—a communications revolution now only in its infancy—affect this problem? Twentieth-century conditions have created a conflict within the First Amendment that was not possible to contemplate two hundred years ago.

Another example is the right to privacy. In the eighteenth century, and for a long while thereafter, private records and other personal information were likely to be kept on one's person or in one's home or place of business. Privacy could be protected by the Fourth Amendment's limits on government's power to enter and search these premises.

Today, most private records and personal information are not kept at home but are maintained by banks, hospitals, employers, insurance companies, schools, the Internal Revenue Service, credit bureaus, motor vehicle departments, the Social Security Administration, and other third parties. Moreover, many of these data banks are increasingly linked through individual Social Security numbers by computer tapes. Yet the Supreme Court has generally refused to apply the Fourth Amendment to private information kept by third parties. The Fourth Amendment still protects one's home and place of business, but the information it was designed to keep private is no longer there. As a result, government officials can often gain access to highly personal information, and a good deal of the privacy originally protected by the Fourth Amendment is being eroded. Special vigilance is required to reestablish the right to privacy under modern conditions.

To a large extent, therefore, the history of constitutional litigation and the political struggles of various civil rights movements may be seen as a continuing process of completing the Constitution: of filling in the gaps in the original Bill of Rights by extending traditional rights to untraditional groups; of searching for effective remedies to persistent, institutionalized violations; and of attempting to adapt old rights to new circumstances. Through such a continuing process, we seek to fulfill the promise of the original vision.

THE CURRENT CHALLENGE
TO CIVIL LIBERTIES

Assaults on civil liberty tend to come in waves, and toward the end of the 1970s a wave of anti–civil liberties sentiment began to build. Great progress had been made during the 1960s in fulfilling the original vision, and so it was perhaps inevitable that a reaction would set in. For not everyone in America shared that vision.

The new movement called itself conservative, but few paused to ask exactly what it was they were trying to conserve. Certainly it did not seem to be the Bill of Rights. They claimed to speak for a restoration of traditional American values, but traditional constitutional values were no part of their plan. They were possessed by a different and more fearful vision.

By late 1980, they had achieved substantial political power. Suddenly, no freedom seemed safe. Book banning became epidemic. Women's rights were threatened. Homosexuals were attacked. Voting rights were endangered. And ominous new laws to weaken the federal courts and to breach the separation of church and state were widely proposed.

The new threat to civil liberties came from four sources. First, there was a highly organized, well-financed private movement, generically characterized as the Moral Majority, but including many other groups, loosely tied together by a similar agenda.

Second, in Congress, men like Sens. Strom Thurmond, Orrin Hatch, and Jesse Helms proposed a broad array of explicit anti–civil liberties legislation, including constitutional amendments, and for a time seemed capable of passing them.[12]

Third, state and local legislatures were poised to pass their own anti–civil liberties legislation. Within the first few months of 1981, for example, over fifteen states introduced nearly identical bills requiring the teaching of "scientific creationism," a euphemism for religious indoctrination designed to blot out the teaching of evolution. Similarly, many school boards sought to ban books in classrooms and libraries all over the country.

Finally, of course, there was the White House itself, where Ronald Reagan functioned as chief moralizer and public relations propagandist for the New Right. Though at first he concentrated primarily on economic issues, his leadership helped fuel the movement to restrict the right of women to choose an abortion, to defeat the Equal Rights Amendment, to impose official prayer sessions in public schools, to encourage laws requiring the teaching of the Biblical story of creation in public schools, to repeal key provisions of the Voting Rights Act of 1965, to attack the independence of the federal courts, and to restrict access by the poor to lawyers.

Although public opinion polls consistently showed no general mandate for those goals, President Reagan consistently spoke as if he were trying to invent one. Utilizing the powerful moral pulpit of the presidency, Reagan seemed to be seeking to alter public belief in many of the values underlying the Bill of Rights. Nowhere was this more evident than in his constant public campaign, continuing to this day, to reestablish doctrinal religion in public schools and to fuse government with particular religious beliefs. This campaign directly threatened—and still threatens—the traditional principle of separation of church and state and the freedom of thought it was designed to protect.

But of the many rights that were endangered during this period, two Reagan administration strategies revealed the degree to which the new movement set itself against the principles that have made constitutional rights work.

The New "States Rights" Movement. The Fourteenth Amendment was enacted after the Civil War to limit the discretion of states to violate individual rights. Soon after coming to power, the Reagan administration launched a campaign to erode federal constitutional standards and return discretion to the states. This campaign focused upon three areas: the rights of racial minorities, the role of federal courts, and the rights of the poor.

The campaign to return discretion to the states in the area of race discrimination began with a struggle over the Voting Rights Act of 1965. Universally acknowledged to be the most effective civil rights legislation ever passed by Congress, the act had proven successful in stopping a wide variety of local discriminatory schemes that diluted minority votes, and was the key weapon in fighting exclusion from equal political opportunity based on race.

For over fifteen months, the president persistently expressed doubts about the continued need for a strong Voting Rights Act, while his Justice Department mounted a strong campaign against its key provisions. Although Reagan eventually signed a strong bill strengthening the act after it had passed overwhelmingly in both houses of Congress, his long indifference to so fundamental a right as the right to vote proved to be part of a pattern that included a systematic effort to weaken and dismantle the civil rights enforcement programs of several federal agencies.

Hiding behind rhetorical catch phrases like "new federalism," Reagan attempted to erode federal standards and remedies governing race discrimination and tried to shift discretion in this area back to the states, whose discretion first caused the problem—and still does. The resurrection of the discredited ideology of states' rights was therefore a direct assault on the principles of the Fourteenth Amendment. The systematic effort to "deregulate" federal standards and limit federal intervention in the area of civil rights, and to return discretion to the states, was an attempt to repeal the constitutional gains of the past two decades.

Perhaps nothing better characterized the new states' rights movement than the alarming effort to dilute the power of federal courts to enforce constitutional rights, an effort the American Bar Association called one of the most dangerous in American legal history. The independence of our federal court system has, as I have said, made it the critical mechanism in enforcing constitutional rights. Yet during the first two years of the Reagan administration, forty bills were introduced in Congress to strip federal courts of their jurisdiction *even to hear* cases in certain areas—abortion, separation of church and state, and racial desegregation. Had any of those bills prevailed, laws violating the Bill of Rights could have been passed and no federal court—including the Supreme Court in some instances—would have had the authority to strike them down.

Such laws, stripping federal courts of their authority to review unconstitutional statutes, would have allowed state legislatures to pass laws free from the fear that they could be challenged in federal court. Of course, such local laws could still have been challenged in state courts. While state constitutional law has had a resurgence in recent years,[13] it is still a fragile reed on which to rely for the protection of threatened liberties. Looking back a few years, how far would Martin Luther King, Jr. and the civil rights movement have gotten if they had been forced to seek redress of their constitutional grievances in the state courts of Alabama, Georgia, and Mississippi?

While these dangerous bills to strip federal courts of jurisdiction were pending in Congress, the Reagan administration was actively pursuing other methods to dilute the independence of the judicial branch. For instance, it sought legislation to limit the federal courts' authority to order appropriate *remedies* for constitutional violations. Examples of this are proposed laws to prohibit courts from ordering transfers of pupils to remedy intentional school segregation and to prohibit courts from excluding illegally seized evidence from criminal trials. In both examples, the substantive rights would remain intact, and the court could declare such rights to have been violated by state and local government officials, but would be prohibited from ordering appropriate remedies.

The third example of the new "states rights" movement—the campaign to erode the rights of poor people—had two elements. First, the administration sought to deny substantive rights to poor people, to erase the gains they had made during the 1960s in applying constitutional standards to the administration of benefit programs. Second, it sought to limit the ability of poor people to challenge the erosion of their rights by denying them lawyers. These two elements appeared to be independent, but were in fact part of a single strategy.

As Prof. Edward Sparer pointed out some years ago, it would be a major error to see the Reagan administration's program in the social-welfare area only in terms of economic cutbacks in government funding. In fact, the administration appeared intent on returning American social welfare to the principles and practices of the English Poor Laws, which governed America's legal approach to the poor until relatively recently in our history. And that involved a question of legal rights.

Under the Poor Laws, poor people *in principle* had no rights. "Due process of law" or "equal protection of the laws" did not apply to them. The right to privacy or confidentiality did not exist. Dependency upon the government for even subminimal levels of subsistence were conditioned upon a waiver of constitutional rights. Survival and individual liberty became mutually exclusive. Without a legal entitlement to assistance based on national standards, relief from starvation or lack of shelter or clothing was an entirely local obligation, to be given, withheld, or ended at the unchallengeable discretion of local officials.

These Dickensian principles continued largely to characterize the public world of social welfare in the United States until the welfare-rights movement began to extend traditional constitutional rights to the poor: entitlements under law, no forced waivers of privacy and other constitutional rights, fair procedures, and equal treatment. The enforcement of such rights, of course, usually required lawyers. It was therefore no accident that the Reagan administration's assault upon the Legal Services Corporation[14] came at the same time as its mean-spirited attempt to unravel the legal rights so recently and minimally won by the dependent poor and to resurrect the degrading principles of the old Poor Laws. This twin assault was nothing less than an attempt to read poor people out of the Constitution and out of the system of laws itself, and make their very survival once again dependent not upon rights, but upon the unlimited and unchallengeable discretion of local officials.

Restricting the Free Flow of Information and Dissent. The First Amendment is the bedrock of our democratic system. It reflects the belief that, in a democracy, people ought to have a say in the decisions that affect their lives. It encourages the free flow of information, and is intended to assure that no important governmental policy decisions are made without open and robust public debate.

For this reason, the First Amendment has always come under attack from those in government who would rather make and implement decisions without bearing the burden of persuading the citizens they represent. Until recently, most attacks on First Amendment rights were obvious and crude. Demonstrations and parades were prohibited by various local laws; people distributing leaflets or making speeches were often arrested; advocates for various causes were prevented from setting up information tables on the sidewalk; meetings and other public assemblies were broken up.

A great many of these problems persisted into the late 1960s. The civil rights movement, first in the South, and then elsewhere in the nation, confronted many of these laws and practices. So did the antiwar movement during the years of American involvement in Vietnam.

Many laws and practices that crudely restricted First Amendment rights were challenged in court. Most of those challenges were successful, and today the right to meet, to speak, to leaflet, and to demonstrate are relatively secure. We don't often confront such direct restrictions on these rights anymore, and, when we do, we can usually obtain a remedy swiftly and effectively.

Now we face what might be called a second generation of First Amendment problems. Where once the primary means of suppressing robust debate was to employ crude restrictions on the rights of assembly and speech themselves, now those who would suppress debate seem content to permit people to talk and meet to their hearts' content, so long as the content of their speech is strictly controlled. The *procedural* rights to speak, publish, hear, and read remain intact. But *what* we are permitted to speak about, publish, hear, and read is increasingly limited to what the government wants us to know. More and more, we are witnessing governmental efforts to restrict, control, and manipulate information that should be available to the public.[15]

A prime example of this effort took place on March 11, 1983, when President Reagan issued a new "secrecy order," forcing thousands of government officials who had access to "sensitive" information to sign contracts that require them to submit *anything* they plan to write or speak about to the government for "preclearance." This order would apply even to fiction and even to federal employees after they leave office! It established, in effect, a lifetime curtailment of free speech.

This "secrecy order" would cut off democratic debate on many critical issues. For example, a recent survey of five major newspapers showed that in 1982 over three hundred columns had been written by former government officials on such subjects as the MX missile, policy toward Central America, military spending, and Soviet intelligence. Had these former officials been covered by the new directive, many of their articles would have been subject to government review and censorship. Similarly, another survey by the Association of American Publishers showed that eighty-five recent books by former officials could have been affected.[16] By strictly controlling the information, analysis, and opinions available for public debate, this executive decree provides the government with an unprecedented system of official censorship.

Nor was this the Reagan administration's only attempt to restrict the free flow of information. In a series of little-known administration actions by the Departments of State and Commerce, the administration moved —without legal authority—to exercise control and censorship of scientists, educators, and students. Astonishingly, it sought to apply the Export Administration Act, which regulates the export of industrial goods, to *ideas* in order to intimidate scientists into submitting their publications to the government for clearance before publishing.[17] By this action, the administration tried to restrict and control information and ideas that were *not* classified and that were already circulating publicly outside the government. In addition to being a frontal attack on academic freedom, the action was significant because it was without legislative authority. Had Congress tried to amend the Export Administration Act to apply its regulations to ideas and information, a great public debate would have ensued over whether such legislation would violate First Amendment limits. But quietly, without debate and without legislation, the Reagan administration just went ahead and enunciated these new rules, and then began to implement them.

In a similar vein, the administration began to restrict the right to travel. Using the Trading with the Enemy Act, which was intended to prohibit industrial trade with enemy nations, the administration announced a new policy prohibiting American citizens from traveling to certain countries, like Cuba, on the ground that money spent there by tourists amounted to trading with the enemy! Again, this enunciation of policy was made without legislative authority, and was subsequently declared illegal by the federal courts.

Finally, the Administration began systematically to deny visitors' visas to many foreign scholars and "controversial" figures, such as the South American novelist Gabriel Garcia Marquez and Mrs. Hortensia Allende, the widow of the assassinated Chilean president, thereby preventing them from accepting invitations to come to the United States to speak. Invoking the infamous McCarran-Walter Act, passed during the fifties, these visa denials to prominent Latin Americans who hold views opposed to United States policy must be seen in the context of the administration's efforts to conduct its Latin American policy covertly, with as little public debate and democratic control as possible. During the same period, visas were also denied to Japanese proponents of a nuclear freeze, to Ian Paisley of Ireland, to the Iranian ambassador to the United Nations, and to a retired general and former NATO commander. These denials seemed similarly designed to prevent the expression of dissent from United States policies.

Taken together, these executive actions were part of an alarming strategy:

• Information and ideas coming into our country were to be restricted by licensing foreign books and periodicals, by barring travel to certain countries, and by refusing visas to foreign scholars and others whose views the government does not want Americans to hear.

• Information and ideas leaving our country were to be restricted by attempts to control the publication of scientific research and limit the education of foreign students.

• Information and ideas circulating within our country were to be restricted by expanding the executive branch power to censor ex-employees, by defining too broadly what can be classified, and by limitations on the Freedom of Information Act.

Not all these attempted restrictions were successful. *But all of them were attempted.* Those in government who supported such restrictions did not share the vision reflected by the First Amendment. They saw the free flow of information as a threat, and sought to insulate official decisions from public debate.

While this trend began before 1980, the Reagan administration accelerated it enormously and seemed to regard restrictions on information as a central strategy of government. Commenting on the denial of visas to certain controversial speakers in 1983, Rep. Fortnoy H. Stark, Jr. of California commented: "I'm beginning to believe that the Reagan administration thinks it cannot survive criticism or free discussion of important issues."[18] Sen. Joseph R. Biden of Delaware, commenting on the Reagan administration's restrictions of information flowing to Congress, said: "Everything is just closing down. The whole attitude is just very, very different."[19]

The executive branch actions did not have the drama of a Bull Connor breaking up a demonstration with police dogs and firehoses. No one was arrested. No one was prevented from speaking. Everything seemed legal. The new tactic of suppression was much quieter, almost stealthy, more difficult to see and therefore harder to resist. But it was no less dangerous to the First Amendment and the tradition of democratic debate.

In August 1981, a few weeks before he died in his ninety-eighth year, Roger Baldwin, who founded the American Civil Liberties Union in 1920, said he thought these were the most dangerous times for civil liberties he had seen. Coming from Baldwin, who had lived through several dark periods in American history, it was a sobering assessment. Yet he remained optimistic about our ability to prevail. And with good reason. For he looked back upon a time when the most radical feminist issue was the right to vote; when blacks were lynched almost every week, and when the destruction of legal segregation seemed impossible; when workers had no legal right to organize unions; when the Supreme Court had yet to uphold a single claim of free speech; and when the idea that the Bill of Rights should apply to such groups as prisoners, mental patients, the handicapped, foster children, homosexuals, or American Indians was not possible to imagine.

For all of the danger civil liberty faces today, the historical tide of expanding liberty should encourage us. There is reason for alarm; but there is no reason for pessimism.

Despite the frightening assault on civil liberties during the past few years, Bill of Rights advocates have prevailed on many of the major issues. In Congress, the Voting Rights Act was strengthened and the Legal Services Corporation was saved. No law restricting the authority of the federal courts was passed. No law restricting the right to abortion was passed. And no law breaching the separation of church and state was passed. In the courts, major victories were won against laws requiring the teaching of the religious doctrine of creationism, against book censorship in public schools, and against laws restricting the right to abortion. There have been defeats too, of course, particularly with respect to executive branch actions, but on the whole it is fair to say that as of late 1983 very little on the agenda of the anti–civil liberties movement had prevailed. Against high odds, Bill of Rights advocates have organized skillfully, and resisted successfully.

The outcome of the next few years may be in doubt. But we will determine it. For what counts is not what they do; what counts is what we do in response. The lesson of our history and indeed of the past few years is clear, as it always has been: the protection of individual rights depends not on the government, not on who gets elected president, not even, ultimately, on the courts, but on private citizens themselves, aware of the fragility of liberty, alert to the forces that threaten it, and prepared to give of themselves and to organize in order to resist those threats.

As Judge Learned Hand said:

> Liberty lies in the hearts of men and women. When it dies there,
> no Constitution, no law, no court can save it.[20]

He was right. The courage and commitment to resist every fundamental violation of liberty is in the end what matters most in the effort to make constitutional rights work.

NOTES

1. William Pitt, Earl of Chatham, *Brangham's Statesmen in the Time of George III*, first series.

2. McCallum, ed., *On Liberty* (1946).

3. For an excellent description of the political climate in which the Bill of Rights was adopted, *see* B. Bailyn, *Ideological Origins of the American Revolution* (1967), and B. Bailyn and J.N. Garrett, eds., *Pamphlets of the American Revolution, 1750–1776* (1965).

4. Although the Fourteenth Amendment was adopted nearly a century later, it continued to reflect the limiting language of the first eight.

5. Declaration of Independence and Preamble to the Constitution.

6. For an excellent theoretical discussion of the doctrine of separation of powers, *see* Neuborne, "Judicial Review and Separation of Powers in France and the United States," 57 *New York University Law Review* 363 (1982).

7. 1 Cranch 137 (1803).

8. For a fuller discussion of judicial review, *see* Neuborne, *supra* note 6.

9. Leonard W. Levy, *Jefferson and Civil Liberties: The Darker Side* (1963).

10. *See generally* W. Gaylin, I. Glasser, S. Marcus, and D. Rothman, *Doing Good* (1978).

11. Report of the National Advisory Commission on Civil Disorders ("The Kerner Commission Report") (1968).

12. For a fuller discussion of the legislative process during this period, *see* Shattuck, *infra* at 46.

13. *See generally* "Special Section: The Connecticut Constitution," 15 *Connecticut Law Review* 7–120 (1982); "Developments in the Law: State Constitutional Law," 94 *Harvard Law Review* (1982).

14. L. Siegel and D. Landau, *No Justice for the Poor* (1983).

15. ACLU, *Free Speech, 1984: The Rise of Government Controls on Information, Debate and Association* (1983).

16. Massing and Peterzell, "Reagan Censors," Op-Ed, *New York Times*, Aug. 8, 1983.

17. Boffey, Op-Ed, *New York Times*, Sept. 5, 1982.

18. *San Francisco Chronicle*, March 4, 1983, at 6.

19. Roberts, *New York Times*, March 17, 1982, at 14.

20. L. Hand, *The Spirit of Liberty* 190 (1974).

THE SUPREME COURT AND THE JUDICIAL PROCESS

BURT NEUBORNE

Burt Neuborne is legal director of the American Civil Liberties Union and professor of Law at New York University School of Law. He is coauthor of Unquestioning Obedience to the President *and* The Rights of Candidates and Voters *and is among the country's most experienced constitutional litigators.*

This book is about the state of our endangered rights on the eve of George Orwell's nightmare vision of a world without them. But a mere catalogue of endangered rights, no matter how accurately drawn or passionately defended, would provide only a snapshot of a more complex phenomenon. What we call "rights" are, after all, not concrete objects which can be made to sit still for an enduring portrait—verbal or otherwise. Rather, they are grand and ambiguous abstractions enmeshed in an institutional matrix which gives them precise articulation and provides for their enforcement against the recalcitrant.

In a very real sense, all rights depend for their ultimate meaning and effect on an institutional structure calculated to provide the individual with an Archimedes' lever to invoke them. If the lever is a strong one, rights are strong as well; if the lever is weak, rights are largely illusory, whatever words may be used to describe them. Witness the hollow grandeur of the rights entombed in most totalitarian constitutions. Thus, before turning to the endangered rights themselves, we should consider the health of the principal means of articulating and enforcing individual rights in our legal structure—the uniquely American phenomenon of judicial review.

Since individual rights are rarely self-defining and are never self-enforcing, any political system which claims to recognize rights must make a fundamental choice about who is to define and enforce them. The choice is between officials whose principal job it is to carry out the political desires of the electorate and a more insulated set of officials who function independently of the wishes of the politically powerful.

Many societies, following Rousseau's conception of popular sovereignty and deference to majority will, have chosen to give politicians—usually legislators or administrators—the last word in deciding the scope of individual rights.[1] We, on the other hand, have chosen to give precise meaning to the concept of individual rights by using insulated officials—usually judges—whose job it is to construe a purposefully ambiguous document called a Constitution.[2] When de Tocqueville noted the extent to which social issues are translated into legal questions in American life, he was merely reporting the fact that our system uses courts, not legislatures, as a principal means of articulating and enforcing individual rights.[3]

Using insulated judges instead of legislators to define and enforce individual rights has one important practical advantage and one obvious theoretical drawback. On the plus side, when the issue is whether an individual possesses a right to do as he or she wishes regardless of the desires of the politically powerful, it doesn't make much functional sense to allow officials beholden to the politically powerful to decide the question. Close cases would, under such an arrangement, almost always be resolved against the individual. Allowing judges who are relatively insulated from public opinion to define the scope of individual rights is thus far more likely to result in the sustained and vigorous enunciation of such rights than a system which relegates the task to representatives of the politically powerful.

On the negative side, the very effectiveness of an insulated judge as a generator of individual rights is in tension with our deeply felt respect for democratic decision making and commitment to majority rule. Of course, a good deal of the tension can be relieved by recognizing that some of what passes for majority rule in any democracy is in fact one transient minority or another which has managed to attain temporary political ascendancy. Allowing judges to check such a powerful transient minority in the name of an existing consensus concerning individual rights is hardly a serious challenge to democratic political theory.

That is especially true since even federal judges appointed for life are not without a democratic imprimatur. They are generally drawn from the political world; they are appointed by the president and must be confirmed by the Senate. As between such a judge and a local police chief, is there much doubt which has the better democratic pedigree?

Occasionally, however, the judiciary does trump a genuine political majority in the name of individual rights. When that happens, majority rule and judicial review may come into real conflict. But even in such situations, much of the conflict is false, since the reviewing court is generally acting on behalf of a "discrete and insular minority"[4] that was unable to participate effectively in the democratic process in the first place.

In any event, whatever the tension—or, perhaps, because of it—judicial review has functioned as a powerful generator of individual rights. Whether it has been invoked by slaveowners seeking to enforce the Fugitive Slave Clause against abolitionist legislatures,[5] by business corporations seeking to enforce Herbert Spencer's *Social Statics* against regulatory initiatives,[6] or by despised minorities—racial,[7] religious,[8] or political[9] —seeking relief from majoritarian overreaching, judicial review has resulted in the sustained articulation and enforcement of many individual rights, the recognition of which would have been inconceivable had the task been left to the political majority. It is, I believe, no exaggeration to suggest that the viability of the endangered rights discussed in this book turn as much on our continued adherence to judicial review as on the substantive arguments marshaled in favor of each particular right.

Not surprisingly, the very effectiveness of courts in protecting unpopular minorities has often provoked resentment and periodic attempts to curb "government by judges." Current political assaults on judicial review are, in fact, merely a cyclical recurrence of populist frustration with the predictable results of the handiwork of John Marshall—the apostle of American judicial review.[10] From the abolitionists' insistence upon jury trials for alleged fugitive slaves;[11] to the populist insistence upon the popular election of judges;[12] to FDR's plan to pack the Supreme Court;[13] to the controversy over reapportionment;[14] to Jesse Helms's "Fetal Life" bills,[15] designed to overturn *Roe v. Wade;*[16] to John East's and Orrin Hatch's assault on federal jurisdiction and remedial authority:[17] the response to vigorous judicial protection of individual rights has often been an attempt by politicians—liberal as well as conservative—to shift the power to define those rights from insulated judges to legislators subject to political pressures.[18] The enduring quality of many of our current rights may well turn, therefore, on the answer to a seemingly esoteric question: How vulnerable is judicial review to attempts to restrict it in the name of fidelity to democratic ideals?

The most striking aspect of any assessment of the vulnerability of judicial review to political attack is the fragility of its textual underpinnings. Despite the very considerable efforts of John Marshall[19] and an array of academics,[20] conclusive support for allowing judges the last word in defining individual rights cannot be found in the text of the Constitution. The accepted justification for judicial review rests, instead, on the reasoning of John Marshall in *Marbury v. Madison* and its repeated adoption as part of our unwritten constitution by the Supreme Court over a 180-year period.

Under John Marshall's model, a judge has no independent authority to overrule decisions of the president, the Congress, or local officials about the meaning of the Constitution. Judicial power to define and protect individual rights flows, instead, from the task of resolving disputes between litigants imposed on judges by Congress. In carrying out that task, a judge is forced to select the governing rule of law from among a number of possible sources urged upon her by the litigants. Since litigants will often point to different sources, a judge must use a hierarchical ranking system to decide which source takes precedence. The ranking rules are simple and are dictated by elementary political theory: judge-made common law rules must give way to valid administrative regulations which, in turn, are outweighed by statutes which may themselves be overridden by the Constitution. According to John Marshall, it is in the inevitable process of deciding whether the rule of law asserted by one litigant (often the government invoking a statute or an administrative regulation) conflicts with a higher-ranking rule of law asserted by another litigant (often an aggrieved individual invoking the Constitution) that judges map the precise scope of individual rights in our system of government. Under *Marbury v. Madison*, therefore, the articulation of an individual right by a judge is an almost accidental byproduct of the judge's primary job of resolving actual disputes referred to her by Congress.

Although Marshall's defense of judicial review is one of our law's great success stories, it leaves judicial review vulnerable to political attack at a number of "pressure points," each of which is currently under siege by those who want to shift power to define individual rights from judges to politicians by asking five troublesome questions.

> First, why should judges have the final word in deciding whether a conflict exists between a statute and the Constitution? Why shouldn't Congress's or the president's or the city council's read-

ing of an ambiguous clause in the Constitution be as authoritative as the Supreme Court's?

Second, how do we distinguish which disputes between litigants should trigger the exercise of judicial power to define individual rights?

Third, can't Congress checkmate judicial review by taking away a court's authority to resolve particular kinds of cases?

Fourth, shouldn't Congress be able to hobble the courts by regulating their enforcement powers?

Finally, isn't the entire process of judicial review dependent upon the availability of lawyers?

WHY SHOULD JUDGES HAVE THE FINAL WORD?

John Marshall's model sums up why judges must have the power to resolve an actual conflict between the Constitution and a statute by refusing to enforce the statute. He does not, however, tell us why, except in obvious cases, a judge's view that such a conflict exists should necessarily prevail over the Congress's, the president's or a local police chief's view that no conflict exists.

The functional answer to the question seems to me to be an easy one. If the purpose of the Constitution is to restrain the politically powerful, it seems self-defeating to name politicians as the final arbiters of the extent of the restraints. Foxes, after all, have never been conspicuously successful at guarding chickens. If the politically powerful could be trusted to construe the ambiguous provisions of the Constitution to place real restraints on their power, there probably would be no need for a Constitution in the first place.

Such a functional answer will not, however, prevent someone who passionately believes that the Supreme Court has profoundly erred from seeking to strip the Court of the power to enunciate a final and binding interpretation of the Constitution.[21] Response to the Supreme Court's 1973 abortion decision—Roe v. Wade[22]—is a textbook example of the process. In Roe, the Supreme Court invalidated state criminal laws forbidding abortion because they conflicted with the due process clause of the

Constitution. As construed by the Supreme Court, the due process clause guarantees women the right to reproductive freedom, at least during the first two trimesters of pregnancy. The crux of Justice Blackmun's opinion was that the State's interest in protecting unborn life did not become compelling enough until the third trimester of pregnancy to warrant interfering with a woman's individual interest in reproductive freedom.

Opponents of reproductive freedom for women, enraged over what they considered to be an erroneous reading of the Constitution, sought to reverse *Roe* by shifting the power to construe the due process clause from the Supreme Court to more "political" bodies.[23] The most notorious attempt was Jesse Helms's "Fetal Life" bill, which sought to give Congress the last word on reproductive freedom by declaring that life begins at conception and not, as the Supreme Court had held, some six or seven months later.[24] As such, it was a frontal assault on the Supreme Court's power to speak the final word on the meaning of the Constitution. Fortunately, the Helms bill was resoundingly rejected, in large part because members of Congress—and an aroused public—came to realize that the integrity of judicial review was at stake.[25]

A more subtle, but equally dangerous, attempt to erode *Roe v. Wade* was attempted by Solicitor General Rex Lee—Ronald Reagan's chief Supreme Court lawyer—who argued that local restrictions on access to abortions should be tolerated by the Supreme Court because, in deciding what the ambiguous provisions of the Constitution mean, the Supreme Court should defer to local politicians in doubtful cases.[26] Since constitutional cases are frequently doubtful cases, the Lee formulation was tantamount to making local political bodies like city councils and state legislatures virtual arbiters of many provisions of the Constitution. Fortunately, Lee's arguments, which were presented to the Supreme Court in support of restrictive abortion regulations adopted by the Akron City Council, were firmly rebuffed by a 6–3 majority.[27]

What links the Helms and Lee approaches is a common desire to shift the power to construe the Constitution from the Supreme Court to politicians. What links the rejection of both is a common perception that to accept either would risk the evisceration of judicial review and a fundamental alteration in the way our rights are defined.

Ironically, one of Richard Nixon's few positive legacies to the nation was the powerful support for the Supreme Court's role as final interpreter of the Constitution that emerged as a result of institutional conflict he precipitated. Nixon's attempt to prevent disclosure of the Watergate tapes was a classic assault on the power of judges to speak the final word on the meaning of the Constitution. Nixon claimed that the Constitution granted the president a privilege to withhold certain information from the courts and Congress in order to make it easier for him to elicit candid discussion from his aides. If, Nixon argued, aides feared that their comments might be turned over to another branch, they would be reluctant to speak openly and frankly. Since significant presidential functions were at stake, he reasoned, the president's reading of the scope of executive privilege implied in the Constitution must be accepted as the final word by the courts and Congress.[28]

Chief Justice Burger, writing for a unanimous Supreme Court, accepted the argument that the Constitution recognized a degree of executive privilege, but firmly rejected Nixon's argument that the president should define its scope. Rather, the Court ruled that when the meaning of the Constitution is at issue, it is "emphatically the province and the duty of the judiciary to say what the law is."[29] The *Nixon* precedent would have made short work of the Helms bill if it had ever been passed.

Thus, whether it has been Jesse Helms on behalf of Congress, Richard Nixon on behalf of the presidency, or Ronald Reagan's chief Supreme Court lawyer on behalf of the Akron City Council, we have repeatedly rebuffed attempts to allow politicians rather than judges to deliver the final word on the meaning of the Constitution. But one thing is certain. Whenever the Supreme Court acts vigorously to protect individual rights, new challenges to its power to interpret the Constitution will erupt and threaten to undermine the structure of freedom in America.

WHAT KIND OF A DISPUTE TRIGGERS JUDICIAL REVIEW?

John Marshall's model ties a judge's power to declare the law to her duty to resolve a dispute between litigants. No dispute, no judicial power. In most situations involving individual rights, the existence of an actual dispute between identifiable litigants (called a "case or controversy"[30] in legal jargon) is obvious, giving rise to "standing" to seek judicial review.[31] In a disturbingly large number of settings, however, individuals asserting constitutional rights cannot point to an individual injury attributable to the government's behavior, and thus may lack the power to trigger judicial review.

For example, in 1983 the Supreme Court was asked to review the constitutionality of Los Angeles police regulations which authorize the use of a potentially lethal chokehold procedure. The Court declined to rule on whether such deadly force could be used because the challenger, who had already been choked within an inch of his life, could not show that he was likely to be choked in the future and thus lacked "standing" to seek injunctive relief.[32] Similarly, several years ago, the Supreme Court declined to rule on the legality of the CIA's failure to make its receipts and expenditures public because the challenger could not point to any special injury that he was suffering which was not also being felt by the public at large.[33] The Court also refused to rule on the legality of granting tax-deductible status to hospitals that refused to serve the poor because no showing could be made that the hospitals would, in fact, serve the poor if deductible status were denied.[34] Similarly, the Court threw out a challenge to exclusionary zoning practices because the challenger could not prove that housing for the poor would, in fact, be built if the practices were invalidated.[35] Finally, the Court refused to pass on the legality of state donations of valuable property to churches because the challenger could not show a particularized injury.[36] In each case, the Court reasoned that the individual interest of the person seeking judicial review was not intense enough to trigger John Marshall's dispute-resolution process.

The unfortunate result, of course, is a species of hyperendangered or, more accurately, extinct rights. Rights without "standing" to enforce them judicially are not rights at all, but revocable gifts from politicians. Without the possibility of judicial enforcement, how valuable is the "right" to inspect the receipts and expenditures of the CIA, or the "right" to be free from racially motivated exclusionary zoning, or the "right" not to have public property given away to churches?

The Court's overly rigid reading in these and similar cases of the dispute requirement inherent in Marshall's model is an excessive exercise in self-denial which prevents judges from protecting many endangered rights. It is nothing less than a back-door mechanism which shifts the final word on many "rights" from judges to organs dominated by the politically powerful.

Of course, expedients like the class action, which treats a single plaintiff as the representative of a similarly situated large group, can help. But while class actions prevent a case from collapsing in midstream because of a change in the plaintiff's status, they do not avoid the need for a plaintiff who qualifies for standing in the first place. What is really needed is a recognition by judges that the dispute requirement, which was imposed by John Marshall as a justification for judicial review, should not be permitted to mutate into a means of stifling judicial review merely because the rights at stake are shared equally by us all.

CAN JUDICIAL REVIEW BE FRUSTRATED BY LIMITING SUBJECT-MATTER JURISDICTION?

John Marshall's model assumes that Congress is relying upon the judge to resolve a category of dispute. We generally describe a judge's power to hear a particular kind of case as the "subject-matter jurisdiction" of the court. Not surprisingly, critics of one or another Supreme Court opinion have sought to reverse it by removing that type of case from the subject-matter jurisdiction of the courts. They hope that if Congress takes away subject-matter jurisdiction over a type of dispute, the judge will lack the power and duty to resolve it and the politician's reading of the Constitution will win by default.

For example, when members of Congress were infuriated by the Supreme Court's insistence that both houses of state legislatures be apportioned under the one-person-one-vote theory,[37] bills proliferated in Congress attempting to revoke subject-matter jurisdiction over reapportionment cases.[38] Similarly, legislators are still attempting to avoid the Supreme Court's school-prayer decisions[39] by seeking to exclude such cases from the court's jurisdiction.[40] Whether the individual right has involved legislative reapportionment, school desegregation,[41] school prayer, criminal procedures,[42] suppression of unpopular dissent,[43] or abortion, foes of vigorous judicial protection of individual rights have sought to exploit its seeming Achilles' heel—the fact that the theory of judicial review put forward in *Marbury v. Madison* assumes the existence of subject-matter jurisdiction over the category of dispute at issue.

Fortunately, in modern times at least,[44] no such political counterattack has succeeded. They have failed for two reasons: First, because Congress realizes that if it tugs on subject-matter jurisdiction as a loose thread in the fabric of judicial review, the entire fabric may unravel;[45] and second, because selective attempts to strip the federal courts of power to hear certain kinds of cases, such as those involving free speech or racial equality, would probably be struck down pursuant to the surviving general grant of jurisdiction to decide cases "arising under the Constitution . . . of the United States."[46]

Of course, a truly determined Congressional majority could go so far as to abolish the general grant of jurisdiction and, indeed, Congress probably possesses the power to abolish the lower federal courts altogether.[47] However, given the pervasive role which the federal courts have come to play in the nation's legal structure, it is extremely unlikely that anyone would be willing to abolish federal jurisdiction over *all* constitutional cases as the price of overturning a single Supreme Court decision. It would be far easier to marshal the political support needed to amend the Constitution directly.[48]

The question of just how far Congress can go in using its broad power to regulate subject-matter jurisdiction as a veto over judicial review has no certain answer. Most observers agree that selective attacks on jurisdiction would probably be unconstitutional.[49] But even as to that point there is disagreement.[50] The constitutional text is not cooperative. The appellate jurisdiction of the Supreme Court is subject to "such exceptions, and under such regulations, as the Congress shall make."[51] The very existence of the lower federal courts was left to the discretion of Congress. And when Congress many years ago removed appellate jurisdiction over a particular case in *Ex parte McCardle,* the Supreme Court passively acquiesced. On the other hand, courts have firmly rebuffed congressional attempts to interfere with the exercise of the judicial function.[52]

Thus, while selective attempts to bar categories of cases would probably fail, the fact remains that determined politicians willing to press the issue to dangerous extremes may well possess the power to dismantle the fundamental mechanism by which our individual rights are protected. Until now, we have had the good sense to resist attempts to use subject-matter jurisdiction as a club to subdue the courts, but there will always be radical court-strippers who are willing to risk one hundred eighty years of judicial protection of individual rights in a blind attempt to overturn a Supreme Court decision with which they disagree.

THE PROBLEM OF REMEDIES

The first three "pressure points"—judicial finality, standing, and subject-matter jurisdiction—all involve overt attempts to transfer the power to decide what rights individuals have from insulated judges to politicians responsive to popular pressure. When an opponent of judicial review is unwilling to confront it openly, a less candid approach is to permit a judge to continue to declare the law while making certain that the power to enforce the decision rests with politically vulnerable bodies. In other words, let the judge declare that public schools are unlawfully segregated, but leave it to the local school board to decide what to do about it. Such a scheme retains the illusion of judicial protection of individual rights while destroying its reality, by denying a judge the remedial power necessary to carry out the decision.

For example, a rash of antibusing legislation has sought to prevent judges from ordering the relief necessary to protect the constitutional right of minority schoolchildren to an education that has not been segregated through government action.[53] Similarly, opponents of vigorous judicial enforcement of the Fourth Amendment's ban on unreasonable search and seizure have sought to remove the court's power to order the exclusion of unlawfully seized evidence.[54] Finally, opponents of school prayer and reapportionment rulings have sought to prevent their implementation by denying judges the power to grant injunctions in such cases.[55]

Unlike the assaults on the first three "pressure points," where John Marshall's model isn't much help in repelling boarders, his theory does help ward off attempts to strip the courts of enforcement powers needed to protect individual rights. After all, under *Marbury*, the judge's power to declare the law in the first place flows from a duty to resolve a dispute. If a judge has the power to declare the law, but not the power to assure that the parties obey the law, many disputes would, as a practical matter, remain unresolved. Thus, a necessary attribute of Marshall's model is the inherent power of a judge to order the parties to take steps necessary to comply with a constitutional decision. Accordingly, the power to grant necessary relief in constitutional cases is as unassailable as *Marbury* itself; any attempt to curb it is almost certainly doomed to failure.

DOESN'T THE WHOLE PROCESS
TURN ON ACCESS TO LAWYERS?

Judicial review requires both independent judges and litigants asserting individual rights. Since judges without litigants are powerless to act, an effective way to undermine judicial review is to limit the ability of people to engage in the complex and expensive process of presenting disputes for judicial resolution. Promoting a rigid view of standing is, as we have seen, one way to keep litigants and judges apart. A second approach is to see to it that poor litigants lack access to lawyers, without whom they cannot possibly appear in court. Recognizing this, opponents of judicial review have in recent years mounted a sustained assault on the availability of counsel in individual-rights cases.

Like Governor Reagan's war on the California Rural Legal Assistance program in the mid 1960s, the current Reagan administration has sought to abolish the federally-funded Legal Services Corporation, which provides free lawyers to poor people seeking to assert rights in court.[56] The Legal Services Corporation was created in 1975 to coordinate efforts to provide lawyers for the poor. Between 1975 and 1981, Legal Services expanded to provide a network of legal assistance to poor persons in every state and county in the country. Linking nation-wide field offices with seventeen national support centers, forty state support centers, a national clearinghouse, and effective training and technical assistance units, Legal Services for the first time allowed judicial review to function for the poor as well as the rich. Then came the Reagan cutbacks. Unable to persuade Congress to abolish the program entirely, the Reagan administration dramatically slashed its funding, forcing the layoff of 30 percent of Legal Services' most experienced lawyers—and making it almost impossible for the remaining lawyers to provide the poor with an adequate chance to participate in the *Marbury* process. Not content with funding cutbacks, Congress imposed a series of limitations on Legal Services lawyers, ranging from prohibitions on representing aliens, homosexuals, or persons seeking abortions, to restrictions on bringing class actions or lobbying on behalf of poor clients.[57]

Despite the funding cutbacks and operating restrictions, dedicated Legal Services lawyers continue to provide thousands of poor people with access to rights for the first time. However, many thousands of other poor Americans cannot take advantage of judicial review. For them, it is meaningless to talk about "rights" or John Marshall's legacy because they have been effectively excluded from the very process by which we define rights and give them practical meaning. If there is a group in America for whom the Orwellian nightmare of a world without rights is a present reality, it is those persons who are too poor to purchase a ticket of admission to an American courtroom.

The Reagan administration seeks to excuse its war on Legal Services by arguing that much of the work performed by Legal Services lawyers could be performed by private lawyers. In fact, private lawyers have traditionally argued most constitutional cases. When litigants asserting constitutional rights are large newspapers or business corporations, the free market can generally be counted upon to produce enough competent lawyers to make the *Marbury* model work. However, most assertions of individual rights—especially in the modern era—have not been by the wealthy and powerful. Were the availability of counsel to turn solely on the marketplace, judicial review would almost certainly be available only to the rich.

For much of the nation's history, the free-market availability of counsel in constitutional cases has been supplemented by lawyers who volunteer their services out of a sense of professional obligation or ideological commitment. Marbury was himself represented without fee by a volunteer lawyer.[58] Most lawyers for fugitive slaves in the first wave of constitutional litigation were volunteers as well. And today, organizations like the American Civil Liberties Union and the NAACP owe much of their legal capacity to thousands of volunteers who carry on a proud tradition of *pro bono* public service litigation.[59] However, reliance solely on volunteer counsel to operate the *Marbury* model simply cannot work. There are far too many cases for the available volunteers. Moreover, when cases are novel, complex, and factually difficult, it is unrealistic to expect volunteer lawyers to expend the substantial resources needed to litigate the case effectively. Congress realized in 1976 that the free market and voluntarism had to be supplemented. The result was the Attorneys' Fee Awards Act of 1976, a statute which permits the prevailing plaintiff in many constitutional cases to collect a reasonable attorney's fee from the losing government defendants.[60] Since 1976, therefore, private lawyers have been able to undertake constitutional litigation in the hope of recovering a reasonable fee if they win. The result has been the slow growth of a self-supporting private bar with expertise in litigating "rights" cases and an economic incentive to do so. Given the purely reactive nature of the *Marbury* judge, the growth of a self-supporting civil rights bar capable of providing the raw material for adjudication is an event of major institutional significance.

Unfortunately, at the same time that it is seeking to defund the Legal Services corporation, the Reagan administration is attempting to undermine the Attorneys' Fee Act by limiting fees in civil rights cases to unreasonably low figures, hoping to remove the economic incentive to litigate constitutional claims.

Legal Services has been severely battered and the fate of the Attorneys' Fee Act is still in the balance. We therefore risk sliding backwards into an era when only the wealthy or the lucky litigant with a volunteer lawyer enjoyed access to judicial review. If that happens, an asterisk should be placed next to every substantive definition of a constitutional right, adding the phrase "if you can afford to pay for it."

Thus, while judicial review appears relatively safe from short-term and short-sighted attempts to sidestep the independent judge in favor of more politically malleable officials, it remains highly vulnerable to attempts to limit the availability of counsel.

Taken as a whole, recent political attacks on judicial review, while troublesome, have not fared well. Attempts to secure legislative reversal of Supreme Court decisions have failed. Attempts to limit subject-matter jurisdiction have failed. Attempts to limit a federal judge's remedial powers have failed. Attempts to abolish Legal Services and to cut off attorneys' fees in constitutional cases have, thus far, failed. Attempts to roll back the "standing" rules have been contained. Opponents of judicial review have simply not succeeded in making much of a dent in John Marshall's handiwork—and that augurs well for the vitality of individual rights in 1984. The continued health of judicial review cannot, however, be taken for granted. The five "pressure points" exist and will, no doubt, continue to be the focus of attempts to shift the power to articulate and enforce individual rights from insulated, and therefore independent, judges to officials more subject to pressure by the politically powerful.

When such assaults come, they should be met, first, with the response that judicial review, whatever its textual underpinnings, is by now a fundamental aspect of our constitutional structure. Such a constitutional argument speaks to the very power of Congress to tamper with the role of judges as ultimate guardians of individual rights and, as things now stand, should be a complete answer to attempts to question the judiciary's ability to have the final word on the Constitution's meaning. It should also be a powerful response to attempts to strip the courts of enforcement powers in constitutional cases and a persuasive check on attempts to use selective curbs on subject-matter jurisdiction to overrule the Supreme Court.

However, given the lack of clear textual support for judicial review, its future cannot be entrusted solely to constitutional argumentation. The textual ambiguity and the "pressure points" inherent in John Marshall's model mean that, at bottom, the survival of judicial review—like the survival of rights generally—is a matter of choice. If we as a society choose to dismantle the system of using insulated and independent judges to define and enforce individual rights, no *deus ex machina* will descend from the text of the Constitution or in the form of John Marshall's ghost to protect us from ourselves. Thus, a second—and ultimately controlling —response to assaults on the "pressure points" should be that attempts to exploit them are not merely legitimate political gambits—they are assaults on the way Americans have learned to govern themselves as a free people.

Since judicial review in part depends upon choice, it is important that supporters not attempt to defend it on indefensible ground. The traditional apology for judicial activism of any kind has been to pretend that judges do not make choices but merely search out a pre-existing "correct" answer to the legal issues before the court. Indeed, most judicial decisions continue to be couched as though they announce the only correct result.

Understandably, supporters of judicial review are occasionally tempted to defend it by arguing that judges merely discover the law, they don't make it. Such a defense is, however, ultimately unpersuasive, because it is demonstrably false. Of course judges make law in some individual rights cases—and everyone knows it. We turn to judges to define and enforce individual rights not because no real choices are necessary, but precisely because hard choices cannot be avoided—and cannot be entrusted to politically vulnerable officials. It is on the recognition of that reality—and not on a negation of choice—that the future of judicial review must turn.

NOTES

1. The British system is, of course, the prime example of allowing elected officials to define the scope of fundamental rights. Until very recently, France followed the same practice of parliamentary supremacy. Beardsley, "Constitutional Review in France," 1975 *Supreme Court Review* 189.

2. American-style judicial review is on the upswing. France has begun to experiment with a variant. See Neuborne, "Judicial Review and Separation of Powers in France and the United States," 57 *New York University Law Review* 363 (1982). Judicial review is also practiced in one form or another in the German Federal Republic, Italy, and Austria. *See* Ohlinger, "Cours Constitutionnelles Européennes et Droits Fondamentaux," Colloquy of the School of Law of Aix-en-Provence on the Protection of Fundamental Rights 376 (1980).

3. A. de Tocqueville, *Democracy in America* (1835).

4. The phrase is from United States v. Carolene Products Co., 304 U.S. 144, 152 n.4 (1938), undoubtedly the most significant footnote in American legal history. *See* J. Ely, *Democracy and Distrust* 75–77 (1980); Sandalow, "Judicial Protection of Minorities," 75 *Michigan Law Review* 1162, 1186 (1977).

5. Ironically, one of the earliest exercises of judicial review in our system was on behalf of slaveowners seeking to invalidate state legislation designed to shield escaped slaves from recapture pursuant to the Fugitive Slave Clause of the Constitution. Prigg v. Pennsylvania, 41 U.S. (16 Pet.) 539 (1842). *See generally* Neuborne, "The Myth of Parity," 90 *Harvard Law Review* 1105 (1977).

6. *See, e.g.,* Lochner v. New York, 198 U.S. 45 (1905).

7. Brown v. Board of Education, 347 U.S. 483 (1954).

8. Sherbert v. Verner, 374 U.S. 398 (1963).

9. Cohen v. California, 403 U.S. 15 (1971).

10. The first explicit recognition of judicial review in our system was John Marshall's famous opinion in Marbury v. Madison, 1 Cranch (5 U.S.) 137 (1803). The opinion is carefully critiqued and placed in historical context in Van Alstyne, "A Critical Guide to Marbury v. Madison," 1969 *Duke Law Journal* 1.

11. *See* R. Cover, *Justice Accused* (1975).

12. *See* Nagel, "Court Curbing Periods in American History," 18 *Vanderbilt Law Review* 925 (1965).

13. S. Rep. No. 711, 75th Cong. 1st Sess. 13–14., explaining the Senate's reasons for rejecting FDR's proposal to appoint one additional Supreme Court Justice for each justice over the age of 75. The plan was FDR's political response to decisions of the Supreme Court that had invalidated key aspects of the first New Deal.

14. H.R. 11926, 88th Cong. 2nd Sess. (1964). *See* McKay, "Court, Congress and Reapportionment," 63 *Michigan Law Review* 255 (1964).

15. The Helms proposals on abortion, discussed *infra*, may be found at S.158, 97th Cong. 1st Sess., 127 *Congressional Record* S.287–88 (daily ed. Jan. 19, 1981).

16. 410 U.S. 113 (1973). Roe v. Wade is discussed *infra*.

17. *See generally* S.583, 97th Cong. 1st Sess. (1981); H.R. 73, 97th Cong. 1st Sess. (1981) (depriving courts of power to issue injunctions against state laws involving abortion); H.R. 867, 97th Cong. 1st Sess. (1981) (depriving the Supreme Court and lower federal courts of jurisdiction in abortion cases); S.481, 97th Cong. 1st Sess., 127 *Congressional Record* S.1284 (daily ed. Feb. 16, 1981) (depriving Supreme Court and lower federal courts of jurisdiction in cases involving "voluntary" prayer in public schools); H.R. 869, 97th Cong. 1st Sess. (1981) (depriving Supreme Court and lower federal courts of jurisdiction in school desegregation cases); S.1147, 97th Cong. 1st Sess. (1981) (depriving courts of power to order busing to achieve racial integration).

18. The classic work on the ability of Congress to strip courts of judicial review power is Hart, "The Power of Congress to Limit the Jurisdiction of Federal Courts: An Exercise in Dialectic," 66 *Harvard Law Review* 1362 (1953). For an excellent recent analysis, see Sager, "Constitutional Limitations on Congress's Authority to Regulate the Jurisdiction of the Federal Courts," 95 *Harvard Law Review* 17 (1981).

19. Marshall sets out the textual basis for judicial review in Marbury at 155–58.

20. *See, e.g.*, "Symposium, Judicial Review," 56 *New York University Law Review* 259 (1981).

21. *See generally* the remarks of Jesse Helms defending his proposals to abolish federal court jurisdiction over school prayer and abortion cases as necessary to rectify "erroneous" judicial interpretations of the Constitution. 125 *Congressional Record* S.4130 (daily ed. Apr. 5, 1979); 127 *Congressional Record* S.1281–84 (daily ed. Feb. 16, 1981); 127 *Congressional Record* S.287 (daily ed. Jan. 19, 1981).

22. 410 U.S. 113 (1973).

23. *See* notes 15 and 17 *supra*.

24. Variations of the Fetal Life bill provided that

   . . . human life shall be deemed to exist from conception for the purposes
   of the constitutional provision that no state shall deprive any person of
   life . . . without due process of law.

   See S.158, 97th Cong. 1st Sess., 127 *Congressional Record* S.287–88 (daily ed. Jan. 19, 1981); H.R. 3225, 97th Cong. 1st Sess. (1981); H.R. 900, 97th Cong. 1st Sess. (1981).

25. The Helms proposals never garnered enough support to warrant a formal floor vote.

26. *See* Brief of United States as Amicus Curiae in City of Akron v. Akron Center for Reproductive Health, Supreme Court 1982 Term Nos. 81–746 and 81–1172.

27. City of Akron v. Akron Center for Reproductive Health, 76 L.Ed.2d 687 (1983).

28. Brief of Richard Nixon in United States v. Nixon, Supreme Court 1973 Term, No. 1766. *See* L. Friedman, ed., *United States v. Nixon: The President Before the Supreme Court* (1974).

29. 418 U.S. 683, 703 (1974). Chief Justice Burger, writing for the Court, quoted Marshall's language from Marbury to emphasize the issues at stake.

30. The phrase "case or controversy" comes from Article III of the Constitution, where it is used to describe the duties and powers of the federal courts.

31. See Dorsen, Bender & Neuborne, *Political and Civil Rights in the United States* 4th ed., vol. 1, ch. 17 §A, for cases discussing the law of standing.

32. Lyons v. Los Angeles, 75 L.Ed.2d 675 (1983).

33. United States v. Richardson, 418 U.S. 166 (1974).

34. Simon v. Eastern Kentucky Welfare Rights Org., 426 U.S. 26 (1976).

35. Warth v. Seldin, 422 U.S. 490 (1976).

36. Valley Forge Christian College v. Americans United for the Separation of Church and State, 454 U.S. 654 (1982).

37. Baker v. Carr, 369 U.S. 186 (1962); Wesberry v. Sanders, 376 U.S. 1 (1964).

38. See McKay, "Court, Congress and Reapportionment," 63 *Michigan Law Review* 255 (1964).

39. Engel v. Vitale, 370 U.S. 421 (1962) (school prayer); School District of Abington Township v. Schempp, 374 U.S. 203 (1963) (Bible reading); Stone v. Graham, 449 U.S. 39 (1980) (Ten Commandments).

40. S.481 97th Cong. 1st Sess., 127 *Congressional Record* S.1284 (daily ed. Feb. 16, 1981); H.R. 2347, 97th Cong. 1st Sess. (1981); H.R. 1335, 97th Cong. 1st Sess. (1981); H.R. 989, 97th Cong. 1st Sess. (1981); H.R. 865, 97th Cong. 1st Sess. (1981); H.R. 408, 97th Cong. 1st Sess. (1981); H.R. 326, 97th Cong. 1st Sess. (1981); H.R. 27 97th Cong. 1st Sess. (1981). For the history of attempts to reverse the school prayer decisions, see Laubach, *School Prayers: Congress, the Courts, and the Public* (1969).

41. *E.g.*, H.R. 869, 97th Cong. 1st Sess. (1981).

42. Opponents of the exclusion of illegally seized evidence and involuntary confessions sought to limit the Supreme Court's decisions in Mapp v. Ohio, 367 U.S. 643 (1961) and Miranda v. Arizona, 384 U.S. 436 (1965) by jurisdictional limitations.

43. Supreme Court protection of radicals during the McCarthy era triggered predictable calls for limitations on jurisdiction. *See* Nagel, "Court Curbing Periods in American History," 18 *Vanderbilt Law Review* 925 (1965).

44. Congress did remove the jurisdiction of the Supreme Court to hear an appeal by a Civil War dissident. *Ex parte McCardle*, 74 U.S. (7 Wall.) 506 (1869). However, habeas corpus relief remained available. *See* Van Alstyne, "A Critical Guide to Ex Parte McCardle," 15 *Arizona Law Review* 229 (1973).

45. *See* Prayer in Public Schools and Buildings—Federal Court Jurisdiction: Hearings on S.450 Before the Subcomm. on Courts, Civil Liberties and the Admin. of Justice of the House Judiciary Committee, 96th Cong. 2d Sess. 361 (1980) (statement of Lawrence Sager); Statement of Telford Taylor on Behalf of the ACLU Before the Subcomm. on the Constitution of the Senate Judiciary Committee 10 (May 20, 1981). *See generally* Sager, "Constitutional Limitations on Congress' Authority

to Regulate the Jurisdiction of the Federal Courts," 95 *Harvard Law Review* 17 (1981).

46. 28 U.S.C. §1331, the general "federal question" grant of jurisdiction provides: "The district courts shall have original jurisdiction of all civil actions arising under the Constitution, laws, or treaties of the United States." See also 28 U.S.C. §1343(3) and (4) (broad jurisdiction over cases involving individual rights).

47. The Constitution does not provide for lower federal courts. Article III states:

   The judicial power of the United States, shall be vested in one Supreme Court and in such inferior courts as the Congress may from time to time ordain and establish.

48. Four Supreme Court decisions have been overturned by Constitutional amendment. Chisholm v. Georgia, 2 U.S. (2 Dall.) 419 (1793) (11th); Dred Scott v. Sandford, 60 U.S. (19 How.) 393 (1857) (14th); Pollock v. Farmers' Loan & Trust Co., 157 U.S. 429; 158 U.S. 601 (1895) (16th); Oregon v. Mitchell, 400 U.S. 112 (1970) (26th).

49. *See* note 45 *supra.*

50. Statement of Paul Bator (currently Deputy Solicitor General of the United States) before the Subcomm. on the Constitution of the Senate Judiciary Committee 7, 9 (May 20, 1981).

51. Article III, clause 2.

52. United States v. Klein, 80 U.S. (13 Wall.) 128 (1872) (invalidating a Congressional attempt to dictate the outcome of pending litigation). See also Battaglia v. General Motors, 169 F.2d 254 (2d Cir. 1948). *See generally* Crowell v. Benson, 285 U.S. 22 (1932); St. Joseph Stock Yards Co. v. United States, 298 U.S. 38, 84 (1936) (Brandeis, J., concurring); Johnson v. Robison, 415 U.S. 361, 366 (1974).

53. S.1147, 97th Cong. 1st Sess. (1981); S.1005, 97th Cong. 1st Sess. (1981); H.R. 3332, 97th Cong. 1st Sess. (1981); H.R. 1180, 97th Cong. 1st Sess. (1981); H.R. 1079, 97th Cong. 1st Sess., 127 *Congressional Record* S.6644–45 (June 22, 1981).

54. *See* note 42 *supra.*

55. S.158, 97th Cong. 1st Sess., 127 *Congressional Record* S.287–88 (daily ed. Jan 19, 1981) (abortion); S.481, 97th Cong. 1st Sess., S.1284 (daily ed. Feb. 16, 1981) (school prayer).

56. *See* Siegel and Landau, *No Justice for the Poor: How Cutbacks Are Destroying Legal Services* (An ACLU Public Policy Report, 1983).

57. Ibid.

58. Francis Pinckney, who had served as Attorney General in the Adams Administration.

59. Ennis, "A.C.L.U.: 60 Years of Volunteer Lawyers," 66 *American Bar Association Law Journal* 57 (1980).

60. 42 U.S.C. §1988.

CONGRESS AND THE LEGISLATIVE PROCESS

JOHN SHATTUCK

> *John Shattuck is legislative director of the American Civil*
> *Liberties Union and director of its Washington office. An*
> *honors graduate of Yale Law School, he served as law clerk*
> *to U.S. District Judge Edward Weinfeld. He is a member of*
> *the Executive Committee of the Leadership Conference on*
> *Civil Rights, and in 1981 he helped organize the National*
> *Coalition to Save the Federal Courts.*

CIVIL LIBERTIES AND
THE 1980 ELECTIONS

The political upheaval that occurred on Election Day 1980 was widely interpreted as a triumph of "conservatism." What kind of conservatism? According to the preamble of the platform on which Ronald Reagan ran, the new era would be defined by "the fundamental conviction of the Republican Party that government should foster in our society a climate of maximum individual liberties and freedom of choice."[1]

But the same platform was full of prescriptions for reducing civil liberty. It urged a constitutional amendment to prohibit a woman from making the private decision to have an abortion.[2] It called for curtailment of religious freedom and a narrowing of the separation of church and state in order to permit governmentally sponsored prayer in public school.[3] It supported "the repeal of ill-considered restrictions" on intelligence agencies adopted after Watergate to protect the rights of Americans against thoroughly documented FBI and CIA abuses.[4] It expressly repudiated the Equal Rights Amendment and the use of busing as a judicial remedy for public school segregation.[5] And it called for a return of capital punishment.[6]

Wielding this platform, well-organized and -financed political action committees succeeded beyond their wildest dreams. They not only captured the White House, but also drove out of Congress some of the staunchest supporters of civil liberties, wresting a dozen Senate seats and majority control of the Senate from the Democrats and taking thirty-three districts in the House of Representatives. The National Conservative Political Action Committee and the Moral Majority poured more than $5 million into an intensive television campaign to bring down four key Senate liberals—Birch Bayh, George McGovern, John Culver, and Frank Church.[7] The most significant loss in the House of Representatives was the third-ranking Democratic leader, John Brademas of Indiana, who as majority whip was often effective in marshaling floor votes on civil liberties issues. At least thirteen other representatives in the House with 1980 civil liberties voting records over 70 percent went down to defeat.[8] On the other hand, forty-two representatives with voting records over 90 percent were reelected. These key supporters—together with thirty surviving senators with ratings over 70 percent—provided the core of a civil liberties defense network in the new Congress.

But raw statistics only begin to tell the story. On January 20, 1981, Sen. Edward Kennedy discharged nearly one hundred Senate Judiciary Committee staff members and turned over the chairmanship of the most important committee for civil liberties in the Congress to Senator Strom Thurmond, whose civil liberties voting record in 1980 was 7 percent.[9] Several days after the election Thurmond stated in an interview that his priorities for the Judiciary Committee in 1981 would be the processing of legislation to bring back the federal death penalty, repeal the Voting Rights Act of 1965, and amend the Constitution to ban abortion and permit school prayer.[10] Thurmond also announced his plan to resurrect the notorious Subcommittee on Internal Security (under a new name, Security and Terrorism), to be chaired by Jeremiah Denton, a Moral Majority–backed freshman Republican from Alabama. The new chair of the Senate Subcommittee on the Constitution was Orrin Hatch, a leader of drives in the previous Congress to ban abortion and authorize school prayer. Hatch replaced the defeated Birch Bayh, who was a prime target of the anti–civil liberties movement because of his consistent leadership on individual rights issues during three terms in the Senate. Bayh's position as chairman of the Senate Intelligence Committee was taken by Barry Goldwater, who had a 13 percent civil liberties voting record in 1979–80.[11]

How seriously the anti–civil liberties prescriptions of the campaign had to be taken depended on what efforts would be made to implement them. The signs were not encouraging. Before the election, Sen. Paul Laxalt, the new president's closest friend in Congress, had drafted and introduced an innocuous-sounding bill entitled the Family Protection Act.[12] The bill incorporated a substantial portion of the New Right agenda: denying federal funds to states unless they allowed prayer in public schools and other public facilities; barring federal aid for the purchase of school textbooks if they "denigrate, diminish, or deny the role differences between the sexes as they have been historically understood in the United States"; and declaring that discrimination against homosexuals or "individuals who proclaim homosexual tendencies" is not an "unlawful employment practice." The Laxalt bill also assaulted the Supreme Court by stripping it of jurisdiction to hear constitutional challenges to school prayer.

The Reagan platform's call for the lifting of "ill-considered restrictions on intelligence agencies," while not specific, soon proved ample cause for alarm. Officials of the Reagan transition team announced in December 1980 that they would "rely heavily" on a controversial and widely publicized report by the arch-conservative Heritage Foundation in mapping new policy for the intelligence community.[13] Recommendations of the report were based on its startling premise that "it is axiomatic that individual liberties are secondary to the requirements of national security and civil order."[14] The report called for stepped-up surveillance of "dissidents" and a revival of federal internal security machinery. At one point it noted ominously that "clergymen, students, businessmen, entertainers, labor officials, journalists and government workers all may engage in subversive activities without being fully aware of the extent, purpose or control of their activities."[15]

Soon after the election it became apparent that the Reagan administration would move quickly to curtail civil rights enforcement, particularly affirmative action and school desegregation, to broaden the powers of the FBI and CIA, and to work closely with the Senate leadership to develop positions on the New Right's "social issues."[16] The immediate battleground for civil liberties would be Capitol Hill. Republican control of the Senate meant quick confirmation for Reagan nominees to the Supreme Court and other judicial and executive positions. It also meant that the Right could take the initiative in drafting and processing anti–civil liberties legislation, which in turn was more likely to get a favorable response in both the Republican Senate and the substantially less-Democratic House.

What, then, would be needed to protect civil liberties from the upheaval of 1980? First, despite the spectacular successes of political action committees in defeating Senate liberals, there was little reason to believe that the national election results were a mandate for constitutional change. Ronald Reagan himself was elected chiefly on the basis of economic issues and the unpopularity of Jimmy Carter, not on the agenda of the Moral Majority.[17] The task of the ACLU and its allies in the civil rights, religious, and legal communities was to impress this crucial political fact upon Republican moderates as well as Democrats,[18] and to bring the Reagan administration to understand that its relations with Congress as a whole would deteriorate quickly if it joined in the crusade to curtail civil liberties.

Second, in surveying the new political landscape in Congress, it was important to remember that blocking or defeating legislation is easier than enacting it. No matter how hostile the leadership might prove to be in the Senate and the Reagan administration, there were civil liberties defenders in both parties and in both houses of Congress to rally opposition to dangerous bills. Although civil libertarians had traditionally looked to the courts for the protection of constitutional rights in times of political stress, the front-line defense of civil liberties against right-wing legislation in the Reagan era had to be in the Congress, not the courts. On some crucial issues—the death penalty, abortion funding, and gay rights, for example—the courts had already reached decisions favorable to the Right that were not likely to be reversed by a Supreme Court with one or more Reagan appointees. Constitutional amendments, of course, have always been beyond the reach of judicial review. Finally, a variety of presidential invocations of "national security" to override civil liberties had been upheld by the Supreme Court in recent years.[19]

Third, any strategy for defending civil liberties in the Reagan years had to take into account the methods used by the Moral Majority, the National Conservative Political Action Committee, and similar political organizations. These groups had achieved their goals by organizing hundreds of thousands of people to communicate directly with elected officials.[20] The civil liberties movement now had to do the same, stepping up its efforts to explain broadly and publicly why civil liberties are important to everyone, not just particular minorities or interest groups. Organizing a defense at the grass-roots level—conducting public forums on the legislative crisis, arranging meetings with legislators and their staffs, stimulating letters and telegrams to Congress from concerned constituents around the country—had to become a major focus of activity for civil libertarians intent on protecting the Bill of Rights from stepped-up attacks in the aftermath of the 1980 elections.

1981: THE FEDERAL COURTS UNDER ATTACK

Early in 1981 a political strategy for achieving constitutional change was unveiled. Counting on the unpopularity of judicial decisions requiring busing for school desegregation, prohibiting prayer in public schools, and permitting abortion, anti–civil liberties organizations and their allies in the new Congress unleashed a sweeping assault on the federal judiciary and began to press for the enactment of legislation stripping federal courts of jurisdiction over a wide variety of constitutional issues. During the early months of the Ninety-seventh Congress they encountered little opposition in the Senate, and their goal seemed to be within reach.

On June 16, 1981, Lowell Weicker, a Republican maverick from Connecticut, rose to his feet in a quiet and nearly empty Senate chamber. The Senate was considering the annual Justice Department authorization bill, and an amendment had been offered by Jesse Helms, a North Carolina Republican and a dominant figure in the new Congress. The Helms amendment would strip the Justice Department of authority to participate in cases in which busing had been ordered as a remedy to cure unconstitutional public school segregation.[21] A similar restriction had twice passed the House of Representatives the year before,[22] and the Helms amendment was widely expected to be adopted quickly by the Senate. On June 17 the New York Times reported that "senators on both sides of the aisle privately estimate that the bill would be approved once Senator Weicker ended his speech-making."[23] Straightening his six-foot-six-inch frame and turning to face his Republican colleague, Weicker slowly began to address the Senate:

> I oppose the amendment of the Senator from North Carolina.
> . . . I suspect that we are going to have much of this kind of

nonsense in the months ahead, and it is for that reason that I
choose this moment and this amendment to draw the line. Nothing of this nature—anti–civil rights, anti–the Constitution—is
going to be achieved easily in this . . . Senate. It is going to be
fought every inch of the way—fought in the parliamentary sense,
fought on the basis of substance or the lack thereof. . . . Because
if this amendment goes through . . . then believe me, there will
be much to follow it.[24]

Weicker's speech, which was delivered intermittently for five legislative
days, had a galvanizing effect on the Senate. The Connecticut Republican, who had already been targeted for defeat by the right wing in the
1982 elections, offered his own amendment to the Helms amendment.
The Weicker amendment stated that "[n]othing in this Act shall be
interpreted to limit in any manner the Department of Justice in enforcing
the Constitution of the United States nor to modify or diminish the
authority of the courts of the United States to enforce it."[25] Since there
was no time agreement limiting debate on the bill, Weicker could continue to hold the floor and attempt to persuade other senators to enter
the debate until cloture was invoked by the votes of sixty senators.[26] On
the third day of debate, a conservative Louisiana Democrat, Bennett
Johnston, joined Helms in offering a substitute for the underlying proposal
which made it very clear how high the stakes were in the growing controversy. Under the Helms amendment, as reformulated by Senator Johnston, the federal courts as well as the Department of Justice would be
barred from ordering busing as a remedy for unconstitutional school
segregation. The stage was set for a far-reaching debate about the judicial
role in enforcing constitutional rights, a debate that eventually dominated
the Ninety-seventh Congress. Following ten months of discussion and
scores of procedural votes, the Helms-Johnston amendment finally passed
in the Senate in March 1982, but it was buried in the House of Representatives and never reached the president's desk for signature into law.

It is difficult to exaggerate what was at stake. During 1981 more than
forty separate bills were introduced in the House and Senate to curtail
lower federal court jurisdiction over such controversial subjects as abortion, prayer in the public schools, school desegregation, and sex discrimination in the military.[27] Some bills would even strip the Supreme Court
of its appellate jurisdiction over these issues. Not since President Franklin
Roosevelt had tried to "pack" the Supreme Court with extra justices in
1937 had the independence and integrity of the federal judiciary come

under such sweeping political attack.[28] If the Helms-Johnston amendment had passed early in the Ninety-seventh Congress, it would have fueled the enactment of much similar legislation.

In addition to the antibusing bills, Senator Helms pursued his course by attempting to overturn the Supreme Court's decision in *Roe v. Wade*, [29] which recognized a woman's privacy right to choose abortion. Separate legislation was offered to strip the Supreme Court and the lower federal courts of jurisdiction to entertain constitutional challenges to governmentally sponsored prayer in public schools.[30] Other proposals that were debated included bills to abolish or limit the exclusionary rule[31]—a judge-made rule for enforcing the Fourth Amendment—and bills to limit sharply the availability of habeas corpus in federal courts.[32]

Most of these congressional attacks on the federal courts were aided and abetted by the Reagan administration. In a widely publicized address in October 1981, Attorney General William French Smith accused the judiciary of invading the domain of the legislatures, state and federal, by reaching decisions that overruled the majority will.[33] He struck at the core of the judicial function by referring to cases in which the courts had decided that a legislative majority had deprived a minority of a constitutionally protected right.[34] Speaking to the American Bar Association in early 1982, the attorney general called upon the courts to heed "the ground-swell of conservatism evidenced by the 1980 elections," warning that the legislative arena would become the focal point of "serious attacks on the independence and legitimacy of the courts by persons who see majority rule being thwarted by the legal system itself."[35] The day before the attorney general's speech, David Brink, president of the ABA, had termed the court-stripping bills pending in Congress "a legislative threat to our nation that may lead to the most serious constitutional crisis since our great Civil War."[36] Brink called upon the Reagan administration to oppose the pending legislation. The attorney general initially declined to take a stand, but soon threw the administration's support behind both the Helms-Johnston antibusing bill and the Helms antiabortion bill.[37]

The clearest statement of the position taken by the Reagan administration and its congressional allies on the role of legislative majorities in interpreting the Constitution can be found in the government's *amicus curiae* brief to the Supreme Court in a 1983 case involving municipal ordinances in Akron, Ohio that sharply curtailed abortion rights.[38] In the government's brief, Solicitor General Rex Lee expressed the remarkable view that interpreting and enforcing constitutional rights is ultimately a question for legislative bodies, not the courts—in essence telling the Supreme Court that it had no business reviewing the constitutionality of the Akron ordinances:

> In our democratic society the government body with the primary authority and responsibility to resolve competing policy views and pressures among citizens is the legislature. . . . The best way to determine who is right and who is wrong on these issues [of constitutional interpretation] is to permit and encourage the opposing sides to exercise their persuasive efforts on . . . legislators.[39]

Under this theory public opinion polls and lobbying campaigns should dictate constitutional law. Justice Harry Blackmun, author of the Court's 1973 abortion decision, was sufficiently perturbed by the government's position to ask the solicitor general during oral argument whether he was requesting the Court to overrule the underlying principle of judicial review established in *Marbury v. Madison.*[40] Taken aback, the solicitor general provided no answer. In its June 1983 decision in the Akron case the Court rebuffed the government's argument.

To put the court-stripping bills in perspective: Congress had enacted limitations on federal court authority in the past, but none that would completely remove the authority of either the lower federal courts or the Supreme Court to hear and decide matters of constitutional dimension or to grant necessary relief in cases of constitutional violation.[41] The post–Civil War statute upheld by the Court in the famous case of *Ex parte McArdle,*[42] relied on by some to support the notion of plenary congressional power to curtail federal court authority, bore little resemblance to the court-stripping bills of the Ninety-seventh Congress. It did not attempt completely to bar federal court consideration of a constitutional issue, but merely to remove Supreme Court jurisdiction over a statutory class of habeas corpus cases, leaving open other avenues of constitutional habeas corpus review by the Court. Shortly after *McArdle* was decided, the Court made it clear in *In Re Yeager*[43] that closing off all avenues of review would be unconstitutional. For example, the Emergency Price Control Act,[44] enacted during World War II, gave exclusive jurisdiction to an Emergency Court of Appeals to enjoin enforcement of price orders, subject to review by the Supreme Court. Congress maintained in an inferior federal court the power to grant injunctive relief, and constitutional claims were left reviewable by the Supreme Court.

It is significant that in the single instance in which Congress, more than a century ago, did attempt to exercise its control over federal court jurisdiction as a means of circumventing a judicial interpretation of the Constitution, the Supreme Court expressly held that Congress had exceeded its authority. In *United States v. Klein*,[45] the Court refused to uphold legislation that prevented persons who had received presidential pardons from suing in federal court to recover property taken by military action during the Civil War. The Court struck down this explicitly court-stripping legislation on the ground that its purpose was not to regulate jurisdiction but to restrict the president's constitutional pardon power.

Early in 1981 the ACLU and other opponents of court-stripping banded together in a National Coalition to Save the Federal Courts. A network of civil liberties, civil rights, women's, civic, religious, labor, and bar organizations was created throughout the country, whose impact was increasingly felt in the Congress.[46] For fifteen months—between June 10, 1981, when proceedings began on the Helms-Johnston antibusing bill, and September 23, 1982, when the Senate voted to table a revised version of the Helms antiabortion bill and to kill Helms's bill barring the Supreme Court from ruling on school prayer cases—the Senate was embroiled in constitutional controversy. The Senate leaders of the opposition to court-stripping—Weicker, Bob Packwood, Max Baucus, and a core group of sixteen others[47]—focused the debate on clear and dramatic questions: Can the national legislature dictate to the federal courts? Can a congressional majority take away the constitutional rights of a minority? Can the Constitution be changed merely by getting a simple majority of the Congress to pass a court-stripping bill without having to persuade super-majorities in the Congress and the state legislatures to adopt a constitutional amendment?

Three years after the 1980 elections the independence and integrity of the federal judiciary appears to have been successfully defended against congressional attacks. Although some federal judges may have been intimidated by the political controversy swirling around the judiciary, the support they received from the Congress and the public was far more significant than the attacks they absorbed from anti–civil libertarians. The very fact that the courts were protected in the Congress showed that an autonomous judiciary in America has greater political support than was believed before the court-stripping attacks were unleashed. That in itself is worth celebrating.

1982: THE LEGISLATIVE DEFENSE

The year 1982 was one of stunning victories and painful defeats for civil liberties in Washington. The strategy developed by civil liberties groups after the 1980 elections for blocking dangerous legislation—grass-roots organizing, coalition building, and public debate—began to take hold in the Congress, but it had no apparent effect on an executive branch which increasingly became the vehicle for efforts to translate anti–civil liberties rhetoric into constitutional change.

Antibusing legislation was blocked in the House of Representatives, but a Department of Justice bent on curtailing federal civil rights enforcement made steady progress toward its goal.[48] An administration determined to operate in greater secrecy failed to persuade the Senate to gut the Freedom of Information Act, but the President by a stroke of his pen instituted the broadest security classification system in American history.[49] A valiant struggle on Capitol Hill saved the Legal Services Corporation and its promise of access to justice for millions of poor Americans, but the delivery of legal services was drastically curtailed by Reagan budget cuts and severe restrictions on legal representation.[50] A reborn civil rights movement overcame all opposition in Congress to the passage of a stronger Voting Rights Act, but the Justice Department filed only two new cases in the voting rights field during its first twenty months, compared to a dozen in the first year of the Carter administration.[51]

A clear pattern emerges from these developments: civil rights and liberties were defended in many areas in Congress by open debate and effective organizing, but the defense was often stymied by the Reagan administration. During much of the summer and fall of 1982, the national media focused on the failure of the New Right to enact any part of its controversial agenda on the "social issues" of religion, family, and race. The defeat of the Right on the Senate floor resulted from a growing consensus among moderates, liberals, and traditional conservatives, such as Sen. Barry Goldwater, that legislation to strip away the authority and independence of the federal courts would have a devastating impact on American constitutional values.

But this message was apparently of little importance to the president and his administration. At every turn their policies called for a shift in the traditional relationship between government and the individual in the United States. Contrary to the Reagan campaign slogan, "keep government off the backs of the people," the administration supported massive government intrusion into private lives in its widely publicized policies on abortion, prayer, and CIA domestic spying, as well as some of its less well-known positions on such issues as the privacy of income tax records. The only promise of governmental withdrawal that the Reagan administration kept was its systematic retreat from the enforcement of laws to remedy race and sex discrimination.

While the administration provided a sturdy vehicle for implementing the anti–civil liberties agenda, the Congress proved to be a remarkably effective mechanism for braking its progress. Three factors contributed to a string of civil liberties victories in the legislative arena during 1982. First, it became increasingly clear in the early months of the Reagan era that the new economic issues would dominate the legislative process. During most of 1981 members of Congress were so preoccupied with positioning themselves on federal tax and budget cuts and other legislative elements of "Reaganomics" that they had little time to devote to the "social issues" of the New Right. The Congressional focus on budget cutting worked to the advantage of civil liberties by creating a lightning rod for political controversy, and by dramatizing the charge that the economic policies of the administration discriminated against minorities and the poor.

A good example was the battle to save the Legal Services Corporation, which had appeared certain to fall victim to the budget axe. As the legal services debate grew in intensity, it became clear that the administration's plan to eliminate the Corporation was being fueled more by right-wing pressure to "defund the left"[52] than by any demonstrable need to cut an additional $300 million from the federal budget. A bipartisan congressional coalition, working with the American Bar Association and a broad spectrum of civil rights organizations, was thus able to shift the congressional debate away from unpopular advocacy by legal services attorneys on behalf of their clients toward the administration's unfairness in cutting off access by the poor to the legal system.

A second major factor contributing to the successful defense of civil liberties in Congress is described by the time-honored adage that it is more difficult to enact legislation than to block it. Any legislative proposal that is voted on by the Congress is bound to generate controversy, but too much controversy at any stage of the process will overwhelm it. The task faced in 1981 was to make any aspect of the anti–civil liberties agenda sufficiently controversial that it would be unable to pass through all the stages of the legislative process. This required systematic monitoring of bills, intensive lobbying of legislators, and daily contact with the press by a core group of Washington-based congressional specialists in the ACLU and other organizations.

An early test for this group came when the National Right to Life Committee and other antiabortion organizations mounted a concerted drive in early 1981 to pass a Human Life Bill, defining "life" subject to constitutional protection as beginning at the "moment of conception."[53] Pro-choice lobbyists seized the opportunity to use the Senate Constitution Subcommittee hearings on the bill as a platform. Point-by-point rebuttals of the medical, religious, and constitutional arguments of witnesses testifying in favor of the bill were offered by a parade of experts assembled by the pro-choice side, and the ranking minority member of the subcommittee, Sen. Max Baucus, engaged the subcommittee chair, Sen. Orrin Hatch, in daily debate over the meaning and likely consequences of the legislation. For nearly a month the press reported the growing turmoil surrounding the Human Life Bill, and when the hearings were over the controversy was so thick that the bill had lost much of its momentum.

The use of congressional procedures to derail anti–civil liberties legislation was a frequent tactic during the first two years of the Reagan administration. The administration's bill to curtail public access to government information under the Freedom of Information Act was buried in a mountain of amendments adopted by the Senate Judiciary Committee after months of subcommittee negotiations and discussions conducted under the prodding of press and civil liberties groups. A similar strategy was used to generate debate on the floor of the House of Representatives around an omnibus immigration bill that was opposed by civil liberties groups because of the likely discriminatory impact of its employer sanctions provisions and its curtailment of federal court jurisdiction over political asylum and other immigration cases.[54] A procedural gridlock was created in the Senate around the administration's package of anticrime bills—to reinstitute a federal death penalty, curtail the exclusionary rule, which bars illegally seized evidence from being introduced in federal criminal trials, cut back the right of state prisoners to file habeas corpus petitions, and otherwise to attack the constitutional rights of persons convicted or accused of crime. Finally, many anti–civil liberties bills were stopped in the House Judiciary Committee, where Chairman Peter Rodino and subcommittee chairs Robert Kastenmeier, Don Edwards, and

John Conyers conducted extensive hearings and deferred final action on court-stripping measures, the death penalty, criminal code revision, constitutional amendments requiring school prayer and barring busing for school desegregation, and a variety of other proposals. Rep. Barney Frank, a politically astute freshman on the Judiciary Committee, observed in November 1981 that a majority of House members were privately pleased that the Committee was becoming a graveyard for controversial bills, because that meant they would not have to vote for or against them.[55]

The third factor behind the surprising success of the civil liberties movement in blocking dangerous legislation was the building of a national communications network committed to defending the Constitution in Congress. Spurred by the need to counter the impact on the legislative process of well-organized grass-roots lobbying campaigns conducted by the Moral Majority, the National Right to Life Committee, and other organizations, civil liberties groups mobilized a nationwide "Bill of Rights Lobby" and created coalitions with new allies. In 1981 and 1982 the ACLU sponsored a series of eighteen Bill of Rights Conferences in major cities around the country, aimed at publicizing the legislative threats to civil liberties and generating a grass-roots response. The conferences were cosponsored by local chapters of the National Organization for Women, the NAACP, the National Urgan League, Common Cause, the League of United Latin American Citizens, the National Abortion Rights Action League, and other organizations, many of which also conducted their own grass-roots campaigns. Legislative newsletters and issue briefs were published and widely circulated. Local telephone and letter-writing campaigns were stimulated to register with congressional offices constituent opposition to the anti–civil liberties agenda. Slowly, members of Congress began to comprehend the strength of this resistance.

By defining the threat to the Constitution in broad terms, the civil liberties movement was able to join forces with many groups who disagreed with it over particular issues, but who could be united in an effort to preserve the country's constitutional structure. For example, two major organizations in the National Coalition to Save the Federal Courts, the American Bar Association and Common Cause, took no position on the underlying issues of school prayer, abortion, and busing; the rest of the coalition, with the exception of the ACLU, was made up of organizations concerned with only one of the substantive issues at stake in the court-stripping legislation. The strength and internal cohesion of the Coalition was demonstrated in the summer and fall of 1982 when for the first time congressional mail began to run strongly against the court-stripping bills. In September pro-choice lobbyists joined the ACLU and national religious groups in rounding up votes in the Senate to table the prayer bill a week after the antiabortion measure had been killed.[56]

Another striking example of the success of coalition politics in countering dangerous legislation was the work of the Leadership Conference on Civil Rights in generating support for the enactment in 1982 of a twenty-five-year extension of a strengthened federal Voting Rights Act.[57] By seeking to weaken the Act, the Reagan Justice Department and its allies in the Senate galvanized a divided and faltering civil rights movement into action. The LCCR, a coalition of 163 organizations often unable to agree on particular issues, quickly reached a consensus that the threat to the Voting Rights Act was so fundamental that if it succeeded a quarter century of civil rights progress would be reversed. United by this perception, the coalition mounted the most effective civil rights lobbying campaign in a decade.

Despite the victories produced by these successful strategies for defending civil liberties in the Congress, the defense did not always hold. On June 23, 1982, President Reagan signed into law the Intelligence Identities Protection Act.[58] The enactment of this statute by overwhelming margins in both Houses was a setback for the First Amendment and an example of the intense pressures against civil liberties in the area of national security. The new statute made it a crime to publish "any information that identifies an individual as a covert agent" of the CIA or FBI —even if the information is unclassified, is a matter of public record, or is derived entirely from public sources. For the first time in American history the press was prohibited from publishing information that is in the public domain, and the executive branch was armed with a sophisticated new censorship device. The Intelligence Identities Act teaches us how fragile are the protections of rights in the intelligence field a decade after Watergate. One of the cosponsors of the identities bill, Sen. Richard Lugar, illustrated this problem when he stated bluntly in an interview, "I don't think on a continuum we are going to be able to have both an ongoing intelligence capability and a totality of civil rights protection."[59]

Even with the setback on the intelligence bill, 1982 proved on the whole to be a successful year for the defense of civil liberties in Congress. The alleged "mandate" to dismantle the Constitution, based on the 1980 election results, evaporated in the cold reality of a Congress dominated by economic issues and an electorate increasingly impatient with the time consumed in congressional debate over the "social issues" agenda.

The 1982 midterm elections proved the point. In contrast to 1980, not a single member of Congress with a favorable civil liberties voting record who had been targeted by the National Conservative Political Action Committee was defeated for reelection.[60] Moreover, the positions of newly elected representatives were far more favorable to civil liberties than the Congress as a whole on such issues as abortion, school prayer, and the Equal Rights Amendment.[61] The most significant political change in the Congress was the Democratic Party's gain of twenty-six seats in the House, more than twice as many as the average seat-shift in a midterm election.[62]

In spite of these developments—perhaps even because of them—the Ninety-eighth Congress convened in January 1983 in an atmosphere of political uncertainty. Having defeated the court-stripping bills, civil libertarians now had to contend with constitutional amendments to prohibit abortion and permit public school prayer, emanating from such moderates as Sens. Mark Hatfield and Tom Eagleton. By early summer it was clear that no constitutional amendment to overturn *Roe v. Wade* would pass the Congress, no matter how liberal its sponsor might be on other issues. On the other hand, a groundswell of support for some form of officially sponsored religious activities in public school appeared to create momentum toward the enactment of various "moderate" bills to achieve that purpose. Finally, the new Congress seemed more likely than the old one to reach agreement on several complex subjects affecting civil liberties, such as the five-year effort to overhaul the nation's immigration laws[63] and the ten-year debate over criminal sentencing procedures.[64]

1983: GOVERNMENT BY EXECUTIVE FIAT

By 1983 it was clear that the political upheaval in Congress resulting from the 1980 election was not likely to produce the revolutionary changes in the legislative framework of constitutional rights that many had predicted would occur during the Reagan administration. The administration itself, however, grew more adamant and inventive in its pursuit of constitutional change, turning increasingly to the vast machinery of the executive branch as the principal instrument of policymaking on issues of civil rights and civil liberties.

During the first three years of the Reagan era executive orders and directives were issued at such a furious pace that the White House became a de facto lawmaking branch of the government.[65] Executive orders are convenient instruments of presidential policy. They can be promulgated without the opportunity for much public debate, and their validity does not depend on congressional approval. More importantly, they provide an aura of legitimacy for presidential actions which might otherwise be challenged as illegal. While an executive order can be invalidated by the courts or overridden by the Congress, its mere issuance tends to insulate the president from charges that he is engaged in abuses of power.

A random sample of Reagan executive orders and directives that infringe on individual rights is alarming. Between 1981 and 1983 the CIA was granted new authority to conduct surveillance inside the United States,[66] the president attempted to replace five out of six members of the historically independent Civil Rights Commission because their views on civil rights did not suit his administration,[67] executive agencies handling classified information were told they could keep much more information secret,[68] guidelines were proposed cutting back affirmative action and other civil rights requirements for federal contractors,[69] the budgets of federal civil rights enforcement agencies were drastically slashed,[70] federal regulations protecting welfare recipients and prisoners against coercive human experimentation programs were narrowed,[71] rules were promulgated requiring birth control clinics that prescribe contraceptives for teen-age patients to inform the teen-agers' parents,[72] guidelines were proposed to ban all lobbying and related First Amendment activities by federal grantees or contractors,[73] tax exemptions were granted to racially discriminatory private schools (until the Supreme Court overruled this executive action),[74] regulations were adopted to permit Secret Service intelligence files to be fed into the FBI's computerized National Crime Information Center,[75] and covert operations in Central America specifically forbidden by Congress were secretly ordered and later publicly defended by the president.[76]

The growth of government by executive order was particularly alarming in areas affecting First Amendment rights. In the spring of 1983 Ronald Reagan announced that he was "up to my keister" with leaks.[77] A decade earlier Richard Nixon had been similarly frustrated. Both presidents took action to try to silence their critics, but there is a substantial difference in the way they went about it. During the spring of 1973 leaking reached floodtide proportions in Washington, from the unauthorized disclosures of Deep Throat to the testimonial confessions of John W. Dean, III. The Congress was prodded by the news media and the public into probing and cataloguing the abuses of power revealed by these leaks and reasserting its legislative prerogatives over a runaway presidency which had enhanced its power at the expense of the Bill of Rights. Thanks in part to the personality of Richard Nixon and his capacity to inspire public distrust, the House Judiciary Committee crystallized a national consensus when it voted articles of impeachment against a sitting president less than two years after the Watergate affair began to unravel.

Ronald Reagan discovered a central truth about the presidency that his Californian predecessor never learned: it is not necessary for a chief executive to break the law in secret if he publicly bends it to suit his purposes by issuing an executive order. On March 11, 1983, the White House released a Presidential Directive on Safeguarding National Security Information.[78] The policy enunciated in this three-page document establishes the broadest secrecy system in United States history, but its public release made it appear more legitimate than Richard Nixon's clandestine and ill-fated leak-plugging operations. Under the Reagan order all executive branch employees who have access to certain categories of classified information must sign lifetime nondisclosure agreements as a condition of employment, obligating them to submit all their writings and speeches for prior review by official censors. Thanks to an earlier Reagan executive order vastly expanding the amount of classified information in the federal government,[79] virtually no area of public policy was immune from censorship under the terms of the order. The secrecy mania went so far that civil rights workers in the Department of Education were for a time required to obtain security clearances in order to process discrimination complaints.[80]

The secrecy order gave the President a powerful tool for quashing public criticism about his policies. Walter Mondale, Henry Kissinger, Cyrus Vance, and thousands of less prominent former officials, had they been forced to sign secrecy agreements when they were in office, could now be threatened with prior restraint when they seek to draw upon their government experience to write or speak about positions taken by the incumbent administration. The result would be an inevitable dampening of public debate on such urgent issues as nuclear weapons, the Middle East, and Central America.

The Congress initially appeared reluctant to respond to the presidential directive on secrecy. The national security aura, combined with typical congressional reluctance to step into territory in which the president had already taken forceful action, relegated Congress at first to a spectator's role in relation to the order. Two House subcommittees conducted several days of hearings to probe its origin and effect,[81] and the Senate Governmental Affairs Committee launched a similar inquiry.[82] Nevertheless, early resistance inside federal agencies to implementing the secrecy program was considerably stronger than organized resistance on Capitol Hill.[83] Eventually, however, the Congress was moved to take action, and it passed legislation shortly before adjourning, in November 1983, to block implementation of the secrecy order until at least April 1984.[84]

Two factors contributed to the ambivalence of Congress in curbing Reagan's national security censorship. First, the order lacked a specific legislative context: it related to no pending legislation and it could be implemented without appropriation of additional funds. By contrast, a related White House directive authorizing federal agency heads to require employees handling classified information to submit to lie detector tests was blocked by the Congress when it inserted a provision in the annual Defense Department Appropriations Bill deleting funds for new polygraph testing.[85] Second, the base of organized public opposition to the censorship order was largely limited to civil liberties organizations and press groups, and there was simply not enough grass-roots pressure on the Congress to offset its normal reluctance to challenge the president on national security issues. When such pressure was brought to bear on the Congress to take action to block another executive order, the result was surprising: in April 1983 the Office of Management and Budget withdrew a controversial proposal to bar political advocacy by the recipients of federal grants and contracts after the House Government Operations Committee, chaired by Rep. Jack Brooks, reacted to an overwhelming public outcry against the proposal by demanding its withdrawal.[86]

Expansion of FBI authority to investigate controversial political speech was another product of Reagan government by executive order. The Justice Department's revision in March 1983 of FBI guidelines for conducting "domestic security" investigations could have a damaging impact on the exercise of First Amendment rights,[87] especially in granting new authority for the FBI to investigate persons or groups based solely on their "advocacy" of illegal conduct[88] and new authority to place informants and undercover agents in political organizations during "preliminary inquiries," when the FBI does not yet have evidence to establish "reasonable suspicion" of any crime.[89] Although FBI Director William Webster, in defending the new guidelines, publicly foreswore any interest in intruding on lawful political activity,[90] the guidelines could be twisted by a less sensitive director into a charter for the kind of political spying that flourished during the J. Edgar Hoover era.

Unlike the Reagan censorship order, the FBI guideline revisions provoked an immediate and modestly effective response in the Congress. Rep. Don Edwards and Sens. Joseph Biden and Patrick Leahy, members of the House and Senate Judiciary Committees, joined the ACLU and other civil liberties groups in publicly criticizing the revisions and calling for the attorney general and the FBI director to make clear that investigations based solely on a person's advocacy would not be conducted. Edwards, who chairs the House Subcommittee on Civil and Constitutional Rights, went further by conducting extensive hearings on the subject and sponsoring an amendment to the Justice Department Authorization Bill, which was adopted by the House Judiciary Committee, barring implementation of the new guidelines for the remainder of 1983.[91] Although the amendment was not offered in the Senate, it served notice that 1960s-style political spying by the FBI would not be tolerated by many members of Congress.

Congressional response to the Reagan secrecy order and the FBI guideline revisions show the advantages enjoyed by a president who acts unilaterally in order to circumvent the legislative process. Curtailment of public information and control over the executive branch often make it possible for the White House to rule by fiat. But there are no political free rides for presidents who issue controversial executive orders, since the Congress is jealous of its prerogatives and wary of appearing tacitly to approve unpopular executive action by failing to challenge it. When an executive order has a direct impact on the legislative process—because it requires additional funding to implement, interprets an act of Congress, or produces a strong public outcry—Congress is likely to become involved. The secrecy order provoked a slower congressional response than the FBI guideline revisions, largely because of the different relationship of these two issues to the funding and authorization process.

Other Reagan executive actions affecting First Amendment rights have become the subject of debate on Capitol Hill when they have interpreted acts of Congress. The control of free speech and the flow of information and ideas across the national borders, for example, is a major Reagan initiative that has faced increasing scrutiny in the Congress because it purports to rely on three statutes: the Export Administration Act,[92] the Foreign Agents Registration Act,[93] and the Walter-McCarran Immigration Act.[94] Although specific actions taken by the administration to control free speech at the borders—such as labeling Canadian films about acid rain and nuclear war "political propaganda," denying visa applications by foreign visitors of whose politics the administration disapproves, and censoring scientific research that might be valuable to "hostile" foreign countries—have been substantially unchallenged in the Congress, these actions have sparked the drafting and introduction of bills to amend the underlying statutes in order to curtail executive discretion.

In addition to freedom of speech and of the press, the Reagan administration, in its effort to alter constitutional rights by executive action, has taken aim at equal protection of the laws.[95] Here, its primary target has been the civil rights enforcement machinery of the federal government, particularly litigation undertaken by the Civil Rights Division of the Department of Justice. One striking example is the field of equal educational opportunity. The law is unequivocal: government at all levels has an affirmative obligation to desegregate public schools, and "freedom of choice" plans are inadequate as remedies for school segregation because they put the burden of change on students rather than on the government.

Nevertheless, "freedom of choice" has been the heart of the Reagan administration's school desegregation policy. William Bradford Reynolds, assistant attorney general for civil rights, told a House Judiciary subcommittee in 1981, "We are not going to compel children who don't choose to have an integrated education to have one."[96] The Justice Department has maintained that the government's only obligation is to remove legal racial barriers so that people can choose whether they want to desegregate. But the Supreme Court has held time and again that government has an affirmative obligation to ensure that public schools are integrated and that no one has a right to choose to attend a segregated public school.[97] Attempting to explain the administration's attitude toward these decisions, Michael Uhlmann, a special assistant to the President for civil rights policy, claimed it was inaccurate to say the administration was not enforcing the law of the land, "unless you call all the decisions of the Supreme Court the law of the land."[98]

As in the case of executive action curtailing freedom of speech, the Congress has been uneven in its response to the Reagan administration's actions in the area of civil rights. Often lacking a specific legislative context, administration policies on school desegregation and affirmative action in employment have been allowed to develop without much effective congressional opposition or oversight. On the other hand, the president has paid a price for his civil rights policies by fostering a perception that he has reversed a quarter-century of bipartisan civil rights progress. This perception has affected the Congress and influenced the outcome of several important debates on civil rights legislation. The overwhelming margin in the House of Representatives in favor of a strengthened Voting Rights Act was one important example, as were the strong votes in both chambers for legislation extending the life of the U.S. Commission on Civil Rights and prohibiting the president from replacing its members without "cause."[99] These votes came after the president had attempted to weaken both the Voting Rights Act, by narrowing its coverage, and the Civil Rights Commission, by replacing five of its six commissioners. Similar congressional responses occurred when the president refused to enforce the laws against sex discrimination. In August 1983, a bipartisan congressional coalition, including prominent Republican Senators Bob Dole and Bob Packwood, filed a brief in the Supreme Court opposing the Reagan administration's position in a pending case that private schools and colleges receiving federal funds do not have to ban sex discrimination in all their programs.[100]

Institutionalized secrecy and surveillance and sharp curtailment of civil rights enforcement are the centerpieces of Ronald Reagan's government by executive order. Some of these presidential edicts have been challenged in the courts and the Congress, but mounting such efforts is a more difficult task than holding a president responsible for a specific illegal act, such as a burglary or a wiretap planned in the Oval Office. In 1974 the House Judiciary Committee unraveled the secret abuses of the Nixon administration on national television. In 1983 several committees of the Congress exposed the evils of the Reagan censorship order, the new FBI guidelines, information control at the national borders, and the failure of the administration to enforce the civil rights laws. But these civil liberties issues were more complex than the crimes of the Nixon era, and the will of Congress to challenge the president was weaker.

The ultimate—and perhaps only—effective method for Congress to hold a president fully accountable for his actions is the remedy of impeachment, but the political incentive to pursue that course, minimal under most circumstances, was further curtailed by President Reagan's strategy of acting under color of his executive orders and presidential directives.[101] Nevertheless, presidential lawmaking at the expense of civil liberties could eventually amount to a usurpation of power as great as the abuses of the imperial presidency a decade ago. On the eve of 1984, a president noted for his ability to "communicate" to the public has mastered the Orwellian art of doublespeak and is arguing that his executive orders are law. By definition, therefore, government by executive order is not lawless. Big Brother could not have stated the case for himself more concisely.

NOTES

1. Republican National Convention Platform, adopted by the Republican National Convention, July 15, 1980, Detroit, Michigan, reprinted in *Congressional Record*, July 31, 1980, at S.10381.

2. *Id.* at S.10383.

3. *Id.*

4. *Id.* at S.10396.

5. *Id.* at S.10382, 10384.

6. *Id.* at S.10386.

7. "Million-Dollar Drive Aims to Oust Our Liberal Senators," *New York Times*, March 24, 1980, at B6, col. 3.

8. *Civil Liberties Alert*, Legislative Newsletter of the American Civil Liberties Union Washington Office, vol. 6, no. 2 (October/November 1982), at 6.

9. *Id.*

10. *Washington Star*, November 17, 1980, at 3.

11. *Civil Liberties Alert*, *supra* note 8.

12. S.1808, 96th Cong., introduced September 24, 1979.

13. *Washington Star*, November 16, 1980, at 12.

14. *Id.*

15. C. Heatherly, *Mandate for Leadership: Policy Management in a Conservative Administration* 940 (1981).

16. *Washington Post*, November 16, 1980, at 6.

17. *New York Times*, November 5, 1980, at 30, col. 1.

18. In a *New York Times* article of December 29, 1980, several moderate Republicans, including Sens. Charles McC. Mathias, Jr., Robert T. Stafford, Lowell Weicker, William S. Cohen, David F. Durenberger, and John H. Chafee, were quoted as saying that "they intend to act as 'watchdogs' in the next Congress and to join with like-minded Democrats to block conservative initiatives they regard as threatening." *Id.* at 15. Senator Cohen stated that "the last thing that President Reagan needs is to get involved in a controversy over school prayer, or abortion or busing. The one thing he has to do is set forth a program to deal with inflation and he can't let other issues divert his energies and those of the House and Senate."

19. *See* Shattuck, "National Security a Decade After Watergate," *democracy*, vol. 3, no. 1, at 56 (Winter 1983).

20. "Christian New Right's Rush to Power," *New York Times*, August 18, 1980, at B7, col. 1.

21. *Congressional Record*, June 16, 1981, at S.6274.

22. *Civil Liberties Alert*, vol. 3., no. 2 (June 1979).

23. *New York Times*, June 17, 1981, at 18.

24. *Congressional Record*, June 16, 1981, at S.6275–S.6276.

25. *Congressional Record*, June 18, 1981, at S.6500.

26. Senate Rule # 22.

27. *Congressional Quarterly Almanac*, vol. 37, 97th Cong., 1st Sess. at 407 (1981).

28. Fink, "Under the High Court," *New York Times*, July 17, 1981, at A23.

29. *Congressional Quarterly Almanac*, *supra* note 27, at 425.

30. *Id.* at 407.

31. *Id.*

32. *Congressional Quarterly Almanac*, vol. 38, 97th Cong., 2nd Sess. at 416.

33. Prepared remarks of Attorney General William French Smith before the Federal Legal Council, Reston, Virginia, October 30, 1981, as quoted in the *New York Times* of that date, at A22.

34. *Id.*

35. As quoted in the *New York Times*, January 26, 1982, at B58.

36. As quoted in the *New York Times*, January 25, 1982, at A19.

37. Letters of Attorney General William French Smith to Senator Strom Thurmond, Chairman, Senate Judiciary Committee, March 26, 1982.

38. City of Akron v. Akron Center for Reproductive Health, Inc., 103 S.Ct. 2481 (1983).

39. Brief for the United States as *amicus curiae*, City of Akron v. Akron Center for Reproductive Health, Inc., *supra* note 38, at 9.

40. 5 U.S. (1 Cranch) 137 (1803).

41. *See* Shattuck and Landau, "Courtstripping: A New Way to Rewrite the Constitution," 21 *Judges' Journal* 16, 19–20 (Winter 1982). *See generally* Sager, "The Supreme Court, 1980 Term-Forward: Constitutional Limitations on Congress' Authority to Regulate the Jurisdiction of the Federal Courts," 95 *Harvard Law Review* 17 (1981).

42. 74 U.S. (97 Wall.) 506 (1869).

43. 75 U.S. (8 Wall.) 85 (1869).

44. Ch. 26, 56 Stat. 23 (1942).

45. 80 U.S. (13 Wall.) 519 (1871).

46. Shattuck, "Civil Liberties Are Safer in Congress's Hands," *New York Times*, November 4, 1982, at A27.

47. Sens. Bill Bradley, Dale Bumpers, John Chafee, Alan Cranston, Barry Goldwater, Gary Hart, Mark Hatfield, Edward Kennedy, Patrick Leahy, Carl Levin, Charles McC. Mathias, Jr., Howard Metzenbaum, George Mitchell, Daniel P. Moynihan, Arlen Specter, and Paul Tsongas.

48. *See, e.g.*, Shattuck, "Malign Neglect," *The New Republic*, Oct. 11, 1982, at 17–19; Taylor, et al., *Without Justice: A Report on the Conduct of the Justice Department in Civil Rights in 1981–82* (Leadership Conference on Civil Rights, 1982).

49. Executive Order 12356 (April 2, 1982). *See also* Presidential Directive on Safeguarding National Security Information (March 11, 1983).

50. *See* Siegal and Landau, *No Justice for the Poor: How Cutbacks are Destroying Legal Services* (American Civil Liberties Union, 1983).

51. Parker and Phillips, *The Justice Department and Voting Rights Act Enforcement: Political Interference and Retreat* (Lawyers Committee for Civil Rights, 1982). *See also Without Justice, supra* note 48, at 6.

52. *See, e.g.*, paid political advertisement of the Conservative Caucus, Inc. in the *Washington Times*, August 3, 1983, at 5A.

53. *Congressional Quarterly Almanac*, vol. 37, at 407 (1981).

54. *See* Shapiro and Henderson, "Justice for Aliens," *infra* at 160.

55. Unpublished speech to Bill of Rights Conference sponsored by ACLU New England affiliates, Boston, Massachusetts, November 8, 1981.

56. *Congressional Quarterly Almanac*, vol. 38, at 416 (1982).

57. Voting Rights Extension Act of 1982, P.L. 97–205, 96 Stat. 131 (1982) (June 29, 1982).

58. Intelligence Identities Protection Act, P.L. 97–200 (June 23, 1982).

59. Quoted in *New York Times*, September 28, 1981, at 24.

60. *New York Times*, November 7, 1982, at 31.

61. *Id.*, November 4, 1982, at 1, 18.

62. *Id.*, November 3, 1982, at 1, 20.

63. See S. 829 and H.R. 1560, "The Immigration Reform and Control Act" (98th Cong., 1st Sess.). *See generally U.S. Immigration Policy and the National Interest, the Final Report and Recommendations of the Select Commission on Immigration and Refugee Policy* (March 1981).

64. *See* S. 668 and H.R. 3128 (98th Cong., 1st Sess.). *See generally* Shattuck and Landau, "Civil Liberties and Criminal Code Reform," 72 Journal of Criminal Law and Criminology 914, 923–34 (1981).

65. *See* Shattuck, "Cutting Back on Freedom by Fiat," *The Nation,* June 11, 1983, at 1.

66. Executive Order 12333 (December 4, 1981).

67. *Washington Post,* May 26, 1983, at 1, 13. In November 1983, the Congress and a federal district court both acted to block the president's firing of two commissioners without cause and his effort to control the appointment of a majority of the commission. *New York Times,* November 12, 1983, at 1.

68. Executive Order 12356 (April 2, 1982).

69. Office of Federal Contract Compliance, "Civil Rights Requirements for Federal Contractors," 47 *Federal Register* 17770 (April 23, 1982).

70. Morisey, *More Is Less: The Reagan Administration's Proposed Civil Rights Budget for Fiscal Year 1984* (American Civil Liberties Union, 1983).

71. 47 *Federal Register* 12276 (March 22, 1982).

72. 47 *Federal Register* 7699 (February 22, 1982).

73. "Proposed Revisions of Office of Management and Budget Circular A-122," 48 *Federal Register* 3348, (January 24, 1983). *See also* Hearings on Proposed Revision of OMB Circular A-122 before the Committee on Government Operations, House of Representatives, 98th Cong., 1st Sess. (March 1983).

74. *See* Bob Jones University v. Internal Revenue Service, 103 S.Ct. 2017 (1983).

75. "Proposed Addition to National Crime Information Center System of Records," 47 *Federal Register* 55343 (1982). *See also* Hearing on Proposed Regulations Concerning Secret Service Access to National Crime Information Center, Subcommittee on Civil and Constitutional Rights, Committee on the Judiciary, House of Representatives, 98th Cong., 1st Sess. (February 9, 1983). The regulations were implemented on April 27, 1983.

76. *See New York Times,* April 15, 1983, at 1; "Can Congress Really Check the CIA?" *First Principles,* May/June 1983, at 1.

77. *Washington Post,* February 23, 1983, at 1.

78. Presidential Directive on Safeguarding National Security Information, March 11, 1983.

79. Executive Order 12356 (April 2, 1982).

80. *Washington Post,* April 8, 1983, at 7.

81. Joint Hearings on Presidential Directive on Safeguarding National Security Information, before the Subcommittee on Civil and Constitutional Rights, Committee on

the Judiciary, and the Subcommittee on Government Employees, Committee on Post Office and Civil Service, House of Representatives, 98th Cong., 1st Sess. (April 21 and 28, 1983).

82. *See* letter from Members of Senate Governmental Affairs Committee to Hon. William Roth, Chairman, June 18, 1983.

83. *See First Principles,* May/June 1983.

84. *New York Times,* October 21, 1983, at 1. *See generally Civil Liberties Alert,* vol. 7, nos. 6–7 (December 1983).

85. *Washington Post,* July 27, 1983, at 5.

86. *See* note 77 *supra.*

87. "Attorney General Guidelines on General Crimes, Racketeering Enterprise and Domestic Security/Terrorism Investigations" (March 21, 1983), superseding "Domestic Security Guidelines" (April 7, 1976).

88. *Id.,* "General Principles," at 3, ¶3.

89. *Id.,* Section 2 B(6).

90. Hearings on Revised FBI Domestic Security Guidelines before the Subcommittee on Civil and Constitutional Rights, Committee on the Judiciary, House of Representatives, 98th Cong., 1st Sess., April 27, 1983 (testimony of William Webster, Director, Federal Bureau of Investigation, at 7).

91. Proceedings on Justice Department Authorization Act of 1984, H.R. 2175, before Committee on the Judiciary, House of Representatives, 98th Cong., 1st Sess., May 10, 1983.

92. 50 U.S. Code, §§ 2401–2413.

93. 22 U.S. Code, §§ 611–621.

94. 50 U.S. Code, §§ 1951–1955, 1961.

95. See Days, "Racial Justice," *infra* at 94–95.

96. Hearing before House Subcommittee on Civil and Constitutional Rights, Committee on the Judiciary, House of Representatives, 97th Cong., 1st Sess., Nov. 19, 1981.

97. *See, e.g.,* Green v. County School Board, 391 U.S. 430 (1968). *See generally Without Justice, supra* note 48 at 16.

98. *Without Justice, supra* note 48, at 16.

99. *Washington Post,* August 6, 1983, at 2; November 15, 1983, at 1.

100. "Congressional Groups Brief Disputes Justice Sex Bias Stand," *Washington Post,* August 9, 1983, at 2.

101. However, a group of five members of Congress introduced an impeachment resolution in the House of Representatives on November 10, 1983, claiming that the president had violated congressional warmaking powers by invading Grenada.

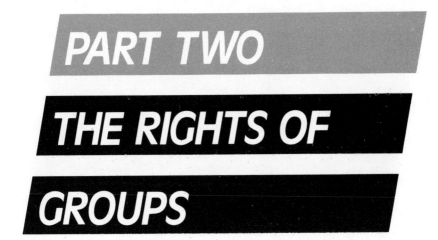

PART TWO
THE RIGHTS OF
GROUPS

RACIAL JUSTICE

DREW S. DAYS, III

Drew S. Days, III, is an associate professor of law at Yale University. Prior to joining the Yale faculty, Mr. Days was a staff counsel for the NAACP Legal Defense Fund and assistant attorney general for civil rights in the Carter administration.

America advanced in race relations during the period from the *Brown* decision in 1954 to the end of the nineteen-sixties farther than it had in the preceding hundred years.[1] In less than a generation, a society that had created and maintained a racial caste system became a place where racial discrimination and segregation constituted offenses to public policy. It would be difficult, consequently, for efforts in any subsequent period to achieve the "strides toward freedom" for blacks and other racial minorities that occurred in the fifteen years following *Brown*. Certainly, events occurring over the past fifteen years can claim no such distinction.

Things could not have started on a worse note, it appeared. The Johnson Administration, which sponsored the most important civil rights legislation in history,[2] was being replaced by that of Richard Nixon, a man with a long record of antipathy to civil rights and civil liberties issues. And the era of the Warren Court, which is justly credited with setting in motion the forces of change in race relations with its *Brown* decision, was drawing to a close. It would shortly be ended by a group of so-called "strict constructionist" Justices who were expected to turn back or at least retard civil rights gains.

Looking back over this more recent period, however, one cannot help being struck by the degree to which both the achievements of the earlier post-*Brown* period have held and actual forward movement in the battle to eradicate racial discrimination "root and branch" has taken place despite the presence of significant obstacles to such progress. For during this period, we discovered just how complicated and difficult the process of achieving racial justice was going to be.

To be sure, the assault upon the institution of segregation leading up to *Brown* and thereafter required the dedication of mind and often body by thousands of persons committed to equality. Some were beaten and killed; churches were bombed; governors stood in schoolhouse doors; and black children needed the assistance of federal troops to get a desegregated education. No one dare minimize the suffering and sacrifice that this campaign required. But it also bears pointing out that several other factors contributed to its success.

First, the wrongs of "separate but equal" in public education, "whites only" in places of public accommodation, and "coloreds to the rear" on common carriers were apparent to all with eyes to see. The solution to these wrongs appeared equally apparent: discrimination in the provision of America's benefits on the basis of race must be prohibited outright. Once that principle was firmly embedded in our laws, arriving at the goal of "equal opportunity for all" would be a relatively simple process, we thought.

Second, it was of no small moment, additionally, that the focus of civil rights activity was on behalf of blacks and directed toward the South, that part of America where the abhorrent institution of slavery flourished for two centuries prior to the Civil War. Northerners and sympathetic Southerners alike could view the struggle to end racial segregation by law or custom as the moral equivalent of the "War Between the States" almost a century earlier. There were no grays, no ambiguities in this piece: blacks were fighting for freedom; racist whites were trying to keep them down. A powerful coalition of blacks, liberal whites (of which a significant proportion were Jewish) and organized labor joined with allies in the federal legislative and executive branches to topple segregation and to urge the judiciary to interpret new civil rights laws broadly to achieve their intended purposes.

Finally, progress on civil rights was aided by the fact that the nation was experiencing during much of this time—before the realities of our "guns and butter" policies of the Vietnam War period became evident —years of economic health and expansion. Unemployment was down, spending for social programs was up, and other economic indicators all pointed to a future in which growth and eradicating racial discrimination could progress hand in hand.

The past fifteen years have taught us just how naive we were to think that future battles would be equally simple. First, we learned that racial discrimination was not only a Southern phenomenon; official racial prejudice and segregation had Northern manifestations as well. Even though no neon signs or statutory provisions proclaimed that blacks were being subjected to discrimination based upon their race, in some Northern communities official action had achieved results so reminiscent of those in the South as to require both areas to be treated alike for constitutional purposes. No longer could Northerners view the fight for civil rights as a Southern problem from which they could stand morally aloof. And remedies that Northerners once called for with the understanding that their effects would be felt "down there" but not "up here" had to be reassessed in terms of these changed circumstances.

We also became painfully aware that remedying the effects of years of racial discrimination would require more than simply declaring that opportunities in education, employment, voting, and housing must be provided without respect to race. Instead, it became increasingly clear that whites would have to be disadvantaged, their expectations altered, and their patterns of life disrupted in order to make the promises of racial equality a reality. While many of these remedial techniques produced strains in the coalition that had proven so effective in fighting for civil rights in the fifteen years after *Brown,* none proved more divisive than the explicit use of race. For some white veterans of the early civil rights struggles, the adoption of racial classifications—even for supposed remedial purposes—represented a rejection of the antidiscrimination principle that the civil rights movement had fought so hard to establish.

The debate over the use of racial criteria intensified, moreover, in the context of voluntary affirmative action plans. In such cases, race was explicitly considered, not to remedy specific acts of discrimination against specific individuals, but rather to ensure the movement of blacks and other minorities into educational institutions, employment opportunities and business ventures in more than token numbers. While remedying specific discrimination through judicial or administrative processes had its place, relying solely on the fortuity of individual or governmental challenges to illegal practices would, it was thought, unduly delay meaningful correction of the effects of racial bias for which the entire society was responsible. The use of racial criteria to remedy proven racial discrimination or for affirmative action purposes would have encountered opposition in any event. Sensitivity to the use of such techniques was heightened during this period, however, by the fact that the economy had begun to falter. With its decline went any hope that opportunities for blacks and other minorities in education, employment, and housing could be provided without limiting those for whites.

And finally, it became apparent that the issue of civil rights was of vital concern not only to blacks. Other racial minorities with compelling histories of discrimination—if not so long-standing and pervasive as that against blacks—also demanded corrective action. Hispanics, Asian-Americans, and native Americans, particularly, presented cases of systematic bias in education, employment, and voting which the nation could no longer deny. What had become an already difficult question of how to ameliorate the condition of blacks after centuries of segregation and exclusion was rendered even more problematic by the appearance on the scene of these additional racial and ethnic minorities.

CIVIL RIGHTS IN THE NORTH

Brown and its companion cases, of course, were Southern cases. What the Supreme Court struck down were state laws or other official government policies that required or permitted segregation of public school children on the basis of race. But it was not long after *Brown* that civil rights lawyers mounted assaults upon Northern school systems in which black children and white children were virtually as segregated from one another as they would have been had the law so dictated. Black plaintiffs in these cases contended, drawing from language in *Brown,* that black children were harmed by racial segregation whatever the cause and were entitled under the Constitution to have such situations rectified. Lower federal judges found such arguments meritless:[3] Northern school systems were segregated for reasons that had nothing to do with official action. The segregation was, consequently, de facto. What the Constitution forbade, they concluded, was de jure segregation, that is, racial separation in public schools mandated by law, ordinance, or other official pronouncement. The United States Supreme Court routinely declined to review these decisions, leaving them for all intents and purposes as the law of the land for over a decade.

In 1973, however, the Supreme Court decided its first Northern school desegregation case. In *Keyes v. School District No. 1.*[4] the Court concluded that Denver public school officials had intentionally segregated black and Hispanic children from whites in violation of the Constitution. This was so, said the Court, even though Denver had never in its history been required or permitted by law or any other official policy to assign children by race. Despite its adherence to the de facto/de jure dichotomy, the Court made it apparent, nevertheless, that Northern school systems were no longer entitled to a conclusive presumption that their segregated patterns were the consequence of adventitious demographic forces. Since *Keyes*, scores of Northern communities have been sued, found guilty of unconstitutional school segregation, and required to implement system-wide desegregation plans.

Contrary to initial expectations, the Burger Court's decisions in the school desegregation field have been generally positive, reinforcing and expanding principles established under Chief Justice Warren's leadership. The movement North in school desegregation, however, has produced its casualties on and off the Court. Insofar as the Court is concerned, the *Keyes* decision brought clearly into the open a split among the Justices over school discrimination remedies that had found muted expression only a year earlier. Since *Keyes*, the unanimity that characterized the Warren Court opinions on school desegregation has become increasingly rare, particularly in Northern cases. Those Justices who dissent from decisions requiring desegregation continue to press two basic arguments. First, they question whether doctrines developed over the years in Southern school desegregation cases to establish constitutional violations have any plausible application to Northern situations. And, second, if so, they reject the notion that certain remedies, particularly busing, offer any realistic prospect of achieving meaningful desegregation, North or South.

On one major issue, however, recent Northern school desegregation litigation has produced a setback very reminiscent of the failure of such suits in the early sixties. In 1974, the Supreme Court reviewed a school desegregation case from Detroit[5] in which lower federal courts had found constitutional violations and required a remedy that included Detroit proper and several surrounding communities. The Court concluded, however, that the required remedy exceeded the constitutional violation since the suburban communities had not been shown to have played any legally cognizable role in creating and maintaining racial segregation in Detroit public schools. Though the State of Michigan was culpable, conceded the Court, its guilt could not be attributed to the suburban communities for purposes of devising a remedy without trenching upon the principle of local school district autonomy. This the Court refused to condone. As a result, financially strapped Detroit was left to educate blacks and other minorities in largely segregated schools surrounded by affluent suburbs serving almost entirely white student bodies. Like the de facto/de jure distinction established by lower federal courts in the early sixties, the Detroit decision has placed an extremely formidable, if not insurmountable, legal barrier in the path of meaningful desegregation in major metropolitan areas.

Opposition to school desegregation in major Southern urban communities had begun to mount within the Congress and in the Nixon Administration in the late sixties and early seventies. But this movement gained impetus as the desegregation process began to reach Northern communities. The target was ostensibly "busing," or the use of transportation for desegregation purposes. In fact, however, for many long-time Southern opponents of the *Brown* decision (and newer Northern converts to this cause), "busing" provided a convenient facade behind which their true objectives could be hidden. For others who had been initially committed to desegregation, opposition to busing represented an expression of their frustration over the extent to which the promises of *Brown* were still unrealized in hundreds of communities almost two decades later. In any event, opposition to busing was the bond that held this "unholy alliance" together. With the help of this new coalition in the Congress, both the Nixon and Ford Administrations were able to obtain legislation designed to limit the extent to which busing could be used for desegregation purposes.[6] Though federal courts have held that these enactments do not affect the degree to which busing can be used to remedy proven violations of the Constitution, the shift in congressional attitudes toward desegregation could not have been made clearer. The same body that authorized, by way of the 1964 Civil Rights Act, a major federal assault upon public school segregation was now trying to reverse the process. Moreover, subsequent congressional action by way of antibusing riders to appropriations bills have proven effective in retarding the desegregation process. Since 1976, the Department of Health, Education, and Welfare (now the Department of Education) has been forbidden to require desegregation remedies that involve busing of children beyond the school nearest their homes, even in cases of proven constitutional violations.[7] Hence, administrative power to withhold federal funding from segregated school districts unless they desegregated fully—an effective tool during the Johnson Administration—was taken away. And efforts continue in the Congress, by way of various proposals—constitutional amendments, limits on federal court jurisdiction and upon the power of the attorney general to bring school desegregation cases—to put an end to the use of busing altogether. So while the law of school desegregation has become for all intents and purposes the same for both the North and South, that uniformity has been gained at the expense of destroying what had been a broad consensus in the North in favor of vigorous implementation of *Brown*.

This shift in attitudes as civil rights battles moved North has occurred in other areas as well. Take, for example, the question of housing discrimination. Enforcement of provisions of the Fair Housing Act of 1968 raised little public controversy so long as it was confined to efforts to ensure that blacks and other minorities had access to rental and sale properties on a nondiscriminatory basis. On the other hand, litigation in recent years, particularly in the North and West, has focused upon certain land use and zoning practices that make it virtually impossible for racial minorities to break the demographic patterns that lock them into deteriorating urban centers surrounded by relatively affluent, largely white suburbs. Mortgaging, financing, and appraising practices that allegedly foster racial segregation *within* urban areas have also come under attack. In the wake of these challenges, support for housing discrimination litigation has waned and recent attempts to strengthen the 1968 act have been rejected by the Congress.

When Congress enacted the Voting Rights Act of 1965, its principal concern was devising enforcement mechanisms that would "shift the burden of time and inertia from the perpetrators of the evil [of voting discrimination] to its victims" in the Deep South where resistance to earlier voting rights legislation had been so vigorous. The coverage formula the Congress adopted, which ensured that states and other political subdivisions in the South were subject to special provisions of the act, had some unanticipated consequences, however. For jurisdictions in the North and West that had no documented history of systematic racial discrimination in voting ultimately found themselves required to obtain approval from the United States attorney general or a special federal court in the District of Columbia before making any changes in their electoral systems. Recognition that the Voting Rights Act had implications for the North as well as the South explains in no small measure why certain members of Congress from the North and West joined their Southern colleagues in opposing, albeit unsuccessfully, 1982 legislation extending the act's special provisions until the year 2009.

Any discussion of the impact of civil rights enforcement in the North would be incomplete, however, without some mention of how Supreme Court doctrine has developed over the past fifteen years with respect to proving constitutional—as opposed to statutory—civil rights violations. In the early years following *Brown,* federal courts were not required to search for the motivations behind practices that segregated blacks from whites: state laws, local ordinances, and official regulations plainly required separation of the races. Thus, there was no occasion for them to address the question of what proof would be required to establish a constitutional violation in the absence of the type of overt evidence of racial discrimination so readily available to plaintiffs in Southern litigation. As civil rights enforcement has moved North, the Supreme Court has been required to devise an answer. The response has not been heartening. Since 1970, the Supreme Court has all but immunized from constitutional attack certain types of so-called "social and economic" legislation despite its significantly negative impact upon blacks and other racial minorities. Consequently, in the early 1970s, welfare programs, housing ordinances, and mechanisms for funding public education that disadvantaged racial minorities survived judicial scrutiny.

The underlying rationale for these decisions was initially obscured by the tendency of commentators to characterize them as evidence of the Court's refusal to elevate poverty to the level of a "suspect classification," thereby requiring that legislation turning on economic status be scrutinized as closely as laws containing racial criteria. Any ambiguity in this respect was removed by two decisions in 1976 and 1977. There the Court announced that governmental actions having a disproportionate negative impact upon racial minorities do not violate the Constitution unless shown to be the result of intentional or purposeful discrimination. In the 1976 decision,[8] the Court found that the intent test was not met in an employment discrimination case and proceeded, in addition, to unceremoniously "reverse" a long list of prior lower court decisions holding unconstitutional a host of employment, zoning, housing, and municipal arrangements. The 1977 case[9] extended the intent principle to allegations of housing discrimination, finding that no constitutional violation could be discerned there either. Since then, the intent test has been extended to uphold certain electoral arrangements[10] despite their significant exclusionary impact upon racial minorities. Only in the area of school desegregation can it be said that the intent test has not set back antidiscrimination litigation.

THE SEARCH FOR EFFECTIVE
REMEDIES

Given the pervasiveness of racial segregation in Southern public schools prior to *Brown*, the focus of the 1954 decision and the 1955 implementation order was upon ending racial assignment policies. It was apparently believed that if school boards ceased assigning students by race and relied upon other criteria such as proximity of a child's home to the school or grade level and course of study required, segregated school systems would desegregate "with all deliberate speed." What the Court discovered, however, was that Southern school boards were not prepared to surrender so readily to its dictates. Racial assignment practices continued unabated in many communities; children were directed in 1956 to the same segregated schools they attended in 1954 and 1955. Black children and their parents courageous (some would say foolhardy) enough to explore the possibility of transfers to previously all-white schools found obstacles placed in their paths at every turn. When the lower federal courts held that school boards would have to provide realistic opportunities to black and white children to transfer into opposite race schools, "freedom of choice" plans sprouted up all across the South.

It became increasingly clear, consequently, more than a decade after *Brown*, that any desegregation plan, "freedom of choice" or otherwise, that placed the primary responsibility for change on the shoulders of black students, parents, teachers, and administrators was unlikely to succeed. Consequently, in 1968 and 1969, the Court issued a series of rulings establishing that school boards—not the black victims of segregation—had an affirmative responsibility to develop desegregation plans that promised to "work realistically and work realistically now."[11] Such plans would, held the Court, most likely have to take into account race in order to ensure that assignment patterns did not simply reinforce the status quo. And where teacher and staff desegregation was concerned, even racial ratios that replicated system-wide black-white proportions in each school were constitutionally permissible.[12] By late 1969, the Court concluded that the standard of "all deliberate speed" for achieving desegregation was "no longer constitutionally permissible."[13]

Two years later, in the *Swann* case involving the Charlotte-Mecklenburg, North Carolina school system, the Court concluded that race must be taken into consideration in developing effective desegregation plans.[14] Though it rejected the notion that every school in a desegregated system must reflect system-wide ratios of black and white students, the Court also left little doubt that wide variations in racial makeups of schools would not be constitutionally tolerated. Despite almost yearly attempts to cut back on the principles underlying its 1971 ruling, the Court continues to adhere to and expand upon that decision to the present day.[15] In its seventeen-year journey from *Brown* to *Swann,* the Court learned that meaningful desegregation could not occur without requiring affirmative efforts on the part of school boards to eradicate the vestiges of their dual systems and without the explicit use of racial criteria in devising and implementing new student assignment plans.

A similar evolution in judicial attitudes toward remedies has occurred in areas other than school desegregation. In employment, for example, passage of Title VII of the Civil Rights Act of 1964 was heralded as establishing once and for all that one could no longer be denied a job or be subjected to terms and conditions of employment on the basis of skin color. The evil the Congress sought principally to remedy by enacting Title VII was the systematic and overt racial discrimination that had deprived blacks and other racial minorities of meaningful job opportunities in the South. As in the case of school desegregation, however, the courts learned that removal of categorical barriers to employment for racial minorities did not necessarily alter the status quo. By using a variety of screening devices such as psychological or aptitude tests, educational requirements, or certain forms of on-the-job experience, many employers could exclude blacks or maintain them in inferior job categories as effectively as they did prior to Title VII's becoming law. Moreover, in the North, employers had been using such screening devices for years with equally devastating consequences for blacks. The federal courts were confronted, consequently, with the question of whether these "facially" non-discriminatory practices would be upheld despite the extent to which approving them would seriously undermine the objectives of Title VII.

The Supreme Court's answer, in the 1971 *Griggs* decision, was to hold that employment requirements that had a discriminatory racial impact presumptively violated Title VII unless such barriers to hiring or promotion could "be shown to be related to job performance."[16] In contrast to its subsequently announced position on constitutional challenges, the Court interpreted the statute "to prohibit not only overt discrimination but also practices that are fair in form, but discriminatory in operation."

In addition to determining as in *Griggs* and several other major cases what constituted violations of Title VII, the Supreme Court and lower federal courts have had to face the issue of what remedies should be authorized for established violations. While simply prohibiting discriminatory practices in the future proved adequate in some circumstances, in others such remedies left proven victims of illegal practices largely uncompensated. The Court concluded that, in most instances, such persons should be entitled to back pay for the effects of their having been denied a job or a promotion in violation of Title VII.[17] Somewhat more controversial was the Court's subsequent determination that the "make whole" purposes of Title VII required that victims of discrimination be given seniority equal to that which they would have enjoyed but for the employer's or union's illegal practices.[18] It became undeniable at this juncture that effective remedies for racial discrimination in employment would, in some instances, conflict with the conditions of employment enjoyed by incumbent whites and frustrate their expectations insofar as promotion and other benefits dependent upon seniority were concerned.

By far the most disputed technique adopted by the federal courts and administrative agencies to remedy employment discrimination has been the use of racial criteria for hiring or promotion. Called variously, depending upon the political persuasion of the speaker, "goals and timetables," "benchmarks," or "quotas," these remedies have been ordered often in cases where the employer has been found to have engaged in systematic racial discrimination over a long period and where serious questions exist as to the employer's willingness or ability to implement truly nondiscriminatory practices. In other cases, such requirements provide the most reliable indications of whether an employer has ceased discriminating. Federal courts and administrative agencies had found, after years of trying, that relying upon employers' "good faith" or "best efforts" to remedy discrimination rarely produced meaningful results. Nevertheless, orders requiring hiring or promotion ratios of so many blacks for every white or setting percentage goals in those respects do not contemplate that an employer will be required to perform the impossible: if adequate numbers of qualified racial minorities are actually unavailable despite diligent efforts to recruit them, then the requirements will be adjusted to comport with reality.

Adoption of these remedies has caused further strain in the historic coalition for civil rights that proved so effective for many years after *Brown*. For those who believed that the movement had been one to banish all considerations of race from decisions affecting education, employment, housing, or voting, the use of racial criteria to remedy Title VII violations was an anathema. For such remedies, in their eyes, rewarded blacks who had not been the victims of discrimination at the expense of whites who had not practiced discrimination solely on the basis of race. Organized labor, too, had its problems with the degree to which Title VII plaintiffs were seeking restructuring of established seniority systems.

In fact, labor's disaffection on this score caused it to mount a major campaign in defense of seniority in the face of attacks by racial minorities that has proven extremely successful. In 1977, the Court held that seniority systems established "pre-act" (prior to Title VII's 1965 effective date) that perpetuate pre-act or post-act discrimination do not violate Title VII unless they can be shown to have had their "genesis in racial discrimination" or to have been "negotiated and maintained with a discriminatory purpose."[19] Since 1977, the Court has further shielded seniority systems from effective attack. First, it broadened the definition of a seniority system in a 1980 case involving a California brewing industry rule granting "permanent" employee status only to those who worked 45 weeks in any calendar year. The Court upheld this arrangement as a bona fide seniority system in the face of allegations that no black had ever gained "permanent" status in the entire history of the industry.[20] In 1982, the protection afforded seniority systems established prior to 1965 was extended to those that were set up after Title VII went into effect.[21] And there is little reason to believe that the debate between organized labor and major civil rights groups over whether seniority and effective remedies for employment discrimination can coexist, particularly in tough economic times, will be resolved easily, if at all.

The experience in the voting rights area over the past fifteen years has paralleled in significant part what has been described earlier with respect to education and employment. The Voting Rights Act of 1965 was directed principally at outright and sometimes brutal opposition in the South to blacks' casting a ballot or running for office. Within a few years after the act became law, courts discovered that a variety of techniques that did not interfere directly with blacks engaging in the physical act of voting nevertheless effectively excluded them from any genuine voice in the political process.[22] Hence jurisdictions have had to submit a number of such practices for approval by the United States Attorney General or the special federal court prior to putting them into effect. In those cases where a proposed change is suspected of having a discriminatory purpose or effect insofar as racial minorities are concerned, it must be disapproved. Conversely, jurisdictions have been encouraged by court decisions to take the racial consequences of their actions explicitly into consideration in order to avoid violating certain provisions of the 1965 law. Thus, the Court held that an annexation plan that proposed to add largely white suburban areas to increasingly black Richmond, Virginia would not pass muster unless the expanded jurisdiction were districted to ensure that black voters had political power consistent with their presence in the population.[23] And three counties in New York gained Court approval for a reapportionment plan that gave certain districts minority populations in excess of 65 percent in order to ensure black and Hispanic voters of a fair chance to elect candidates of their choice.[24] That Hasidic Jews were allegedly disadvantaged by the New York plan underscored the tension between civil rights and some Jewish organizations over the morality, if not the legality, of explicit racial criteria to remedy discrimination.

AFFIRMATIVE ACTION

Even the introduction of racial criteria in remedies for proven discrimination, however, could not be expected to alter segregated patterns overnight. Besides, litigation or administrative action seeking remedies for discrimination had too much of a "hit-or-miss" quality to offer much hope of any systematic attack upon exclusionary practices. That some employers were subjected to Title VII suits while others with worse records in hiring and promoting racial minorities were left alone, or that school desegregation litigation was similarly haphazard, contributed to the general sense that additional approaches had to be devised. Moreover, the modern civil rights statutes embodied the hope that much of the change from a segregated to an integrated society would occur voluntarily.

Affirmative action was such an alternative. Though affirmative action has taken on many manifestations over the past fifteen years, the least controversial has involved voluntary "outreach" efforts, by employers and educational institutions particularly, to ensure that racial minorities were adequately informed of available opportunities and fairly considered when admissions or employment decisions were made. Such programs were generally embraced by those interested in seeing progress on race relations; and since whites did not appear to be disadvantaged even though racial considerations played a part, there seemed to be no serious conflict with the antidiscrimination principle. Moreover, even where the Supreme Court approved in principle voluntary desegregation plans that attempted to achieve a reflection of system-wide black/white ratios in every school,[25] no great outcry resulted. For there, too, the sense was that no child had an inalienable right to attend any particular school; racial balance plans would only introduce a new criterion in the everyday process by which school administrations assign pupils. In no event would a child be deprived of a public education under such arrangements.

Difficulties arose, however, once affirmative action programs introduced racial considerations into the actual allocation of limited resources. The first challenge to such practices reached the Supreme Court in 1973. That case, brought by a white applicant denied admission to the University of Washington Law School, allegedly because of the school's affirmative action program, was resolved without any decision on the merits.[26] But the battle lines had been drawn over the constitutionality of admissions programs that employed racial criteria. Put simply, opponents of such programs contended that race could never be used to make admissions decisions except in cases of proven discrimination, and then only to compensate actual victims of such discrimination. Washington Law School made no claims to be rectifying its own discriminatory actions or to be aiding identifiable victims of discrimination by way of its plan. Those in favor argued, among other things, that blacks and other minorities had been discriminated against historically not as individuals, but as groups. Consequently, voluntary efforts to correct the effects of this class-based discrimination could properly take race into account. Proponents took a range of positions with regard to the extent to which race could be used in the admissions process and the degree to which specific numbers of seats in an entering class could be set aside for minority students. Another case presenting these issues was not long in coming along, however. Allan Bakke, a white medical school applicant, sued the University of California at Davis, alleging that he had been denied admission in favor of less qualified minority students because the Medical School had set aside sixteen out of one hundred seats in the entering class for which only blacks and other minorities could compete.[27] The Supreme Court's decision in *Bakke* gave both sides of the argument something to celebrate. By votes of five to four, the Court held the Davis program invalid but rejected

Bakke's contention that any consideration of race in the admissions process would violate the Constitution or federal statute.

In 1979, the Supreme Court addressed in the *Weber* case the question of whether labor and management could legally agree to establish an employee training program that set aside half of the openings for black workers.[28] It rejected a challenge to such a plan set up by Kaiser Aluminum and the United Steelworkers. Instead, it held that Title VII did not bar efforts by "the private sector voluntarily to adopt affirmative action plans designed to eliminate conspicuous racial imbalance in traditionally segregated job categories." The Court noted, in approving the Kaiser plan, that it had three important redeeming features. First, it did not require the discharge of white workers and their replacement by blacks. Second, it did not create an absolute bar to the advancement of white workers, since half of those trained would be white. Last, the plan was a temporary measure, not designed to maintain racial balance but simply to eliminate a manifest racial imbalance.

A year later, the Court upheld the constitutionality of the Federal Public Works Employment Act of 1977.[29] In that legislation, the Congress directed that 10 percent of the $4 billion program to assist states and localities with capital construction projects should be earmarked for racial minority contractors. The Supreme Court held in the *Fullilove* case that Congress had acted within its constitutional authority in legislating to ensure effective participation of minority contractors in federally funded programs from which they had historically been excluded.

Though *Weber* and *Fullilove,* and *Bakke* to a lesser extent, must be regarded as progressive steps in the movement to make racial minorities first-class citizens, these lawsuits had certain unfortunate consequences as well. First, the very fact that the Supreme Court took these cases for review, with all the media coverage and public debate that attends such grants, tended to foster a distorted sense of what was really happening in the field of racial discrimination. Based upon the *Bakke* suit, some were undoubtedly led to conclude that blacks were entering other medical schools at such high rates as to begin squeezing out white applicants in large numbers. In truth, blacks accounted for less than 5 percent of medical school enrollments as the *Bakke* case reached the Supreme Court, despite a significant expansion in the number of seats available in medical schools during the late sixties and early seventies. One would have thought from the arguments Brian Weber made that Kaiser Aluminum's Gramercy, Louisiana plant had provided unnecessary assistance to black workers at the expense of whites. Instead, the Gramercy plant, located in an area where the labor pool was almost 40 percent black, employed only a 15 percent black work force and a less than 2 percent black craft work force. And because an association of white contractors sought to have the 10 percent Minority Set-Aside provision declared unconstitutional, many were probably led to believe that minority contractors had succeeded in cornering the market on federal construction contracts. As of 1977, however, minority firms were getting less than 1 percent of the federal public works budget; white contracts were getting the rest, with one group, the Association of General Contractors of America, getting an average of eighty cents of every federal public works dollar. In sum, though the evidence of the continuing unaddressed effects of deep-seated prejudice against blacks and other racial minorities was everywhere to be seen, *Bakke, Weber,* and *Fullilove* tended to skew public discussion away from how to remedy "just plain old discrimination" to the questions of so-called "reverse discrimination."

Secondly, this trilogy of affirmative action cases has raised almost as many questions as it has answered. Not one has given a clear, clean answer as to where and when racial criteria may be used consistent with constitutional and federal statutory requirements. Though *Bakke* did hold that race may, in some circumstances, be a criterion in the university admissions process, the deciding vote was cast by a Justice who thought that achieving "ethnic diversity" was the only persuasive justification. *Weber* seemed to reject the need for an employer to establish that its affirmative action plan was necessitated by a desire to avoid Title VII liability; yet a concurring Justice voted to uphold the Kaiser/Steelworkers' approach precisely because he thought that the record contained evidence of "arguable violations" of the federal statute. And the decision explicitly avoids providing any guidance on the degree to which public employers, limited by the provisions of the Equal Protection Clause as well as of Title VII, may institute programs like Kaiser's. *Fullilove,* certainly a ringing endorsement of Congress's power to establish racial classifications, leaves to another day whether legislative bodies at the state or local level may act similarly. While good and sufficient explanations exist for the circumspect way in which the Court has approached these issues, the fact remains that those seeking to move forward in this area must often do so at their peril.

Third, deep rents in the civil rights coalition have resulted. This has been particularly true with respect to the historic alliance between black and Jewish groups. Despite efforts by voices of reason on both sides to maintain the dialogue, misunderstandings and recriminations have been difficult to avoid. On the one hand, some blacks regard opposition by Jews to programs like those at issue in *Bakke, Weber,* and *Fullilove* as anti–affirmative action and, indeed, anti–civil rights. Some Jews, on the other hand, believe that black insistence upon the use of race in the allocation of university seats, jobs, and government contracts reflects a crass disregard for their legitimate fears of the *numerus clausus,* given the long and sordid history of anti-Semitism. Neither side has come out of this dispute a winner; the wounds have yet to heal.

OTHER RACIAL MINORITIES

Brown made it impossible for white Americans to ignore any longer the moral blight of racial segregation. But only in the past few years has the nation been forced to come to grips with the fact that blacks are not the only victims of racial and ethnic discrimination.

Ironically, the same year that the Supreme Court decided *Brown* it also concluded in a criminal case from Texas that "persons of Mexican descent" had been sufficiently subjected to discrimination to qualify as an "identifiable class" for constitutional purposes.[30] Yet, in so many other respects, it was difficult to analogize the condition of Hispanics to that of blacks. First, they were not brought to America in chains. Second, the term "Hispanic" masks a great diversity in national origins, colorations, and degrees of assimilation into the "Anglo" culture. Some Hispanics are as dark as the darkest black; others are as blue-eyed and fair-haired as any Nordic. And often it was these physical characteristics that determined how they would be treated by non-Hispanic whites. Very few blacks could look forward to such "discriminating" reactions. Third, for the most part, prejudice against Hispanics had not relied upon legal institutions for its maintenance; deeply embedded custom sufficed.

Finally, the realities of racial discrimination against Hispanics and certain other minority groups, such as Asian-Americans, have been obscured by at least two other factors. It is often argued that such groups do not enjoy equal status with whites not because of racial animus but because many of their members have not been willing or able to master the English language. Their legal status has been complicated also by problems associated with illegal immigration. For those determined to deny opportunities to members of these other racial and ethnic minorities, "helping stem the tide of illegal aliens" has provided a handy rationalization.

Nevertheless, we have finally confronted in many important respects the truth about these other victims of discrimination. Federal courts have ordered the desegregation of not only all-black and all-white schools, but of all-Hispanic schools as well, holding the principles of *Brown* and its progeny fully applicable to such tri-ethnic situations.[31] Hispanics have won important victories in constitutional challenges to discriminatory electoral systems.[32] The Voting Rights Act was amended in 1975 to include coverage for language minorities, a change that subjected Texas entirely and portions of other states in the West and Southwest to its special preclearance provisions.[33] Title VII and many of the other modern civil rights statutes have been effective tools in the fight against national origin and ethnic discrimination.[34] And affirmative action programs have come to include uniformly not only blacks but also Hispanics, Asian-Americans and native Americans, as was true of that struck down in *Bakke* and that upheld in *Fullilove.*

The addition of these other minorities to the civil rights picture has not been greeted with universal approval. Blacks, for one, have feared that their efforts to obtain increased status might be blunted by this proliferation. In fact, interests among these various groups, particularly blacks and Hispanics, have diverged on occasion. For example, in both 1965 and 1970, black groups decided against pressing for including language minority provisions in the Voting Rights Act, though Hispanics desired such coverage. They felt that to do so would arouse opposition to the legislation on the part of congressional delegations from the West and Southwest whose votes were needed for passage. Since 1975, moreover, blacks and Hispanics have not agreed on remedies for certain forms of voting rights violations. Because blacks are often found in compact and concentrated areas in most major American cities, they have tended to favor ward systems to at-large arrangements. Hispanics living in the Southwest, on the other hand, are often diffused residentially, making it difficult, if not impossible, to create wards which they can control electorally. Officials in areas where both ethnic groups are present have not been reluctant to exploit this disagreement in hopes of maintaining the status quo.

Language differences have also presented difficulties. One of the most important developments in the last fifteen years has been the recognition that the denial of information and materials in their native language can deprive certain minority groups of equal opportunity as effectively as outright exclusion. Consequently, the Supreme Court has held that school districts receiving federal financial assistance must afford children who do not speak English with a meaningful opportunity to obtain a basic education.[35] Coincidentally, however, this development has created problems in the school desegregation process. Some Hispanics resist reassignment of their children because of the disruptive effect they believe desegregation will have upon bilingual education programs. This resistance has been compounded by the fact that some Hispanics reject certain basic premises underlying desegregation since *Brown,* namely, that bringing black and white children together in public schools serves to remedy the constitutional violation of segregation and to prepare both groups for responsible citizenship in a pluralistic society. Certain Hispanic groups, in contrast, believe that their children can be prepared most effectively in facilities where they are in the majority and where significant attention is paid to imparting knowledge of the Spanish language and Hispanic culture. For those who subscribe to this philosophy, desegregation holds no attraction whatsoever. Moreover, the degree to which public school children should be allowed to receive instruction in their native language for purposes other than facilitating the transition to English and the place of bicultural components in the education process have become subjects of polarizing national debate, desegregation aside.

Finally, any attempt to allocate finite resources among several groups rather than solely to one will inevitably create problems. A 10 percent Minority Set-Aside Program for "Negroes, Spanish-speaking, Orientals, Indians, Eskimos and Aleuts," as anyone can see, means that no one group has any assurance of getting the entire allocation. Indeed, the various minorities are invited, in effect, to compete against one another for a piece of this limited pie. The same has been true of other mandatory and voluntary programs designed to remedy discrimination against more than one minority group at a time.

The upshot of all of this is not that the civil rights movement has been left a shambles as a result of the arrival of these other minorities onto the scene. Blacks, Hispanics, and other racial minorities are not at one another's throat. In fact, the degree of concerted action among these groups, given their varying priorities, has been quite remarkable. But the differences described above have meant that, on some issues, coalitions have been difficult to form and opportunities for civil rights advancement have sometimes not been adequately exploited.

THE REAGAN ADMINISTRATION

Despite these difficulties, there would be reason for some optimism about the future of civil rights were it not for significant threats posed to advancement by the Reagan administration. Since 1981, administration officials have waged a systematic campaign to reverse civil rights gains in America that took almost three decades to achieve. Rather than providing the type of support and guidance lent by prior administrations, Reagan appointees have sought to exploit and exacerbate many of the difficulties that have attended civil rights advancement over the past fifteen years.

On school desegregation, this administration has declined to utilize court-created rules of evidence to establish liability of school districts for illegal segregation, categorically rejected busing as a remedy, and sought to place back on the shoulders of minority victims of segregation primary responsibility for its eradication. With respect to employment discrimination, its position has been that racial criteria may never be used as a remedy for violations of Title VII, no matter how pervasive the violation and no matter how resistant to taking corrective action the employer may be. Voluntary affirmative action plans using racial criteria have become primary targets for attacks by the Reagan administration. According to its principal civil rights official, for example, the *Weber* case was wrongly decided and must be overturned. In one of the cases where it hopes to achieve that reversal, the Reagan Justice Department has sided with Hispanic employees against blacks.

In 1981 and 1982, when the Congress was considering a further extension of the 1965 Voting Rights Act, the Reagan administration took no public position on this important issue for almost a year. Once it did speak, what the administration proposed was a series of amendments that would have weakened the Act; it advanced them adamantly and unsuccessfully for an additional six months. The extension was ultimately voted out without the Reagan provisions by wide margins in both the House and Senate, after most members of Congress concluded that the administration's objections were unprincipled. Given such strong congressional support for the measure, President Reagan had very little choice but to sign it into law. But he attempted, nevertheless, to characterize the extension as a victory for his administration. And on the question of discrimination by recipients of federal funds or other financial assistance, the Reagan administration has, in numerous instances, interpreted federal laws in ways that would allow funds to continue flowing despite evidence of exclusionary practices. It was in that spirit that this administration concluded that the Internal Revenue Service's denial of tax-exempt status to segregated schools was illegal, reversing a Government position established during the Nixon administration and adhered to under both Ford and Carter.

The federal courts and the Congress have refused, thus far, to yield to the Reagan administration's revisionist views of federal civil rights law and the realities of eradicating the lingering effects of long-standing racial discrimination. The Supreme Court has declined, for example, to accept for review a school desegregation case this administration had hoped would provide a vehicle to cut back on requirements in this area.[36] It has run into similar difficulties in seeking to roll back the use of racial criteria as remedies for employment discrimination and as part of affirmative action programs.[37] And, in a powerful reaffirmation of the law prior to its "reinterpretation" by the Reagan administration, the Supreme Court voted 8–1 that the Internal Revenue Service's denial of tax-exempt status to segregated educational institutions was both legal and consistent with the nation's "fundamental and overriding interest in eradicating racial discrimination in education."[38] But the assaults of this administration are bound to have long-term negative consequences, particularly if President Reagan wins a second term. For its policies have already reopened old wounds, sowed confusion in the public mind as to the state of civil rights law, and chilled voluntary efforts to address problems of discrimination.

CONCLUSION

The last fifteen years have not been easy. But America has, generally speaking, maintained a forward momentum on civil rights. Whether we will experience further progress between now and the end of this century, however, will depend upon a complex mixture of realism, creativity, and sheer luck.

We must be realistic, first, about the fact that a society that condones the continued segregation of black and other racial minorities in deteriorating cities surrounded by affluent, largely white suburbs is unlikely to advance appreciably on civil rights. Remedies for school and residential segregation must be addressed on a metropolitan basis. Second, we must acknowledge that racial minorities have been left socially and economically vulnerable by centuries of discrimination and that government policies that affect such groups negatively perpetuate that vulnerability. Prohibiting only those policies *intended* to discriminate against racial minorities is no prescription for progress.

We must be creative in developing remedies that will more effectively accommodate the legitimate interests of organized labor in job security with the compelling need to eradicate the effects of racial discrimination. We must also devise safeguards to ensure that the legitimate use of racial criteria for remedial or affirmative action purposes does not degenerate into a new form of racism. Such techniques should be invoked selectively, not on a wholesale basis.

And we need luck to bring about a return to a healthy economy. Without this precondition, all the realism and creativity in the world may well be beside the point.

NOTES

1. Brown v. Board of Education, 347 U.S. 483 (1954).

2. The Civil Rights Act of 1964, 42 U.S.C. §§ 2000 et seq.; the Voting Rights Act of 1965, 42 U.S.C. §§ 1971 et seq.; and the Fair Housing Act of 1968, 42 U.S.C. §§ 3601 et seq.

3. Bell v. School City of Gary, Ind., 324 F.2d 209 (7th Cir. 1963); Springfield School Committee v. Barksdale, 348 F.2d 261 (1st Cir. 1965); and Deal v. Cincinnati Board of Educ., 369 F.2d 55 (6th Cir. 1966).

4. 413 U.S. 189 (1973).

5. Milliken v. Bradley, 418 U.S. 717 (1974)

6. Education Amendments of 1972, 20 U.S.C. §§ 1651–1656; Education Amendments of 1974, 20 U.S.C. §§ 1701 et seq.

7. Eagleton-Biden Amendment to the Labor-HEW Appropriations Act, H.J. Res. 662, Pub. L. No. 95–205 (§ 101).

8. Washington v. Davis, 426 U.S. 229 (1976).

9. Village of Arlington Heights v. Metropolitan Housing Development Corporation, 429 U.S. 252 (1977).

10. City of Mobile v. Bolden, 446 U.S. 55 (1980).

11. Green v. County School Bd., 391 U.S. 430 (1968).

12. United States v. Montgomery County Board of Educ., 395 U.S. 225 (1969).

13. Alexander v. Holmes County Board of Educ., 396 U.S. 19 (1969).

14. Swann v. Charlotte-Mecklenburg Board of Educ., 402 U.S. 1 (1971).

15. Columbus Board of Educ. v. Penick, 443 U.S. 449 (1979); Dayton Board of Educ. v. Brinkman, 443 U.S. 526 (1979).

16. Griggs v. Duke Power Co., 401 U.S. 424 (1971).

17. Albermarle Paper Co. v. Moody, 422 U.S. 405 (1975).

18. Franks v. Bowman Transportation Co., Inc., 424 U.S. 747 (1976).

19. Teamsters v. United States, 431 U.S. 324 (1977).

20. California Brewers Assn. v. Bryant, 444 U.S. 598 (1980).

21. American Tobacco Co. v. Patterson, 456 U.S. 63 (1982).

22. Perkins v. Matthews, 400 U.S. 379 (1971).

23. City of Richmond v. United States, 422 U.S. 358 (1975).

24. United Jewish Organizations v. Carey, 430 U.S. 144 (1977).

25. McDaniel v. Barresi, 402 U.S. 39 (1971).

26. DeFunis v. Odegaard, 416 U.S. 312 (1974).

27. Regents of the University of California v. Bakke, 438 U.S. 265 (1978).

28. United Steelworkers of America v. Weber, 443 U.S. 193 (1979).

29. Fullilove v. Klutznick, 448 U.S. 448 (1980).

30. Hernandez v. Texas, 347 U.S. 475 (1954).

31. Keyes, *supra* note 4.

32. White v. Regester, 412 U.S. 755 (1973).

33. Briscoe v. Bell, 432 U.S. 404 (1977).

34. Teamsters, *supra* note 19.

35. Lau v. Nichols, 414 U.S. 563 (1974).

36. Metropolitan County Board of Educ. of Nashville and Davidson County, Tenn. v. Kelley, *cert. denied,* 103 S.Ct. 834 (1983).

37. Boston Firefighters Union, Local 718 v. Boston Chapter, NAACP, *dismissed as moot,* 103 S.Ct. 2076 (1983).

38. Bob Jones University v. United States, 103 S.Ct. 2017 (1983).

SEXUAL JUSTICE

SUSAN R. ESTRICH AND VIRGINIA KERR

Susan R. Estrich is an assistant professor of law at Harvard Law School. She teaches, writes, and practices in the areas of criminal law, labor law, and constitutional law.

Virginia Kerr is an assistant professor of law at the University of Pennsylvania Law School. She teaches, writes, and practices in the areas of sex discrimination, equal employment opportunity law, and civil procedure.

In 1949, Margaret Mead observed that "every known society creates and maintains artificial occupational divisions and personality expectations for each sex that limit the humanity of the other sex."[1] Although she stressed that the conventions by which the sexes are differentiated vary from society to society, she observed that in every society the differentiation seems to be accompanied by a hierarchy of value in which the activities and characteristics defined as "male" are regarded as superior to or more important than the activities and characteristics defined as "female." This sexual asymmetry means that

> men may cook, or weave, or dress dolls or hunt hummingbirds, but if such activities are appropriate occupations of men, then the whole society, men and women alike, vote them as important. When the same occupations are performed by women, they are regarded as less important.[2]

Mead's basic observations have been confirmed by other cross-cultural investigators. Writing in 1974, for example, Michelle Rosaldo summed up the evidence:

> Everywhere we find that women are excluded from certain crucial economic or political activities, that their roles as wives and moth-

ers are associated with fewer powers and prerogatives than are the roles of men. It seems fair to say then, that all contemporary societies are to some extent male-dominated and although the degree and expression of female subordination vary greatly, sexual asymmetry is presently a universal fact of human social life.[3]

America in the 1980s is no exception. Gender continues to shape the limits and experiences of our lives, and to predict economic, social, and political status.

Despite ever-increasing numbers of women working outside the home there has been no progress at all in reducing the disparity between male and female earnings.[4] In 1955, women earned $.64 for every $1.00 men earned; by 1980, this had dropped to $.59 for every $1.00. A person who is both female and black earned $.54 for every $1.00 earned by a white man, and Hispanic women earned $.50 for every $1.00. The labor market still consists of occupations divided along gender lines. Women workers *are* the workforce for the lowest paying jobs: they constitute 94 percent of all secretaries, 95 percent of all household workers, and 96 percent of all nurses. It is these jobs that remain largely nonunionized. Household workers are not even protected by the workers' compensation system. Management and union positions remain the province of men—less than 6 percent of all women in the labor force hold management positions— and only 2 percent are in the skilled trades.

While the political voice of women has begun to be heard over the last decade, national offices continue as male enclaves. Only 2 percent of United States senators are women; under 5 percent of the members of the House of Representatives are women, and only one woman serves as a governor. The judiciary presents no better a picture. In the higher state courts, for example, only 1.3 percent of the judges are women.

Women, in short, constitute an underclass in this society. Sixty-three percent of all Americans living below the official poverty line are women, and that percentage increases with age. Notwithstanding the idealizations of traditional motherhood that have been brought back into fashion by the New Right, the gap between the ideal and the real is breathtaking. The woman who invests in a traditional marriage and thus relies on her husband's earnings for economic security in exchange for her work in the home does so at the risk that the marriage will fail, in which case she can expect her husband's standard of living to go up while hers goes down.[5] Families with female heads have a poverty rate six times greater than male-headed families. Women who perform the critical task of nurturing young children, whether they do so for love, money or both—at home, in child-care centers, or in elementary schools—are among the least esteemed—in terms of respect, not simply of money—members of our society.

Economic and political facts barely begin to sketch the story of sexual asymmetry in this society. On the job, women are likely to be the targets of sexual harassment: they are expected at least to endure sexual innuendo if not explicitly to exchange sexual favors for promotion or the simple ability to retain their jobs.[6] On the streets, the threat of sexual assault is sufficiently grave that many women live under a de facto curfew in which they do not go out at night, or if they do, they do not go without an escort. The woman who is raped continues to be treated by many police and court officers as if she invited it. And even in their most intimate relationships, 50 percent of all women will face violence from their husband or boyfriends.[7] As with rape, the institutional response to domestic violence against women is not always reasoned: women are not infrequently blamed for their wounds and bruises.

From their earliest moments, children are exposed to this web of political, economic, and private injustice. Our schools are a clear example.[8] Like the rest of the labor market, schools are occupationally segregated, with the number of women teachers declining at each level of education, until we find few teaching in universities. Women who teach are concentrated in the arts and humanities; the sciences remain a male-dominated preserve for student and teacher alike. Control over our educational institutions—through administrators, school boards, and boards of trustees—is a male prerogative despite the vast numbers of women who teach elementary-age children or who are students. Schools, as an integral part of a child's socialization, reflect cultural expectations and assumptions about gender, identity, and role, as illustrated by stereotyped images of women and men in textbooks, continued math and science anxiety in girls, and stereotyped vocational education.

While the facts of women's lives tell one story, law in the United States would seem to tell another—a story of access to justice and to many rights long enjoyed by men. During the last twenty years, legislation at both the federal and state level—now covering all substantial sectors of the job market—has been enacted to prohibit discrimination on the basis of sex in hiring, compensation, and in the terms and conditions of employment.[9] During the same period, legislation designed to provide access for women in education, in the credit industry, and in housing has also been enacted.[10] State family law codes have been revised to provide for more equitable distribution of marital property upon divorce and to address the economic plight of displaced homemakers who are disadvantaged upon divorce due to their investment in traditional marriage.[11] Many states now provide civil remedies and make use of criminal sanctions in instances of domestic violence.[12] Finally, as a result of the 1973 Supreme Court decision in *Roe v. Wade*, women—or at least women who are over eighteen and able to afford the service—now have what is commonly described as a "right" to terminate an unwanted pregnancy, at least during its early stages, free of criminal sanctions imposed by the state.[13]

How do we explain the apparent gap between these legal norms, which promise equal opportunity without regard to gender, and the realities of sexual asymmetry in American society? A soothing explanation lies in the fact that this country's experience with a norm of equal opportunity for women is too short to have made a substantial dent in a system that has formidable historical, social, and psychic roots. Laws designed to undo sex-based discrimination can be effective only if their proscriptions are accepted and honored and—if not honored—vigorously enforced. The federal statutes that form the basic legal framework for the equal-employment and educational rights women now enjoy—Title VII of the Civil Rights Act of 1964 and Title IX of the Education Amendments of 1972—have been in effect for less than a generation, and much of the effort under those statutes during the 1970s was devoted to the basic project of ensuring that prohibitions against sex discrimination were taken seriously. Those efforts had only begun to bear fruit in the late 1970s when, with the election of Ronald Reagan, the women's rights and civil rights community was forced to turn its attention to the task of preventing outright administrative nullification of the principles that had been so recently established.

This explanation carries a necessary reminder of the fragility of the framework that has afforded American women alive today legal freedoms. To the extent that the framework is largely statutory, it can all too easily be ravaged by the political process. To the extent that the framework is constitutional, it is less vulnerable to erosion. Yet, as demonstrated by the political ascendancy of the New Right, with repeal of *Roe v. Wade* and resistance to adoption of the Equal Rights Amendment high on its agenda, the liberty guaranteed to women by the Constitution is by no means secure.

Even apart from these reminders that the liberties of women rest upon a precarious political foundation, there is ample reason for caution and concern about the future. For the law itself mirrors the dominant views of gender in our society. The decisions of the Supreme Court interpreting the Constitution and the equal opportunity statutes, which will be our focus, have played a critical role in affording women greater freedom. Yet at the same time, those decisions—and the concept of "equality" that informs those decisions—leave unchallenged the hierarchy of value that characterizes sexual asymmetry in our society. An examination of those cases makes clear both the potential and the limits of law in addressing sexual asymmetry—and thus advancing sexual justice.

While the primary emphasis of this paper is on gender, no discussion of sexual justice would be even minimally adequate if it ignored the monumental injustices faced by gay men and lesbian women on account of their sexual orientation. The number of homosexual persons in our country can only be roughly estimated, not only because of definitional uncertainties but also because our society for so long has equated homosexuality with deviance and has chosen to blind itself to the reality that millions of Americans do not share the dominant sexual orientation. For those gay men and lesbian women who in recent years have increasingly refused to abide by the social mandate that their sexual orientation must be invisible, the consequences can be severe: criminal liability, discrimination in housing and employment, loss of custody of one's children, to mention only a few of the possible and all too common reactions. And the fact that, absent a local law to the contrary, such consequences are legal is, at least in part, a product of the continued legal existence of the very same sexual asymmetry which limits the freedom of all of us based on our gender.

THE IDEOLOGY OF "SEPARATE SPHERES"

Until 1971, when the Supreme Court for the first time struck down a state law on the basis of sex discrimination, the Court's decisions explicitly subscribed to an ideology that defined women and men as having substantially different roles in the scheme of human existence. Women, because of their physical structure and child-bearing function, were seen as wife and mother, confined to the private domestic sphere of the home. Men were thought to belong in the public world of ideas, commerce, and government, where they were assumed to have support obligations toward their families but no significant responsibility for the daily care of children; they were assumed to respond with either lust or greed towards women encountered in the public world. Women who departed from the role and place ascribed to them were regarded as anomalous, in need of special protection either to compensate for the double burden of market work and domestic duty or to preserve their chastity in the face of male sexual aggression.

The ideology of separate spheres was called into play by the Court in 1873 to justify an Illinois ruling denying a woman qualified in all respects except her sex admission to the bar; according to one Justice, it was the "divine law of the Creator" that Myra Bradwell not practice law.[14] By the turn of the century, references to scientific and sociological materials thought to establish an inexorable link between female biology and female dependency replaced divinity as authority for the ideology; it was on this basis that the Court in 1908 upheld an Oregon law restricting hours of work of women, but not of men.[15] After the Second World War, the Court began to retreat behind the veil of deference to legislative judgment to explain its refusal to invalidate laws enforcing the ideology; the legislature, the Court held in 1948, could reasonably conclude that women who were not the wives or daughters of tavern owners should not work as bartenders.[16] Yet, while the justifications for the ideology may have shifted as society and consciousness changed, the legal doctrine endured. In *Hoyt v. Florida*—decided seven years after the Court in *Brown v. Board of Education* had declared "separate but equal" to be inherently unequal in the case of race—the Supreme Court continued to enforce the view that

> Despite the enlightened emancipation of women from the restrictions and protections of bygone years, and their entry into many parts of community life formerly considered to be reserved to men, woman is still regarded as the center of home and family life.[17]

Hoyt is an instructive precedent for later treatment of gender by the Supreme Court. A woman accused and convicted by an all-male jury of murdering her husband—during a quarrel in which she said he flaunted his infidelity and humiliated her—argued that female peers might have better understood her defense of temporary insanity. Her legal claim was that Florida's exemption of women from compulsory jury registration, which had the effect of creating a primarily male jury pool, deprived her of her right to the equal protection of the laws guaranteed by the Fourteenth Amendment. Her argument was premised on the assumption that women and men would bring different perspectives to the jury box and the case. The Court, emphasizing that the Fourteenth Amendment only protected Hoyt against sex-based classifications that were arbitrary or unreasonable, concluded that because of women's "special responsibilities" as the "center of home and family life," Florida's decision to make jury duty for women discretionary was not irrational.

The legislative decision to which the Court deferred in *Hoyt* was explicitly grounded upon the separate spheres ideology. In its brief to the Supreme Court, the State of Florida argued:

> The rearing of children, even if it be conceded that the socio-psychologists have made inroads thereon, nevertheless remains a prime responsibility of the matriarch. The home, though it no longer be the log cabin in the wilderness, must nevertheless be maintained. The advent of "T.V." dinners does not remove the burden of providing palatable food for the members of the family, the husband is still, in the main, the breadwinner, child's hurts are almost without exception, bound and treated by the mother.[18]

Under this ideology, both men and women have family obligations. Yet the work of men in the paid labor force to provide necessary support income may be interrupted when the state calls for jury duty. For jobs regarded as sufficiently critical to social well-being—for example, that of physician—the state often permits an automatic opt-out. A male physician must register for jury service, but upon a statement that he is a physician, the man is stricken from the pool of registrants. Under the jury system in force at the time *Hoyt* was decided, however, a man who had ongoing responsibility for child care would be required to make a special showing of undue hardship in order to opt out.

By contrast, women—because of their identification as mothers—are relieved of the obligation even to register for jury service. And all women, regardless of their actual status vis-à-vis men and children, are treated as wives and mothers. If the woman is a physician, the system treats her as a mother. If the woman has no children, she is still treated as a mother. Any other roles are made invisible.

The system thus regards both the man and the woman who depart from conventional role assignments as, in some sense, deviant. Men who have child-care obligations are strange. Women who do not or who identify themselves in other terms are equally strange. For the woman who is, in fact, both a worker and a mother the message is particularly harsh: her "duty," as expressed in Florida's brief, is one that the state would not ask her even to consider delegating—not to a babysitter, not even to the father who, by Florida's account, is a domestic incompetent, incapable of cooking a meal or applying a Band-Aid to a cut finger.

In this sense, *Hoyt* encapsulates essential features of our system of sexual asymmetry. It treats child-bearing functions as overdeterminative for women and reproductive functions as meaningless for men, and it labels individual women and men who depart from gender role assignments as deviant or, to use a gentler adjective, exceptional. To the extent that legal rules and constitutional norms reflect and perpetuate the role allocations resulting from this grossly over- and under-determined view, the system is in conflict with an individual's interest in self-determination.

A second feature, however, and one often overlooked, is also present in *Hoyt.* On its face, the Court's opinion appears to rest on contradictory premises about the significance of gender roles and sex differences. On the one hand, the Court seems to have assumed that men and women are interchangeable as jury members. Certainly this assumption would explain the apparent belief that Hoyt received a fair trial, notwithstanding the use of a jury selection system that led to the underrepresentation of women on jury panels, and, in Hoyt's case, produced an all-male jury. On the other hand, if men and women are so alike that it is not unfair to a defendant for the state to exempt women from jury service, how can it make sense to justify such an exemption on the ground that women are, after all, special?

The apparent answer is that women's viewpoint is at once regarded as distinct and at the same time as unnecessary to the fact-finding and moral judgments juries make. Indeed, under the scheme the Supreme Court approved in *Hoyt,* the closer a woman comes to living the life ideology assigns to her, the more likely she is to be regarded as different from men and the less likely she is to be regarded as having a voice that should be heard in the public realm. What is public and male establishes the valued norm; the private world, despite the support it gives to the public, is discarded. There is no need for women to sit in the jury box and no part for them in the hierarchy of public discourse.

Were Hoyt's case to arise today, her attorney might argue that she was the victim of battered wife syndrome. In some jurisdictions that argument might be allowed to go to the jury. In all jurisdictions, women would undoubtedly sit as jurors, for as a result of two Supreme Court cases decided in the mid-70s states are now prohibited by the Sixth Amendment guarantee of a fair trial from employing the system condoned in *Hoyt.*[19] However, *Hoyt's* analysis of the permissible scope of discrimination under the Fourteenth Amendment has not been repudiated, and its underlying logic cannot be dismissed as a relic of the past.

Of the two major legal approaches that have been used to challenge legislation that enforces sexual asymmetry, the first—equality doctrine—has been reasonably successful in eliminating the types of formal gender-based barriers to public opportunity for women condoned in such cases as *Bradwell, Muller,* and *Goesart.* Yet, under the contemporary version of that doctrine, traditional distinctions between male and female realms have survived to sustain either the outright exclusion of women from some parts of the public world or to sustain conditions upon their access to that world that penalize them for their reproductive role. Where women have sought rights in the private realm—particularly the right to control reproduction—a second strand of doctrine, privacy doctrine, has emerged to support claims to immunity from state involvement. Under that doctrine, gender equality is never explicitly an issue. The application of that doctrine has accordingly incorporated considerations of wealth, age, and tradition to constrain the freedom of those whose activities are thought to conflict most sharply with socially prescribed gender role norms—to those who, in other words, are in most need of constitutional protection.

EQUALITY DOCTRINE

The Court's modern response to cases involving sexual asymmetry began with the use of equality doctrine in 1971. The first case, *Reed v. Reed,* involved a challenge to an Idaho estates administration law that gave fathers an absolute preference over mothers whenever a dispute arose over who would handle the assets of a deceased child.[20] Idaho defended the statute on the ground that men, because of their greater familiarity with business, would on the average be better qualified than women. It also contended that an automatic preference for men would reduce family conflict and the need for probate hearings to resolve such conflict. A unanimous Court invalidated the law, reasoning that Idaho's ultimate objectives, while they might be legitimate, could not be pursued by dissimilar treatment of men and women who were otherwise in the same relationship to the decedent. The mandatory preference for fathers (men), the Court said, was "the very kind of arbitrary legislative choice forbidden by the Equal Protection Clause of the Fourteenth Amendment."[21]

Viewed in its political and social context, *Reed* seems in many respects unremarkable. The year 1971 may be regarded as a high-water mark of national political activity and legislative recognition of the principle of equal rights for women. In that year, the National Women's Political Caucus was founded for the express purpose of achieving parity in the political representation of women. In the same year, the Equal Rights Amendment to the Constitution—which had foundered in different Congresses for almost fifty years—was favorably reported in the House; the amendment was approved by joint resolution in 1972.

Viewed against the background of legal precedent, however, *Reed* marked a dramatic change. It invalidated, for the first time in the history of the Supreme Court, a law using gender as a means of defining rights. The victory of *Reed*, however, becomes muted when seen against the Court's treatment of other classifications, particularly racial ones. Following its 1954 decision in *Brown v. Board of Education*, [22] the Court developed what is often termed a two-tier equal protection analysis. Under that analysis, the Court defers to legislative line-drawing unless the state uses a classification that the Court regards as "suspect." If it does, the Court will strictly scrutinize the law by placing upon the state the burden of demonstrating that the classification is necessary to further a compelling state interest. The burden carried by the state is so stringent that it can rarely be met. After *Brown*, race became the paradigm suspect classification. In invalidating the Idaho law in *Reed* the Court employed equal protection analysis, but it failed to declare sex a "suspect" category. It simply struck down the law. The community of legal scholars who attempt to make sense of the Court's work concluded that the Court, some thought unwittingly, had created a middle-tier of review for gender classifications. It would apply to sex-based lines a scrutiny that was neither strict nor completely deferential but heightened—a sort of maybe yes, maybe no message to women about their rights under the Constitution.

In 1973, with the Court's decision in *Frontiero v. Richardson* [23] that the military's policy of denying automatic benefits to the husbands of servicewomen while granting them to the wives of servicemen was unconstitutional under the equal protection component of the Fifth Amendment, it was clear that *Reed* was not an aberration. And the *Frontiero* opinions cast some light on the judicial terrain of the middle tier. A plurality of four Justices, characterizing the separate-spheres ideology of the premodern cases as "romantic paternalism," argued that sex, like race, should be considered a suspect classification for purposes of equal protection analysis. Four other Justices concluded that the *Reed* approach was entirely adequate to support the result, with Justice Powell, writing separately for three of the four, suggesting that the Court should await the results of the ERA ratification process before making up its mind whether gender should be regarded as a suspect ground for state allocation of public burdens and benefits. Only Justice Rehnquist dissented.

The debate in *Frontiero* over the proper constitutional standard for reviewing legislation treating women and men differently appears to mask a more fundamental agreement among the eight Justices about the nature of the problem of sexual asymmetry and the appropriate legal response to it. Both approaches—concededly in different degrees—tend to define gender inequality as a problem of nonneutrality that robs otherwise deserving women of an opportunity to experience the public world on the same terms and conditions that men experience that world and that robs men of equivalent opportunities in the private realm. Both approaches either ignore or underestimate the extent to which the public power that men have long monopolized has influenced the design of the public and the private realms. And both approaches, implicitly if not explicitly, maintain the distinctions between public and private worlds and the value hierarchy that ranks the male public world as more significant than the female private world. The Court's equality doctrine, then, has permitted individual women and men to cross boundaries without changing the boundaries themselves.

Sex-based differentials in the age of majority,[24] the drinking age,[25] the respective rights of men and women and their spouses to Social Security[26] and workers' compensation benefits,[27] the rules defining the respective rights of husbands and wives to seek alimony[28] or to control jointly owned property,[29] and the respective rights of unwed mothers and fathers to maintain relationships with their children[30] have all been struck down by the Court. Only last term—over Justice Powell's statement in dissent that the Court was "bow[ing] deeply to conformity," a majority of Justices joined the opinion by Sandra Day O'Connor in *Mississippi University for Women v. Hogan* holding unconstitutional a Mississippi statute excluding males from enrolling in a state-supported professional nursing school.[31]

All of these cases—involving as they did relatively unsubtle legislative expressions of the ideology that treats men and women differently on the basis of characteristics that are only group averages—also involved clear penalties against individuals who fail to conform to gender roles. In that sense, they fit squarely within the Court's equation of gender equality with gender neutrality in law. Yet as Justice Powell's dissent in the Mississippi nursing case illustrates, individual claims to enforcement of that definition may be perceived as in conflict with the need to take into account norms of fairness for the group as a whole.

In the Mississippi case, Justice Powell characterized the women-only admissions policy invalidated by the majority as an affirmative policy designed to expand the educational options available to women. Because the state offered coeducational nursing study opportunities in other locations, state support of a female-only nursing program was viewed as a legitimate response to the interests of women who wished to study in an all-female environment, harming neither the male plaintiff nor those women who preferred coeducational learning. Under this vision no significance was given to the absence of all-male nursing school programs since men had not sought these opportunities. History, which teaches that women formed single-sex colleges in the nineteenth century as a response to their exclusion from a higher educational system reserved to men and that teacher-training and nursing schools for women were welcomed under an ideology that identified those professions as suitable for women, provides an instructive counterpoint to this vision. Similarly, economic analysis linking the depressed salaries of nurses to the fact that nursing is "women's work" indicates how the symbolic constraints placed on men by the Mississippi female-only scheme might inflict economic harm on women. These factors, although mentioned in the majority opinion, were disregarded by Justice Powell and the three other Justices who dissented from the majority's ruling, in favor of the idea that the sex-segregation in the Mississippi system reflected a healthy pluralism, not sexual asymmetry.

To the extent that the dissenters in the Mississippi case meant to suggest that the diverse experience and perspective of women should be accounted for in any equality analysis that hopes to promote gender equality, the point is well-taken. But we cannot at the same time disregard a social and economic history that instructs that laws separating women from men in the public realm reflect and reinforce the basic boundaries that devalue women and their perspective.

That the state in the Mississippi nursing case was able to persuade four Justices that a law firmly grounded in the separate spheres ideology was "benign" evidences the deep roots of that ideology and the increasing sophistication with which it is defended. The case, as well, provides a useful introduction to the problem presented by gender-specific laws that claim legitimacy as efforts to compensate women for the discrimination that they have faced in social and economic life. In *Hogan,* the majority readily recognized such a claim as false.

The line between laws that compensate women for past disadvantage and laws the perpetuate current structures of disadvantage is not, however, always so easy to draw. In the 1974 case of *Kahn v. Shevin,* [32] for example, the Court declined to find unconstitutional sex discrimination in a Florida law that granted all widows but no widowers a $500 tax exemption. The state argued that the exemption was intended to reduce "the disparity between the economic capabilities of a man and a woman" and to further "the state policy of cushioning the financial impact of spousal loss upon the sex for which that loss imposes a disproportionately heavy burden." In view of overwhelming evidence that women as a group did suffer greater financial difficulties than men, particularly when widowed, the Court upheld the law, refusing to yield to Mr. Kahn's claim that he as an individual was in fact just as, if not more, needy than some of the widows who received a tax break, and refusing to question the norms of female dependency and male self-reliance fostered by Florida's tax law. The state's concern for the plight of older widows was both reasonable and commendable. But the classification did not have to be drawn on the basis of sex to serve Florida's goal. A need-based line would in fact have produced results which helped women as a group, without excluding needy men or perpetuating traditional images of both sexes.

The Court, in post-*Kahn* challenges to gender-specific statutes defended as valid efforts to address the economic problems of women, has displayed a heightened ability to recognize the costs inflicted upon women by statutes that appear to accommodate their interests. In *Weinberger v. Wiesenfeld,* [33] it refused to follow *Kahn* and thus invalidated a Social Security Act provision that offered survivor's benefits to both the widows and minor children of deceased male wage earners but only to the children of deceased female wage earners. The Court recognized that widows are much more likely to be dependents, but recognized as well that the scheme discriminated against the female wage-earner by giving her family lesser protection and at the same time discriminated against the widowed father by depriving him of an opportunity to stay at home to care for his young children. In *Califano v. Webster,* [34] a unanimous Court—although following *Kahn* in upholding a Social Security provision that established a more favorable basis for computing benefits for female than for male retirees—stressed that the sex-specific rule at issue was an interim measure (it was repealed in 1972) designed by Congress to directly address the economic disparity in female earnings attributable to discrimination against women in the job market.

Yet, in other so-called "benign discrimination" cases, ones that require a more searching examination of the complex structures of identity and value that characterize sexual asymmetry, the Court's performance has been far less auspicious. In *Schlesinger v. Ballard,* for example, the Court upheld the Navy's practice of affording women officers a longer period of service before subjecting them to mandatory "up-or-out" attrition rules.[35] It reasoned that Congress might "quite rationally have believed that women line officers had less opportunity for promotion than did their male counterparts, and that a longer period of tenure for women officers would, therefore, be consistent with the goal to provide women officers with 'fair and equitable career advancement programs.' "[36] Missing from the majority analysis was any challenge to the explicit gender discrimination in Navy assignments and structure that limit the promotional opportunities of women and type women as ancillary participants in military life. The just remedy for the discrimination against women in the military would have been to eliminate the discrimination, not mask it with discretionary rules for favored treatment for women.

Indeed, on closer examination, virtually every "benign" classification favoring women that the Court has examined emerges as an effort partially to patch over fundamental systems of de jure and de facto discrimination which under no circumstances can be termed "benign." What is rarely acknowledged by the Court's opinions is that the conflict between individual and group justice which these cases seem to present is largely a product of the boundaries of work and value that continue to separate men and women as groups in our society. Absent challenge to the underlying social and cultural structures that regard women as a group as less valuable than men and leave them more needy, there will continue to be a seemingly intractable conflict between a norm of equal treatment of individual men and women, without regard to the prescriptions of sex-role stereotyping, and equal outcomes for women as a group. Yet, in cases presenting direct challenges to these fundamental boundaries, the Court's equality analysis has left them untouched.

MODERN SEPARATE SPHERES: WAR/SEXUALITY/REPRODUCTION

In cases that have directly challenged the most basic organizing principles of sexual asymmetry in this society, the Court has continued to enforce separate spheres as a matter of law.[37] War is for men, and reproduction for women. As for heterosexual intimacy, which is the only approved sexual intimacy in the modern version of separate spheres, the state is permitted to regulate along sex-based lines that enforce a vision of the male as aggressive sexual subject and the female as dependent sexual object.

The three key cases that we examine here are *Rostker v. Goldberg*,[38] *Michael M. v. Superior Court*,[39] and *Geduldig v. Aiello*.[40] They involved, respectively, challenges to a male-only draft registration law, to a statutory rape law prohibiting acts of consensual sex with teenage girls, and to a state disability statute that provided income protection for virtually all disabilities except those attributable to pregnancy. In each, the Court concluded that the gender line did not violate the Fourteenth Amendment.

Rostker, in many senses, presents a striking modern analogue to *Hoyt*, the Florida jury case. At issue in both was a registration system which automatically exempted all women and no men from the duty to register. In both cases, women could serve only if they volunteered, while men were required to serve unless they could individually establish that they fit within a legislative exception. The difference, of course, is that by 1981 when *Rostker* was decided, our society and our law had evolved to the point where jury service was no longer considered a male province in which the participation of women was unnecessary or undesirable. The same, however, is not true for military service.

The image of male as warrior and aggressor and female as dependent and nurturer is among the most powerful in the separate spheres ideology.

As Professor Williams has recently noted, men's experience has been most divided from women's in the area of physical combat and its modern equivalents.[41] The Congressional debate leading to the enactment of the registration statute provides a helpful refresher course in the contemporary rationale for that division. Congress—focusing on the idea of a mandatory female presence in the military—was concerned that sexually mixed units might experience morale problems, that the presence of women in combat roles might dangerously interfere with the willingness of male officials to wage and win necessary wars, that imposing military service obligations on women would wrench children from their mother's care (or force them into the incompetent arms of their fathers),[42] and that the administrative changes (including housing and bathroom arrangements) needed to accommodate a substantial female presence in the military would far outweigh the benefits. The reasoning is reminiscent of Florida's defense of its male-only jury registration statute, with the same explicit message that women are contingent, not essential, players in military life and policy.

Similarly, in the military context as in *Hoyt*, legislative reluctance to interfere with the private work of women renders the public work of women invisible or insignificant. Women who do not conform—women who are in fact serving in the military as volunteers, as they have been since World War II—are penalized by less promising careers. Women outside the military are limited in their ability to participate in the public sector as full participants in the formation of national defense policy and in the paid labor force.

The Supreme Court is presumptively aware of these costs. Some of the facts about the competitive position of women in the military were spelled out in *Schlesinger v. Ballard*, the benign classification case in which the Court found the Navy's exclusion of women from combat and ship assignments sufficiently detrimental to their promotional opportunities to justify more favorable promotion rules for women. Some of the facts about the impact on civilian employment opportunities for women, in a society that since the Civil War has awarded preferential treatment to veterans in the competition for governmental civil service jobs, were spelled out in *Personnel Administrator of Massachusetts v. Feeney*,[43] in which the Court upheld a lifetime absolute preference for veterans in civil service job competition whose effect was to promote a male monopoly of the highest-ranking civil service positions. Finally, a textbook review of the biographies of many of this society's political leaders attests to the significance of military service as a positive factor in the competition for political office. Domestic service does not have the same public or political value; the only homemaker preference with which we are familiar is not a public employment preference but a preference that women be homemakers.

Against this background, the Court in *Rostker v. Goldberg* explained its ruling upholding the all-male registration law on the ground that the purpose was to prepare for a draft of combat-ready troops. Because women are statutorily excluded from combat, it reasoned that "[m]en and women . . . are simply not similarly situated for purposes of a draft or registration for a draft."[44] The exclusion of women from registration, the Court concluded, was thus not an "accidental by-product of a traditional way of thinking about females,"[45] but rather a considered judgment as to how to meet military needs. All of the evidence would indicate that the Court was correct in saying that the judgment was not accidental. To the contrary, it is clear that the judgment was a deliberate product of a traditional way of thinking about women and men and their appropriate social, sexual, and reproductive roles, and that its effect is to perpetuate those roles.

Both the majority and dissenting opinions in *Rostker* studiously avoided close examination of the norms that define war, combat, and, for that matter, combativeness as uniquely masculine activities. *Michael M. v. Superior Court,* the second in our trilogy, produced similarly elliptical opinions. The statutory rape law challenged in *Michael M.* by a teenage male charged with a violation defined the crime as "an act of sexual intercourse accomplished with a female not the wife of the perpetrator, where the female is under the age of eighteen years."[46] The issue for the majority under the formulaic equality analysis of the middle tier was whether the sex-based line, punishing only men for statutory rape, bore a fair and substantial relationship to the goal of the regulation. Accepting the state's suggestion that the law was designed to reduce teen-age pregnancy, the majority upheld the statute. Because "[o]nly women may become pregnant," and "because virtually all of the significant harmful and inescapably identifiable consequences of teen-age pregnancy fall on the young female," the Court concluded that a legislature acts "well within its authority when it elects to punish only the [male] participant who, by nature, suffers few of the consequences of his conduct."[47]

That the California statute had long been justified in the state courts as a means of preserving the chastity of innocent young girls troubled four of the five Justices who voted to uphold it not at all. But Justice Blackmun, the fifth vote for the Court's judgment, intimated in his concurring opinion that the statute should be upheld and applied only in those instances in which the girl could be regarded as "innocent"—that is, in which she resisted male sexual overtures. Thus, he thought, "it is only fair" to observe that Sharon, the young woman complainant in the case, "appears not to have been an unwilling participant in at least the initial stages of the intimacies," making the case "an unattractive one to prosecute at all, and especially to prosecute as a felony." There followed a footnote reference to Sharon's record testimony that described a teen-age party in which she and Michael M. had departed from the group to engage in what was known in the 1950s as petting. He wanted to engage in intercourse, she didn't, and when she said no, he slapped her in the face several times at which point Sharon just "said to [her]self 'forget it,'" and acquiesced.[48] Apparently, in Justice Blackmun's view, this was a typical sexual encounter—male as aggressor, female acquiescing—which should not be punished even under a statute that makes no pretense of concern with consent or mutuality.

The Rehnquist majority opinion, in contrast, assumes that the statute could be appropriately or justly applied to *any* act of heterosexual intercourse in which a girl under eighteen might engage, regardless of her consent or her chastity. The notion was that California, recognizing that nature suppresses female sexuality by imposing upon women the potential punishment of pregnancy, had elected to create for males the legal equivalent of pregnancy: the threat of a statutory rape prosecution. But one crucial point is left out of the majority's analysis: the fact that the non-physiological consequences of pregnancy—the "punishment" of pregnancy itself as well as the additional constraints that punishment may place on female sexuality—are socially created, as much the product of governmental action as the criminal sanction imposed on Michael M.

The dissenting opinions did not discuss this point. Instead, those opinions suggest that Michael M. and Sharon, at least under the legal definition of statutory rape, had engaged in the "same act" and therefore should have been treated identically.[49] Under that claim, either both should have been regarded as wrongdoers or both should have been free from criminal sanction. Given the assumption that the intimacy proscribed by the statute was mutually willed, the argument is compelling. Given the reality that statutory rape prosecutions are commonly brought in nonconsensual situations—where the sexuality is neither free nor mutual but physically or emotionally coerced by a stepfather or boyfriend—the argument is flawed.

The problems underlying the *Michael M.* case go to the core of how our society has defined and shaped sexual roles, and the social significance that it has attached to pregnancy. Neither the majority nor the dissents chose to recognize, let alone confront, those problems. And the Court's result reflects an accommodation to separate social spheres rather than any serious challenge to them.

The third case in our trilogy, which deals explicitly with the issue of female reproduction, provides an excellent example of a legally sanctioned punishment of pregnancy. In *Geduldig v. Aiello,* the Court reached the surprising conclusion that a California disability scheme—providing workers with income loss protection for time lost due to a wide range of nonoccupational disabilities (including disabilities associated with male reproductive anatomy) with the striking exception of disabilities associated with pregnancy—did not constitute unconstitutional sex-based discrimination. The result is perhaps less startling than the reasoning. Although the case was decided in 1974 after the Court had heightened its scrutiny of sex-based classifications, the majority opinion did not apply that scrutiny. Instead, the majority concluded that the classification before it was not a gender-based classification at all: California had merely drawn a line between "pregnant persons"—to be sure an all-female class —and "nonpregnant persons," a class that included both men and women; women, it reasoned, were not singled out by that line since "[t]here is no risk from which men are protected and women are not. Likewise, there is no risk from which women are protected and men are not."[50]

The majority claim that California treated women and men even-handedly by limiting coverage to risks they have in common was belied by the record showing coverage of risks that are unique to men such as the risk of prostate disease. Yet, even putting aside that difficulty with *Geduldig,* the Court's reasoning suggests an understanding of gender equality that is ominously narrow. *Geduldig* yields a rule of equality that requires identical treatment of men and women for characteristics that they have in common, and that justifies—through the stance of deference to the state judgment—gender bias with regard to the characteristics that divide them. This analysis inevitably works to draw the equality line at the biological divide.

The gender-bias condoned by *Geduldig* is clear. Women, to the extent that they are free from the "burden" of pregnancy, enjoy the same employment rights as men. Women who cannot or do not wish to free themselves from that burden—and its attendant obligations of child care —enjoy only those benefits government wishes to extend; equality does not require that it extend any. Men, in contrast, have never been asked to choose between parenthood and paid employment nor regarded as "special" or problematic when they choose both. And, when individual men have made the more problematic choice to give equal or greater priority to homework than to market employment, the Court's equality analysis, as is evidenced by dependency benefits cases like *Frontiero v. Richardson* and *Weinberger v. Weisenfeld,* has been adequate to protect their decisions.

Thus, it seems that the claims of men to the dependency rights that have been reserved to women have fared better under the Court's equality doctrine than the claims of women to rights essential for support of self and family. For *Geduldig,* after all, presented precisely such a claim. The question that interests us is why. The answer seems to be that the doctrine is itself gender-biased. Although both men and women are essential to reproduction—each playing roles that are necessary but undeniably different—*Geduldig* labels the female reproductive role as "unique" and implicitly treats the male reproductive role as inconsequential to its definition of shared human characteristics. The discourse in *Michael M.* is similarly slanted towards the view that women are uniquely responsible for reproduction—the male stake in reproduction, according to that case, is too tenuous to place serious constraints on male sexuality. This discourse suggests that the standard used by the Court for evaluating the equality claims of women is a male standard: male characteristics, both social and biological, become the floor and the ceiling for the allocation of employment rights. Under the equality logic of *Geduldig,* the normal worker is a person, either male or female, who is neither pregnant nor subject to the physiological and social risks of pregnancy, and the ancillary worker is a pregnant or potentially pregnant person. This is the vision of sexual asymmetry.

What is new in *Geduldig,* of course, is the neutrality language, a language that was surely obligatory given the *Reed/Frontiero* departure from the overt separate spheres thinking approved in the Court's premodern cases. Yet, as we have already suggested, the results of the *Reed/Frontiero* line of cases are entirely consistent with *Geduldig.* For those cases, while they have afforded individual men and women the precious freedom from legally imposed gender-role prescriptions, have done so on reasoning that returned with a vengeance in *Geduldig* to justify that thinking. That reasoning works well to permit some women to try out what men have formerly done and to free men to pursue activities that have formerly been identified as female. It has, however, done little to challenge the basic value dichotomy that labels the male world as more valuable than the female and that asks women to adopt the norms of that public world in order to claim an equal voice in it. Indeed, the reasoning—not unlike the underlying message of *Hoyt*—tends inevitably toward the thought that women are entitled to equality with men in the public sphere only to the extent that they arrange their lives and priorities in the way that men have traditionally arranged theirs. *Geduldig* made this thought explicit, using neutrality language that, however unintentionally, seemed to say that the price of equality in the workplace for women is childlessness.

In *Gilbert v. General Electric*, [51] the *Geduldig* reasoning was imported into the interpretation of Title VII of the Civil Rights Act of 1974, with the result that America's private employers were legally free not to take the needs of pregnant workers into account in plans providing for disability and other benefits. Although the Court in a subsequent Title VII case confined its rationale in a way that prevented employers from forcing women to take a maternity leave and depriving them of their seniority,[52] the primary message of *Geduldig/Gilbert* was sufficiently at odds with established Title VII doctrine and any just concept of public employment rights for women as to provoke a legislative amendment to Title VII that overruled *Gilbert*. [53] Thus, under Title VII, but not under the Constitution, a line drawn on the basis of pregnancy is regarded as a gender-based line, and it is clear that disabilities associated with pregnancy may not be singled out for disfavored treatment in a fringe-benefit plan that accommodates other non-work-related disabilities. Whether an employer is affirmatively required by Title VII to provide basic leave time that is minimally adequate to accommodate the normally short period of pregnancy disability is still an open question.

Still, even under Title VII, which pays far less deference to employers than is afforded legislatures by the constitutional equality doctrine, the Court's scrutiny of the fundamental organizing features of sexual asymmetry, particularly as they relate to female sexuality and reproduction, remains limited. The Court, applying a Title VII theory that requires an employer to show a business necessity for neutral rules that have a discriminatory impact on women,[54] has invalidated a height/weight qualifying requirement for prison guard positions, a requirement that set the physical norm in terms of a male average with the result that disproportionate numbers of women could not qualify for the job. Yet in the same case, *Dothard v. Rawlinson,* [55] the Court concluded that the prison system could rely upon an overt gender rule to disqualify all women from maximum-security guard jobs. Title VII provides that overt male- or female-only employment rules can be defended if the rule reflects one of those "certain instances" in which being male or female is a bona fide occupational qualification (BFOQ) for the job. Although that exception had been narrowly construed by most lower courts, the Court in *Dothard* sustained the defense. Being male, the Court reasoned, was a BFOQ for the job of guarding dangerous male inmates in the "particularly inhospitable setting" of Alabama's unconstitutionally overcrowded prisons. Why? A woman's "very womanhood" would undermine her capacity to provide security because of the "likelihood that inmates would assault [her] because she was a woman."[56] The Court insisted that its reasoning was not paternalistic, that it was not attempting to protect women from male sexuality, but instead asserted that women were excluded because, as potential sexual targets, they might provoke sexual violence and thus pose a threat to prison security. This logic, fortunately, has not been extended to the problem of sexual harassment, which—at least in the lower federal courts—is now recognized as actionable sex discrimination under Title VII.[57]

Even if the Alabama prison situation is dismissed as a unique case, opportunities remain under Title VII to exclude women from the workplace through more subtle means than those employed successfully by the Alabama Corrections Commission. In the Supreme Court's first Title VII sex-discrimination case, it swiftly rejected an employer's argument that a refusal to hire mothers of preschool children was a "sex-plus" rule that should not even have to be justified under Title VII;[58] unlike pregnancy, in cases like *Geduldig* and *Gilbert,* parenting is a characteristic shared by both sexes. Yet, while employers are thus forbidden by Title VII to overtly exclude mothers, the accepted male design of the public world of business is replete with success criteria—such as constant availability, willingness to travel on short notice and work overtime, and the like—that handicap any person who has significant noneconomic obligations for the care of children almost as effectively as a blanket exclusion of mothers or primary caretakers of young children.

Finally, notwithstanding the legislative overruling of *Gilbert,* women continue to face explicit discrimination in the workplace because of health risks in the environment to their unborn—and in some cases unconceived —children. In jobs identified as "women's work" (e.g., nursing), environmental problems have been handled by developing methods to permit women to remain on the job. But in more traditionally male-dominated blue-collar industry, the response has often been to exclude *all* women of child-bearing age (unless they undergo sterilization or sign notices acknowledging the reproductive risks of the job)—even though there is increasing scientific evidence to suggest that many of the toxic substances adversely affecting the female reproductive system also harm male reproductive health. And one court that has addressed this issue has suggested, despite evidence that the hazard harmed men and women alike, that a policy of excluding women only could be defended as a business necessity under Title VII if reasonably related to the goal of protecting the health of unborn children of women workers.[59] The reproductive function of women, in short, continues to be treated as a justification for treating the woman worker as problematic and for limiting her employment rights.

PRIVACY

Given the Court's inability to understand reproduction within a framework of gender equality, it is not surprising that the most important women's rights decision of the decade was decided not under the Equal Protection Clause and an equality analysis but instead under the substantive due-process right to privacy. The case is *Roe v. Wade.*[60] Its well-known holding is that the Constitution locates the abortion decision in the pregnant woman, as advised by her physician, and thus the state cannot criminalize first-trimester abortion, can regulate the second trimester only to preserve and protect maternal health, and in the third trimester can prohibit abortions to protect fetal life but must permit them when necessary to preserve the life or health of the woman. In *Roe v. Wade* the Supreme Court, like the Court in *Brown v. Board of Education,* took a leadership role in asserting constitutional protection against majoritarian overreaching.

As a decision about the scope of constitutional protection of privacy, *Roe* was both very radical and very traditional. The traditional aspect of *Roe* inheres in its definition of the context of privacy protection. *Roe's* precursors, dating back as far as *Pierce v. Society of Sisters*, [61] had recognized home and family, traditionally defined, as the sphere protected from governmental intrusion. The equation of privacy with family, and the derivative recognition that the protection of sexual intimacy is required if individuals are to be free to decide to establish families, was clearly drawn in *Griswold v. Connecticut*, [62] where the Court, striking down a law prohibiting the use of contraceptives by married couples, protected the privacy of the marital bedroom and decisions for or against reproduction made within it. *Eisenstadt v. Baird*, [63] which invalidated a law that barred the distribution of certain contraceptives to unmarried individuals, might appear at first glance to have severed the connection between privacy and family, at least if the latter concept is defined by a marital relationship. Yet *Eisenstadt* reinforces the emphasis on reproduction, protecting the freedom of those who engage in heterosexual intimacy to decide whether and when to reproduce.

Roe stands squarely within this tradition. As in *Griswold* and *Eisenstadt*, the Court in *Roe* invoked the right to privacy in a context of heterosexual intimacy to establish constitutional protection for the reproduction decision—albeit post- rather than preconception. Indeed, in 1980, the Supreme Court described the liberty protected by *Roe* as a "freedom of personal choice in certain matters of marriage and family life."[64] Within that definition, as we discuss in more detail in the section that follows, there has been little room for those who are led to form intimate relationships with members of the same sex.

What was radical about *Roe v. Wade*—at least considered in its doctrinal context—was its identification of the woman (in consultation with her physician) as the individual within the family with the ultimate power over the decision to reproduce. That power—to determine whether a pregnancy should be continued and thus to control commitments to family—is one that had long been exercised by the state or delegated to men alone (under traditional property law that treated both a married mother and her child as the property of the father) or to the family as a unit, with the father acting as its de jure or de facto source of moral authority. *Roe*, as elaborated by the 1976 case of *Planned Parenthood Ass'n v. Danforth*, [65] dramatically altered this legal allocation of power, identifying the woman as the authoritative decision-maker as against the state, at least in the earlier stages of pregnancy, and as against the potential father at all stages.

On one level, *Roe*'s identification of the woman as the authority on the abortion issue could be seen as a reinforcement of separate spheres and of the equation between women and the private sphere. But that interpretation is misguided. First, the separate spheres tradition has not included authority for women to structure the private sphere: that authority belonged either to men or to the state. Second, the continuing social punishment of pregnancy means that the abortion issue is not simply a private-sphere question; for many, it is determinative of public-sphere participation. Finally, while some might still argue that in a truly "equal" world the abortion decision is one that should be shared by the woman and man (as is undoubtedly the fact in many cases), we can imagine no situation in which it would be tolerable for a man either to force a woman to bear a child or to force her to abortion.

In recent years, however, the traditional aspects of *Roe v. Wade* have imposed substantial limits on its more radical message of empowerment. Liberal political theory suggests that the essence of a right to privacy or autonomy is a right to be free of state intrusion and influence in protected decisions. But privacy doctrine's continued emphasis on family has left room for the states to impose, and the Court to tolerate, severe constraints on the autonomy of the most vulnerable women in our society—those who are young and those who are poor. In the case of the former, the Court has held that a state may constitutionally require a physician to give notice to a girl's parents before an abortion,[66] and it may even require her to obtain the consent of both, so long as it provides for an alternative proceeding in which the girl can, for instance, bring a lawsuit and ask a judge to determine either that she is mature enough to decide on her own to terminate an unwanted pregnancy or that an abortion—in the judge's view—would be in her best interests.[67] Thus, it is the family, rather than the minor daughter herself, that is authorized to make the abortion decision free from governmental interference; where unanimity in the family unit is lacking, the state, in the form of a judge, then makes the so-called "private" decision.

In the case of poor women, the Court has permitted Congress to exempt from Medicaid coverage just one medically necessary health-care service, that of abortion, out of all the health care covered by Medicaid.[68] For the Court, the "financial constraints that restrict an indigent woman's ability to enjoy the full range of constitutionally protected freedom of choice are the product not of governmental restrictions on access to abortions, but rather of her indigency."[69] Thus, the state is permitted to assert control over the reproductive lives of a group of women who, because of their poverty, are economically dependent on the state and thus particularly vulnerable to economic coercion at its hands.

Reproduction thus continues to be overdeterminative of the role of women in our society, not because of a biological dictate but because of social and legal rules. The Court's equality doctrine—which has failed to seriously question the link that has historically been drawn between reproductive difference and gender-inequality[70]—allows the state to identify reproduction and sexuality as reasons for treating women as ancillary to the public world of men or excluding them altogether from certain activities within it. *Roe* powerfully undermines this vision, but in the awkward framework of a privacy doctrine that itself reflects conventional thinking about reproduction, a framework that provides the least protection to the women who are the most vulnerable to efforts to deny their autonomy as individuals.

JUSTICE AND SEXUAL ORIENTATION

The continued legality of discrimination on the basis of sexual orientation provides stark evidence of the extent to which the Court's equality and privacy doctrines have left undisturbed the calculus of gender-identity and value that informs our system of sexual asymmetry—a calculus that affirms those who are comfortable with its premises and that punishes those who are not. Several of the secondary terms of that calculus—ones that script the normal heterosexual relationship according to a vision of the male as aggressive, instrumental, and dominant in the public realm and the female as destined by her reproductive role for a passive, expressive, and emotionally supportive activity in the private realm—have been discussed at length in this essay. Homosexuality, or at least homosexuality that is acknowledged without apology or embarrassment, presents an apparently formidable threat to the basic ground rule of the gender script: real women seek intimate relationships with men or none at all; real men seek intimate relationships with women or none at all. Substantially unprotected by federal equal opportunity statutes, gay men and lesbian women have looked with little success to the federal Constitution and the courts to enforce their claims to freedom from blatant discrimination in the labor market and to freedom from a criminal and civil sanctioning system that treats same-sex intimacy, however mutual, as an occasion for the imposition of draconian penalties.

The Supreme Court has addressed the issue of sexual orientation only once, and in so doing tacitly approved the notion that its equality and privacy doctrines—notwithstanding their apparent sensitivity to the individual costs of sex-role stereotyping and of governmental oversight of the intimate expressive lives of citizens—are not intended to question the basic gender norms that separate men and women in the public realm and require them to integrate in the private. In the 1976 case of *Doe v. Commonwealth's Attorney*,[71] the Court affirmed without opinion a district court decision upholding the constitutionality, as against a challenge brought by homosexual men, of a statute that criminalized consensual sodomy. Although some lower courts,[72] and indeed some members of the Supreme Court,[73] have sought to read that decision narrowly, numerous states continue to criminalize sexual intimacy between consenting adults of the same sex, and *Doe* stands as a precedent that is constantly invoked to justify rulings that characterize the right to privacy as a right available to heterosexuals only.[74]

Even where homosexual intimacy has been decriminalized, civil law and civil courts deny to lesbian women and gay men the rights and protection afforded to those whose sexual orientation conforms to traditional norms.[75] Decisions involving the private realm of "family"— defined as it has been with reproduction in the context of traditional relationships as its determining factor—make this clear. In no state are lesbian women and gay men permitted to create a legally recognized marriage; challenges to this fundamental restriction on intimate association have been uniformly unsuccessful. In Washington, for example, two male plaintiffs challenged the denial of a marriage license as unlawful sex discrimination under both the state Equal Rights Amendment and the Equal Protection Clause of the Fourteenth. Rejecting that challenge, the Washington Supreme Court concluded that the plaintiffs had not been denied a marriage license because of their gender, but rather because of the impossibility of reproduction from a union between them:

> [I]t is apparent that the state's refusal to grant a license allowing the appellants to marry one another is not based upon appellants' status as males, but rather it is based upon the state's recognition that our society as a whole views marriage as the appropriate and

desirable forum for procreation and the rearing of children. This is true even though married couples are not required to become parents and even though some couples are incapable of becoming parents and even though not all couples who produce children are married. These, however, are exceptional situations. The fact remains that marriage exists as a protected legal institution primarily because of societal values associated with propagation of the human race. Further, it is apparent that no same-sex couple offers the possibility of the birth of children by their union. Thus the refusal of the state to authorize same-sex marriage results from such impossibility of reproduction rather than from an invidious discrimination 'on account of sex.'[76]

Such a result, convoluted though it may seem, nonetheless follows from the equality analysis approved in cases like *Geduldig* and from a privacy doctrine that works to reinforce, even as it challenges, the sexual asymmetry implicit in that analysis. By identifying reproductive biology as a justification for different treatment of men and women, without regard to the impact of the distinction on either the self-determination rights of individual men and women or their relative standing as groups in this society, the Court's equality doctrine provides a prosperous setting for law that defines appropriate intimacy by reference to reproduction. And, as we have seen, the Court's privacy doctrine, even as it has afforded women essential control over reproduction, has left undisturbed the equation between that privacy and traditional forms of heterosexual intimacy.

The practical impact of legal refusal to recognize same-sex intimacy ranges far beyond denial of the psychic and sexual security that is typically associated with formalized marriage. Numerous jurisdictions continue to impose limits on the ability of "unrelated" individuals to live together— limits that provide an affirmative legal basis for the widespread discrimination against gay people in housing. Property and inheritance rights, social security and pension entitlements, standing to sue for wrongful death, to cite only a few economic status examples, all turn on the existence of a legally recognized marriage or family bond. In a very few jurisdictions, these consequences of legal intolerance for same-sex commitments have been somewhat ameliorated by decisions permitting gay couples to establish relationships by adoption.[77] Such decisions, however, while they compensate for some of the pragmatic consequences of legally sanctioned intolerance, merely highlight the uniform rule of nonrecognition. To qualify for tolerance, same-sex relationships must be cloaked in forms that render the relationships invisible.

When the civil family law has been forced to confront individuals whose relationships defy the categorical thinking promoted by our sexual and gender-labeling system, its judgment has been both categorical and punitive.[78] Under the highly discretionary rules that govern contested parent-child relationships, a parent whose nontraditional sexual orientation is known faces formidable odds. These rules typically direct judges to resolve disputes between natural parents according to the "best interests of the child" and to permit state interruption of an ongoing parent-child relationship only upon a showing that the parent is unfit. Until recently, the family law system regarded homosexuality as per se evidence of parental unfitness. Thus, it is not surprising that until the mid-1970s, cases involving the rights of homosexual parents were rare: added to the myriad collateral consequences that public disclosure of homosexuality might bring was the almost certain knowledge that such disclosure would jeopardize established relationships with children.

As a result of the increasing unwillingness of women and men whose sexual orientation is nonconforming to conceal their relationships, many more of these cases have been litigated in the last few years: lesbian mothers typically fight to retain custody of their children and gay fathers typically fight for visitation rights. Yet, while a number of jurisdictions have now abandoned the per se rule that a homosexual parent is an unfit parent, sexual orientation continues to overshadow the inquiry in most of the cases. When custody is denied, sexual orientation—not the quality of the parent-child relationship—is almost always the controlling factor. When custody is awarded to lesbian mothers, it is typically on the condition that they maintain a household separate from their life-partner. Similar restrictions, virtually unprecedented with respect to heterosexual parents, are commonly placed upon the visitation rights of a gay father or of a lesbian mother. Indeed, some courts have gone further, conditioning visitation on the "reform" or "cure" of the parent whose sexual orientation is out of step with that of the majority.

Predictably enough, some psychological experts who are enlisted to support efforts to deny custody to or restrict the visitation rights of gay parents, particularly when young children are involved, assert that the nonconforming sexual orientation of an otherwise loving parent may interfere with the child's ability to develop a normal gender-identity.[79] Apart from the rank stereotyping of lesbian mothers as too masculine and gay fathers as too feminine that acceptance of this empirically unsupported reasoning may mask, the courts that adopt the gender-identity rationale, and many do, engage in a logic that is self-contradictory. Central to the legal justification for disfavored treatment of men and women who are homosexual is the notion that the law merely reflects what is naturally ordained by biology. Yet, the fear that children will copy the sexual orientation of their nonconforming parent, if that parent is permitted to be open about his or her sexual preference, squarely contradicts this biological determinism with its apparent presumption that heterosexual orientation is both a learned and a fragile aspect of gender-identity. The identity rationale, with its emphasis on adult sexuality as determinative of the child's best developmental interests and its corresponding de-emphasis on the everyday aspects of child care for which women have been socially responsible, also stands squarely in a cultural tradition that devalues the importance and difficulty of the nurturing activity that has been assigned to women.

Legal hostility to the parent with a nonconforming sexual orientation can impose particularly severe costs on the lesbian mother. Given the disparity between male and female earning power, the lesbian mother, like most women, is likely to be in a weaker economic position than the father in a custody dispute. This economic inequality may enable the father to punish the mother through custody litigation focused on her sexual orientation or to negotiate for lesser support obligations in return for an agreement not to litigate a custody case that he has a statistically high chance of winning. The father whose homosexual orientation is not publicly known and who has been involved in a conventional relationship that places the mother in a position of economic dependency—and we stress the relative nature of this observation—may enjoy greater immunity from disruption of his relationships with his children if he seeks only visitation and not physical custody. Because she depends upon him for economic support, the mother may be dissuaded from making his sexual orientation an issue by the prospect that disclosures will lead to retaliation against him on the job and economic deprivation for her and her children.

The penalties that condition access to the private realm on conformity to traditional sexual norms are paralleled by similar conditions on access to a public world defined by the norms of "real"—that is heterosexual—men. Efforts to invoke Title VII's ban on sex discrimination to protect gay people who have been discharged because of their sexual preference or failure to display personal characteristics that are regarded as gender-appropriate have been uniformly unsuccessful. Thus, in one illustrative Title VII decision, a court found that a man who had been fired from a janitorial job because he was too "effeminate" had not suffered from sex-based discrimination proscribed by Title VII.[80] Federal law, in short, permits employers to enforce highly conventional gender-personality stereotypes and to treat all persons whose sexual preference is nonconforming as unfit.

Nowhere is the discrimination against lesbian women and gay men harsher than in the military. In the 1970s, it was estimated that between two and three thousand individuals annually were being discharged—less than honorably—from the military for reasons involving sexual orientation.[81] While lawsuits since that time have at least required the military to state explicitly the reasoning behind such a discharge,[82] exclusion continues to be the dominant practice. The justifications, ranging from morale problems to the need for "efficient" operations, are more than vaguely reminiscent of those advanced in *Rostker* to justify a single-sex draft. Nevertheless, it is estimated that between 75 percent and 80 percent of all gay soldiers do complete their terms of duty,[83] but only at the price of concealing their sexual orientation.

Men and women who are led to choose same-sex sexual intimacy are, as this brief account has suggested, subjected to the severest sanctions if they reveal their preferences in an economic or personal setting that makes them vulnerable to reprisal. That the law both tolerates and implements this sanctioning system is, in our estimate, a prime indicator of the manner in which the Court's equality and privacy doctrines bow deeply to sexual asymmetry even as they question it.

CONCLUSION

As a result of the changes in law, consciousness, and technology over the past three decades, women in America now enjoy an unparalleled measure of freedom. The legal doctrines that we have examined in this essay have at once played a vital role in securing that freedom and at the same time have failed to seriously question the primary structures that continue to rank the activities of men and women as different in kind and disparate in value. In this sense, both equality doctrine and privacy doctrine accept sexual asymmetry.

The result is that the private world of women continues to be under-valued, and the public world remains closed to all but the few women who have both the opportunity and the willingness to adopt the male norm. For this minority, the choice can be a costly one. For the majority—particularly working-class women who do not easily have access to the escape routes of education and advancement and black women who suffer the additional burden of racism—the choice is often illusory. And for lesbian women, as well as gay men, access even to the private sphere alone is limited, if not foreclosed. Gays and lesbians, perhaps more than any other group, pay the price of the continued realities of separate spheres, and of a privacy doctrine that ratifies traditional norms of sexuality and gender-identity.

Our criticism of those doctrines does not signal our belief that they cannot be transformed. Vital to that transformation is the perspective that has so long been missing from public discourse on law—the perspective of women. The fundamental problem of gender discrimination is not that it has labeled women as different when they are in fact the same—although we by no means intend to suggest that that problem has not been grave. The fundamental problem, as we see it, is that the perspective of women, precisely when it is the farthest from that of men and therefore absolutely essential to the joint human project of designing the world, has been silenced. Just as men now seek joint custody in the private realm, women's claim to joint custody in the public world must be recognized if either sex is to enjoy real freedom of choice in how they structure their lives.

NOTES

1. M. Mead, *Male and Female* 349 (1968).

2. *Id.* at 168.

3. M. Rosaldo & L. Lamphere, eds., *Woman, Culture and Society* 3 (1974).

4. The data in this section on the economic status of women are derived from U.S. Comm'n on Civil Rights, *A Growing Crisis: Disadvantaged Women and Their Children* (1983); "Women in Poverty," 15 *Clearinghouse Review* 925–934 (1982).

5. Weitzman, "The Economics of Divorce: Social and Economic Consequences of Property, Alimony, and Child Support Awards," 28 *University of California at Los Angeles Law Review* 1181, 1241 (1981).

6. C. MacKinnon, *Sexual Harassment of Working Women* 25–32 (1979).

7. J. Fleming, *Stopping Wife Abuse* 155 (1979).

8. *See generally* Graham, "Expansion and Exclusion: A History of Women in American Higher Education," 3 *Signs: Journal of Women in Culture and Society* 759, 768 (1978); U.S. Comm'n on Civil Rights, *supra* note 4, at 37–38.

9. Title VII of the Civil Rights Act of 1964, 42 U.S.C. §§2000e–2000e–17 (1976 & Supp. IV 1980); Equal Pay Act of 1963, 29 U.S.C. §206(d) (1976).

10. Title IX of the Education Amendments of 1972, 20 U.S.C. 1681–1686 (1976); The Equal Credit Opportunity Act, 15 U.S.C. §1691 (1976 & Supp. IV 1980); Fair Housing Act of 1968, 42 U.S.C. §§3604–3606 (1976).

11. *See generally* S. D. Ross & A. Barcher, *The Rights of Women: The Basic ACLU Guide to a Woman's Rights* (1983).

12. S. Schechter, *Women and Male Violence: The Victims and Struggles of the Battered Women's Movement* 157–183 (1982).

13. 410 U.S. 113 (1973).

14. Bradwell v. Illinois, 83 U.S. (16 Wall.) 130 (1873).

15. Muller v. Oregon, 208 U.S. 412 (1908).

16. Goesart v. Cleary, 335 U.S. 464 (1948).

17. 368 U.S. 57, 61–62 (1961).

18. Brief of Appellee at 11.

19. Duren v. Missouri, 439 U.S. 357 (1979); Taylor v. Louisiana, 419 U.S. 522 (1975).

20. 404 U.S. 71 (1971).

21. *Id.* at 76.

22. 349 U.S. 294 (1954).

23. 411 U.S. 677 (1973).

24. Stanton v. Stanton, 421 U.S. 7 (1975).

25. Craig v. Boren, 429 U.S. 190 (1976).

26. Califano v. Goldfarb, 430 U.S. 199 (1977)

27. Wengler v. Druggists Mutual Insurance Co., 446 U.S. 142 (1980).

28. Orr v. Orr, 440 U.S. 268 (1979)

29. Kirschberg v. Feenstra, 450 U.S. 455 (1981).

30. Caban v. Mohammed, 441 U.S. 380 (1979).

31. 458 U.S. 718 (1982).

32. 416 U.S. 351 (1974).

33. 420 U.S. 636 (1975).

34. 430 U.S. 313 (1977).

35. 419 U.S. 498 (1975).

36. *Id.* at 508.

37. For the discussion of what follows, we are indebted to the insights provided by Freedman, "The Equal Protection Clause, Title VII, and Differences Between Women and Men: A Critical Analysis of Contemporary Sex Discrimination Jurisprudence," *Yale Law Journal* (forthcoming 1984); Frug, "Security Job Equality for Women: Labor Market Hostility to Working Mothers," 59 *Boston University Law Review* 55 (1979); MacKinnon, "Feminism, Marxism, Method, and the State: An Agenda for Theory," 7 *Signs: Journal of Women in Culture and Society* 515 (1982); Olsen, "Statutory Rape: A Feminist Critique of Rights Analysis," unpublished manuscript; Olsen, "Family and the Market: A Study of Ideology and Legal Reform," 96 *Harvard Law Review* 1497 (1983); Powers, "Sex Segregation and the Ambivalent Directions of Sex Discrimination Law," 1979 *Wisconsin Law Review* 55 (1979); Scales, "Toward a Feminist Jurisprudence," 56 *Indiana Law Journal* 375 (1981); Taub & Schneider, "Perspectives on Women's Subordination and the Role of Law," in *The Politics of Law,* D. Kairys, ed. (1982); Wildman, "The Legitimation of Sex Discrimination: A Critical Response to Supreme Court Jurisprudence," manuscript; Williams, "The Equality Crisis: Some Reflections on Culture, Courts and Feminism," 7 *Women's Rights Law Reporter* 175 (1982).

38. 453 U.S. 57 (1981).

39. 450 U.S. 464 (1981).

40. 417 U.S. 484 (1974).

41. Williams, *supra* note 37, at 183.

42. In evaluating this argument, it is interesting to recall that during World War II, as a result of the need for women workers in the defense industry, the government engaged in a massive propaganda campaign to convince mothers that working outside the home was patriotic and not harmful to children. That campaign was backed up by substantial federal financial and administrative support for child-care programs, many of which operated on a twenty-four-hour basis and provided such amenities to mothers as take-home hot meals. See Kerr, "One Step Forward, Two Steps Back: Child Care's Long American History" in Roby, ed., *Child Care: Who Cares?* 162–165 (1973). The separate-spheres ideology, like other belief systems, is amenable to an override by the exigencies of economics.

43. 442 U.S. 256 (1979).

44. 453 U.S. at 78.

45. *Id.* at 74 (quoting Califano v. Webster, 430 U.S. 313, 320 [1977]).

46. 450 U.S. at 466.

47. *Id.* at 471, 473.

48. *Id.* at 481, 483–487 and n. *.

49. *Id.* at 488–502.

50. 417 U.S. at 496–497.

51. Gilbert v. General Electric, 429 U.S. 125 (1976).

52. Nashville Gas Co. v. Satty, 434 U.S. 136 (1977) at 142.

53. 42 U.S.C. §2000.

54. In Griggs v. Duke Power Co., 401 U.S. 424 (1971), a Title VII race case, the court held that neutral rules wich produce unequal results must be justified by the employer as a business necessity. The Griggs approach to equality stands in sharp contrast to the constitutional rule. In Personnel Administrator of Massachusetts v. Feeney, 442 U.S. 256 (1979), the Court sustained an absolute lifetime preference for veterans in civil service employment—not withstanding its effect perpetuating a male monopoly on jobs—on the ground that the Fourteenth Amendment guarantees "equal laws, not equal results."

55. 433 U.S. 321 (1977).

56. Id. at 336.

57. Barnes v. Costle, 561 F.2d 983 (D.C. Cir. 1977); Bundy v. Jackson, 641 F.2d 934 (D.C. Cir. 1981).

58. Phillips v. Martin Marietta Corp., 400 U.S. 542 (1971).

59. See Wright v. Olin, 30 FEP 889 (4th cir. 1982), see generally Williams, "The Reconciliation of Fetal Protection With Employment Opportunity Goals Under Title VII," 69 Georgetown Law Journal (1981).

60. 410 U.S. 113 (1973).

61. 268 U.S. 510 (1925).

62. 381 U.S. 479 (1965).

63. 405 U.S. 438 (1972).

64. Harris v. McRae, 448 U.S. 297, 312 (1980).

65. Planned Parenthood of Missouri v. Danforth, 428 U.S. 52 (1976).

66. H.L. v. Matheson, 450 U.S. 398 (1981).

67. Bellotti v. Baird, 443 U.S. 622 (1979).

68. Harris v. McRae, 448 U.S. 297 (1980).

69. Id. at 316.

70. For an insightful discussion of the manner in which issues of reproduction should be treated under equality theory, see S. Law, "Rethinking Sex and the Constitution," Pennsylvania Law Review (forthcoming 1984).

71. 403 F. Supp. 1199 (E.D. Va. 1975), aff'd, 425 U.S. 901 (1976).

72. See, e.g., Baker v. Wade, CA 3-79-1434-R (N.D. Tex. Aug. 17, 1982), noted at 51 United States Law Week 2149 (1982); New York v. Onofre, 434 N.Y.S. 2d 947 (1980), cert. denied, 451 U.S. 987 (1981).

73. Carey v. Population Services, 431 U.S. 678, 688 n.5, 694 n.17 (1977) (plurality opinion).

74. See T. Stoddard et al, The Rights of Gay People, Appendix A, "Criminal Statutes Relating to Consensual Homosexual Acts Between Adults" (1983).

75. *See generally,* Rivera, *Our Straight-Laced Judges: The Legal Position of Homosexual Persons in the United States,* 30 *Hastings Law Journal* 799 (1979); Rivera, *Recent Developments in Sexual Preference Law,* 30 *Drake Law Review* 311 (1980–81) (both cited below as Rivera).

76. Singer v. Hara, 11 Wash. App. 247, 522 P.2d 1187, 1195 (1974).

77. *In re* Adult Anonymous II, 88 A.D. 2d 30, 452 N.Y.S. 2d 198 (1st Dept. 1982).

78. While many, if not most, of these decisions are unpublished, all known cases involving the custody of children of homosexual parents, as of 1980, are detailed in Stoddard et al., *supra* note 73a, and Rivera, *supra* note 74.

79. *See, e.g.,* S. v. S., 608 S.W. 2d 64 (Ky. Ct. App. 1980).

80. Smith v. Liberty Mutual Insurance Co., 395 F. Supp. 1098, 1099 n.2 (N.D.Ga. 1975).

81. *See* C. Williams & M. Weinberg, *Homosexuals and the Military* 28 (1971). *See generally* Rivera, *supra* note 74.

82. *See, e.g.,* Matlovich v. Secretary of Air Force, 591 F.2d 852 (D.C. Cir. 1978).

83. C. Williams & M. Weinberg, *supra* note 79, at 60.

We would like to thank Harriet Dichter, University of Pennsylvania Law School class of 1984 and Jane Schacter, Harvard Law School class of 1984 for their assistance.

SYLVIA A. LAW

Sylvia A. Law is a professor of law at New York University Law School, where she is co-director of the Arthur Garfield Hays Civil Liberties Program. She has engaged in legal and political work in the areas of health, poverty, and women's rights and is the author of The Rights of the Poor *and* Blue Cross: What Went Wrong?

The predecessor to this book, *The Rights of Americans: What They Are —What They Should Be,* commemorated the fiftieth anniversary of the American Civil Liberties Union. The prior years had seen an extraordinary expansion in the rights of many Americans traditionally subordinated by law and political practice, notably blacks and other racial minorities, women, and the poor. At the same time, members of and advocates for these groups saw the expansion that had taken place as seriously incomplete and gravely threatened by conservative trends in all three branches of government.

The Rights of Americans reflected both of these themes. It stated a bold vision of expanding democracy and equality, captured in essays on "traditional" civil liberties such as the right to protest, associate, and publish, and on new rights related to "the essentials of life" such as housing, welfare, legal services, a habitable environment, and equal opportunities in employment and education. On the other hand, many of the essays acknowledged resistance to both traditional civil liberties and the newer equality rights. As Norman Dorsen put it in his eloquent introduction to the volume, "government at every level attempts to solve serious community and national problems by restricting the rights" of the unpopular.[1]

Opposition to, or at least doubts about, rights to economic equality were not confined to the Nixon Administration and its wealthy primary constituency. Many members of "the comfortable middle class" and the "newly secure skilled worker" had "enough of social change and judicial activism." Today the policies of the Reagan administration and the Ninety-seventh Congress powerfully reject the legitimacy or feasibility of economic equality. Further, many liberals today see concern with economic equality as subordinate to concern with productivity and profits.[2]

Within the ACLU there has been ongoing debate as to whether to regard issues of economic justice as equivalent in importance to more traditional civil liberties. As Professor Dorsen noted, the essays on various "essentials of life" were "open to the charge of wandering from the traditionally narrow road of civil liberties to the broad avenues of social justice and economic policy." He rejected this charge as resting on a "false dichotomy" between liberty and economic justice, observing that the effective exercise of liberty depends upon material resources and a substantial degree of economic and social equality. He said there is no need to "apologize for including among individual rights the enjoyment of minimal economic security."[3] Indeed, fundamental rights should include such matters as the right to useful work at a decent wage, the right to participate in workplace and community governance, as well as the rights to essential material goods and services explored in the 1971 volume.

Civil libertarian ideas embody some of the grandest and most liberating visions of our individual and collective human potentiality. The rights to speak, to dissent, to develop and express independent conscience, to associate with others in communities of mutual concern, to control our bodies, all reflect a vision of ourselves and others as free, self-governing people. Further, these noble concepts about who we are directly support a deep civil libertarian commitment that each person be treated with equal concern and respect.

The core social issue of our time is whether liberal civil liberties will serve values of human self-realization, community, and equality or whether these liberal rights will rather legitimate the entrenched power of bureaucratic and market institutions that deny those values. The goal of this essay is to participate in the debate about American social policy and law by focusing on one theme: that economic justice and civil liberties are not only compatible, but mutually reinforcing.

HISTORIC CONCEPTS OF ECONOMIC
ARRANGEMENTS AND CIVIL LIBERTY

The nation's founders understood that civil liberties and economic arrangements are closely related. John Adams said, "Property must be secured or liberty cannot exist . . . The moment the idea is admitted into society that property is not as sacred as the laws of God, and that there is not a force of law and public justice to protect it, anarchy and tyranny commence."[4] Even in the simpler society of revolutionary America, in which property was more widely distributed, some of those who shaped our constitutional charter recognized that people born without material resources could not participate in market, political, and social life. For example, Thomas Paine proposed a "national fund" raised through heavy inheritance taxes, to distribute fifteen pounds to each person at age twenty-one, and ten pounds a year to everyone over fifty, "as compensation in part, for the loss of his or her natural inheritance, by the introduction of the system of landed property."[5] Benjamin Franklin maintained that "All the Property that is necessary to a Man, for the Conservation of the Individual and the Propagation of the Species, is his natural Right, which none can justly deprive him of: But all Property superfluous to such purposes is the Property of the Publick. . . ."[6]

In the mid–nineteenth century, with the rise of industrialism, a new view of civil liberties and economic relations came to dominate American thinking. Classical liberalism emphasized that the principal function of political and economic institutions was to protect individual autonomy. The only legitimate bases of legal obligation to others were personal fault or voluntary contract. The core of economic freedom was the right to buy and sell, to retain the earnings of labor and capital, and to accumulate wealth. Free-market exchange would promote both individual benefit and general public good, and provide an essential protection against concentrated political power. The primary function of government was as an umpire to protect the economic status quo and to prevent people from injuring one another. Government regulation was viewed as an evil that interfered with free-market exchange.

This classical liberal view of the relation between economic arrangements and political liberty is still advanced, and is generally called conservatism in the United States today. Milton Friedman argues that a free competitive market secures the right to dissent because "the employee is protected from coercion by the employer because of the other employers for whom he can work. . . . Since the household always has the alternative of producing directly for itself, it need not enter into any exchange unless it benefits from it."[7]

In this defense of capitalism, Friedman assumes that freedom to contract will allow people to secure the material goods necessary for support and security. But in a complex society freedom to contract often does not enable people to secure economic subsistence. Most households are not in fact free to produce directly. In the 1960s many people attempted to build a life outside the money economy. Often they were people richly blessed with skill, energy, physical strength, and initial material resources. Few succeeded.

By contrast, in opposing socialism, Friedman does not focus on the possibility of obtaining a job and material subsistence but rather on actual economic power. He observes that "[i]n order for men to advocate anything, they must in the first place be able to earn a living. This already raises a problem in a socialist society, since all jobs are under the direct control of political authorities."[8] Friedman is correct that liberty and dissent inextricably require economic support, but wrong in asserting that the unfettered freedom to buy and sell necessarily makes either political freedom or economic support possible.

From the mid–nineteenth century until the late 1930s the Supreme Court enforced the classical liberal view and struck down as unconstitutional laws enacted for the common good that inhibited freedom of contract or restricted property rights.[9] If this meant suffering for those who lost in free-market struggles, it was the unfortunate price of both liberty and productivity. Nevertheless, contrary to Friedman's assertion, free-market ideology did not provide even theoretical protection for First Amendment freedom of speech. No right of free speech, either in law or practice, existed until well into the twentieth century. It was not until 1931 that the Supreme Court held that the First Amendment restrained state and local officials.[10] "Before [1939], one spoke publicly only at the discretion of local, and sometimes federal, authorities, who often prohibited what they, the local business establishment, or other powerful segments of the community did not want to hear."[11] American history does not support the view that political freedom goes hand in hand with laissez-faire economics.

THE NEW DEAL

Since the 1930s a different political ideology, one that both builds upon and modifies that which went before, has dominated our thinking. The economic collapse of 1929 supported greater federal action to regulate economic institutions and to soften some of the harshest consequences of the free market. But New Deal liberalism retains the assumption that free markets, private accumulation of resources, and freedom to contract are desirable economic arrangements. It retains much of the prior distrust of the government.

Some New Deal programs, such as the Agricultural Adjustment Act, subsidized essential industries that failed in the free market. The banking and securities industries were regulated in the wake of widespread bank closings. The National Labor Relations Act encouraged economic peace by routinizing labor-management relations, without interfering with management prerogatives to determine the content and organization of work. Other New Deal programs provided relief in forms least disruptive of dominant economic interests. Hence, the Social Security Act minimized governmental interference with the wage-labor market by targeting subsistence benefits to groups defined as unemployable, such as the elderly, the disabled, and women with children. Public works projects provided temporary jobs for the unemployed doing work that the private market did not seek.[12]

The New Deal program was inconsistent with prior constitutional concepts protecting property, contracts, and the economic status quo. The economic conditions and political unrest that produced the New Deal legislation made it untenable for the Supreme Court to continue to protect the economic status quo. Further, Legal Realists such as Karl Llewellyn and Jerome Frank had demonstrated that classical liberal concepts of property rights, whether in land or freedom of contract, were not natural and God-given, but rather were simply social and legal arrangements, and that the legal arrangements protected by the Court in the name of natural law had a strong class bias.[13] Natural rights fell, in the most dramatic shift in constitutional doctrine in American history. Since the 1930s the Supreme Court's approach to civil liberties and economic arrangements has drawn a sharp distinction between social and economic legislation and laws affecting civil liberties. This approach presumes that the legislature possesses a greater institutional competence to set social and economic policy than do the courts, because legislatures express democratic will.[14] Courts should defer to legislative judgment on "social and economic legislation" because such laws involve political choices rather than issues of constitutional principle. But when legislation impinges upon freedoms of speech, conscience, association, blocks access to the legislative process, or burdens racial or other "discrete and insular minorities," courts must look more searchingly at the legitimacy of the asserted legislative goals, the fit between the asserted goals and the means chosen to achieve them, or both.[15]

Although the distinction between economic legislation and fundamental rights has intuitive appeal, in practice, like the classical liberal concepts of natural right, it has also proven to be self-contradictory and class-biased. For example, a law denying additional welfare payments to families of more than five people was upheld as mere "economic and social legislation," despite the obvious adverse impact on family autonomy and compositional choice, which in other contexts the Court recognizes as an aspect of constitutionally protected liberty.[16] Denying welfare to those who resist unannounced "home visits" from investigating bureaucrats does not violate Fourth Amendment rights, but surprise inspections to enforce basic workplace safety under the Occupational Health and Safety Act do.[17] And perhaps most egregiously, a law limiting campaign spending for Congressional elections violates the First Amendment because money is a form of speech, while a law excluding payment for medically necessary abortions from the otherwise comprehensive Medicaid program does not burden any fundamental right.[18] The list could go on.[19]

A NEW PROPERTY CONCEPT OF ECONOMIC ARRANGEMENTS AND CIVIL LIBERTY

Since the 1930s an ever-increasing amount of individual economic resource has taken the form of largess from the government as licenses, franchises, subsidies, taxi medallions, TV channels, and liquor permits. Until the late 1960s the assumption was that the government could grant or deny such largess on whatever terms it chose. The result was that the basic material support and security of increasing numbers of people depended upon explicit government power that often seemed arbitrary and unchallengeable.

In 1964 Prof. Charles Reich formulated a new approach to the relation between economic arrangements and civil liberty, appropriate to the growing welfare state. He focused on one function that property serves in human life. Property maintains

> independence, dignity and pluralism in society by creating zones within which the majority has to yield to the owner. Whim, caprice, irrationality and "anti-social" activities are given the protection of the law; the owner may do what all or most of his neighbors decry. The Bill of Rights also serves this function, but while the Bill of Rights comes into play only at extraordinary moments of conflict or crisis, property affords day-to-day protection in the ordinary affairs of life. Indeed, in the final analysis the Bill of Rights depends upon the existence of private property.[20]

Reich also recognized that today the "property" upon which many citizens depend takes the form of government largess. Further, "[T]here can be no retreat from the public interest state. It is the inevitable outgrowth of an interdependent world . . . If private property can no longer perform its protective functions, it will be necessary to establish institutions to carry on the work that private property once did but can no longer do."[21]

In 1971 the Supreme Court adopted Reich's analysis, holding that welfare is a form of property that cannot constitutionally be taken away without due process of law. The case, *Goldberg v. Kelly*, involved the claim of welfare recipients that the constitutional provision prohibiting the state from taking life, liberty, or property without due process of law required that they be given notice and an opportunity for a hearing prior to the termination of aid.[22] In characterizing welfare as property the Court recognized that property rights are not natural, immutable, or inherent, but only grant their possessors such power as the courts and legislatures choose to recognize. Property, whether in the form of land, wages, welfare, or a license to practice law, is what the society defines it to be. At the same time, the Court held that the government is not entirely free to dictate the terms and conditions upon which welfare is granted. Due process requires fundamental fairness, whatever that might mean in a particular context. The idea that property is whatever we say it is squarely conflicts with the idea that the Constitution protects individuals from forfeiture of "property" without due process of law. This flat and open inconsistency is a good, healthy thing, for it forces us to confront the substantive political values at stake.

The Supreme Court in *Goldberg* did just that, saying:

> From its founding the Nation's basic commitment has been to foster the dignity and well-being of all persons within its borders. We have come to recognize that forces not within the control of the poor contribute to their poverty . . . Welfare, by meeting the basic demands of subsistence, can help bring within the reach of the poor the same opportunities that are available to others to participate meaningfully in the life of the community. . . . Public assistance, then, is not mere charity, but a means to "promote the general Welfare, and secure the Blessings of Liberty to ourselves and our Posterity."[23]

At a conceptual level, *Goldberg* contains the seeds of two ideas that could radically alter relationships between individuals and the ground rules of collective relationships. First, if poverty is not the fault of the individual but rather the product of economic relationships that benefit some at the expense of others, the poor have a stronger moral claim for aid in the courts and the legislatures than if we believe that people are poor because of their own sin or voluntary choice. Second, the recognition that property is both socially defined and constitutionally restrained demands closer examination of the functions of property. Taken seriously, these ideas could lead to a significant reordering of social relations.

At a practical level the importance of *Goldberg* is that it makes poor people more free to speak and act by expanding their opportunities to resist some forms of retributive action against them. This principle protects not only the poor, but others who rely on government largess. Perhaps in a society characterized by more cooperative, mutually supporting relationships the bureaucratized protection of *Goldberg* would not be necessary. But that is surely not the world in which we live. Even in more cooperative groups individuals have a powerful interest in knowing the grounds for and having a chance to resist collective action against them.

However, the larger transforming potential of *Goldberg* has not been realized, and to understand why we must look beyond Supreme Court cases. Charles Reich provided the intellectual basis for *Goldberg*. The Court cited him in support of the proposition that welfare is property protected by the Constitution; indeed they did not cite anything else on the point.[24] But the Reich/*Goldberg* concept of the relation between economic arrangements and civil liberties, while brilliant, is limited. It correctly recognizes that one function of property is to provide the material support that makes individual liberty possible. But property arrangements play other social functions. They structure the complex human relations that we know as work. They facilitate the accumulation of material resources that makes it possible to undertake enterprises that no one person can accomplish alone. To understand the individual-support function of property requires examination of the other functions that property serves, i.e., the organization of work and accumulation of material resources. The transforming potential of *Goldberg* has not been realized, in part, because the idea of property it embodies is limited.

The other reason the transforming potential of *Goldberg* has not been realized is that the social movement that supported the Court's 1971 decision declined. Ideas made manifest in action shape constitutional doctrine even more profoundly than ideas on paper. The Court would not have adopted Reich's theory in *Goldberg* without the welfare rights movement of the late 1960s in which poor people acted as if they had a right to subsistence and decent treatment. Significant Supreme Court actions protecting the political and economic rights of common people often come during periods of social struggle by those people. The transformation in constitutional doctrine in the 1930s in relation to both First Amendment rights and economic regulation would not have occurred without the labor and other social movements. Similarly, the Supreme Court decision that legalized abortion was not merely the result of an intellectual concept but rather the response to tens of thousands of women acting as if they had a right to control their bodies and lives.[25]

Many reasons account for the decline of the civil and welfare rights movements that made *Goldberg* possible. Important leaders died—Martin Luther King, Malcolm X, George Wiley. The war in Vietnam led many who were active in other social struggles to concentrate their attention on the antiwar movement. New Deal and Great Society social programs are structured on categorical lines that divide people from one another. The working poor are separated from the "unemployables"; the aged are separated from women and children; regional conflicts abound.[26] The FBI harassed and destablized large numbers of groups and individuals working against the war and for civil rights and economic justice.[27] The commercially oriented and corporate-controlled mass media profoundly shape social movements, and contributed to their decline.[28] Finally, because for many the 1960s concept of economic relations and political liberty did not address the work and material-accumulation functions of property, it could not sustain commitment to protecting individual interests in material support.

TOWARD A NEW IDEA OF ECONOMIC RELATIONS AND CIVIL LIBERTIES

Today, while more Americans experience economic distress and insecurity than at any time since the Great Depression, the political mood of the nation, particularly in relation to issues of economic arrangements, is conservative. There are two main explanations for this. First, people are skeptical as to whether the New Deal/Great Society vision of America is workable. There are good reasons for this skepticism. James O'Conner argues that the present public fiscal crisis results from the effort simultaneously to aid the accumulation of private capital and to legitimate the free market by relieving the most egregious human suffering that the market generates.[29] Further, as discussed below, social and public services are financed largely on the basis of regressive state, local, and payroll taxes, and middle-income people who bear the burden of these taxes are justly resentful. Work is not organized to enhance productivity, quality, or worker satisfaction. Technology has made many jobs obsolete, and we have not developed the capacity to either spread work around or to expand opportunities for people to work providing needed social services. It is possible to solve these problems. But our history strongly suggests that solutions demand a popular political movement, and that movement is lacking.

The second reason for our conservative political climate is that the political process is distorted in favor of concentrated economic power. The issues presented in electoral politics are shaped by increasingly concentrated corporate power and wealth. Communications technology and capital-intensive campaign techniques have made the political impact of money more potent than ever before in our history. As Judge J. Skelly Wright observes, "Financial inequalities pose a pervasive and growing threat to the principle of 'one person, one vote,' and undermine the political proposition to which this nation is dedicated—that all men are created equal."[30] Within the past several years the Burger Court has gone far to deny that corporations are creations of public power and subject to public control. In 1976 the Court held that Congress could not limit corporate campaign contributions;[31] in 1978 the Court struck down a Massachusetts law limiting corporate spending to influence voting on referendum issues unrelated to corporate business.[32] According to the Court, money talks, corporations are people, and the legislature has little power to limit the power of corporate influence in the political process.

It is not only the power of concentrated wealth that distorts the political process. At the other end of the spectrum, large numbers of people do not participate in electoral politics. In 1980, 76.5 million eligible voters, or 47 percent, stayed away from the polls. There is a systematic class bias in voter nonparticipation. This is not inevitable. In other times and places, people with little money or education voted.[33] Nonvoting reflects features of the American political system, e.g., the perception that electoral politics do not offer choices that matter and that individuals cannot influence those choices.[34] Despite pervasive economic insecurity and government and corporate policies that hurt the majority of people who are not among the rich, there are few signs of rebellion. This is both understandable and distressing. Ordinary people cannot be optimistic about the possibility of challenging the power of concentrated wealth. Too little in our daily experience allows us to develop our capacities as self-governing and democratic people.

Developing a politics that comes to grips with the inadequacies of the New Deal vision of a just society requires that we go beyond Reich and address the other functions of property and their relation to liberty, i.e., work and the accumulation of material resources.

WORK, ECONOMIC ARRANGEMENTS, AND CIVIL LIBERTY

The dominant view in the United States, today and always, conceives of work as an exchange relationship. Work is a burden, i.e., the giving up of "leisure" in return for compensation. The utility of work is defined by the user, initially the employer as the direct purchaser of labor, ultimately the consumer. The employer decides what it contracts to buy; the employee "fills the job." The worker has a role defined by the job and does not own the job. The value of work for the worker is only as a means toward self-sufficiency separate from work. The worker has no legitimate interest in the product, but only in the pay and working conditions, which affect him or her personally. Individuals are morally obligated to make themselves employable, to change themselves to meet whatever the market may require. If you cannot get the job you want, you must take the job you can get.[35]

For most of our history this concept of work was constitutionally protected from legislative alteration. For example, in 1915 the Supreme Court struck down a state law prohibiting employers from requiring workers not to join a union. The law was held unconstitutional because it limited the worker's "right" to bargain away his liberty to associate with his fellows. The exchange relation was constitutionally protected and the legislature could not redress inequalities in bargaining power which were "the normal and inevitable result" of the right to contract.[36]

As discussed earlier, the notion that the liberty and property of the exchange relationship was a natural right immune from legislative alternation fell in the 1930s when the Supreme Court was forced to recognize that the economic status quo is not constitutionally protected against democratic alteration. Since then, legislatures have enforced some modifications of the pure exchange relation. Employers are prohibited from discriminating on the basis of race or sex.[37] The law recognizes the right of most workers to organize and to bargain about terms and conditions of their work.[38] The law limits entrepreneurial freedom to pollute the environment[39] and to expose workers to physical danger.[40]

But the legislative modifications of the exchange relation have been limited. At present approximately 70 percent of all nongovernmental employees—those who are not covered by collective bargaining agreements—have virtually no protection against unjust dismissal.[41] A worker who expresses well-grounded concern for the safety of the product he or she produces can be dismissed as a troublemaker.[42] An employer can adopt policies that have the effect of discriminating on the basis of race or sex, but unless an injured worker can meet the difficult burden of proving intent to discriminate, the remedies available are limited.[43] Workers can unionize, but they cannot bargain about the content or quality of the product or service they provide, or the organization of the work itself.[44] Even doctors can legally demand bargaining only on wages, hours, and terms and conditions of employment, not the larger issues that determine their ability to provide decent care.[45] Interns and residents have no legal right to organize.[46] The corporate employer, not the human healer, defines the job.

Further, workers' interests in their jobs have not received even the minimal constitutional protection afforded poor people's interest in subsistence. After *Goldberg* opened our constitutional ideas of property and fundamental fairness, it would not be a large leap to insist that corporations, created and subsidized by the state and wielding power greater than many governments, must also act with fundamental fairness in making decisions that affect the economic survival of individual workers and communities.[47] Recognizing a constitutionally protected right of workers to know the justification for employer actions that affect them adversely and assuring workers an opportunity to object does not guarantee a job, just as *Goldberg*'s requirement of due process does not guarantee a substantive right to eat. But it would be important. Workers would be freer to act and speak without fear of retaliatory discharge if the Constitution guaranteed a protective process and a substantive right not to be discharged for the exercise of constitutionally protected rights. Providing at least some procedural due-process protection to worker and community interests in learning the reasons for corporate relocation decisions, and assuring a forum to protest those decisions, would not ordinarily prevent a corporation from abandoning a community in search of higher profits, but it would facilitate a broader understanding and participation in these decisions that might lead to more responsible corporate action.

The major legal, doctrinal obstacle to applying even *Goldberg*'s minimal due-process protections to employee and community interests in work is the law's distinction between the public and private spheres. The classical liberal view distrusted "public power" but saw "private exchange" as wholly beneficial. "In the public sphere . . . basic concepts of freedom, democracy, and equality are applicable. However, in the private sphere, which encompasses almost all economic activity, we allow no democracy or equality and only the freedom to buy and sell."[48]

The presumption that public power is always dangerous and private power always beneficial is false. Stories of chemical dumps, workers knowingly exposed to toxic chemicals, acid rain, and products sold with deadly, correctable defects remind us that concentrated private power is often arbitrary, sometimes life-threatening. More basically, the distinction between public and private is not sharp; it may indeed have no coherent meaning. For example, corporations are the creation of the state, perform public functions, and are often highly dependent upon government subsidies and tax expenditures. For another example, tens of thousands have been transformed by the feminist insight that the personal is political; the allocation of responsibility in the home is a "private" decision that profoundly affects "public" participation in work and politics. Yet the public/private distinction persists in constitutional doctrine, and indeed the sphere of public accountability seems to be shrinking.[49] Applying standards of public accountability to concentrated private economic power, either through legislation or through constitutional interpretation, would be an important reform. However, it accepts the legitimacy of the concept of work as an exchange relationship and seeks merely to limit the more oppressive aspects of the exchange.

The exchange-relationship view of work has profound implications for government efforts to assure the material support that is the necessary requisite to liberty. If work is only a means of obtaining money to allow the worker to engage in activities outside of work that give life meaning, then government subsistence programs threaten the wage labor structure. This threat demands that income-security programs be targeted to the unemployable. But the definition of the "unemployable" is elusive and often destructive to those people defined as socially useless. The distinction divides the working poor and those defined as unemployable. The threat to wage labor incentives demands that we devote significant public resources to enforcing wage work requirements against recipients of public aid, even in times of high unemployment. Most seriously, if work is seen simply as a means to the end of economic sufficiency, income-maintenance programs must be kept meager and demeaning to minimize disincentives for wage labor.

The exchange relationship is not the only way of thinking about work. Pope John Paul II in his Encyclical Letter *On Human Work* says work is not simply "merchandise" that the worker sells to the possessor of capital, but is rather something

> that corresponds to man's dignity, that expresses this dignity and
> increases it . . . Through work man not only transforms nature,
> adapting it to his own needs, but he also achieves fulfillment as
> a human being and indeed, in a sense, becomes more a human
> being.[50]

Marx too protests against the exchange view of work:

> for labour, life activity, productive life itself, appears to man in the
> first place merely as a means of satisfying a need—the need to
> maintain physical existence. Yet the productive life is the life of
> the species. It is life engendering life. The whole character of a
> species—its species-character—is contained in the character of its
> life activity, and free conscious activity is man's species character.
> Life itself appears only as a means to life.[51]

Both Marx and the Pope urge that we conceive of work as an expression
of basic human need and character. The value of work is defined not
simply by the buyer, but also by the worker. Prof. Howard Lesnick argues,
"Work is not *merely* the sale of a sale-able piece of oneself, in return for
self-sufficiency; it is an expression of one's energy, one's capacity and
desire to be useful, one's responsibility and connection to fellow hu-
mans."[52]

This view has profound implications. If one without work is without
an essential aspect of his or her humanity, there is a moral basis not simply
for a claim for material support but also for a right to work and to a role
in shaping work. In this concept of work, economic and civil liberty are
indistinguishable. Self-expression and realization through political speech
or through the activity of work are one. Political and workplace solidarity
are unified.

MATERIAL ACCUMULATION,
ECONOMIC ARRANGEMENTS
AND CIVIL LIBERTIES

Civil liberties and economic justice are inextricably linked in that the
exercise of political liberty requires a source of material support. They are
also linked in that the "free conscious activity"—whether work, speech,
or association—is characteristic of all human beings. But it is incomplete
and therefore distorting to address issues of subsistence or work relations
without also addressing the issue of accumulation of material resources.

Every society has some means of facilitating the bringing together of
human and material resources to achieve objectives that no single person
can achieve alone. In a complex industrial world, with a money-based

economy, the process we know as the accumulation of capital serves this function.

The traditional view of accumulating material resources was that everything that an individual earns, through labor or use of capital, belongs to him, as a matter of natural right. For example, in 1895 the Supreme Court heard a challenge to the constitutionality of the Income Tax Act of 1894. The arguments against the tax were both technical and moral. The moral argument was that any departure from the principle that what is mine is mine was "communistic, socialistic . . . populistic."[53] By a 5–4 vote the Court held the tax unconstitutional, rejecting cases that had for over one hundred years approved such taxes.[54] In 1913 the decision was repudiated by the Sixteenth Amendment to the Constitution.

While it is today clear that Congress has broad constitutional power to tax progressively and otherwise to impose social controls over the accumulation of material resources, it often fails to do so. Three aspects of prevailing government policy in this area demand attention. First, our tax system is both regressive and systematically unaccountable. Second, profitable activities are left to the private profit-making sector, while essential but unprofitable enterprises are public responsibility. Third, our commitment to militarism precludes economic justice. The discussion of these issues is merely suggestive of the ways in which the economic relations we know as material accumulation affect other economic relations such as work and subsistence and civil liberties.

TAX POLICY

As a technical and constitutional matter Congress has broad authority to use progressive taxation to reduce the disparities in wealth and income that now so pervasively undermine our democracy.[55] Poverty is both an absolute state of deprivation—the inability to purchase a nutritionally adequate diet—and also a relative deprivation—having dramatically less than other people in a culture.[56] Addressing the problem of relative poverty inescapably requires consideration of where money comes from as well as issues of benefits paid. Further, as a practical matter it is not reasonable to expect middle- and working-class people to finance services for the poor—jobs, day care, education, health—that the middle class cannot obtain for themselves.

At present, our tax system is systematically skewed to provide stable public financial support to concentrated economic power and to relegate essential human services to regressive and unstable sources of public support. The most stable form of public financial support is the tax expenditure.[57] Once adopted, a tax expenditure provides profitable enterprise with a reliable public subsidy, without the inconvenience or uncertainty of public accountability or periodic legislative appropriation. In 1984 federal tax subsidies for oil and gas corporations alone will cost $3.9 billion.[58] Tax expenditures have grown quickly in recent years. In 1967 tax expenditures produced a revenue loss of $36.6 billion, amounting to 20.5 percent of total federal direct outlays. In fiscal year 1981, the cost of tax exemptions reached a total of $228.6 billion, amounting to 34.6 percent of outlays.[59]

The primary justification for these tax expenditures is that they serve a public purpose. But when it is suggested that they should be subject to regular congressional review, to ascertain whether they in fact serve their intended purpose, the "natural law" notion that what is mine is mine of right reemerges. For example, Sen. Russell Long, questioned about his opposition to legislative review of tax exemptions, and his personal gain of $300,000 in oil-depletion allowances, said that when a person receives a depletion allowance, "he has it because somebody worked for it. And whoever it was who worked for it has that as a reward. He did something, he tried to achieve something, he made a contribution."[60] Of course, Senator Long "earned" his depletion allowance simply by investing in a government-subsidized industry. If we are ever to finance essential public services, provide work for Americans who need it, or support those who cannot work, we must subject the tax appropriations process to democratic control.

At the other end of the spectrum, the economically vulnerable depend upon regressive and unstable sources of public aid. For example, Social Security and Medicare are financed through a regressive tax on payroll. Aid to Families with Dependent Children (AFDC) and Medicaid rely on even more regressive state and local taxes. States and localities lack the power to levy progressive taxes based on ability to pay. If they do, businesses and the wealthy people move. Governors and mayors simply cannot afford to lose their wealthiest citizens and so rely heavily on regressive revenue sources like sales and property taxes. As a practical matter, the federal government has a much greater power to tax income and wealth on a progressive basis for it is much more difficult for capital to leave the United States.[61]

Experience in the past decade with the Supplemental Security Income (SSI) program for the aged, blind, and disabled, and the AFDC program for needy women and children is illustrative. Since 1974 the SSI program has been financed through general federal revenues, while the AFDC program depends in significant part upon more regressive state and local taxes. Today SSI benefits exceed AFDC benefits for families of comparable size in every state. In twenty-two states, SSI benefits exceed benefits for needy women and children by more than 100 percent. In six states SSI benefits exceed AFDC benefits by more than 400 percent.[62] AFDC is the only major subsistence program that is not indexed for inflation. In the past decade the real value of already meager AFDC grants has declined by 56 percent. The federal government is not inherently more humane toward the poor than the states. But the federal government does have a greater power to tax progressively to raise funds to provide the material support that is the necessary requisite of liberty.

MISALLOCATION OF PUBLIC AND PRIVATE RESPONSIBILITY

A second way government policy vitally affects economic justice is the decision to leave profitable activities to private enterprise and to assume public responsibility for unprofitable essential services. There are many examples of this pattern. Private enterprise retains the profitable freight rail service, and the public Amtrak gets the unprofitable but essential passenger service. Private hospitals take care of patients with insurance, and dump those patients on the public hospitals when the insurance runs out. Private enterprise sells cheese for profit; the government buys excess supply to keep the price high and distributes surplus to the hungry. If distribution of surplus affects private profit, free distribution stops. When public services are costly or of low quality, the failure is seen as evidence of inherent incompetence.

Democratic control of accumulation is important because profitability is not the only criterion by which social good is measured. Clean air and safe streets do not produce private profit, but few would disagree that they are desirable. There is tremendous need, not simply among the poor, for a variety of human services—day care, home health care, education, transport and escort for the handicapped and infirm. Ten percent of the population is actively seeking work, and many more have given up the search because they know jobs are not to be found. Providing human services, particularly for those who are not rich, is not an attractive option for corporations organized for the sole purpose of maximizing return on investment. The federal government could use expanded, progressively raised, tax revenue to support locally accountable organizations in providing necessary human services to a broad spectrum of people.

The misallocation of public and private responsibility for the accumulation of material resources necessarily affects our capacity to make work democratically accountable. Staughton Lynd argues powerfully that we cannot address the problem of plant closings without considering "the problem of investment decision making based solely on profit maximization." Steelmaking, for example, is highly capital-intensive and "the rate of profit to be made by investing in steel is likely to be lower than the rate of profit to be derived from investments in chemicals, real estate, or oil. Thus, U.S. Steel, while telling Congress that it lacks the money to modernize its steel mills, [had] spent more than $6 billion to buy Marathon Oil." A system of investment decision making that looks only to the investor's rate of profit "may deprive society of essential goods and services like steel by investing in more profitable but less socially needed opportunities."[63]

MILITARISM

Much of the future that Orwell envisioned in *Nineteen Eighty-Four* has not come to pass. In part it is a tribute to our deep democratic and civil-libertarian traditions; in part a tribute to the indomitability of the human spirit. The portion of Orwell's vision that rings most true today relates to the military.

> [T]he Superstates are permanently at war, and have been so for the past twenty-five years. War, however, is no longer the desperate, annihilating struggle that it was in the early decades of the twentieth century. It is a warfare of limited aims between combatants who are unable to destroy one another. . . . [No] superstate

could be definitely conquered. . . . They are too evenly matched, and their natural defenses are too formidable. . . . The primary aim of modern warfare . . . is to use up the products of the machine without raising the general standard of living. . . . If it once became general, wealth would confer no distinction. It was possible, no doubt, to imagine a society in which *wealth*, in the sense of personal possessions and luxuries, should be evenly distributed, while *power* remained in the hands of a small privileged caste. But in practice such a society could not long remain stable. For if leisure and security were enjoyed by all alike, the great mass of human beings who are normally stupefied by poverty would become literate and would learn to think for themselves; and when once they had done this, they would sooner or later realize that the privileged minority had no function, and they would sweep it away. *In the long run, a hierarchical society was only possible on a basis of poverty and ignorance.* . . . Goods must be produced, but they must not be distributed. And in practice the only way of achieving this was by continuous warfare.[64]

Orwell paints with a broad brush. But without denying either the necessity of military defense, or the technical complexity of defense choices, the point remains that defense spending inescapably has a profound impact on economic arrangements and civil liberties. The Reagan administration today seeks to build 226 MX Densepack Ballistic Missiles, at a cost of about $100 million each. A conservative estimate is that the MX program will cost over $10 billion a year for over a decade.[65] By contrast, for example, the entire federal cost of the SSI program was less than $6 billion in 1979.[66] Military expenditures are a significant source of public subsidy to concentrated private power; in 1978, for example, ten companies each did more than $1 billion worth of business with the Pentagon.[67] Further, expenditures have the effect of transferring wealth from the many to the few because military spending, in either the public or private sector, creates far fewer jobs than comparable expenditures for civilian purposes.[68]

In the permanent war of Orwell's *Nineteen Eighty-Four* the Superpowers "are not divided by any genuine ideological difference."[69] Today both the United States and Soviet superpowers are devoted to militarism and more generally to concentrated control of capital accumulation. In the United States public policy strengthens the power of concentrated private capital, while in the Soviet Union concentrated power is exercised by bureaucratic and managerial elites.[70] But Orwell was wrong in envisioning no "genuine ideological difference" between the superstates. Our public commitment to civil liberties, democracy, and equality, at least within our borders, makes the United States freer and more open to alternative futures than the Soviet Union.

It is convenient for governments, both capitalist and communist, to foster the belief that economic justice and civil liberties are antithetical. If Socialist states can convince their citizens that suppression of dissent is the inevitable price of economic security, all but the most iconoclastic might well believe that sacrifice of bourgeois civil liberties was worthwhile. Obviously, it is easier to govern without troublemakers challenging the concentrated power of the state. But without free expression the egalitarian ideals of socialism are not realized for it is too easy for wealth and power to concentrate in the hands of the bureaucratic elite.[71]

Similarly, if liberal/capitalist government can convince its citizens that economic inequality and insecurity are the inevitable price of individual rights of dissent, association, and movement, even those who are most economically oppressed might well believe that the price is worth paying. Again, the benefit of this belief is obvious—it is much easier to govern in the interests of the wealthy if people believe that systemic concern for economic equality and security is somehow antithetical to broadly shared civil libertarian values.

CONCLUSION

Economic justice and civil liberties are mutually reinforcing in many ways. Because individual material support is a prerequisite to the exercise of all rights, civil libertarian values support individual claims against the state for subsistence. Because work is a means of support and a central form of human self-actualization, commitment to civil libertarian values also demands concern that people have opportunity for work and for a voice in the control of work. Civil libertarian values cannot be realized by focusing exclusively upon the real threat of abusive government power. It is also necessary to apply ideals of fair process, free expression, equality, and democracy to concentrated private economic power. Only by doing so can we hold concentrated economic power accountable to general democratic will and to particular individuals. As a practical matter it is not possible to assure individual economic support or to provide opportunities for work without also considering more generally the way in which public monies are raised and used.

Most of the agenda advocated here cannot be realized in the courts. But civil libertarian concerns are broader than those rights that can be enforced through litigation. For example, even though placing limits on the power of the FBI and CIA to engage in covert operations apparently cannot be accomplished through litigation on behalf of individuals, it is nonetheless a matter of legitimate civil libertarian concern. For a second example, although prevailing constitutional principles do not restrain private employers from discriminating on the basis of race or sex, civil libertarian concern for equality opposes discrimination by such employers. A concept of civil libertarian values limited to that which can be achieved through a lawsuit at any particular moment in history demeans the importance of individual interests in free speech, dissent, association, conscience, and equality, and misunderstands the relationship between litigation and other forms of social decision making. If judicial recognition of civil libertarian rights occurs most frequently when organized social movements demand recognition for such rights, then concern with civil liberties inescapably demands concern and support for social movement.

Property serves many functions. It is necessary to make concentrated economic power more democratically accountable in order to realize civil libertarian values. At the same time, the property that provides an individual material support and security is valuable precisely because it protects the individual's ability to march to a different drummer, without having to account to the collective will. This essay attempts to articulate one approach to the distinction Benjamin Franklin drew between property necessary "for the Conservation of the Individual" and the "Property of the Publick." Others have described distinctions between property that is necessary to liberty and property that is a means of exercising power.[72] Such distinctions are inevitably uncertain in particular application, but it is essential that they be made if civil libertarian values are to serve human goals of self-realization, community, and equality. Corporations are not people. They are socially created means to an end, while we are all ends in ourselves. "Neutrality" does not require that we pretend that the property of General Motors is equivalent to the property of the welfare check.

NOTES

Most of what I know about economic justice I first learned from Edward V. Sparer. His article, "Fundamental Human Rights, Legal Entitlements and the Social Struggle: A Friendly Critique of the Critical Legal Studies Movement," 36 *Stanford Law Review* (1984), presents a sophisticated treatment of the issues addressed here. He provided helpful criticism of an early draft of this paper, just prior to his death in June 1983. The complexity of his insight was such that I know this would be a different essay if he had lived.

I am also grateful for the help provided by: Hal Candee, Noel Cunningham, Norman Dorsen, Barry Ensminger, Brian Glick, Cynthia Kern, Lewis Kornhauser, Howard Lesnick and Rand Rosenblatt.

1. N. Dorsen, ed., *The Rights of Americans* XV (1971).

2. *See* G. Hart & P. Tsongas in Bowles, Gordon & Weisskopf, *Beyond the Waste Land: A Democratic Alternative to Economic Decline* 267 (1983).

3. *The Rights of Americans, supra* note 1.

4. Adams, *Discourses on Davila (1789–90)*, quoted in Coker, *Democracy, Liberty, and Property* 466 (1947).

5. T. Paine, *Agrarian Justice*, quoted in S. Lynd, *Intellectual Origins of American Radicalism* 75 (1968).

6. B. Franklin letter to Robert Morris, Dec. 25, 1749 in Smyth, ed., *Writings*, IX, 138 quoted in S. Lynd, *Id.* at 69.

7. M. Friedman, *Capitalism and Freedom* 14–15 (1962).

8. *Id.* at 16.

9. L. Tribe, *American Constitutional Law* 439 (1978).

10. Stromberg v. California, 283 U.S. 359 (1931); Near v. Minnesota, 283 U.S. 697 (1931).

11. D. Kairys, "Freedom of Speech," in *The Politics of Law* 140 (1982), discussing Hague v. CIO, 307 U.S. 496 (1939).

12. H. Zinn, *New Deal Thought* (1966).

13. K. Llewellyn, "The Constitution as an Institution," 34 *Columbia Law Review* 1 (1934); J. Frank, *Law and the Modern Mind* (1930); Cohen, "The Basis of Contract," 46 *Harvard Law Review* 553 (1933).

14. *See* Tribe, *American Constitutional Law, supra* note 9, arguing that the Court should have rejected the natural law theories on grounds of substantive justice not on grounds of institutional competence.

15. United States v. Carolene Products Co., 304 U.S. 144, 152 n. 4 (1937).

16. Dandridge v. Williams, 397 U.S. 471 (1970) and Moore v. City of East Cleveland, 431 U.S. 494 (1977).

17. Wyman v. James, 400 U.S. 309 (1971) and Marshall v. Barlow's, Inc., 436 U.S. 307 (1978).

18. Harris v. McRae, 448 U.S. 297 (1980) and Buckley v. Valeo, 424 U.S. 1 (1976).

19. *See* Tribe, *American Constitutional Law, supra* note 9, at 522–532, 1122–1135.

20. C. Reich, "The New Property," 73 *Yale Law Journal* 733, 771 (1964).

21. *Id.* at 778.

22. Goldberg v. Kelly, 397 U.S. 254 (1970).

23. 397 U.S. at 264.

24. 397 U.S. at 262, n. 8.

25. Roe v. Wade, 410 U.S. 113 (1973).

26. E. Sparer, "Gordian Knots: The Situation of Health Care Advocacy for the Poor Today," 15 *Clearinghouse Review* 1 (1981).

27. F. Donner, *The Age of Surveillance* (1980), especially ch. 6, "Aggressive Intelligence."

28. *See* T. Gitlin, *The Whole World is Watching: Mass Media in the Making and Unmaking of the New Left,* (1980); G. Hodgson, *America in Our Time* (1976), *especially* chs. 7 and 15.

29. J. O'Conner, *The Fiscal Crisis of the State* (1973).

30. J. Skelly Wright, "Money and the Pollution of Politics: Is the First Amendment an Obstacle to Political Equality?" 82 *Columbia Law Review* 609, 610 (1982).

31. Buckley v. Valeo, 424 U.S. 1 (1976).

32. First National Bank v. Belloti, 435 U.S. 765 (1978).

33. N. Nie, S. Verba, & J. Petrocik, *The Changing American Voter* (1976); E.E. Schattschneider, *The Semi-Sovereign People* (1960).

34. R.A. Cloward and F.F. Piven, "Toward a Class-Based Realignment of American Politics: A Movement Strategy," 13 *Social Policy* 3 (1983).

35. This paragraph paraphrases the words of H. Lesnick, "The Interaction Between the Consciousness of Work and Our Understanding of Law, Lawyering and Learning," unpublished essay 1–10 (1981). More generally, this section is illuminated by Prof. Lesnick's course and unpublished teaching materials on law and work.

36. Coppage v. Kansas, 236 U.S. 1, 18 (1915).

37. *See discussion* N. Dorsen, P. Bender, B. Neuborne & S. Law, *Political and Civil Rights in the United States,* vol. 2, ch. 29, "Discrimination in Employment" (1979).

38. *See* C. Summers & R. Rabin, *The Rights of Union Members* (1979).

39. *See* W. H. Rodgers, Jr., *Environmental Law* (1977).

40. *See* G. Z. Nothstein, *The Law of Occupational Safety and Health* (1981).

41. S. Estreicher and B. Wolff, for the Committee on Labor and Employment Law, Bar

Ass'n of the City of New York, "At-Will Employment and the Problem of Unjust Dismissal," 36 *The Record* 170 (1981).

42. *See, e.g.,* Geary v. United States Steel Corp., 456 Pa. 171, 319 A.2d 174 (1974).

43. *See* N. Dorsen, P. Bender, B. Neuborne & S. Law, *Political and Civil Rights in the United States, supra* note 37.

44. J.B. Atleson, *Values and Assumptions in American Labor Law* (1983).

45. For example, in New York City, which bargains with interns and residents working in the public hospitals, the doctors can negotiate about the hours of their own shift, but they cannot bargain about the staffing levels needed to avoid the twenty-four-hour shift. Decision # B-10-81, Office of Collective Bargaining, City of New York. In the Matter of the City of New York v. Committee of. Interns and Residents (1981).

46. NLRB v. Committee of Interns and Residents, 566 F.2d 810 (2d Cir. 1977), *cert. denied,* 435 U.S. 904 (1978).

47. On due process for individual workers *see* Estreicher and Wolff, *supra* note 4. On due process and plant relocation see Bluestone and Harrison, *The Deindustrialization of America* (1982); *Note* "Advance Notice of Plant Closings: Toward National Legislation," 14 *University of Michigan Journal of Law Reform* 283 (1983).

48. D. Kairys, "Freedom of Speech," in *The Politics of Law* 163–64 (1982).

49. *See generally* "Symposium on the Public/Private Distinction," 130 *University of Pennsylvania Law Review* 1289–1609 (1982).

50. Encyclical of Pope John Paul II on Human Work, Sept. 14, 1981 in Carter, *The Papal Encyclicals* 305–07 (1981).

51. K. Marx, "Economic and Philosophical Manuscripts, 1844" in K. Marx & F. Engels, *Collected Works,* vol. 3 276 (1975).

52. Lesnick, *supra* note 35, at 11.

53. A.T. Mason & W.M. Beaney, *The Supreme Court in a Free Society* 131 (1959).

54. Pollock v. Farmer's Loan and Trust Co., 158 U.S. 601 (1895).

55. On the negative impact that wealth disparity and concentrated economic power have upon democratic values, *see generally* C.E. Lindblom, *Politics and Markets* (1977). On the controversial nature of the idea of progressive taxation *see* W. Blum and H. Kalven, *The Uneasy Case for Progressive Taxation* (1963).

56. For a discussion of concepts of poverty, *see* Sparer, *supra* note 26.

57. The Congressional Budget Act defines tax expenditures as ". . . those revenue losses attributable to provisions of the Federal tax laws which allow a special exclusion, exemption or deduction from gross income or which provide a special credit, a preferential rate of tax or a deferral of the tax liability." U.S. Joint Committee on Taxation, *Estimates of Federal Tax Expenditures for Fiscal Years 1982–87* 2 (1982). *See also* S.S. Surrey, "Federal Income Tax Reform: The Varied Approaches Necessary to Replace Tax Expenditures with Direct Governmental Assistance," 84 *Harvard Law Review* 352 (1970).

58. *Estimates of Federal Tax Expenditures for Fiscal Years 1982–87, supra* note 57, at 10.

59. P.F. Harstad, "Budget Committee Explores Limits on Tax Expenditures," 13 *Tax Notes* 1405 (1981).

60. Quoted in Goodwin, "Bridging the Gap Between Social Research and Public Policy," 9 *Journal of Applied Behavioral Science* 85,108 (1973).

61. J. Pechman, *Federal Tax Policy* 219 (1971).

62. *Background Material and Data on Major Programs Within the Jurisdiction of the Committee on Ways and Means,* Committee on Ways and Means, 98th Cong., 1st Sess. (1983), AFDC data, table 5 at 259; SSI data, table 16 at 330.

63. S. Lynd, "Comment on Management Prerogatives, Plant Closings and the NLRA," 11 *Review of Law and Social Change* 113, 116 (1983).

64. G. Orwell, *Nineteen Eighty-Four* 186–92 (1949).

65. J. Fallows, *National Defense* 66 (1981).

66. *Statistical Abstract of the United States* 317 (1983).

67. Fallows, *supra* note 65, at 36.

68. S. Melman, *The Permanent War Economy* (1974).

69. Orwell, *supra* note 64, at 186.

70. Michael Harrington characterizes the Soviet Union by saying "The state owns the means of production and a bureaucratic elite owns the state." *Socialism,* at 4 (1970). This may be an oversimplification. *See, e.g.,* J. Burns, "Moscow Will Try Again to Widen the Powers of Factory Managers," *New York Times* 1, col. 1 (July 27, 1983).

71. C. E. Lindblom, *Politics and Markets* (1977) documents the unequal distribution of income in states that are nominally Socialist.

72. M. Radin, "Property and Personhood," 34 *Stanford Law Review* 957 (1982); L.T. Hobhouse, "The Historical Evolution of Property in Fact and in Idea," *Property: Its Duties and Rights,* 2d ed. 3, 9–11 (1922); B. Ackerman, *Private Property and the Constitution* 116–18, 156 (1977); A. Berle, "Property, Production and Revolution," 65 *Columbia Law Review* 1, 2–3 (1965); Cohen, "Property and Sovereignty," 13 *Cornell Law Quarterly* 8 (1927).

JUSTICE FOR ALIENS

STEVEN R. SHAPIRO AND WADE HENDERSON

Steven R. Shapiro is a staff attorney with the New York Civil Liberties Union who has participated in several lawsuits challenging the constitutionality of immigration practices.

Wade Henderson is legislative counsel to the American Civil Liberties Union. He served as assistant dean of Rutgers Law School and as executive director of the Council on Legal Education Opportunity. He has published articles on affirmative action and public interest law.

America is a nation of immigrants that is distrustful of foreigners. Perhaps no more so than other countries, but more paradoxically so, given our heritage. This ambivalence toward aliens has been a constant strand in American history. The result has been a cycle of tolerance and intolerance that has revolved, in large measure, around our economic well-being and political security. America perceives itself as a haven for immigrants and that self-image is supported by a great deal of evidence. Repeatedly, however, in periods of national stress, this hospitality has been replaced by active hostility that has often produced disastrous consequences for civil liberties in America.

Only seven years after the Bill of Rights was ratified, Congress enacted the Alien Act of 1798, which granted the president unilateral power to expel any alien on national security grounds without even the semblance of judicial review. Following the Russian Revolution, the infamous Palmer Raids led to the deportation of numerous aliens whose left-wing political views were deemed an intolerable threat by the United States government. And during World War II, thousands of persons of Japanese ancestry (including many American citizens) were forcibly detained under military guard in "relocation centers" surrounded by barbed wire.

Even today, it is undoubtedly true that aliens possess fewer legal rights than virtually any other segment of American society. The courts in this country have traditionally served as a last resort for such disenfranchised groups. For aliens, however, this uniquely American process of seeking legal equality as a means of social acceptance has not generally worked. While exceptions exist, the courts have largely deferred to the political branches of government in defining the rights that should be granted to aliens. The political system, in turn, has been slow to respond to the problems of people who cannot vote.

Immigration, nonetheless, is a highly political and partisan issue. The Reagan administration has demonstrated a selective concern about immigration problems that is largely determined by its political agenda. Both nationally and internationally, the immigration policies of the Reagan administration have been shaped to meet political needs. As so often in the past, the result of that decision-making process has been an immigration program that is inconsistent, incoherent, and generally ineffective.

The contradictory impulses pushing the Reagan administration are most apparent in Latin America. The tide of immigrants coming to this country in recent years from El Salvador and Nicaragua is inextricably tied to the Reagan administration's policy of promoting confrontation rather than conciliation in the region. People flee war. Yet the Reagan administration has sought increased American military expenditures in Latin America by arguing that America will otherwise be overrun by millions of refugees seeking a safe haven from violence. This explanation is worse than illogical; it is an implicit appeal to the racism and nativism that have stained this country throughout its history.

Haiti offers another example of the close relationship between the Reagan administration's foreign policy and what purports to be its immigration policy. In cooperation with the Haitian government, the United States Coast Guard is now intercepting boats at sea and returning them to Haiti before they can land in Florida. The immigration gains from interdiction are slight and its legality is questionable. Its rationale cannot be understood in immigration terms, however. Rather, interdiction was conceived by the Reagan administration as a means of placating a Haitian dictatorship that, while notoriously repressive, is seen as a stronghold of anticommunism in the Caribbean.

On a global scale, the immigration policies of the Reagan administration are similarly affected by its political concerns. The economic difficulties of the developing world have not been a high political priority. Consequently, issues of overpopulation, world hunger, and poverty have received only minimal attention. Until these problems are addressed, immigration to America is unlikely to decrease no matter how strict our laws become.

CONSTITUTIONAL RIGHTS
OF ALIENS

Any effort to understand the status of aliens in this country must begin with the term "alien" itself. It is not a term that was chosen because of its legal precision. It includes within its broad sweep at least the following categories: (a) individuals outside the United States who seek permission to enter the country; (b) individuals who attempt to enter the country and are stopped at the border; (c) individuals who enter the country illegally; (d) individuals who enter the country legally but remain here unlawfully; (e) individuals who visit the United States on a temporary basis for work or school or simply vacation; and (f) individuals who live in the United States permanently but never become American citizens. Each of these groups has different rights in different situations.

As a symbolic statement, however, use of the word "alien" is both precise and powerful. In almost a primitive sense, it draws a line between members of the community and those on the outside. Moreover, it implies a wariness toward outsiders, which supplies linguistic justification for departing from customary notions of fairness. In American law, the concept of equality has been interpreted to grant similar groups the right to be treated alike. Since aliens are different by definition, they can be treated unequally without seeming to offend the basic principles which we like to think as a nation remain intact.

Adopting this perception of the alien as outsider, the Supreme Court has concluded that certain classes of aliens may not even claim the right to constitutional protection. Thus, under present law, the Constitution does not apply to aliens who have not yet entered the United States. A citizen of France, for example, may not invoke the Constitution if he is denied a visa by the American embassy in Paris, no matter how arbitrary or capricious that denial may seem. Similarly, the government is not bound by any constitutional constraints in excluding an alien who arrives in this country without proper documentation. In such circumstances, the Supreme Court has said: "Whatever the procedure authorized by Congress is, it is due process as far as the alien denied entry is concerned."[1]

It is impossible to imagine the Supreme Court making a similar statement in any other context under our constitutional system. Even in the immigration context, that statement is possible only by asking the wrong question. Plainly, the Constitution was not drafted to aid the citizens of other countries. It was drafted, however, to limit the power of the United States government. Our constitutional values are jeopardized when those limits are exceeded regardless of who the victim may be.

The problems inherent in the Supreme Court's approach are perfectly illustrated by a 1972 case involving Dr. Ernest Mandel, a Belgian Marxist scholar who was invited to speak in the United States by several leading American universities. Mandel's application for a visa was denied, under a provision of the Immigration and Nationality Act that prohibits any Communist or person advocating the tenets of Communism from entering the United States without an express waiver by the attorney general.[2] When the attorney general refused to grant a waiver, Mandel sued, along with a group of Americans who had hoped to participate in conferences with him, alleging that the government's action violated the First Amendment.[3] The Court began its opinion by acknowledging that First Amendment rights were "implicated." Nevertheless, it refused to order Mandel's admission on the theory that the government had presented a bona fide explanation for his exclusion—namely, that on a previous trip he had attended a fund-raising party, although his visa entitled him only to lecture. The Court also ruled that Mandel himself had no right to sue as a foreigner, no matter what the government's reason for excluding him.

The decision in *Mandel* has indisputably curtailed the free and robust discussion of public issues in the United States. More than any of its predecessors, the Reagan administration has seen *Mandel* as a way of curbing debate to suit its policy goals. Conveniently for the administration, the anti-Communist bias of the Immigration Act coincides with its own political ideology.

Thus, in the spring of 1982, the Reagan administration barred nearly three hundred members of a Japanese disarmament organization from attending a disarmament conference at the United Nations. The government defended its decision by alleging a link between the Japanese delegates and the Soviet Union. In the spring of 1983, at a time when United States policy in Latin America was being fiercely debated, Mrs. Salvador Allende, wife of the slain Chilean president, was barred from accepting a speaking engagement in California on the ground that her political beliefs and associations made her presence in the United States "prejudicial to the public interest." In the fall of 1983, a former Italian general was prohibited from attending a rally in Boston in opposition to the placement of American missiles in Europe. With demonstrations against the deployment of those missiles occurring throughout Europe and the United States, the general was informed by American officials that the time was not right for his admission. Implicit in the terms of the denial was the suggestion by the Reagan administration that, once the missiles were deployed and the debate concluded, the general would again be allowed to visit the United States.

Three days before deciding *Mandel*, the Supreme Court wrote in another case that, "above all else, the First Amendment means that government has no power to restrict expression because of its message, its subject matter, its ideas or its content."[4] Nothing in the *Mandel* decision directly contradicts that fundamental principle. Indeed, the actual holding of *Mandel* is simply that an alien's failure to abide by a prior visa constitutes sufficient reason for barring his return. The government, however, has chosen to view *Mandel* as an open invitation to engage in ideological exclusions. Whether that interpretation will ultimately prevail remains an open question. In the meantime, the government has demonstrated its willingness on several occasions to limit debate in this country by invoking *Mandel*. It is difficult to see how that result can be reconciled with the First Amendment.

The notion of alien as outsider also pervades the Supreme Court's current thinking on the rights of permanent resident aliens, who are no longer as free as they were just a few years ago in selecting the career they wish to pursue. Job discrimination against resident aliens has a long heritage in this country. One of the earliest equal-protection opinions written by the Supreme Court invalidated California's practice of banning Chinese immigrants from the laundry business by denying them permits that were routinely granted to American citizens under similar circumstances.[5] With the development of modern constitutional law, it became established that alienage was a suspect classification and, like race, could not be used by government as a distinguishing characteristic except for the most compelling reasons. As the Supreme Court explained in 1973, resident aliens "pay taxes, support the economy, serve in the armed forces and contribute in myriad ways to our society. It is appropriate that a state bear a heavy burden when it deprives them of employment opportunities."[6]

Applying this strict scrutiny, the Supreme Court struck down a series of state statutes that prohibited resident aliens from becoming lawyers,[7] from receiving welfare,[8] and from holding any state civil service position.[9] The Court objected, particularly in the civil service case, to the indiscriminate sweep of the citizenship requirement. At the same time, the Court acknowledged that society could appropriately insist on citizenship for some public officials because of their important policy function. The Court recognized, in effect, that a community's political leaders should properly belong to the political community they lead.

In the past several years, that exception has nearly swallowed the rule of nondiscrimination. In 1978, the Court upheld a statute that barred resident aliens from becoming state troopers on the theory that "the right to govern is reserved to citizens."[10] New York's right to deny a teaching license to resident aliens was upheld in 1979.[11] And in 1982, the Court upheld a California law that required all "peace officers" to be American citizens.[12] Although nominally adhering to its distinction between policy positions and other government jobs, the Court's present view is that "the classification need not be precise."[13]

This growing hostility to even resident aliens can probably best be understood as a consequence of the country's increasing preoccupation with the problem of illegal aliens. By conservative estimate, there are between three and six million illegal aliens living in the United States.[14] The question of what to do with those who are here, and how to prevent others from coming, is an extraordinarily vexing one. It has absorbed the attention of Congress, the Supreme Court and a blue-ribbon panel jointly appointed by Congress and the president. As a result, immigration has become a major item on the national agenda in the 1980s. This reexamination has been further prompted by an economic recession that has made jobs more scarce and services more difficult to fund.

Generally speaking, illegal aliens are not entitled to government benefits. Under federal law, for example, illegal aliens are excluded from the food stamp program, old age assistance, aid to families with dependent children, aid to the blind, aid to the permanently and totally disabled, Medicaid, Medicare, and the Supplemental Security Income program.[15] The rationale for this limitation is not an economic one. The statistical evidence that has been compiled convincingly shows that illegal aliens contribute their fair share to public services through income tax, sales tax, and property tax assessments. On the other hand, they underutilize those services for fear of exposure.[16] Nor is there any reason to believe that illegal aliens will be deterred from coming to the United States by the denial of benefits. It is the prospect of jobs and not the availability of benefits that lures illegal aliens to this country.[17] Given this reality, the refusal to grant these often life-sustaining benefits can be explained only by a desire to punish illegal aliens for breaking the law.

The limits of that justification were explored by the Supreme Court in a 1982 case striking down a Texas statute which denied free public education to the children of illegal aliens.[18] The Court carefully refrained from disturbing the state's power to treat illegal aliens differently. Indeed, it recognized that an alien's illegal status is a legitimate factor that a state may take into account in the distribution of benefits. But the Court was unwilling to accept the notion that children should be penalized for the illegal conduct of their parents. As the Court noted, "imposing disabilities on the . . . child is contrary to the basic concept of our system that legal burdens should bear some relationship to individual responsibility or wrongdoing."[19] Moreover, the Court was heavily influenced by the fact that education was at stake. "We cannot ignore," the Court held, "the significant social costs borne by our Nation when select groups are denied the means to absorb the values and skills upon which our social order rests."[20]

The opinion in the Texas education case was of enormous significance, primarily because of the Court's practical recognition that a contrary result would have led to the creation of a permanent underclass in this country. Experience has taught that the government faces a virtually impossible task in detecting and apprehending illegal aliens. Approximately 85 percent of the illegal aliens who enter the United States come across a Mexican border that is two thousand miles long and uninhabited desert for much of its length.[21] The difficulty of patrolling such a vast stretch of land has proved insurmountable. The government has responded by employing a variety of search-and-seizure techniques meant to maximize the effect of its limited resources. In the process, constitutional constraints have not always been respected.

Three cases decided by the Supreme Court in the mid–1970s define the present scope of the government's search power in the immigration context. The first case in this trilogy concerned the government's right to stop cars on a random basis away from the border to search for illegal aliens through the use of so-called "roving patrols."[22] To the government, the value of these patrols primarily lay in their random quality. Yet, that randomness is also what made them constitutionally suspect. As traditionally interpreted by the Supreme Court, the Fourth Amendment requires individualized suspicion as a basis for any search or seizure. Indeed, the Fourth Amendment was adopted largely to prohibit the sort of general searches favored by the British during colonial times. Accordingly, the government defended its use of roving patrols more as a matter of necessity than a matter of principle.

That expedient view of the Fourth Amendment was properly rejected by the Supreme Court, which stated: "It is not enough to argue, as does the Government, that the problem of deterring unlawful entry by aliens across long expanses of national boundaries is a serious one. The needs of law enforcement stand in constant tension with the Constitution's protections of the individual against certain excesses of official power. It is precisely the predictability of these pressures that counsels a resolute loyalty to constitutional safeguards."[23]

Despite this seemingly unequivocal language, the Court began to retreat from its steadfast adherence to constitutional safeguards only two years later. It has long been settled that the police cannot stop a car or question its passengers without probable cause to believe that a crime has been committed. In 1975, the Court nevertheless ruled that immigration officials are free to stop the same car on less than probable cause so long as they have a reasonable suspicion that illegal aliens may be inside.[24] The Court was unwilling to go as far as the government wanted, however, expressly rejecting the government's claim that it could stop any car whose occupants appeared to be Mexican.

Finally, in 1976, the Court upheld the use of fixed immigration checkpoints on major highway routes near the Mexican border.[25] The Court concluded that the privacy invasion was minimal (in the majority of cases it involved only a visual inspection as the car slowly drove past a permanent roadblock) and easily overshadowed by the law enforcement need. In short, the Court engaged in exactly the sort of balancing that it had decried only a few years before.

The lower federal courts have struggled to apply these principles in reviewing other immigration practices. Most notably, the courts have divided on the constitutionality of what the immigration service terms "area control operations." In the typical area control operation, immigration officers enter a factory, seal off its exits, and question all of its employees. Any employee who cannot establish his or her right to work in the United States through the proper documentation is then arrested. Focusing on the lack of individualized suspicion, one appellate court has declared these operations unconstitutional.[26] A second court has insisted that a warrant be obtained but has not required individualized suspicion.[27] And a third court has sustained the validity of area control operations with neither a warrant nor individualized suspicion.[28] The matter is now before the Supreme Court, which must decide once again whether the magnitude of the government's immigration problem is sufficient reason for diluting settled Fourth Amendment standards.[29]

Area control operations have increased in recent years as unemployment increased. It is widely believed, although there is little evidence to support this view, that illegal aliens are taking jobs at substandard wages that would otherwise be held by American citizens. The pressure of that belief has prompted Congress to undertake a reexamination of the immigration laws.

THE LEGISLATIVE RESPONSE

Several years ago, amidst growing dissatisfaction with America's ability to manage its immigration "problem," Congress began to reconsider the basic approach to immigration policy. The debate provoked by that reconsideration has centered ever since on the Simpson-Mazzoli bill. Originally introduced in 1982, the bill was conceived as a comprehensive revision of the immigration law that has been in effect since 1952.[30] After two years of controversy, the bill was tabled in the House of Representatives in the fall of 1983 as opposition mounted to some of its central provisions.

Notwithstanding this legislative setback, the issues raised by the Simpson-Mazzoli bill are unlikely to disappear in the ongoing debate over immigration reform. Whatever the future of the bill, therefore, its approach to immigration cannot be ignored.*

Based in part on the recommendations of the Select Commission on Refugee Policy,[31] the Simpson-Mazzoli bill endeavored to solve two problems at once: first, it proposed a host of new immigration controls in an effort to reduce the number of illegal aliens entering the United States; second, it provided a one-time-only amnesty program for millions of illegal aliens residing in the United States. Acknowledged by its sponsors as a

---

*As this book goes to press, there are still inconclusive discussions about reviving the Simpson-Mazzoli bill in the next Congressional session beginning in January, 1984.

compromise, the bill initially received broad bipartisan support. Yet, from the outset, portions of the bill were actively opposed by an equally broad coalition concerned that individual rights were not fully protected in the rush to achieve legislative consensus. As the bill was scrutinized more carefully, that opposition solidified and, thus far at least, has proved decisive.

The Simpson-Mazzoli bill was designed to restrict what is widely viewed as an immigration system that is poorly enforced and easily evaded. That sentiment is typically expressed in almost apocalyptic terms, as illustrated by the following quote from a Senate report in favor of the bill:[32]

> . . . current U.S. immigration policy is no longer adequate to deal with modern conditions, including the growing immigration pressures on the United States. Immigration to the U.S. is "out of control" and it is perceived that way at all levels of government and by the American people—indeed by people all over the world.

Describing the situation, of course, is easier than solving it. The approach adopted by the drafters of the Simpson-Mazzoli bill can be divided into four parts. First, the bill reduced the number of legal immigrants permitted to enter the United States annually. Second, it attacked the problem of illegal immigration by allowing summary exclusion of undocumented aliens by border patrol guards, limiting judicial review of immigration decisions, and authorizing civil and criminal penalties for employers who knowingly hire undocumented workers. Third, the bill expanded the program of temporary foreign labor, primarily migrant farmworkers, but subjected it to greater regulation. Fourth, the bill provided a general amnesty to illegal aliens who have lived in the United States for a designated period of years in the hope of eliminating a shadow population that is now forced by necessity into an underground existence.

Economic issues predominated the legislative debate provoked by the Simpson-Mazzoli bill. In particular, the concept of employer sanctions was justified by its sponsors as a way of preserving jobs for Americans. Conversely, the "temporary worker program" (that permits foreigners to enter the country on a day-to-day basis) was intended to ensure a steady labor supply for American businesses that have difficulty recruiting American workers, generally because of the low wages they pay.

Employer sanctions were the cornerstone of the Simpson-Mazzoli package. By eliminating the economic incentive of American jobs, the bill sought to reduce the flow of undocumented workers into the United States. Thus, the bill required employers to verify the legal status of all prospective employees or face potential civil and criminal penalties. The goal of assisting American labor during a period of high unemployment is undoubtedly a laudable one. During debate over the Simpson-Mazzoli bill, however, it proved impossible to propose a system for achieving that goal that did not also produce substantial civil liberties problems.

The most commonly proposed solution, and the one suggested by the Simpson-Mazzoli bill, presumed the creation of a national identity card tied, most probably, to a computerized data bank. To work, a system of that sort must contain personal information on virtually every adult in the work force. In the symbolic year of 1984, the alarm that such a proposal has caused among civil libertarians is easily understood. Nor are civil libertarians alone in expressing that concern. Indeed, the privacy threat inherent in a centralized data-collection system was explicitly noted in a 1977 report by the Privacy Protection Study Commission.[33]

Even without a national identity card or computerized data bank, a system of employer sanctions poses serious civil liberties risks. Most importantly, it increases the probability of discrimination against Hispanics. A cautious employer anxious to comply with the law against hiring illegal aliens is less likely to hire any employees who "look foreign" or speak with an accent, especially Spanish. Other employers, motivated by the desire to avoid federal supervision, are likely to fear that their business affairs will be monitored more closely by federal officials if they employ large numbers of Spanish-speaking workers. At the very least, the possibility of sanctions will encourage many employers to conduct identity checks of their Hispanic employees, thereby further dividing a society that is already too polarized by race and ethnicity.

Proponents of the bill responded to these charges by pointing to the antidiscrimination provisions that already exist in federal law. The most significant of those provisions is contained in Title VII of the 1964 Civil Rights Act, which prohibits discrimination in employment on the basis of race, sex, or national origin.[34] Unfortunately, Title VII is unlikely to offset the discriminatory potential of employer sanctions, for several reasons. Title VII does not cover seasonal workers and thus exempts many of the traditional jobs that attract illegal aliens, including migrant farmwork.[35] It does not cover small businesses.[36] It does not prohibit an

employer from hiring only English-speaking employees.[37] And it is enforced by an agency that cannot order employers to halt even those
practices found to be discriminatory.[38] Accordingly, efforts were under
way to include an antidiscrimination provision within the Simpson-Mazzoli bill itself and to provide an enforcement mechanism specifically
tailored to the discriminatory potential of employer sanctions, before the
bill was removed from the legislative agenda in 1983.

Yet another concern raised by critics of the bill was that a program of
employer sanctions might prove counterproductive to its stated objective
of securing new jobs for American workers. Under current law, the National Labor Relations Board has consistently held that illegal aliens are
entitled to the full protection of the national labor laws.[39] It is uncertain,
however, whether this protection would survive new legislation making it
a crime to hire illegal aliens. If not, those illegal aliens who remain in the
workforce would be stripped of their ability to bargain collectively and the
Simpson-Mazzoli proposal would paradoxically make the employment of
illegal aliens even more profitable for American business.

Despite the central role of employer sanctions in the Simpson-Mazzoli
scheme, it would be a mistake to see the current push for stricter immigration laws solely in economic terms. The debate in Congress over the
Simpson-Mazzoli bill revealed, as well, a fundamental unease about the
impact of extensive and continuing immigration on the national character. In the midst of that debate, it was rarely noted that the national
character so jealously guarded against foreign dilution was formed by the
immigrants of another generation. Instead, proponents of the bill consistently painted a mythical picture of a homogeneous society whose future
is threatened by the arrival of outsiders.[40] In a symbolic response to this
fear of foreign encroachment, the Simpson-Mazzoli bill passed by the
Senate in 1983 contained a nonbinding provision declaring English to be
the official language of the United States. It was a clear message speaking
to the latent fears of a national character under siege.

A very different impulse led Congress to enact the Refugee Act of
1980.[41] Prompted by the refugee crisis that followed the fall of Vietnam
in 1975, the Act "reflects one of the oldest themes in American history
—welcoming homeless refugees to our shores."[42] Like so much else in our
immigration history, however, America's welcome for those fleeing persecution was often an ambivalent one. Indeed, some victims of persecution
were hardly welcomed at all. The Refugee Act harmonizes American law

with international standards in the refugee field for the first time and, in theory at least, both liberalizes and rationalizes America's refugee program.

Refugee affairs in this country have always been marked by a tension between those who perceive the subject of refugees as a foreign policy question and those who regard it as a human rights issue, separate and apart from ideological concerns. Until passage of the Refugee Act, there was no American refugee policy in any real sense. Instead, America had a foreign policy that sometimes was implemented through refugee decisions. Thus, American law gave a preferential status to persons fleeing Communist aggression because American policy makers wanted to exploit the flow of Communist refugees as a foreign policy triumph. By contrast, the human rights abuses of non-Communist regimes, no matter how brutal, provided no basis for refugee status under prior law.

This discrimination has been eliminated under the Refugee Act, which focuses on the individual rather than the country from which the individual is fleeing. That change is most evident in the decision to incorporate into American law the internationally recognized definition of a refugee as a person possessing "a well-founded fear of persecution based on race, religion, nationality, membership in a particular social class or political opinion."[43]

In analyzing the Refugee Act, it is important to distinguish between two groups of people. Persons outside the United States who claim "a well-founded fear of persecution" in their home country are classified as refugees. The number of refugees who may be admitted each year is established by the president after consultation with Congress.[44] In addition, the president must inform Congress annually of "the anticipated allocation of refugee admissions."[45] Within these parameters, refugee applications are processed on a first-come, first-served basis. Persons already in the United States who claim "a well-founded fear of persecution" as a basis for remaining are classified separately as political asylum applicants. The standard is the same but there is no numerical ceiling on the number of asylum applications that can be granted.

The Refugee Act represents a clear repudiation of past refugee policy and administrative practice. Through its provisions, Congress sought to curtail the politicized nature of executive decision-making in the refugee area, and to protect the substantive and procedural rights of those fleeing repression, whether from the right or the left. Those purposes have now been acknowledged in judicial decisions that provide that political asylum cannot be denied without due-process safeguards.[46]

The need to depoliticize the refugee process was rapidly confirmed by world events. Shortly after the act's passage, approximately 125,000 Cubans arrived in the United States as part of the "Mariel boatlift." While the boatlift was originally portrayed as a freedom flotilla in the American press, expressions of concern increased in proportion to the number of refugees. As the political situation in Latin America deteriorated, and Cubans were followed by Haitians and Salvadorans, the welcome mat that had been laid down was quickly withdrawn. In its place, the Reagan administration announced a strict detention policy and, eager to divert attention from an economic recession, fed the perception that hordes of refugees were on the verge of destroying the American way of life. This shift in attitude illustrates again the cyclical nature of American immigration policy. It also raises enduring questions about America's commitment to racial equality, since the country has never been confronted before by such a large-scale migration of nonwhite refugees.

This feeling that the nation is being overrun exerts obvious pressure on the political process and magnifies the importance of judicial review to ensure that executive authority is properly restrained. The Simpson-Mazzoli bill was based on precisely the opposite assumption. Under the original Senate proposal, the federal courts were stripped of all jurisdiction to review asylum decisions except for the constitutional right of habeas corpus, which cannot be suspended by legislation.[47] In later versions, the bill restored judicial review but carefully described its permissible scope. The relevant language stipulated that decisions on asylum applications could be reversed if they were arbitrary or unlawful but omitted any mention of asylum decisions that were unsupported by evidence and, therefore, just wrong.

Moreover, the structure of the Simpson-Mazzoli bill virtually assured that many asylum decisions would never come to light and never be brought to court. Specifically, the bill would have allowed an immigration official stationed at the border to exclude summarily any undocumented alien who did not explicitly request political asylum. A determination of the alien's right to political asylum under those circumstances would not have been subject to judicial review.

Such a drastic change in current law could potentially jeopardize the life or liberty of countless refugees. Present law affords an alien the opportunity to present his case through counsel at an adversarial hearing before an immigration judge.[48] A summary exclusion procedure has none of these safeguards and is therefore susceptible to political manipulation in violation of the Refugee Act and American treaty obligations.[49]

The plight of Salvadoran refugees illustrates that danger. Once in this country and informed of their rights, many Salvadorans have applied for political asylum. Those applications pose an awkward problem for the Reagan administration, which supports the current regime in El Salvador. Were a summary exclusion procedure available, the government could easily avoid embarrassing an ally by simply rejecting Salvadoran refugees at the border. These fears, articulated by the Salvadoran community in the United States, are hardly fanciful. Indeed, a federal court has already enjoined the immigration service from engaging in practices tantamount to a summary exclusion of Salvadorans without the benefit of due process of law.[50]

The argument generally offered in support of the effort to limit judicial review of asylum claims is that the courts are responsible for the administrative backlog that now exists. Approximately 150,000 asylum claims are presently pending before the immigration service. The existence of an asylum backlog is therefore undeniable. It is not, however, the fault of the courts. In fact, less than 2 percent of the current backlog results from litigation.[51] Rather, the delays occur within the administrative process for political reasons and because its management techniques are unable to keep pace with a burgeoning caseload. Accordingly, the assertion that judicial review must somehow be limited in the interest of efficiency is a disingenuous one. The hidden agenda behind that proposal is a desire to halt undocumented immigration by any means, even at the cost of stampeding the rights of asylum applicants.

In a parallel effort, the Reagan administration has been asking the courts to tighten the standard for obtaining asylum under the Refugee Act. As already noted, the statutory predicate for asylum is "a well-founded fear of persecution." The government has argued that this standard can be satisfied only if the alien establishes a "clear probability" that he or she will be persecuted upon return home—a standard that was in effect before the Refugee Act was passed.[52] Two federal courts have rejected that argument, noting that the risk of an erroneous judgment can sometimes be fatal, and that a "reasonable belief" of persecution is sufficient to satisfy the United Nations Convention and Protocol on the Status of Refugees, which served as a model for the Refugee Act.[53] The issue is now before the Supreme Court and its answer will go a long way to determining the future significance of the Refugee Act.[54]

Thus far, the promise of the Refugee Act has not been fulfilled. If anything, the experience of asylum-seekers has gotten worse rather than better. Three years after enactment of the law, the Reagan administration has yet to produce final asylum regulations of the sort contemplated by Congress. In the absence of clear guidelines, the law's humanitarian goals have not been achieved.

The treatment of Haitian boat people is a particularly vivid example of the Reagan administration's attitude toward political asylum. It is an attitude that views political asylum as a foreign policy tool and, therefore, disdains the individual evaluations contemplated by the Refugee Act. Until the federal courts intervened on behalf of the Haitians, thousands of boat people were unlawfully detained for more than a year in what has since been declared an act of intentional discrimination. They were not informed of their right to apply for political asylum by immigration officials. Many were hindered in their ability to meet with lawyers who could advise them of that right. And some were rushed through mass hearings while still unrepresented in an effort to expel them before asylum applications could be filed.[55] Given this prelude, it is hardly surprising that virtually no Haitian boat people have been granted asylum by the Reagan administration notwithstanding the fact that Haiti has been described by the International Commission of Jurists as the "most ruthless and oppressive regime in the world."[56]

Once again, this country is experiencing a period in which concern over the problem of aliens has largely replaced concern over the plight of aliens in the national consciousness. Civil liberties rarely prosper in such an atmosphere. History also instructs that lost rights are not easily regained.

NOTES

1. United States ex rel. Knauff v. Shaughnessy, 338 U.S. 537, 543 (1950).

2. 8 U.S.C. §1182(a) (28).

3. Kleindienst v. Mandel, 408 U.S. 753 (1972).

4. Police Department of the City of Chicago v. Mosley, 408 U.S. 92, 95 (1972).

5. Yick Wo v. Hopkins, 118 U.S. 356 (1886).

6. In re Griffiths, 413 U.S. 717, 722 (1973).

7. *Id.*

8. Graham v. Richardson, 403 U.S. 365 (1971).

9. Sugarman v. Dougall, 413 U.S. 634 (1973).

10. Foley v. Connellie, 435 U.S. 291, 297 (1978).

11. Ambach v. Norwick, 441 U.S. 68 (1979).

12. Cabell v. Chavez-Salido, 454 U.S. 432 (1982).

13. *Id.* at 442.

14. Select Commission on Immigration and Refugee Policy, Report of Conclusions and Recommendations (1981).

15. Plyler v. Doe, 457 U.S. 202, 251 (1982).

16. *Id.* at 228.

17. *Id.*

18. Plyler v. Doe, *supra* note 15.

19. *Id.* at 220, quoting Weber v. Aetna Casualty & Surety Co., 406 U.S. 164, 175 (1972).

20. *Id.* at 221.

21. United States v. Martinez-Fuerte, 428 U.S. 543, 551–52 (1976).

22. Almeida-Sanchez v. United States, 413 U.S. 266 (1973).

23. *Id.* at 273.

24. United States v. Brignoni-Ponce, 422 U.S. 873 (1975).

25. United States v. Martinez-Fuerte, *supra* note 20.

26. ILGWU v. Sureck, 681 F.2d 624 (9th Cir. 1982), *cert. granted sub nom;* INS v. Delgado, 51 U.S.L.W. 3770 (April 25, 1983).

27. Blackie's House of Beef v. Castillo, 659 F.2d 1211 (D.C. Cir. 1981), *cert. denied,* 445 U.S. 940 (1982).

28. Babula v. INS, 665 F.2d 293 (3d Cir. 1981).

29. INS v. Delgado, *supra* note 26.

30. 8 U.S.C. §1101, *et seq.*

31. *See* note 14 *supra.*

32. S. Rep. No. 62, 98th Cong., 1st Sess. 2–3 (1983).

33. Privacy Protection Study Commission, *Personal Privacy in an Informational Society* (1977).

34. 42 U.S.C. §§2000e, *et seq.*

35. Section 701(b) of the Civil Rights Act of 1964, 42 U.S.C. §2000e(b).

36. *Id.*

37. Garcia v. Gloor, 618 F.2d 264 (5th Cir. 1980), *cert. denied,* 449 U.S. 1113 (1981); *see also* Garcia v. Rush-Presbyterian St. Luke's Medical Center, 660 F.2d 1217 (7th Cir. 1981); cf. Vasquez v. McCallen Bag and Supply Co., 660 F.2d 686 (5th Cir. 1981).

38. Section 706(b) of the Civil Rights Act of 1964, 42 U.S.C. §2000e-5.

39. 29 U.S.C. §151, *et seq. See also,* Amay's Bakery and Noodle Co., 227 N.L.R.B. 214, 94 L.R.R.M. 1165 (1976).

40. That sentiment is capsulized in the Senate report, note 32 *supra.*

   We see evidence that if the newcomers to a community do not excessively disrupt or change the attributes of a community which make it familiar to its residents and uniquely their 'home' . . . then the newcomer may be welcome, especially if they make positive contributions to the community's economic and general well-being. On the other hand, it is seen that if the newcomers remain 'foreign,' they may not be welcome, especially if they seek to carve out separate enclaves to embrace only their own language and culture if their numbers and the areas of the community which they affect are great. This should not be so in the 'ideal' world, but it is real.

41. Pub. L. No. 96-212, 94 Stat. 102 (1980), codified at 8 U.S.C. §§1157-59.

42. S. Rep. No. 256, 96th Cong., 2nd Sess. (1979).

43. 8 U.S.C. §§1101(a)(42)(A) and 1158.

44. 8 U.S.C. §1157(a)(1).

45. *Id.*

46. Jean v. Nelson, 711 F.2d 1455 (11th Cir. 1983); Haitian Refugee Center v. Civiletti, 503 F.Supp. 442 (S.D.Fla. 1980), *modified,* 676 F.2d 1023 (5th Cir. 1982); Orantes-Hernandez v. Smith, 541 F.Supp. 351 (C.D.Cal. 1982); Nunez v. Boldin, 537 F.Supp. 578 (S.D. Tex. 1982).

47. United States Constitution, Art. I, Sec. 9, Cl. 2 *See also* "Developments in the Law —Federal Habeas Corpus," 38 *Harvard Law Review* 1038 (1970).

48. 8 U.S.C. §§1158, 1225, 1226, and 1362.

49. The United States became a party to the United Nations Convention and Protocol Relating to the Status of Refugees in 1968, 19 U.S.C. §6257, T.I.A.S. No. 2322, 606 U.N.T.S. 268.

50. Orantes-Hernandez v. Smith, 541 F.Supp. 351 (C.D. Cal. 1982); Nunez v. Boldin, 537 F.Supp. 578 (S.D.Tex. 1982).

51. "Although there are some 150,000 asylum applications pending, less than 500 of these are in the courts." Letter from Sen. Edward M. Kennedy to members of the United States Senate, April 28, 1982.

52. McMillen v. INS, 658 F.2d 1312, 1316 (1981); Manriquez v. INS, unreported, (3d Cir. Jan. 27, 1983), *petition for cert. docketed,* 51 U.S.L.W. 3759 (April 19, 1983).

53. Stevic v. Sava, 678 F.2d 401, 409 (2d Cir. 1982), *cert. granted,* 51 U.S.L.W. 3627 (March 1, 1983); Reyes v. INS, 693 F.2d 597 (6th Cir. 1982).

54. Stevic v. Sava, *supra* note 53.

55. These practices were documented and enjoined in a series of federal court decisions. *See* Jean v. Nelson, 711 F.2d 1455 (11th Cir. 1983); Louis v. Meissner, 530 F.Supp. 924 (S.D.Fla. 1982); Haitian Refugee Center v. Civiletti, 503 F.Supp. 442 (S.D.Fla. 1980), *modified*, 676 F.2d 1023 (5th Cir. 1982).

56. Haitian Refugee Center v. Civiletti, *supra* note 55, 503 F.Supp. at 475.

ACADEMIC FREEDOM

THOMAS I. EMERSON

Thomas I. Emerson is Lines Professor of Law Emeritus at Yale Law School, a former official in the federal government, the author of The System of Freedom of Expression *and other books, and a participant in important free speech cases in the federal courts.*

The concept of academic freedom, as we have come to know it in the United States, holds that members of educational institutions should have the utmost freedom to inquire, to search for the truth, to teach, and to publish the results of their labors. At the same time they are participants in an academic community and owe that group certain obligations. They are also members of the larger society and have the rights and obligations of all citizens. This set of rights and responsibilities grows out of our view of the functions of educational institutions in a democratic society. On the one hand the educational structure is intended to reflect and transmit the values, the knowledge, the traditions, and the culture of the past. It is also intended to develop independent-minded citizens, expand knowledge to new vistas, and operate as a bold and insistent critic of the society. Such a system is obviously a complex one, loaded with tensions, and requiring a sophisticated balance.

Those features of our educational system that stress the traditional are, of course, supported by the whole apparatus of government and the pervasive forces of inertia in the society. It is the leavening features that demand constant attention. These have found support partly in the growth of professional organizations, such as the American Association of University Professors, which have assisted in the formulation of the principles of academic freedom and in the creation of a kind of common law of academic freedom through the application of those principles in specific cases. This development has continued during the past decade and the standards urged by the teaching profession for assuring academic freedom have received wide acceptance. In addition, certain legislative measures, such as laws prohibiting discrimination on account of race or sex, have advanced the cause of academic freedom.

As in the case of other democratic rights, however, a major source of support for the system of academic freedom rests upon our judicial institutions. To an increasing extent the principles of academic freedom have been incorporated into our constitutional structure. Thus, although the Supreme Court has never reached the point of finding an independent constitutional right to academic freedom, the requirements of the First Amendment have frequently been applied to support claims of academic freedom. Due-process and equal-protection doctrines have likewise been invoked in academic freedom cases. And, apart from constitutional principles, the courts have relied to some degree upon common law doctrines —tort, contract, and fiduciary relationships—to give judicial sanction to the tenets of academic freedom. Intervention of the courts in protecting academic freedom has, of course, hazardous aspects; it may infringe unduly upon the autonomy of the very institutions sought to be protected. Yet the decisive trend over the past decades has been in the direction of an expanding role for the courts in maintaining the system of academic freedom.

At the same time, pressures upon the system, from government as well as from economic and social forces within the nation, have been accelerating. The resulting conflicts are being fought in five principal areas. They are: (1) the rights of faculty members; (2) the rights of students; (3) control of the curriculum and textbooks, and censorship of library books; (4) attempts by government to limit the dissemination of information on national security grounds; and (5) commercial exploitation of university research.[1]

RIGHTS OF FACULTY MEMBERS

The rights of faculty members in educational institutions constitute the heart of the system of academic freedom. It is the individual faculty member who carries the main burden in the educational structure, and upon whom chief reliance must be placed for achieving the goals of the educational process. In particular, teaching students independence of thought and the ability to engage in effective criticism of the society depends upon according the faculty member a sufficient measure of autonomy.

A constitutional structure for protecting the rights of faculty members has gradually begun to take form. The earliest cases involved restrictions imposed by government, from outside the educational structure, in such forms as loyalty programs and legislative-committee investigations into "subversive activities." The safeguards of the First Amendment and other constitutional provisions were, of course, available to the faculty member as to any other citizen. It is noteworthy, however, that in applying these constitutional protections where educational institutions were involved the courts frequently laid special emphasis upon considerations derived from the theory of academic freedom. Thus in *Sweezy v. New Hampshire,* in which the Supreme Court rejected the efforts of a New Hampshire legislative committee to probe into the contents of a lecture on socialism at the University of New Hampshire, Chief Justice Warren observed:

> The essentiality of freedom in the community of American universities is almost self-evident. No one should underestimate the vital role in a democracy that is played by those who guide and train our youth. To impose any straight jacket upon the intellectual leaders in our colleges and universities would imperil the future of our Nation. . . . Teachers and students must always remain free to inquire, to study and to evaluate, to gain new maturity and understanding; otherwise our civilization will stagnate and die.[2]

Justice Frankfurter, concurring, quoted from a statement issued by a group of South African scholars:

> In a university knowledge is its own end, not merely a means to an end. A university ceases to be true to its own nature if it becomes the tool of Church or State or any sectional interest. A university is characterized by the spirit of free inquiry, its ideal being the ideal of Socrates—"to follow the argument where it leads." This implies the right to examine, question, modify or reject traditional ideas and beliefs. Dogma and hypothesis are incompatible, and the concept of an immutable doctrine is repugnant to the spirit of the university. The concern of its scholars is not merely to add and revise facts in relation to an accepted

framework, but to be ever examining and modifying the framework itself.[3]

Loyalty programs and legislative committees that impinged upon the academic freedom of faculty members were not flatly outlawed by the Supreme Court. But they were sharply circumscribed, mainly on grounds of vagueness and overbreadth, and thereby rendered considerably less intrusive.[4] In the past decade these issues have faded into the background. It is quite possible, however, that they would be revived in a period of tension or crisis.[5]

In 1968 and 1969, in two seminal decisions, the Supreme Court extended the First Amendment rights of faculty members from protection against outside restrictions to protection against infringements emanating from within the educational structure itself. *Pickering v. Board of Education* involved the dismissal of a high school teacher who had written a letter to the local newspaper critical of the manner in which the school board had, unsuccessfully, attempted to raise additional revenue for the schools. Some of the statements in the letter were inaccurate. The Illinois courts upheld the dismissal on the ground that the school board could reasonably conclude that publication of the letter was "detrimental to the best interests of the schools." The Supreme Court unanimously rejected the Illinois court's position that "teachers may constitutionally be compelled to relinquish the First Amendment rights they would otherwise enjoy as citizens to comment on matters of public interest in connection with the operation of the public schools in which they work." The Court acknowledged that "the State has interests as an employer in regulating the speech of its employees that differ significantly from those it possesses in connection with the regulation of the speech of the citizenry in general." But it ruled that the First Amendment demanded that a balance be struck "between the interests of the teacher, as a citizen, in commenting upon matters of public concern and the interest of the State, as an employer, in promoting the efficiency of the public services it performs through its employees."[6]

The penetration of the First Amendment to the internal operations of the educational system was confirmed the following year in *Tinker v. Des Moines Independent Community School District.* The issue before the Supreme Court in that case involved the suspension of three high school students for wearing black armbands to school in protest against the

Vietnam War. Upon finding that there was no disruption of school activities the Court overruled the action of the school authorities, saying:

> First Amendment rights, applied in the light of the special characteristics of the school environment, are available to teachers and students. It can hardly be argued that either students or teachers shed their constitutional rights to freedom of speech or expression at the schoolhouse gate.[7]

The principle that the First Amendment protects the faculty member against internal as well as external sources of restriction is now fully accepted. Special considerations arise, however, when the First Amendment is applied in an academic setting: the academic institution is designed to perform certain sensitive functions; the faculty member has obligations as a participant in that organization; and there are a number of competing interests to be taken into account, including those of colleagues, students, administration, staff, and parents, as well as the general public. For this reason more specific rules for governance under the First Amendment are required. The Supreme Court has not as yet moved very far into this territory, but a brief sketch of its topography may be ventured.[8]

So far as concerns the conduct of the faculty member in the classroom, the problem is to draw the line between the macrolevel of control, which is the prerogative of those who establish the basic policies of the institution, and the microlevel of classroom operation, which is the area where the faculty member is entitled to substantial leeway. The line will be drawn at different points, of course, depending upon the nature of the academic institution. In an elementary school context the faculty member will have less independence in the classroom than in a university or graduate school context. The Supreme Court has never addressed these issues. The state and lower federal courts have come to mixed results, but the right of the faculty member to autonomy in presentation of the subject has received substantial recognition.[9]

Freedom of the faculty member to engage in research and publication poses less difficult problems. The earlier battles fought over the right of university faculty members to expound unorthodox ideas have been largely won, at least in principle. It is now generally agreed that, at all levels of the educational process, there is no legitimate basis for the exercise of control over faculty research and publication other than professional competence.

This is not to say, of course, that practice conforms to principle. Although no formal claims are made that appointment, promotion, tenure, or dismissal decisions should be influenced by nonprofessional factors, there is little doubt that such considerations frequently lurk beneath the surface. The paucity of Marxist scholars on university faculties is not an accident. Yet there is very little that the law can do to change this situation. It is to be hoped that, while diversity within a particular educational institution may be difficult to achieve, there will be sufficient diversity among institutions to meet the goals of a democratic educational process.

The rights and responsibilities of faculty members as citizens of an academic community have frequently been a matter of controversy. The problem involves the conduct of faculty members outside the classroom but inside or affecting the academic institution. The issues are difficult to reduce to precise rules because the relationship of the faculty member to the academic community is more intimate than that of the citizen to the general policy, and a variety of interests must be taken into account. The governing principles, however, were laid down in the *Pickering* and *Tinker* cases. In *Pickering*, as previously noted, the Supreme Court applied a balancing test, but with some specification of what factors were important to the balancing process. On the one hand the Court considered to what extent the conduct involved was "detrimental to the interests of the schools," in that it "impeded the teacher's proper performance of his daily duties in the classroom" or "interfered with the regular operation of the schools generally," such as by promoting disharmony. On the other hand the Court took note of the importance of "free and unhindered debate," pointing out that the issue involved discussion of "matters of public concern" on which teachers were "most likely to have informed and definite opinions."[10]

In *Tinker* the Supreme Court confirmed that expression within an educational institution could not be constrained unless it "materially disrupts classwork or involves substantial disorder or invasion of the rights of others." The Court went further, however, and added a vital element to the balance. It made clear that "undifferentiated fear or apprehension of disturbance is not enough to overcome the right to freedom of expression." In other words the Court would view claims of disruption with a skeptical eye and demand proof of harm based on more than mere speculation. The importance of the *Tinker* element is difficult to overestimate. In the absence of such an approach the balancing test affords little protection.[11]

It is possible for members of an academic community to enjoy substantial freedom of expression under the protection of the *Pickering* and *Tinker* principles. Much depends upon the extent to which the courts define and refine the factors entering into the balancing test, apply the *Tinker* element with firmness, and otherwise display hospitality for the values of academic freedom. Within the past few years the Supreme Court has shown some signs of withdrawing the warmth of support evidenced by the *Pickering* and *Tinker* decisions. In *Mt. Healthy City School District Board of Education v. Doyle,* the Court dealt with the refusal of a school board to rehire a teacher for a variety of reasons, one of which was that the teacher had made a call to a radio station concerning the school's adoption of a dress code. The Court upheld the lower court in finding a violation of the teacher's First Amendment rights but ruled the teacher was not entitled to reinstatement or back pay if the school board could show that it would have reached the same decision apart from its reliance upon the protected conduct. Clearly the adoption of such a rule, as a practical matter, makes the possibility of obtaining redress for infringement of academic freedom somewhat remote.[12]

Finally, there remains the question of the faculty member's rights, as citizen of the larger community outside the academic walls, to engage in conduct not directly connected with the academic institution itself. These issues, like the loyalty and legislative-committee restrictions imposed from the outside, have not been actively raised in recent years. On the whole, the principle that faculty members have the same rights as ordinary citizens, except where their conduct is so egregious as to directly impair their job performance, seems to be accepted.[13]

The substantive rights accorded faculty members have been supplemented by procedural rights granted under due-process principles. Thus procedural safeguards are available when a faculty member claims deprivation of a constitutional right, is subject to disciplinary action, asserts violation of the terms of express or implied tenure, or can show infringement of any other property or liberty interest. The procedures to which the faculty member is entitled include, at a minimum, a statement of reasons and an opportunity to be heard upon disputed questions of fact. Procedural requirements are, of course, subject to sophisticated circumvention. Nevertheless they do afford valuable protection. As Justice Marshall has pointed out, when the academic institution "knows it may have to justify its decisions with sound reasons, its conduct is likely to be more cautious, careful, and correct."[14]

The foregoing array of constitutional rights supporting academic freedom of the faculty member is strictly available, of course, only with respect to educational institutions that satisfy the requirements of "state action," that is, that are publicly operated or financed. Yet the principles of academic freedom that have been formulated in constitutional terms have spread to wide areas of the private sector. This is due partly to the fact that the courts can often derive the same set of safeguards from common law doctrines of contract, tort, and fiduciary relationships, regardless of "state action." In addition, private institutions tend to accept voluntarily the constitutional rules laid down for the governance of public institutions.[15]

All in all, the academic freedom of faculty members is now sustained by a substantial legal framework. Moreover, the American Association of University Professors and other professional organizations continue to be active in further development of the rules and in securing adherence to them in practice. By and large, the overt violations which take place, at least at the university level, appear to be confined to smaller and more isolated institutions. Nevertheless, weaknesses in the structure are evident. The legal doctrines are stated in such broad terms, and contain such wide loopholes, that the system could crumble under heavy pressure. And, while the diversity achieved is significant, it does not extend very far beyond the mainstream of the current academic world.

RIGHTS OF STUDENTS

Academic freedom for students has undergone a slower development than that for faculty members. Initially students started at a point where, under the doctrine of *in loco parentis*, they had virtually no rights recognized by the school authorities or by the courts. Gradually the situation changed as the status of children and youth in our society changed. From a legal standpoint, the turning point came in the Supreme Court's decision in *Tinker*, previously described. After holding broadly that students "did not shed their constitutional rights to freedom of speech or expression at the schoolhouse gate" the Court went on in more specific terms:

In our system, state-operated schools may not be enclaves of totalitarianism. School officials do not possess absolute authority over their students. Students in school as well as out of school are "persons" under our Constitution. They are possessed of fundamental rights which the State must respect, just as they themselves must respect their obligations to the State. In our system, students may not be regarded as closed-circuit recipients of only that which the State choses to communicate. They may not be confined to the expression of those sentiments that are officially approved. In the absence of a specific showing of constitutionally valid reasons to regulate their speech, students are entitled to freedom of expression of their views.[16]

In *Tinker* the Supreme Court upheld the right of high school students to engage in symbolic expression—the wearing of armbands—so long as the school authorities could not demonstrate that the conduct materially disrupted school activities or invaded the rights of others. A few years later the Court dealt with an allied right—the right of association—at the college level. In *Healy v. James* a group of students had formed a local chapter of Students for a Democratic Society but the president of the college refused to grant their organization recognition, thereby denying them use of the college facilities and other privileges. The president's action was based on several grounds: that the local chapter would be affiliated with the national organization of SDS, a group which advocated "a philosophy of violence and disruption"; that the chapter would be "a disruptive influence"; and that the chapter would not agree to abide by the rules of the college. The Supreme Court reiterated the *Tinker* position that "state colleges and universities are not enclaves immune from the sweep of the First Amendment"; rejected the first ground stated by the president for the reason that First Amendment principles did not allow guilt by association or punishment for "advocacy" as distinct from "action"; rejected the president's second ground under the *Tinker* doctrine that no concrete evidence of disruption had been shown; and remanded the case for development of the facts as to whether the chapter had refused to agree to abide by reasonable campus rules. While the Court's holding that First Amendment rights can be made conditional upon an advance agreement to obey the rules is, to say the least, dubious, the great significance of the decision is that it measures the First Amendment rights of students by the doctrines applicable to citizens generally. The Court made this explicit, saying:

... the precedents of this Court leave no room for the view that, because of the acknowledged need for order, First Amendment protections should apply with less force on college campuses than in the community at large. Quite to the contrary, "[t]he vigilant protection of constitutional freedoms is nowhere more vital than in the community of American schools". . . . The college classroom with its surrounding environs is peculiarly the "marketplace of ideas," and we break no new constitutional ground in reaffirming this Nation's dedication to safeguarding academic freedom.[17]

A third decision of the Supreme Court reinforces the *Healy* position. In *Papish v. Board of Curators of the University of Missouri*, a graduate student was expelled for distributing a campus newspaper that contained "indecent" material. The Court overruled the action of the university authorities. Holding that the material involved could not be found "constitutionally obscene or otherwise unprotected," the Court declared that "the First Amendment leaves no room for the operation of a dual standard in the academic community with respect to the content of speech." Although the Court has not abandoned the requirement that student conduct not be "disruptive" or infringe on the rights of others, its willingness to measure the content of student expression by regular First Amendment standards is a major step forward.[18]

The Supreme Court has also extended substantial due-process rights to students. In the leading case, *Goss v. Lopez*, the Court held that students were entitled to a hearing before serious disciplinary measures, such as suspension, were taken against them. The required hearing did not have to be fully formal, but due process did require that "the student be given oral or written notice of the charges against him and, if he denies them, an explanation of the evidence the authorities have and an opportunity to present his side of the story." More recently, the Court has shown some reluctance to expand due process requirements in student cases. In *Ingraham v. Wright* it declined to recognize the right to a hearing prior to the use of corporal punishment. And in *Board of Curators of the University of Missouri v. Horowitz* it held that dismissal of a student on academic, as distinct from disciplinary, grounds did not necessitate a hearing.[19]

The fortunes of students who seek to vindicate their rights through the judicial system have varied. Obviously there is considerable leeway available to the courts in applying the rules developed in *Tinker, Healy*, and *Papish*. And at the lower levels of the educational structure the rights accorded students tend to diminish. Moreover, numerous instances of denial of student rights undoubtedly go unchallenged in the courts. Nevertheless, on the whole student academic freedom, so far as it is exercised, does seem to receive a growing measure of protection.[20]

CURRICULUM, TEXTBOOKS, AND LIBRARIES

Control over the curriculum, textbooks, and school libraries rests primarily with the school authorities at the appropriate level. Frequently their decisions are challenged by other interested parties—teachers, students, parents, or the general public—as failing to conform to the principles of academic freedom. By and large these issues are settled through a political process—usually local but at times statewide or national. In some cases an accommodation can be reached by parents exercising their constitutional right to send their children to a private school. Occasionally the school authorities will provide an exemption for a particular student or group. In an increasing number of cases, however, these issues are being brought before the courts.

In certain forms, questions relating to curriculum, textbooks, and libraries do not raise any unusual problem for the courts. Thus a state law forbidding the teaching of the German language in the public schools, or requiring the teaching of "creationism," can be dealt with in the traditional judicial manner. But judicial review of other kinds of issues, such as whether to use a certain textbook, or whether to add a certain book to the school library, presents the courts with difficult choices. It is not that persons with sufficient interest to challenge the school authorities are lacking. Nor is there an absence of applicable legal doctrine, whether it be freedom of expression, equal protection, privacy, substantive or procedural due process, or statutory interpretation. The principal issue is whether the courts have the resources and capacity to play a major role in supervising the actions of innumerable school authorities in their day-to-day judgments. Clearly the role of the courts must be a limited one. Just how limited is a matter of much dispute.[21]

Two current controversies illustrate the issues. One relates to the use of racially or sexually biased textbooks. The other concerns censorship of library books.[22]

There is widespread feeling that the curriculum and textbooks used in school systems throughout the country are racially biased in that they present materials exclusively from a white point of view and ignore the history, culture, and contributions to society of blacks and other minorities. A similar feeling exists that teaching materials are also biased in terms of gender, in that they portray females in stereotyped roles that are patronizing, demeaning, and give a negative and limited image of female potential. There appears to have been no effort to rectify sex bias in teaching materials by resort to judicial action. But at least one case, which presents the complex of problems involved, has sought to challenge racial bias.

In *Loewen v. Turnipseed* a group of teachers, students, and others brought a suit under the Federal Civil Rights Acts to compel school authorities in Mississippi to approve a certain textbook, *Mississippi: Conflict and Change,* for use in a junior high school history course. The school officials, who had power to recommend as many as five texts for the history course, had approved only one, a book entitled *Your Mississippi.* It was alleged that *Your Mississippi* depicted Mississippi history from a racist point of view while *Mississippi: Conflict and Change* contained a more balanced presentation. The trial court found that rejection of *Mississippi: Conflict and Change* was "motivated and influenced by racial issues," and ordered the Mississippi authorities to make the book eligible for use in the history course. The court did not, however, grant the plaintiffs' request to enjoin the defendants "from engaging in policies or practices which discriminate against textbooks containing perspectives on history at odds with those traditionally acceptable in Mississippi."[23]

The trial court's theory of the case was that the action of the school authorities violated the First Amendment in that it infringed upon "the teacher's free choice of curriculum," the "editor's right to distribute his book," and the "student's right to obtain an education." Ultimately, however, the trial court based its decision upon a procedural ground, namely that the school authorities had not provided "a method by which those affected by such decisions may oppose them."[24]

The trial court skipped rather hastily over some difficult First Amendment questions. The First Amendment right of a junior high school teacher to choose the basic textbook for a history course is clearly a limited one, if it exists at all. Likewise, a First Amendment right in editors or authors to have their books chosen by the school authorities in preference to others has thus far not been recognized by the courts. The chief First Amendment interest infringed would clearly be the "student's right to obtain an education," and a plausible argument can be made, based on right-to-know doctrine, to support this theory. A biased, rather than a balanced, presentation hardly fulfills the obligation of the state in operating a compulsory educational system. But the trial court did not elaborate its position. Moreover, although the evidence suggested a violation of the Equal Protection Clause, the court did not address that issue.

Assuming a constitutional right to have been established, however, the trial court's emphasis on procedure may point toward a solution of some of the difficulties inherent in cases of this kind. The courts cannot supervise every curriculum and textbook decision made by the school authorities. Nor are they in a position to survey the field and compare one textbook with another to see which better satisfies the standard of a balanced presentation. However, where a specific alternative to the school board's choice is proposed, the interested parties are given a chance to advance their positions, and the school board states explicitly the reasons for its decision, the case comes to the court in a much more manageable form. Using such a combination of consumer, scholarly, and judicial action, some progress in reducing race and sex bias from curriculum and textbooks might be achieved.

The banning of books from school libraries on the ground they conflict with traditional values has reached alarming dimensions in recent years. Reports of such censorship are widespread and increasing. In 1982 more than 50 percent of high school librarians responding to a national survey reported some form of censorship pressure. The effect is, of course, to thwart the goals of the educational process, especially the goal of encouraging independent and innovative thought. Such a narrowing of horizons is plainly incompatible with the principles of academic freedom.[25]

The main counterforce to book banning must, as in the case of curriculum and textbooks, rest upon political action, particularly at the local level. Still, there remains an important role for the judicial system.

The difficulties in seeking relief through the courts should not be underestimated. School library facilities are limited and hence a selection has to be made. Legitimate reasons for excluding or removing books are manifold. Decisions by the school authorities necessarily involve judgments on the contents of the book, the merit of the ideas expounded, and the establishment of priorities in subject matter and form. And the individual decisions made day by day are almost without number.

On the other hand, the theoretical case for the existence of constitutional limitations in the operation of a public school library is strong. The administration of a library is a governmental function and, like all activities of the government, must be performed within the boundaries of the Constitution. In the case of banned books, as in the case of a biased curriculum, the constitutional restrictions flow from the First Amendment doctrine of the right to know—the right of a citizen to receive information. While the parameters of right-to-know doctrine are obscure, its application to this situation is relatively clear. Because of the compulsory education laws, the student is a member of a captive audience. As such the student has a special right to obtain materials necessary to fulfill the goals of the educational system. The school library is, of course, a major instrument for broadening the scope of the ideas and information available. The student's right to know thus encompasses the right to a school library that provides the necessary diversity.[26]

Controversies over the banning of books have been brought to the courts with increasing frequency, and with mixed results. The issues finally reached the Supreme Court in *Board of Education, Island Trees Union Free School District No. 26 v. Pico*, decided in 1982.[27]

In *Pico*, after certain members of the Board of Education had attended a conference of "a politically conservative organization of parents" and obtained a list of "objectionable books," the Board conducted a search of the high school and junior high school libraries. Thereafter the Board ordered the removal of nine books as being "anti-American, anti-Christian, anti-Semitic, and just plain filthy." The banned books included *Slaughterhouse Five*, by Kurt Vonnegut, Jr.; *The Naked Ape*, by Desmond Morris; *Down These Mean Streets*, by Piri Thomas; *Black Boy*, by Richard Wright; and *The Fixer*, by Bernard Malamud. A group of students brought suit to enjoin the removal, alleging infringement upon their First Amendment rights. The district court granted a motion for summary dismissal but the Court of Appeals for the Second Circuit reversed and remanded the case for trial. The Supreme Court, by a vote of five to four, affirmed the ruling of the court of appeals but was unable to agree upon a majority opinion.[28]

Justice Brennan, writing for himself and Justices Marshall and Stevens, held the First Amendment applicable upon right-to-know grounds, saying:

> In sum, just as access to ideas makes it possible for citizens
> generally to exercise their rights of free speech and press in a

meaningful manner, such access prepares students for active and effective participation in the pluralistic, often contentious society in which they will soon be adult members.[29]

Justice Brennan then went on to consider the standard to be utilized in determining whether the school board's action violated the First Amendment right. Here he found the issue to be one of the intention of the school board to deny students a right of access to ideas with which it disagreed:

> In brief, we hold that local school boards may not remove books from school library shelves simply because they dislike the ideas contained in those books and seek by their removal to "prescribe what shall be orthodox in politics, nationalism, religion, or other matters of opinion."[30]

The only effort made by Justice Brennan to make this standard more concrete was to say that the school board's discretion "may not be exercised in a narrowly partisan or political manner."[31]

Justice Blackmun concurred with Justice Brennan in remanding the case for trial but disagreed on First Amendment theory. He declined to apply right-to-know doctrine, analyzing the problem as one of reconciling "the schools' 'inculcative' function with the First Amendment's bar on 'prescriptions of orthodoxy.'" The standard advanced by Justice Blackmun for applying his First Amendment theory, however, was not essentially different from that of Justice Brennan. "In my view," he said, "we strike a proper balance here by holding that school officials may not remove books for the *purpose* of restricting access to the political ideas or social perspectives discussed in them, when that action is motivated simply by the officials' disapproval of the ideas involved." Justice White concurred in the judgment to remand the case for trial, but felt it unnecessary to reach the constitutional issues.[32]

Chief Justice Burger and Justices Powell, Rehnquist, and O'Connor, dissenting, would have affirmed the district court in granting the motion for summary judgment. They rejected the right-to-know theory, asserted there was no First Amendment right of access to particular books in a school library, and argued that decisions on the appropriateness of retaining materials in libraries were matters for the elected school boards, not the courts.

After the remand the Island Trees School Board, apparently in order to avoid further legal costs, restored the books to the school libraries. Thus the issues were never judicially resolved and the ultimate position of the Supreme Court remains uncertain.[33]

Justice Brennan's opinion is an important contribution to the legal debate. It strongly supports the position that school authorities must operate within the confines of the First Amendment in the administration of school libraries. Yet it does not do much to clarify the standards that the courts should use in judging whether the First Amendment has been violated. In the first place, Justice Brennan's standard entails proof of "intent" to deny students access to ideas. While the motivation of the school authorities is relevant, and as a practical matter will frequently be articulated in book-banning cases, such a requirement could operate to limit the area in which judicial relief could be granted. A little more sophistication on the part of school officials could easily result in effective concealment of purpose. Consequently a more objective standard would seem essential.

Moreover, the core of the Brennan standard—that school officials may not suppress ideas they dislike—does not provide a satisfactory criterion. Frequently and necessarily the decision of the school authorities will be based on a judgment as to the worth of the ideas expressed in the book. Justice Brennan's subsidiary rule—that the discretion of the school authorities be not exercised "in a narrowly partisan or political manner"— goes somewhat further in focusing the issues. Yet ultimately the formulation of standards must be in terms of whether or not, based on professional criteria, the decision of the school authorities unduly restricts the space which the educational institution should afford the student for growth and development.

CONTROL OF THE DISSEMINATION OF INFORMATION ON NATIONAL SECURITY GROUNDS

Perhaps the gravest threat to academic freedom at the present time arises from attempts by the government to control the dissemination of information on national security grounds. These restrictions are one phase of the increasing tendency of recent administrations to reduce the flow of information available to the public concerning the activities of government. Thus proposals to curtail the coverage of the Freedom of Information Act, to provide criminal penalties for government officials who "leak" information to the press or public, and to expand the investigating powers of the intelligence agencies, are all designed to protect and enlarge the area of governmental secrecy. Such policies not only diminish the information needed by the public to participate in decision making but seriously handicap the scholar or student who seeks to describe, analyze, or criticize governmental conduct. The restrictions now being imposed in the name of national security, however, carry the secrecy process one ominous step further. They are designed not only to safeguard information in the possession of the government but to limit the communication of information and ideas generated in the private, or nongovernmental, sector.

The measures involved are described in Paul Bender's article in this volume. They comprise a network of statutes, regulations, directives, and informal actions that tighten the restrictions on access to information in the possession of the government, through such devices as expansion of the classification system, compelling government employees to sign secrecy agreements, and using lie detector tests to ferret out the source of "leaks." In addition they seek to impose ever-broadening control over the dissemination of scientific and technical information developed in the private sector. These controls are exercised through conditions imposed upon research funded by the government, through statutory provisions embodied in the Atomic Energy Act and the export control laws, through the denial of visas to foreign students and visitors, and through pressures on scientists to submit voluntarily to government censorship. The extent to which they impinge on academic freedom is evidenced by the government's claim that a university lecture attended by a foreign student or the delivery of a paper at a conference where a foreign scholar is present constitutes an export of information subject to the export-control laws.[34]

The objective sought by the government in attempting to stem the free exchange of scientific and technical information is, of course, to prevent foreign countries, particularly the Soviet bloc, from using the information to strengthen their military and economic positions. Secrecy with regard to information in the possession of the government that has a direct and identifiable bearing on military uses may be justified. But the efforts by the government to extend secrecy controls beyond this point undermine the whole system of academic freedom as we have known it up to the present. The reasons are apparent, and need only be briefly summarized:

1. The government controls are in diametric conflict with the basic tenets of the scientific method. The advance of scientific knowledge has always rested upon full freedom to inquire, to publish, to build upon the work of others, and to test results through uninhibited exchange of ideas. Scientific progress depends upon living and working in an atmosphere of creative intellectual dialogue, not in intellectual isolation.

2. Governmental limits upon the ability of teachers to obtain full access to information and ideas seriously diminishes the capacity of the university to train incoming students and thereby jeopardizes future progress.

3. Curtailment of publication and discussion prevents the academic community from informing the public about matters of concern to all citizens.

4. Attempts to force a university to impose special restrictions upon what a foreign student may learn, or to exclude foreign scholars from participation in research, conferences, or other university activities, destroys the open and free spirit that should characterize an academic community.

5. Any governmental restriction on the subjects of research or the publication of results inevitably has an impact beyond its intended boundaries as the persons affected tend to avoid borderline areas and accept self-censorship.

The government's program thus exacts a costly price in terms of academic freedom. On the other hand, the gains achieved are tenuous at best. The sources of information and ideas which might affect our national security are too voluminous and scattered to be kept under control, except perhaps through the mechanisms of a police state. Moreover, as is generally conceded, the most that the government can expect is that its efforts will bring about a short delay in the transmission of the material it seeks to withhold. Finally, while the Supreme Court has not yet addressed these issues, the validity of the restrictions under the First Amendment, except as they seek to maintain the secrecy of information in the government's possession, is open to serious doubt.

In the end the question is whether national security will be better promoted by a policy of encouraging scientific progress through open interchange or by a policy of containment through secrecy. All our experience to date suggests that the latter course is ineffective and self-defeating.

COMMERCIAL EXPLOITATION OF ACADEMIC RESEARCH

Lastly, our present system of academic freedom is threatened from within by developments in the commercial exploitation of academic research. For many years there has existed a kind of unofficial division of labor between the academic community and the business world. The function of the university has been to engage in basic research, which advances the state of our knowledge at the theoretical level. Application of that knowledge through commercial enterprise has been the function of private industry. This arrangement leaves the academic community free to pursue its inquiries wherever they may lead, unencumbered by the demands and seductions of monetary gain.

In recent years marked changes have begun to take place. The time lag between theoretical discovery and practical application has narrowed and the former division of functions has commenced to break down. The result has been that academic research and commercial exploitation have tended to merge, so that the university and its scholars are drawn into the arena of big business and private profit. Faculty members are lured into lucrative consultantships, or acquire financial interests in private corporations, or even participate actively in their management. Such developments have been particularly acute in the fields of genetic engineering and computer science.

The impact upon academic freedom is obvious. The time and energy devoted to business interests cuts into the time and energy available for students. Private funding of university research tends to concentrate upon subjects of immediate interest to private enterprise. The very atmosphere of the academic community—one of free and open pursuit of knowledge

—is at odds with the business objective of making a profit from the exclusive control of newly developed information.

This encroachment of the business world upon the academic community, and the resulting conflicts of interest, raise far-reaching issues for the future of academic freedom. Fortunately the solution lies in the hands of the universities themselves. It is within their power to draw the lines between academic inquiry and commercial exploitation, and to insist that the academic community remain true to its ideals. Many universities are already engaged in the process of formulating and enforcing such guidelines. To what extent they will succeed remains to be seen.

THE FUTURE OF ACADEMIC FREEDOM

The system of academic freedom is a fragile one. Public educational institutions are created by government and subject to its control. Private institutions are increasingly dependent on government grants, scholarships, and other public funding. So far as private institutions finance themselves they look largely to the generosity of the economic establishment. Ultimately all academic institutions are dependent upon the acceptance and support of the community in which they exist. Yet, according to the principles of academic freedom, it is the function of academic institutions to criticize the government, the establishment, and the society, to expose their shortcomings, and to propose uncomfortable change. Moreover, the individuals accorded the right of academic freedom must maintain an equally precarious balance. They are entitled to independence in teaching, research, and publication, but they must avoid isolation, elitism, and unconcern with social responsibility.

Despite these tensions and complexities, the basic principles underlying the system of academic freedom are broadly accepted in the United States. It is true that practice does not always match theory, and the area of actual freedom tends to fall within the boundaries of mainstream academic modes of operation. Nevertheless the theory of academic freedom has definitely become part of our liberal heritage.

Moreover, the legal framework supporting the system of academic freedom has been substantially strengthened in the last several decades. Thus the principles of academic freedom are given significant weight in

First Amendment decision making. Constitutional protections extend not only against restrictions imposed from outside the educational system but to limitations emanating from within the system. The rights of faculty members in the classroom, in research and publication, as members of the academic community, and as citizens of the outside world, are all given some measure of substantive and procedural protection. Likewise, the rights of students are beginning to receive wider recognition. While the legal doctrines enunciated by the courts remain vague in important respects, and contain loopholes that could be widened under pressure, on the whole the legal foundations of academic freedom are now sufficiently established to provide a workable system.

On the other hand serious threats to the system of academic freedom lie ahead. A major source of danger can be expected from the encroachments of government. The gradual expansion of governmental powers, the increasing volume of regulation, the extension of bureaucratic controls, all reduce the autonomy of institutions dealing with the government. The increasing dependence of academic institutions upon government financing makes them more vulnerable to government demands. The growing tendency of government to attach conditions to its grant of funds, such as the requirement that students who have not registered for the draft become ineligible for federal financial aid, results in the intrusion of government into the internal operation of academic institutions. More broadly, failures by the government to meet and solve the pressing problems of the day create a political climate where criticism is not tolerated and democratic procedures are short-circuited. And the recent government emphasis on national security, amounting to a search for "total" security, leads to restrictions that seriously curtail the exchange of information and ideas.

If these and similar tendencies persist, the system of academic freedom could be hard pressed. The reality of the danger is evidenced by the government's current program to control the dissemination of technological information through the export laws. Such cavalier indifference to the elementary rules of scientific inquiry and the requirements for scientific progress casts a shadow over the future of academic freedom.

Other dangers to academic freedom are posed by the dependence of academic institutions upon corporate largess. The inclination of the commercial establishment to infiltrate the campus seems to be gaining ground. Unless universities are prepared to offer a coordinated resistance to this threat the impact upon academic freedom is likely to be disastrous.

Beyond the dangers emanating from government and the business establishment, the future of academic freedom will depend upon broad political and social developments. In recent years traditionalist social forces, fundamentally opposed to innovation and diversity, have become better organized, increasingly articulate, and politically more influential. If, by such a move to the right, the society closes in, refuses to face the causes of its troubles and the need for change, loses its tolerance for dissident viewpoints, and is moved by fear and panic to preserve the present status regardless of the demands of social justice, then academic freedom will not survive.

Finally, much will depend upon how academic institutions and supporters of academic freedom conduct themselves. They must educate the public in the functions and values of a sophisticated system. They must defend the system against attacks from government and seduction by commercial enterprise. And above all they must justify the system in action by demonstrating that individual freedom responds to the needs of the community and works also for the public good.

NOTES

1. On the general theory and operation of academic freedom in the United States, *see* Machlup, "On Some Misconceptions Concerning Academic Freedom," 41 *American Association of University Professors Bulletin* 753 (1955), and the collection of materials in N. Dorsen, P. Bender, & B. Neuborne, 1 *Emerson, Haber & Dorsen's Political and Civil Rights in the United States*, 4th ed., ch. 10, and 1980 supplement (hereafter cited as *Political and Civil Rights*). For an account of the trend toward judicialization of academic freedom, *see* Finkin, "Toward a Law of Academic Status," 22 *Buffalo Law Review* 575 (1973).

2. Sweezy v. New Hampshire, 354 U.S. 234, 250 (1957).

3. 354 U.S. at 262–63.

4. *See* Keyishian v. Board of Regents, 385 U.S. 589, 603 (1967); Wieman v. Updegraff, 344 U.S. 183, 195–97 (1952); Barenblatt v. U.S., 360 U.S. 109, 129 (1959).

5. For an account of the loyalty and legislative committee decisions of the Supreme Court, *see* T. Emerson, *The System of Freedom of Expression* chs. 7, 8, and 16 (1970).

6. Pickering v. Board of Education, 391 U.S. 563, 567, 568 (1968).

7. Tinker v. Des Moines Independent Community School District, 393 U.S. 503, 506 (1969).

8. Application of the First Amendment to internal restrictions on faculty members was taken for granted in Mt. Healthy City School District Board of Education v. Doyle, 429 U.S. 274 (1977), and Givhan v. Western Line Consolidated School District, 439 U.S. 410 (1979). *See also* Perry v. Sindermann, 408 U.S. 593 (1972).

9. For discussion of the state and lower federal court decisions, *see Political and Civil Rights* 821–23; Miller, "Teachers' Freedom of Expression Within the Classroom: A Search for Standards," 8 *Georgia Law Review* 837 (1974); Project, "Education and the Law: State Interests and Individual Rights," 74 *Michigan Law Review* 1373, 1447–55 (1976); R. O'Neil, *Classrooms in the Crossfire* ch. 6 (1981). *But cf.* Goldstein, "The Asserted Constitutional Right of Public School Teachers to Determine What They Teach," 124 *University of Pennsylvania Law Review* 1293 (1976).

10. 391 U.S. at 571, 572–73, 574.

11. 393 U.S. at 513, 508. Rights of the faculty member as citizen of the academic community were also upheld in Madison School District v. Wisconsin Employment Relations Commission, 429 U.S. 167 (1976). For lower court decisions see *Political and Civil Rights* 833–39; *Note* "Teachers' Freedom of Expression Outside the Classroom: An Analysis of the Application of Pickering and Tinker," 8 *Georgia Law Review* 900 (1974).

12. Mt. Healthy City School District Board of Education v. Doyle, 429 U.S. 274 (1977). The Supreme Court applied the same rule in Givhan v. Western Line Consolidated School District, 439 U.S. 410 (1979).

13. On the rights of faculty members as citizens, *see* Emerson and Haber, "Academic Freedom and the Faculty Member as Citizen," 28 *Law and Contemporary Problems* 525 (1963).

14. The main Supreme Court decisions on procedural rights for faculty members are Perry v. Sindermann, 408 U.S. 593 (1972), and Board of Regents of State Colleges v. Roth, 408 U.S. 564 (1972). The quotation from Justice Marshall is in his opinion in the *Roth* case, 408 U.S. at 592. For a compilation of lower court decisions, see *Political and Civil Rights* 848–70.

15. See Finkin, *supra* note 1, at 588–601.

16. 393 U.S. at 511.

17. Healy v. James, 408 U.S. 169, 187, 188, 180, 188, 180–181 (1972).

18. Papish v. Board of Curators of the University of Missouri, 410 U.S. 667, 670, 671 (1973).

19. Goss v. Lopez, 419 U.S. 565, 581 (1975); Ingraham v. Wright, 430 U.S. 651 (1977); Board of Curators of the University of Missouri v. Horowitz, 435 U.S. 78 (1978).

20. For a summary of the lower decisions on student rights, *see Political and Civil Rights* 879–90 and Levine, Cary and Divoky, *The Rights of Students* (1975).

21. For a sampling of the discussion see Note, "Challenging Ideological Exclusion of Curriculum Material: Rights of Students and Parents," 14 *Harvard Civil Rights-Civil Liberties Law Review* 485 (1979).

22. Two other issues of current concern—school prayers and the teaching of "creationism"—are dealt with in Norman Redlich's article on religious liberty in this volume.

23. Loewen v. Turnipseed, 488 F.Supp. 1138, 1149, 1142 (N.D. Miss. 1980).

24. 488 F.Supp. at 1153.

25. The survey of librarians is reported in Office for Intellectual Freedom of the American Library Association, *Newsletter on Intellectual Freedom*, vol. 32, no. 1 at 1, 18 (Jan. 1983). The Newsletter contains monthly accounts of all incidents of library censorship. *See also* O'Neil, *supra* note 9, ch. 7.

26. For further discussion of the application of right-to-know doctrine to school libraries *see* Emerson, "The Affirmative Side of the First Amendment," 15 *Georgia Law Review* 795 (1981).

27. Board of Education, Island Trees Union Free School District No. 26 v. Pico, 102 S. Ct. 2799 (1982). For a discussion of the lower court cases, *see* Estreicher, "Schoolbooks, School Boards, and the Constitution," 80 *Columbia Law Review* 1092 (1980); *Note*, "Removal of Public School Library Books: The First Amendment Versus the Local School Board," 34 *Vanderbilt Law Review* 1407 (1981); *Note*, "Not on Our Shelves: A First Amendment Analysis of Library Censorship in the Public Schools," 61 *Nebraska Law Review* 98 (1982).

28. 102 S.Ct. at 2802, 2803.

29. 102 S.Ct. at 2808.

30. 102 S.Ct. at 2810.

31. 102 S.Ct. at 2810.

32. 102 S.Ct. at 2814 (italics in original).

33. The decision of the Board of Education not to continue the case is reported in the *New York Times*, Aug. 15, 1982 at 24.

34. *See* H.R. Rept. No. 34, 96th Cong., 2d Sess., *The Government's Classification of Private Ideas* (1980); Cheh, "Government Control of Private Ideas—Striking a Balance Between Scientific Freedom and National Security," 23 *Jurimetrics Journal* 1 (1982).

CRIMINAL JUSTICE: THE ACCUSED

DAVID RUDOVSKY

*David Rudovsky is first assistant defender at the Defender
Association of Philadelphia. He is an instructor in Trial
Advocacy at the University of Pennsylvania Law School and
the coauthor of* Police Misconduct: Law & Litigation *and*
The Rights of Prisoners. *Mr. Rudovsky was for ten years
Philadelphia counsel for the National Emergency Civil Liberties Committee.*

It has been a historical commonplace for government officials and others
to exploit the public's legitimate concerns about crime and criminal violence for partisan and political purposes. Fear of crime has been used to
deflect consideration of other seemingly intractable social issues, to denigrate political, minority, and ethnic movements, and to justify regressive
legislation and arbitrary police controls. The end result of these law-and-order campaigns usually has been enhancement of state power at the
expense of individual rights, but virtually no reduction in crime.

In recent years a new variation on this theme has sounded: adherence
to constitutional protections for the accused is incompatible with effective
law enforcement. In a turnabout that distorts public dialogue and decision
making, aspects of the criminal justice system that secure fairness and
equality are now blamed for aggravating crime and violence. Illustrative
of this approach is the report of the Reagan administration's Task Force
on Violent Crime, which proposes a substantial modification of the exclusionary rule (the doctrine that prohibits the use of illegally obtained
evidence), and endorses preventive detention, restrictions on the remedy
of habeas corpus, and restoration of the death penalty.[1] The "war on
crime," it would appear, should be fought almost exclusively by restricting
civil liberties.

Demonstrably, however, these measures would have only the most incidental impact on crime and violence. Consider bail and pretrial release.

Not only has the debate on this issue focused almost exclusively on those who are released and arrested for new crimes (as opposed to those who spend months in jail only to be found not guilty at trial), but the danger to the public has been greatly exaggerated. In a recent study in Washington, D.C. it was determined that only 2 percent of persons charged with violent crime were arrested for a violent or property crime while on bail.[2] Indeed, given the extreme difficulty of predicting dangerousness with any accuracy, to be confident of preventing one person from committing a violent crime while on bail we would have to incarcerate up to ten who would not.[3] Preventive detention would cause many innocent persons to be jailed in order to incapacitate very few guilty persons. Speedy trials would provide greater protection, both to the public and the accused.

Similarly, the exclusionary rule does not cause the release of significant numbers of defendants. Recent studies show that evidence was excluded in federal prosecutions in only 1.3 percent of all cases (0.5 percent were dismissed because of the rule) and that in state prosecutions only 0.8 percent of all arrests were declined for prosecution for reasons of improper searches.[4]

Furthermore, it is incorrect to characterize rules of the criminal justice system—and particularly the remedies that are afforded for violations of constitutional rights—as mere technicalities whose sole beneficiaries are guilty persons unfairly escaping the law. In our system of law, constitutional rights are not self-enforcing. The remedies provided by the exclusionary rule, federal habeas corpus, and civil injunctive suits are often necessary to vindicate personal liberties; they are the principal means by which we seek to deter officials from engaging in unconstitutional conduct. It is, of course, true that many persons who invoke these remedies are those accused or convicted of crime (they have the greatest incentive to litigate), but in so doing they act as constitutional surrogates for the citizenry at large. Thus, the dramatic retrenchment of the rights of people accused of crime restricts our common entitlement to civil liberties.

THE WARREN AND BURGER COURTS—AN OVERVIEW

Many of the protections that currently exist in the criminal justice system were first mandated by the Warren Court. These include right to counsel at all critical stages of criminal cases; exclusion of physical, identification, and confession testimony where the police violated the due-process, privacy, or self-incrimination rights of defendants; the right of confrontation of adverse witnesses; disclosure of certain evidence favorable to the defense; and appellate and federal remedies to challenge unfair convictions.[5]

This is not to suggest that the Warren Court always favored the accused or that there was a complete turnabout on criminal justice issues by the Burger Court. In fact the Warren Court rejected several important constitutional challenges. For example, it limited the defense of entrapment by adopting a rule that focuses on the intent or predisposition of the defendant to commit a crime, rather than upon the conduct of the government agent.[6] The Court authorized broad overreaching by agents —that would entrap even the law-abiding into criminal activity—if the defendant had some "predisposition" toward criminal activity. Similarly, the Court declined to restrict police use of agents and stoolpigeons to manipulate personal and business relationships and to intrude into homes and offices.[7]

In addition, the Court framed several of its significant rulings in a manner that allowed the police, prosecutors, and lower courts to ignore or undermine constitutional protections. A notable example was the Court's failure to require disclosure and identification of police informers who allegedly provided information in support of search warrants.[8] Many warrants are issued on the assertion of a police officer that an "informant" observed certain criminal activity. By crediting this assertion without determining whether the informant exists, the Court, in the words of one observer, winked its eye at the police "perjury routine."[9] Similarly, the refusal in the *Miranda* case to require counsel's presence before questioning of a suspect has led to "swearing contests" between police and defendants as to whether the proper warnings of the right to remain silent were given. Since trial judges invariably believe police testimony, the *Miranda* protections are often illusory. If the Court had intended to fully protect the accused from police overreaching, it would not have permitted waiver of *Miranda* protections without counsel.

The record of the Burger Court on criminal justice issues, while regressive, is not totally negative. Warren Court precedents have been limited, but rarely directly overruled; on a few occasions, the current Court has reaffirmed constitutional principles.[10] Overall, however, the record of the past fifteen years is discouraging. Individual rights—the hallmark of the constitutional decisions of the 1960s—have been subordinated to state interests of efficiency, order, and conformity.

This process, reflecting the profound differences in values and assumptions between the Warren and Burger Courts, has not been limited to the judicial arena. On the legislative level, the Congress has long debated a new criminal code that would substantially restrict individual rights. While this legislation has not yet passed, the civil liberties struggle is made even more difficult when courts function against a conservative legislative backdrop, particularly where serious attempts have already been made to "strip" the federal courts of their duty to resolve certain constitutional questions.

On one issue—sentencing codes—there has been a vigorous and sustained effort to impose mandatory sentences and to increase the length of prison sentences. This has led to a substantial increase in the nation's prison population and related problems of overcrowding. Similarly, most states have passed new death-penalty statutes and there are now over twelve hundred persons on death row. Given the increasing resort to the penal sanction, it is perplexing that there is still the widely held perception that the criminal justice system is too lenient and too solicitous of the rights of the accused. We send a higher proportion of our people to prison for longer periods of time than any industrialized country other than South Africa. In 1981, over five hundred thousand persons, or 250 for every hundred thousand in the general population, were in our prisons and jails; the rates in Britain and West Germany were each less than one-third of the American rate.[11]

Mandatory-sentencing laws were passed with the laudable goal of preventing disparity in sentencing. On balance, however, these schemes have undermined civil liberties since they cause the incarceration of many persons for whom a probationary or short prison sentence may in fact be appropriate, both from the standpoint of protecting society and of ensuring fair treatment for the offender. Moreover, the resulting prison overcrowding has increased the debilitative effects of prison life. Some may derive satisfaction from such retribution, but such practices will hardly lead to safer streets.

JUDICIAL EROSION OF
CONSTITUTIONAL PROTECTIONS

It is in the courts, however, that most civil liberties issues are ultimately decided. In examining how the current Court has breached the constitutional promises of an earlier era, I have grouped and analyzed the substantive legal changes in terms of the judicial processes by which they have been made—direct retrenchment, judicial door closing, and manipulation and avoidance of legal doctrine.

The Court's retrenchment from earlier decisions protecting against illegal searches, seizures, and arrests has been dramatic. In *Mapp v. Ohio*, [12] the Warren Court applied the exclusionary rule (requiring suppression of illegally obtained evidence) to state prosecutions. That Court also gave a broad reading to the Fourth Amendment. It resolved a long-standing historical dispute over the proper interpretation of the Amendment's warrant clause by requiring that prior judicial approval be obtained in advance of all searches, unless compelling circumstances made this course of action impossible.[13] Further, the Court determined that with limited exceptions (e.g., stop-and-frisk of suspicious persons), the police need probable cause to effect an arrest, secure a warrant, or conduct a search. In *Katz v. United States*, [14] the Court, in ruling that electronic surveillances were "searches" within the meaning of the Fourth Amendment, gave explicit recognition to the right of privacy. By so doing, the Court not only broadened the protections of the Amendment, but also enlarged the class of persons who had legal standing to object to unlawful governmental intrusions.

The Burger Court has seriously eroded these protections. *Katz* sought to enhance our right to be free from governmental intrusion in areas and situations where one has a reasonable "expectation of privacy." But who is to define when one has this expectation of privacy? Can the government defeat privacy interests by simply stating that it will search all persons in particular areas (e.g., airports or "high crime areas")? How do we decide whether our private conversations with friends or associates are protected from governmental overhearing, bugging, or the use of informers? Must we draw curtains around our lives to assert an expectation of privacy for personal matters in homes and offices?

Predictably, the Burger Court has given this principle a very narrow reading. We are told that we have no legitimate expectation of privacy in personal bank accounts,[15] that we should not be surprised if the telephone company makes our records available to the police,[16] and that as passengers in cars or guests in homes, we may not have a sufficient interest to object to unlawful police intrusions.[17] Perhaps of greatest concern, by affording law enforcement free reign to use informers and agents, the Court has told us not to expect privacy in our personal and business relationships. The distortion of Fourth Amendment doctrine that results is succinctly put by Prof. Anthony G. Amsterdam:

> I can conceive of no rational system of concerns and values that restricts the government's power to rifle my drawers or tap my telephone but not its power to infiltrate my home or my life with a legion of spies.[18]

Consider in this regard the Court's decision in *United States v. White*,[19] where a government informer, without a warrant or other court order, engaged the defendant in conversations that were transmitted via a hidden radio to federal agents. The Court ruled that "however strongly a defendant may trust an apparent colleague, his expectations in this respect are not protected by the Fourth Amendment when it turns out that the colleague is a government agent regularly communicating with the authorities."[20] The Court assumed that only "wrongdoers" would be risking arrest by placing their confidence in police agents. As Justice Harlan demonstrated in dissent, however, the issue is not simply whether *criminals* place unjustified reliance on so-called friends:

> [I]t is too easy to forget—and, hence, too often forgotten—that the issue here is whether to interpose a search warrant procedure between law enforcement agencies engaging in electronic eavesdropping and the public generally. By casting its "risk analysis" solely in terms of the expectations and risks that "wrongdoers" or "one contemplating illegal activities" ought to bear, the plurality opinion, I think, misses the mark entirely. . . . The interest [to be protected] is the expectation of the ordinary citizen, who has never engaged in illegal conduct in his life, that he may carry on his private discourse freely, openly, and spontaneously without measuring his every word against the connotations it might carry when instantaneously heard by others unknown to him and unfamiliar

with his situation or analyzed in a cold, formal record played days, months, or years after the conversation.[21]

The entire range of Fourth Amendment protections are even more seriously endangered by proposals to eliminate or modify the exclusionary rule. The Supreme Court has recently ordered argument on whether the exclusionary rule should be subject to a "good-faith" exception.[22] Over the past several years the Court has limited the kinds of judicial proceedings in which the exclusionary rule can be applied,[23] and one court of appeals has adopted a "good-faith" exception to the exclusionary rule.[24] This issue has become symbolic for law-and-order advocates, and the message that a modification or elimination of the doctrine would send to police officers is troubling to contemplate.

We need not speculate on the serious consequences of a good-faith exception to the exclusionary rule since we have substantial experience with the detrimental impact that an identical doctrine has had in civil rights litigation. The Supreme Court has ruled that government officials may defeat civil rights damages suits by proving that their unconstitutional actions were performed in "good faith."[25] As a practical matter, this standard has wholly insulated proven constitutional violations.

For example, in cases involving arrests or searches, where the police acted without probable cause and, therefore, in violation of the Fourth Amendment, the officer can still avoid liability by showing he had a mistaken notion of whether probable cause existed—that is, that he reasonably made an unreasonable decision! The potential reach of the defense is illustrated by a recent case in which a court of appeals ruled that a plaintiff "was not only required to show that his arrest was illegal. . . . [but] that it was so *illegal*" as to constitute "egregious" conduct.[26] Apparently, the law is not offended by "routine" constitutional violations.

Extension of this doctrine to criminal cases will cause similar adverse consequences for civil liberties. Deterrence of police misconduct will be diminished because good faith will become a substitute for the Fourth Amendment's specific requirements of probable cause and a warrant. Since the issue for decision would be an officer's intentions, not only would unconstitutional acts be condoned, officers could continue to profess ignorance and thereby continue to make "reasonable mistakes" in the future.

Furthermore, if a defendant contends that a well-trained officer would have acted differently, the prosecution could argue that the officer was ignorant or untrained and therefore acting in good faith. Perhaps the courts would reject such a subjective test, but experience teaches otherwise. As a result, police officers would in some situations testify that they did not know that their actions were in violation of the Constitution. More seriously, this defense could lead some police departments to provide ambiguous training on search-and-seizure law to lend support to such testimony.

The Warren Court not only established substantive rights for suspects and defendants, but it provided the means for enforcement of the rights by federal courts. Most dramatically, it resurrected the ancient remedy of habeas corpus. Although explicitly recognized in the Constitution, this remedy had lain dormant for decades due to restrictive judicial interpretations. In 1963, the Warren Court appreciably broadened the power of federal courts to issue the "Great Writ" as a prompt and efficacious remedy for whatever society deems to be "intolerable restraints."[27] The Court went on:

> Its root principle is that in a civilized society, government must always be accountable to the judiciary for a man's imprisonment: if the imprisonment cannot be shown to conform with the fundamental requirements of law, the individual is entitled to his immediate release. . . . [28]

The Supreme Court ruled specifically that state prisoners may submit their constitutional claims to federal courts unless they had "deliberately bypassed" state remedies. Under this standard, procedural mistakes that were the result of the ignorance or incompetence of the defendant's lawyer at a state trial would not bar federal relief; the vindication of constitutional rights was more important than deference to state procedural rules.

The Burger Court has made deep inroads on this doctrine with decisions that share a common theme with the Court's philosophy in other areas—the limitation of federal judicial power in correcting or reforming unconstitutional state practices. In *Stone v. Powell*,[29] for example, the Court overruled prior cases and held that federal habeas corpus cannot be invoked to challenge a state conviction because evidence obtained in violation of the Fourth Amendment was admitted at trial. This limitation on the exclusionary rule was justified in part on the theory that only constitutional violations that concern questions of guilt or innocence should be grounds for habeas relief. It will not be surprising if the Court extends this rationale to preclude review of violations of other constitutional provisions.

The Court has also jettisoned the *Fay v. Noia* procedural test for determining whether defendants who failed to raise certain issues in the state courts will be allowed federal relief. Stressing the "social costs" of this remedy, the Court has ruled that the failure to present the issue to the state court will bar federal habeas review unless the defendant can show both adequate cause for not having presented the issue and substantial prejudice.[30]

This standard has ominous implications with regard to a defendant's right to effective assistance of counsel. The Court appears willing to allow a defendant to forfeit constitutional rights where the trial lawyer has failed because of negligence or inexperience to recognize and litigate constitutional issues. Thus, the Court has denied habeas review where the lawyer did not challenge exclusion of blacks from an indicting grand jury,[31] failed to raise a *Miranda* claim,[32] and did not object to his client being compelled to wear prison garb at trial,[33] even though in each case constitutional rights were denied.

Indeed, the Court has gone to an extreme in applying this "waiver" standard. In *Engle v. Issac,*[34] defendants challenged a state rule of criminal procedure requiring them to prove self-defense by a preponderance of the evidence. Their lawyers had not objected to this rule at trial because it had already been upheld by state appellate courts. Some time after their convictions, the rule was reinterpreted to place the burden of disproving self-defense on the prosecution. The Supreme Court denied relief on the grounds that the lawyers' failure to object constituted a waiver, even though any objection at trial obviously would have been futile.

The Court's insistence that defense counsel raise and argue all possible issues at trial would be unobjectionable—indeed it would be commendable—if the Court as a corollary also recognized that such diligence was an element of the Sixth Amendment right to effective assistance of counsel. But there is no indication that the Court will make the standards reciprocal; to the contrary, in many cases a lawyer's negligence or incompetence will be grounds for barring appellate or habeas relief, but will not be deemed egregious enough to contravene the Sixth Amendment.

By way of contrast, one may compare attempts to hold government officials liable for violation of constitutional rights. The Court has provided these defendants with a broad good-faith defense that will defeat liability upon a showing that the right violated was not "clearly established" at the time.[35] Thus, while officials' disregard of constitutional rights will be excused if reasonable, criminal defendants will be denied relief if their lawyers, because of incompetence or lack of clairvoyance, make mistakes in representing their clients.

The habeas decisions are only one aspect of the failure of the criminal justice system to confront the widespread problem of inadequate defense of criminal cases. In part, this problem results from the failure to take seriously in individual cases the constitutional requirement that counsel be effective and competent. Structural discrimination, based on factors of race, wealth, and class, also contributes. Most defendants are too poor to retain counsel and are provided appointed counsel, usually public defenders. These lawyers, though dedicated and resourceful, are handicapped in their efforts for institutional reasons, including understaffing and lack of continuity of representation. Legal assistance to the poor is simply not measured by the standards of adequacy and competency that anyone with financial resources would rightfully demand from a lawyer.

The Warren Court took limited steps to ameliorate the difference that financial resources would have on a defendant's right to a fair process. In *Griffin v. Illinois*, [36] for example, the Court ruled that indigent defendants be furnished transcripts of their trials in order to obtain full appellate review of their convictions. Justice Black stated: "[I]n criminal trials a state can no more discriminate on account of poverty than on account of religion, race, or color."[37] Of course, if the true implications of this pronouncement were fully explored, the criminal justice system would need to be completely overhauled. But the Warren Court failed to do so, and the Burger Court has essentially repudiated the equality principle. Indigent defendants have been denied appointed counsel to prepare discretionary appeals, including petitions to the Supreme Court, and the Court has substituted a far less stringent "fairness" test to determine whether state procedures that discriminate between defendants on the basis of wealth are permissible.[38]

Moreover, while the Chief Justice has spoken with some force—off the Bench—with respect to the major task of ensuring capable, trained, and effective counsel, both he and the Court have failed to address the structural discrimination in the system that causes inadequate lawyering. Good advocacy training is simply not sufficient, and the Court has declined to use its powers to require states to provide the resources necessary to ensure, through institutional change, that poor people's lawyers will be diligent and zealous in their representation.

JUDICIAL "DOOR CLOSING"

The tactic of dismissing lawsuits on technical, procedural grounds has become an increasingly popular method of avoiding judicial enforcement of rights.[39] This process has been most commonly invoked in "class actions"—cases seeking systemic compliance with established constitutional principles.

For example, in *Rizzo v. Goode,*[40] the record showed a widespread pattern of police abuse of citizens, and the district court ruled that the police department must establish a formal internal administrative procedure to handle civilian complaints of police misconduct. The Supreme Court rejected this remedy, stressing principles of "federalism"—deference to local officials—despite the proven refusal of these officials to act to prevent these constitutional violations. The failure of the Court to draw the most obvious of inferences—that police officials are aware of and responsible for system-wide abuses—is, of course, grounded more in the judgment that police departments should be free from judicial or other restraints than in any legal or constitutional principle.

More recently, in *Los Angeles v. Lyons,*[41] the Court manifested even greater judicial deference to police misconduct—this time with respect to lethal practices. In *Lyons,* the plaintiff had been rendered unconscious as a result of a police "choke hold," after the police stopped his car for a motor vehicle violation. The plaintiff had offered no threats or resistance. Accordingly, he sued for an injunction against the use of this police practice in similar situations and supported his claim with evidence of fifteen deaths that had occurred (mostly of blacks) as a result of the practice. The Court refused to issue an injunction since Lyons could not prove that he would be subject to such a hold in the future. If he was, the Court assured him, he could sue for damages (or, if he was so unfortunate as to die, his family could sue). Showing little concern for the existence of an unconstitutional police practice, the Court blithely reasoned:

Of course, it may be that among the countless encounters between the police and the citizens of a great city such as Los Angeles, *there will be certain instances in which strangleholds will be illegally applied and injury and death unconstitutionally inflicted on the victim.* As we have said, however, it is no more than conjecture to suggest that in every instance of a traffic stop, arrest, or other encounter between the police and a citizen, the police will act unconstitutionally and inflict injury without provocation or legal excuse. And it is surely no more than speculation to assert either that Lyons himself will again be involved in one of those unfortunate instances, or that he will be arrested in the future and provoke the use of a choke hold by resisting arrest, attempting to escape, or threatening deadly force or serious bodily injury.[42]

AVOIDING PRECEDENTS

In providing constitutional definition to the procedural rights of suspects, the Warren Court formulated broad principles as well as specific rules of criminal justice. The Burger Court has been able to manipulate and redefine legal doctrines and thereby restrict, limit, and undercut these principles.

Evisceration of rights through a process of distinguishing precedent is well illustrated by the Court's response to earlier decisions establishing fair identification procedures.[43] Many criminal cases, of course, turn on the question of identification, and convictions for the most serious felonies—murder, robbery, rape, and burglary—can be obtained solely on the eye-witness identification of a single person. Notwithstanding the numerous instances of misidentification caused by impermissibly suggestive confrontations, it was not until 1967 that the Court placed some restrictions on the methods police use to secure identification testimony. The Court announced two important principles: first, that a formal, postindictment, lineup is a critical stage of criminal proceeding, thus necessitating the assistance of counsel; second, that the police may not conduct identification procedures that are "unnecessarily suggestive and conducive to mistaken identification." Animating the Court's decisions was the understanding that even the fairest trial was meaningless if the police had used deceptive identification procedures in its investigation.

In a series of decisions the Burger Court has severely restricted these cases. In *Kirby v. Illinois,* [44] the Court ruled that there is no right to counsel at a lineup that occurs after arrest but before indictment or formal charging since, in the Court's view, the right to counsel attaches only at the point that adversary *judicial* proceedings have been initiated. To reach this result, the Court had to ignore the primary rationale for the rule—to protect suspects from unfair police lineups by providing them with counsel and a meaningful opportunity to cross-examine witnesses at trial. The timing of the lineup is obviously irrelevant, since the dangers and hazards inherent in the identification process are present whenever it is conducted. Most identification procedures are conducted after arrest but *before* judicial proceedings have started. Moreover, there are no law-enforcement interests that are adversely affected by fair identification procedures. The Court's formalistic, technical interpretation of the Sixth Amendment demonstrates that legal doctrine can easily be manipulated to undermine prior precedent without the necessity of overruling.

In *United States v. Ash,*[45] the Court again retreated when it ruled that postindictment *photographic* displays containing an accused's picture are not covered by the Sixth Amendment. To reach that result, the Court again had to distinguish *Wade,* although no functional distinction of significance can be drawn between a lineup and a photographic display.

Constitutional mandates are not always respected by those involved in what the Court has called the "often competitive enterprise of ferreting out crime."[46] Many participants in the system, including police, prosecutors, and judges, are hostile to the notion of "defendants' rights" and have found ways of circumventing Supreme Court decisions.

Consider, for example, the experience involved in enforcing decisions like *Miranda v. Arizona*[47] and *Mapp v. Ohio,*[48] which require the suppression of evidence obtained by illegal methods. Most suppression claims involve factual disputes, and the protections are undermined by a fact-finding process that slants decision making in favor of particular classes of litigants. For example, these constitutional rights hinge on such questions as: Were the *Miranda* warnings given? Did the suspect waive his right to counsel? Did the defendant act in a manner that gave the police officer "probable cause" to arrest? As our earlier discussion of the *Miranda* decision makes clear, resort to often unreliable fact determinations is avoidable in some cases. In others, we should at least be aware that judges regularly choose to accept even blatantly unbelievable police testimony. For example, after the *Mapp* decision, defendants who had previously submitted to police searches apparently altered their behavior patterns such that, upon seeing an officer, they felt compelled to toss away incriminating evidence. Judicial acceptance of such testimony allows the police to circumvent *Mapp* with a technicality: one who throws away evidence has "abandoned" it and cannot claim that he was unlawfully searched; but he can be convicted of having possessed it.

The issue of a defendant's right to a trial by jury provides another example of how constitutional guarantees are negated in practice. As a doctrinal matter, the Supreme Court has permitted states to make inroads on the jury trial right. Juries may now be composed of as few as six persons;[49] there can be less than unanimous verdicts;[50] and prosecutors may use peremptory challenges to exclude black and other minority representation on the jury.[51] But more important, trial courts have been permitted to punish defendants for the exercise of their right to trial by jury. It is not unusual for local criminal courts to impose more severe sentences for persons who demand a jury trial, as opposed to pleading guilty or acquiescing in a trial before a judge. Judges routinely hand down longer sentences to those who exercise their right to a jury trial and, in some jurisdictions, jury trials are assigned to the harshest judges in an effort to discourage such requests.

The Supreme Court has sustained such trial court and prosecutorial vindictiveness. In one case, after having charged the defendant with forgery, the prosecutor stated that he would recommend a five-year sentence if the defendant pleaded guilty, but would reindict him under a habitual-offender statute with a mandatory life sentence if he caused the "inconvenience" of a jury trial by pleading not guilty. The defendant refused to plead guilty, was convicted, and the Supreme Court found nothing impermissible in the resulting life sentence: the prosecutor's actions might "deter" exercise of a constitutional right, but they were part of "plea bargaining," were not "retaliatory," and were not proscribed by due process.[52]

ALTERNATIVE RESPONSES TO CRIME

The Supreme Court's devaluation of constitutional rights has not gone unanswered. In a significant development, a number of state courts, interpreting their own constitutions and laws, have refused to acquiesce in constitutional retreat. For example, the privacy principle has been invoked to thwart seizure of bank records, the right to counsel under state law has been used to reject the Court's distinction between pre- and postindictment lineups, and state constitutional protections against unreasonable searches have been invoked to protect persons stopped for traffic violations from undergoing full body searches.[53]

This ironic development—the Warren Court, after all, was reacting in part to state refusals to protect individual rights—has prompted a change in civil liberties litigation tactics. It remains to be seen whether reliance on state law will continue and what the ultimate effect may be. Unfortunately, these decisions affect only a limited number of criminal-justice issues and are controlling in only a small number of states. What we have surely learned, however, is that the protection of civil liberties cannot be left to one governmental institution. The issues are political in nature and therefore can be addressed in numerous forums. Ultimately, the articulation and enforcement of rights requires a consensus that can be achieved only by a combination of legal, legislative, and political efforts.

Effective measures are available that would help control crime without restricting civil liberties. A critical aspect of any anticrime program is an understanding of and a program to address crime's root causes—including poverty, unemployment, dissolution of family relationships, and lack of community support. Attributing crime to man's propensity for "evil," as President Reagan has done, simply avoids the hard questions. The sad fact is that our society's social incohesiveness, lack of a sense of shared purpose, and social and economic inequalities will make it extremely difficult to substantially reduce crime.

This is not to suggest that even in the short run we cannot provide a greater measure of security and protection. To do so, we must make more effective those institutions upon which we rely in fighting crime. The police, for example, will not achieve full effectiveness unless they develop the trust of the communities they serve. Significant hiring and training changes will be necessary to ameliorate the crippling effects of racial prejudice in police departments. In addition, cooperation with the community can be enhanced through the reintroduction of foot patrols, expansion of community-police programs such as citizen block-watches, and a more serious treatment of domestic violence.

In the sentencing and corrections fields, we must provide alternatives to incarceration (e.g., community service or direct aid to victims for nonviolent offenders) and reclassification of prisoners to ensure that the limited number of maximum-security cells are used only for those who require such confinement. Uniformity in sentencing should be achieved under reasonable sentence guidelines, rather than the often draconian and inflexible mandatory sentencing laws that have been passed in recent years. Further, rehabilitation efforts will succeed with some persons if conducted on a voluntary basis with a guarantee of employment upon release. We should not expect reduction in recidivism if we continue to parole prisoners into communities with 40 percent unemployment rates.

Finally, we should recall the substantial costs of white collar and corporate crime. Historically, we have not vigorously enforced the criminal laws in these areas; prosecutions are seldom brought, for example, where an employer's failure to comply with health and safety regulations has resulted in the injury or death of workers or consumers. This differential treatment has been raised to the definitional level in the proposed new federal criminal code, which initially included an "endangerment provision" that would have criminalized violations of certain environmental and safety laws. This provision, directed at corporate decisions that would "knowingly place a person in imminent danger of death or serious bodily injury," was deleted as a result of corporate lobbying.

It has always been tempting to pare down the laws of criminal procedure to make it easier to get at criminals. But while simple solutions may win elections, they will not solve the serious problem of crime. The current emphasis on fighting crime by diluting constitutional protections is seriously misdirected. And if civil liberties continue to be viewed as a cause of crime, we will have neither safety nor liberty.

NOTES

1. U.S. Department of Justice, *Attorney General's Task Force on Violent Crime, Final Report* (1981).

2. *Pretrial Release: An Evaluation of Defendant Outcomes and Program Impact* (1981), cited in Bazelon, "The Crime Controversy: Avoiding Realities," 35 *Vanderbilt Law Review* 487, 494 (1982).

3. *Id.*

4. U.S. General Accounting Office, *Impact of Exclusionary Rule on Federal Criminal Prosecutions* (1979); Brosi, *A Cross-City Comparison of Felony Case Processing* (1979).

5. Gideon v. Wainwright, 372 U.S. 335 (1963); United States v. Wade, 388 U.S. 218 (1967); Mapp v. Ohio, 367 U.S. 643 (1961); Miranda v. Arizona, 384 U.S. 436 (1966); Brady v. Maryland, 373 U.S. 83 (1963); Fay v. Noia, 372 U.S. 391 (1963).

6. Sherman v. United States, 356 U.S. 369 (1958).

7. *See, e.g.,* Hoffa v. United States, 385 U.S. 293 (1966).

8. McCray v. Illinois, 386 U.S. 300 (1967).

9. Younger, "The Perjury Routine," *The Nation* 596–97 (May 8, 1967).

10. *See, e.g.,* United States v. United States District Court, 407 U.S. 297 (1972); Brewer v. Williams, 430 U.S. 387 (1977).

11. National Institute of Justice, *American Prisons and Jails* (1980); American Institute of Criminal Justice, *Just the Facts* (1980); Elliot Currie, "Crime and Ideology," *Working Papers* (May 1982).

12. 367 U.S. 643 (1961).

13. Chimel v. California, 395 U.S. 752 (1969)

14. 389 U.S. 347 (1967).

15. United States v. Miller, 425 U.S. 435 (1976).

16. Smith v. Maryland, 422 U.S. 735 (1979).

17. Rakas v. Illinois, 439 U.S. 128 (1978).

18. Amsterdam, "Perspectives on the Fourth Amendment," 58 *University of Minnesota Law Review* 349, 365 (1974).

19. 401 U.S. 745 (1971).

20. *Id.* at 749.

21. *Id.* at 789.

22. United States v. Leon, 103 S.Ct. 3535 (1983).

23. *E.g.,* United States v. Calandra, 414 U.S. 338 (1974).

24. United States v. Williams, 622 F.2d 830 (5th Cir. 1980).

25. *E.g.,* Harlow v. Fitzgerald, 102 S.Ct. 2727 (1982).

26. Saldana v. Garza, 684 F.2d 1159, 1165 (5th Cir. 1982).

27. 372 U.S. 391, 401–402 (1963).

28. *Id.*

29. 428 U.S. 465 (1976).

30. *E.g.,* Wainwright v. Sykes, 433 U.S. 72 (1977).

31. Davis v. United States, 411 U.S. 233 (1973).

32. Wainwright v. Sykes, *supra* note 30.

33. Estelle v. Williams, 425 U.S. 501 (1976).

34. 102 S. Ct. 1558 (1982).

35. Harlow v. Fitzgerald, *supra* note 25.

36. 351 U.S. 12 (1956).

37. *Id.* at 19.

38. *See, e.g.,* Ross v. Moffitt, 417 U.S. 600 (1974). In a recent case the Court relied on equal-protection principles to deny states the right to automatically revoke probation where the probationer was too poor to pay a fine. Bearden v. Georgia, 103 S.Ct. 2064 (1983).

39. *See, e.g.,* Rizzo v. Goode, 423 U.S. 362 (1976); O'Shea v. Littleton, 414 U.S. 488 (1974); Laird v. Tatum, 408 U.S. 1 (1972); Younger v. Harris, 401 U.S. 37 (1971).

40. 423 U.S. 362 (1976).

41. 103 S.Ct. 1660 (1983).

42. *Id.* at 1668 (emphasis added).

43. United States v. Wade, 388 U.S. 218 (1967); Stovall v. Denno, 388 U.S. 293 (1967).

44. 406 U.S. 682 (1972).

45. 413 U.S. 300 (1973).

46. Johnson v. United States, 333 U.S. 10, 14 (1948).

47. 384 U.S. 436 (1966).

48. 367 U.S. 643 (1961).

49. Williams v. Florida, 399 U.S. 78 (1970).

50. Apodaca v. Oregon, 406 U.S. 404 (1972).

51. Swain v. Alabama, 380 U.S. 202 (1965).

52. Bordenkircher v. Hayes, 434 U.S. 357 (1978).

53. Burrows v. Superior Ct., 529 P.2d 590 (Cal. 1974); Commonwealth v. Richman, 458 Pa. 167 (1974); Zehrung v. State, 569 P.2d 189 (Alaska, 1977).

CRIMINAL JUSTICE: PRISON AND PENOLOGY

ALVIN J. BRONSTEIN

Alvin J. Bronstein is the executive director of the ACLU Foundation's National Prison Project, and has litigated many prisoners' rights cases throughout the country. He has written and edited articles and books on the rights of prisoners.

For almost a century, the prevailing view in our society and in our courts was that prisoners suffered a total deprivation of liberty and that their rights were nonexistent. The penitentiary inmate was considered "the slave of the state."[1] Although that particular language became a bit too raw for most judges, the concept that prisoners had no rights persisted until fifteen years ago, in what became known as the "hands off" doctrine. Conditions inside prisons were off-limits to judicial scrutiny, and a refusal to interfere with internal prison administration became the basis for a persistent and virtually uniform refusal to enforce barely any constitutional rights for prisoners.

As a natural outgrowth of the post–World War II civil rights and civil liberties movements, and aided by the public awareness that resulted from the explosion at Attica in 1971, judicial attitudes began to move away drastically from the notion of de facto rightlessness that had been almost universally accepted for prisoners. Although the principle prevailed that a prisoner's rights and civil liberties were diminished to some extent by virtue of incarceration, it was recognized that "there is no iron curtain drawn between the Constitution and the prisons of this country."[2] Thus, for almost ten years, the courts carefully examined what went on behind the curtain, and set limits on the government's curtailment of the rights and civil liberties of prisoners. In addition to a series of decisions protecting the civil liberties of prisoners in narrow single-issue cases, such as disciplinary due process and the right to uncensored communication with the outside world, by the early part of this decade there were thirty states in which the entire state prison system, or one or more major prisons in the state, were operating under a federal court order because of a finding that the totality of conditions in that system or prison constituted cruel and unusual punishment.

Experienced observers acknowledged the important role of the courts. Prof. James Jacobs wrote that "Prison litigation may be the peaceful equivalent of a riot in bringing prisoners' grievances to public attention and in mobilizing political support for change."[3] Federal Bureau of Prisons Director Norman Carlson said that "the federal judiciary as a whole is the most effective force for constructive change in prisons."[4] According to Allen Breed, director of the National Institute of Corrections, "the role of the courts over the past fifteen years in acting as a catalyst for much needed change in our nation's prisons cannot be overemphasized."[5]

However, beginning in the last half of the 1970s, the Burger-Rehnquist Court has moved us, though not full circle back to the slave-of-the-state era, two-thirds of the way back. In what is best characterized by Justice Rehnquist's callous comment that "nobody promised them a rose garden,"[6] a majority of the Supreme Court has seen as its principal role the halting of the doctrinal expannsion of prisoners' rights law. In a series of cases beginning in 1976, we began to see a return to the "hands off" doctrine with language about "a wide spectrum of discretionary actions that traditionally have been the business of prison administrators rather than federal courts,"[7] and to the effect that "the day-to-day functioning of state prisons" involves "issues and discretionary decisions that are not the business of federal judges."[8] In *Rhodes v. Chapman*, the first case in which the Supreme Court considered the limitations that the Eighth Amendment imposes upon the conditions in which a state may confine prisoners, the Court discussed the deference that should be given to prison administrators. It added that "to the extent that such conditions are restrictive and even harsh, they are part of the penalty that criminals pay for their offenses against society."[9] And one federal court of appeals judge has recently said that "the *Rhodes* opinion, in my view, is a clear signal that the federal judiciary should, absent inaction by state courts, legislatures and executive officials where dire circumstances exist in a state penal system, practice a hands-off policy."[10]

THE END OF JUDICIAL HANDS-OFF

The courts first began to look behind the iron curtain of prison secrecy in the late 1960s and, continuing on through the 1970s, set out various limitations upon historic intrusions into the civil liberties of prisoners. Prisoners were afforded the right to some procedural due process in disciplinary proceedings, parole hearings, and before they could be transferred to harsher conditions. Corporal punishment was abolished and restrictions were imposed upon the length and conditions of solitary confinement. The right to correspond with lawyers, courts, and government officials, and to be free from arbitrary censorship of mail and publications, was established. Prison officials were required to insure that prisoners had meaningful access to the courts. Restrictions on the free exercise of religion, particularly for nontraditional religions, were enjoined and racial discrimination was prohibited de jure, if not de facto. Prisoners were protected in their right to express political beliefs and to engage in limited forms of political activity. A limited right to privacy and to freedom in personal appearance was established. The right to be free from deliberate indifference to serious medical needs and to be protected from harm was made clear.[11]

In 1975, a federal court in Alabama added a new dimension to the scrutiny of prison conditions and practices by examining every aspect of prison life in the entire state prison system. After looking at overcrowding, environmental conditions, idleness, levels of violence, staffing, classification, medical and mental health care, and restrictions on visitation, the court found that the totality of conditions violated the Eighth Amendment's prohibition against cruel and unusual punishment and that the "prison conditions are so debilitating that they necessarily deprive inmates of any opportunity to rehabilitate themselves or even maintain skills already possessed."[12] This statement was one of the first clear recognitions that prisons make those confined within their walls worse off than when they arrived.

The court then ordered the state of Alabama to comply with various "minimum constitutional standards." Among other things, it required the state to reduce its prison population to the designed capacity of each institution (a reduction of 42 percent); to provide each prisoner with a minimum of sixty square feet of living space; to provide each prisoner with a meaningful job, the opportunity to participate in recreational, educational, vocational training, and prerelease transition programs; to provide each prisoner with certain minimum personal articles, such as linens, toilet articles, and reading and writing materials, as well as hot and cold water; to provide necessary medical and mental-health care according to certain published standards; to provide minimum staff in various specific locations, at all times, to prevent violence; and to provide certain minimum food, public health, correspondence, visitation, and other physical standards.

In addition, the court set forth a timetable for bringing each of the major institutions into compliance with the standards; a plan for the hiring of appropriately trained and educated staff, whose racial and cultural background was more similar to those of the prisoners; and a plan for the reclassification of all Alabama prisoners to identify those for whom transfer to community-based facilities would be appropriate, ordering the state to establish those facilities.

Finally, the Alabama court said that inadequate funding or claimed lack of resources was no answer to the existence of unconstitutional conditions, and warned that failure to comply with the minimum standards would necessitate the closing of those "several prison facilities herein found to be unfit for human confinement."[13]

A number of other courts followed this lead, and, by the early 1980s, 60 percent of the states had similar court orders dealing with their entire system or one or more major prisons. However, even those rights that are guaranteed by the courts are often illusory for many prisoners. Litigation is costly and time-consuming, and implementation and enforcement of these rights rest primarily in the hands of prison officials, who often resist change. Like most bureaucrats, they prefer the status quo and, more recently, the political climate has made it increasingly difficult for them to obtain the resources needed to accomplish meaningful change.

A CASE STUDY OF FRUSTRATION AND REFORM

In some states, the years of prisoner frustrations combined with political shenanigans resulted in tragic human and economic costs. In 1978, the

National Prison Project of the American Civil Liberties Union Foundation joined with local counsel in a case challenging the totality of conditions at the New Mexico State Penitentiary in Santa Fe. Although the New Mexico attorney general attempted to negotiate a meaningful settlement of the case, he and the attorneys for the prisoners were hampered by a reluctant governor and state legislature. The federal judge assigned to the case, who had been active in state politics, appeared less than anxious to move the case along. In February 1980, after almost two years of little progress in the lawsuit, the prison exploded in a horrendous riot, which resulted in the deaths of thirty-three prisoners.

In a report mandated by an emergency statute passed by the state legislature, the attorney general of New Mexico wrote:

> Throughout its history, the Penitentiary of New Mexico has suffered from neglect. The New Mexico prison has always waited at the end of the line for public money, and elected officials have turned their attention to the ugly problems of the penitentiary only when the institution has erupted in violence and destruction. Lack of space, inadequate programs, and understaffing have all been part of the prison's tradition. . . . The penitentiary can be repaired and even a bureaucracy can be repaired. But the men who, day by day for year after year, have to look over their shoulder for the man with the knife, who lack enough opportunity to make decisions in their daily lives that they forget how to decide—these men cannot be repaired. They are forever broken by a system designed to correct them.[14]

In July 1980, motivated by the national publicity resulting from the riot and spurred by the state attorney general, a comprehensive agreement settling the lawsuit was entered into by state officials and incorporated in a consent decree. The attorney general stated:

> Corrections officials were influential in getting the state to agree to a series of reforms, including population ceilings, uniform disciplinary procedures, basic services and personnel levels. Other corrective actions guaranteed by the consent decree included redefinition of all offenses; elimination of vague "catch all" offenses, such as "disruptive conduct"; limitation of punishment; provision for 8 hours of meaningful daily activity for inmates and the implementation of a classification system that will insure proper program participation and housing assignments.[15]

However, by the spring of 1981, it became clear that the governor, the legislature, and the state corrections officials were not interested in seriously complying with the provisions of the settlement and consent decree. The attorney general refused to represent state officials any further because of his perception that they were unwilling to comply with the consent decree, and for the next year very little progress was made. In early 1982, while engaging in preparation for a trial at which the issue of noncompliance was to be heard, the attorneys for the prisoners discovered that the federal judge had received *ex parte* communications about some of the matters in controversy from a friend who was an employee of the defendant prison officials. A recusal motion was filed, and after a trial before a federal judge from another state appointed by the United States Court of Appeals, the court decided that the judge's impartiality could reasonably be questioned and ordered the case transferred to another judge.

In the fall of 1982, a new governor and a host of other state officials were elected and, together with the presence of a judge who made it clear that he would hear and decide the case expeditiously, led the state to enter a new agreement in the spring of 1983. This agreement also resulted in the appointment of a special master to monitor and oversee compliance with the settlement. It has been apparent in this case that politics often has more to do with the results of prison litigation than the Constitution.

THE PROBLEM OF OVERPOPULATION

During a period when there have been fewer resources available as a result of the financial problems of government at every level, we have experienced a phenomenal growth in our federal, state, and local prison and jail population. On December 31, 1982, there were almost forty-three thousand more inmates under the jurisdiction of state and federal prisons than the year before, the largest one-year increase in history. This 11.6 percent increase brought the nation's prison population to 412,303. When added to the 1981 record 12.5 percent growth, it caps a remarkable surge in imprisonment in the past decade. From 1972 to 1982, the nation as a whole has more than doubled its prison population. The nation's local jail population, at 210,000 as of June 30, 1982, has risen as fast as the prison population over the past four years.[16]

The magnitude and strength of the population boom has defied attempts to explain it, but most experts agree that one significant factor is the hardening of public attitudes. Demographics and the movement towards mandatory and longer sentences have certainly had an impact, but of greater significance is the fact that we have become a very punitive society. There is a sense of futility and despair in the country and it is appealing to turn to the Ronald Reagan level of solutions, rewarding and punishing individuals, rather than looking at underlying causes and wider social reform. In addition, the public is being pandered to and lied to and fed enormous portions of rhetoric instead of some insight into reality. Without serious challenge, public officials at every level of government are telling us that more imprisonment for longer periods of time will impact crime rates and make our streets safe. In a country that already has the highest rate of incarceration in the world, with the exception of the Soviet Union and South Africa, maintaining those myths is a pervasive threat to civil liberties.

Perhaps in response to the get-tough attitudes of the public, and certainly contributing to it, a majority of the Supreme Court has halted the trend of careful protections for the civil liberties of prisoners and has, in a number of areas, actually cut back on the protections ordered by most lower federal courts.

CONDITIONS OF CONFINEMENT

Prior to 1976, the lower federal courts were unanimous in holding that a change in the conditions of confinement, such as transfer, that has a substantial adverse impact on the prisoner involved was sufficient to invoke the protection of the Due Process Clause of the Fourteenth Amendment. The Supreme Court, however, in *Meachum v. Fano*, [17] held that it was the nature of the interest involved rather than its weight which determined whether the Due Process Clause was implicated. The Court went on to say that there was no independent liberty interest that flowed from the Constitution, and no matter how grievous the loss resulting from changed conditions, the protections of the Due Process Clause could not be invoked unless the state first created a liberty interest by law or policy. Prison officials were therefore free to transfer prisoners anywhere for any reason or for no reason.

Then in a First Amendment case, *Jones v. North Carolina Prisoners' Labor Union,* [18] the Court held that the burden was on the prisoner plaintiffs to disprove the speculative predictions by prison officials that recognizing prisoner First Amendment claims will lead to impairment of security. Justice Rehnquist made deference to prison administrators a virtual principle of decision. Standing traditional First Amendment law on its head, he wrote that "The District Court, we believe, got off on the wrong foot in this case by not giving appropriate deference to the decisions of prison administrators and appropriate recognition to the peculiar and restrictive circumstances of penal confinement."[19]

Because even the most conservative judges would not baldly go back to the slave-of-the-state concept and must concede that the Constitution does protect prisoners in certain gross situations,[20] merely shifting the burden of proof was not enough. What they needed, in a sense, was a substantive equivalent of *Jones* which would make difficult, or even preclude, a factual showing by prisoner litigants of the real harm of prison conditions.[21]

It was not unexpected, then, that the first jail-conditions case taken by the Supreme Court came from a modern federal facility. As a new facility, it was completely atypical of the sort of jail in which conditions suits are ordinarily brought. Moreover, the courts tend, with some reason, to think of federal facilities as generally benefiting from more enlightened administration than most state or local institutions.[22] Thus, in *Bell v. Wolfish,* [23] the Supreme Court was setting standards for all conditions cases in an institution that did not reflect the physical reality of the overwhelming majority of jails in the nation. Similarly, the Court, in *Bell,* in a decision also written by Justice Rehnquist,. endorsed an artificial distinction between constitutional minimum standards and actual practice. When, for example, Justice Rehnquist upheld visual body-cavity searches, he did so while explicitly ignoring the district court's findings that the searches had been conducted in an abusive manner and that such abuses were predictable.[24] While in his discussion of double-celling, the placing of two prisoners in a cell designed for one, he stressed the atypical amenities present in the facility, in the case of body-cavity strip searches he ignored the actual record made by the prisoner plaintiffs in order to uphold the defendants' policies. In a startling departure from the reasoning of all the lower courts with respect to the rights of pretrial detainees, Justice Rehnquist stated that "The presumption of innocence is a doctrine that allocates the burden of proof in criminal trials"; but "it has no application to a determination of the rights of a pretrial detainee during confinement before his trial has even begun."[25]

Although the *Wolfish* court had found double-celling constitutionally permissible under the unusual circumstances of the case, the burgeoning prison populations continued to lead to additional court orders enjoining double-celling. When the Supreme Court next considered double-celling, in a prison rather than jail conditions case, it again granted review in an unusual case. The state prison at Lucasville, Ohio, was one of only a handful of maximum-security prisons constructed in the 1970s. Most of the trial court's factual findings were favorable to the prison officials and the judge's ultimate decision enjoining double-celling was heavily linked to generalized expert testimony regarding the negative impact of overcrowding.

When the Supreme Court did hand down its decision in *Rhodes v. Chapman*, [26] it reluctantly endorsed specific decisions of lower courts that had granted relief in grossly unconstitutional totality-of-conditions cases, but reversed the lower court in this case by focusing on the trial court's failure to find specific harms at the prison resulting from the overcrowding and by rejecting that court's reliance on generalized expert opinion. By limiting the use of expert witnesses, the Court was able to continue to articulate a concern for minimum constitutional standards in prisons while making it much more difficult for prisoners to show that these standards had been violated. In short, *Rhodes* was a sort of substantive equivalent in the law for the procedural burden placed upon prisoner plaintiffs in *Jones*. The Supreme Court raised the ante in prison litigation by requiring proof directly related to harm from overcrowding at the particular institution in question.

But *Rhodes* also raises as many questions as it answers. One can view with a certain amount of skepticism the Court's characterization of Lucasville as an essentially benign institution. The prisoner plaintiffs in the trial court had attempted unsuccessfully to broaden the case from a simple overcrowding suit to raise other totality-of-conditions claims. Had they been able to do so, it is possible that the judge's ultimate findings would have presented the institution in a different manner. Justice Marshall's dissent argues that the majority had misread some of the trial court's findings to make them appear more favorable to the defendants.[27] Moreover, one cannot keep from believing that the evidence of harm in Lucasville was there but that for some reason, possibly because of overconfident reliance on the generalized expert testimony, the plaintiffs did not present it.

Still, *Rhodes* presents a number of critical issues for the future development of the civil liberties of prisoners in the courts. To what extent has the Court created special standards for the receipt of expert testimony that do not apply in other areas of the law? Where there is a scientific body of evidence about, for example, the public health effects of overcrowding of a quality that would be accepted in other contexts, must each plaintiff in an overcrowding case nonetheless prove that the predicted impact on communicable diseases and stress-related diseases has in fact occurred at the institution in question, possibly with an appropriately controlled study? Will lower courts really require proof that serious injury has occurred to identifiable individuals rather than proof that conditions make the probability of serious harm overwhelming?

Beyond these questions, however, is the general impact on litigation strategy of *Rhodes*. Just as we suspect that there really was evidence of concrete harm in Lucasville, the general importance of *Rhodes* is that cases will be lost because the plaintiffs lack the resources to find and prove the harm. In short, it is likely that cases will succeed or fail not on the basis of how unconstitutional the conditions are, but on the basis of how resourceful the lawyers and experts are. There are few relatively well-financed and -staffed prisoners' rights offices, and they will have to play an even more important role in the future. Reform litigation by offices funded through the Legal Services Corporation has been severely curtailed by the Reagan administration and the efforts of the Civil Rights Division of the United States Department of Justice have been reduced to the point where they are relatively meaningless. By the summer of 1983, three years after the passage of the Civil Rights of Institutionalized Persons Act[28], the Department of Justice had filed only one case involving prison conditions under the act, and that case was dismissed shortly thereafter because of the department's failure to comply with the technical jurisdictional provisions of the Act.

CONCLUSION

What then might we look to in the future? We must devote even more of our efforts toward the goal of a uniform acceptance by all branches of government, as well as the media and the public, of the principle that prisoners must be afforded certain fundamental rights if we are to regard ourselves as a civilized society.[29] Those rights must include:

1. The right to personal safety. Large, overcrowded prisons in this country are dangerous places and a person in custody is generally helpless to protect himself. The obligation of the state to provide safe custody is imperative.

2. The right to care. Decent, clean housing, adequate diet, enough clothing, and medical care are basic needs of all citizens and they must be provided for prisoners who cannot provide for themselves.

3. The right to personal dignity. Self-respect is hard to come by in the poor and racially disadvantaged persons who fill our prisons, and a prisoner's sense of worth must not be further damaged by the humiliations of confinement.

4. The right to work. Idleness is a disease of America's prisons. A prisoner should be provided work if he wants it and he should be paid on the same basis as he would be in the free labor market. He should meet his responsibilities for housing and dependents like the rest of us.

5. The right to self-improvement. There should be a range of educational, vocational, recreational, and artistic programs available to every prisoner so that we do not perpetuate the lack of opportunity which drives so many poor people to criminality in the free world.

6. The right to vote. Electoral disability, unique to this country in the free world, protects no one and serves as

a pointless humiliation to the prisoner. Participation in the democratic process should be encouraged in the interest of making citizenship a real and vital feature of the prisoner's future life.

7. The right to a future. A person who is isolated from the outside world can hardly plan for or even conceive of a future. Existing barriers should be removed and contact with families, friends, and the general outside community should be encouraged.

We should do no less if we believe that the Bill of Rights applies to all persons, and if we expect prisoners to return to the free society as lawful and productive citizens.

The future development and recognition of the rights of prisoners depends as much on political leadership and public education as it does on the courts. The courts in this country have never been the ideal vehicle for social change, but they have been a catalyst and created the pressure for change in the other branches of government. When public policy makers begin to acknowledge that we are wasting vast amounts of scarce resources in our bankrupt corrections systems, and the public hears this message loud and clear, we may begin to see some real change.

What is needed was stated simply by Jeff Bingaman, former attorney general of New Mexico:

> Prisons simply do not deal with the basic problems of crime in our society. Prison is a dehumanizing experience, and most persons come out the worse for being in. Nearly all criminals, even under the strictest sentencing practices will return to society. Even a well managed bureaucracy, necessary to run prisons, cannot change these basic truths. . . . If New Mexico's heritage of rich and deep familial and community roots is to be realized, communities must play a part in housing, resocializing and accepting persons who have violated the community's laws. If New Mexico does not dramatically change its philosophy and practices about how to deal with criminals, there will be more tragedies and the need for more reports by Grand Juries, by Citizens' Panels, and by the Attorney General. Ultimately, there will be more bureaucracy, more waste of taxpayers' money for architects and buildings, more more crime and more human waste.[30]

The question for the United States is whether, as the richest society in history, it will take steps within its means to rectify a festering and dangerous situation in its prisons, or whether it will pay an even heavier price, sooner or later, for neglecting it.

NOTES

1. Ruffin v. Commonwealth, 62 Va. 790, 796 (1871).

2. Wolff v. McDonnell, 418 U.S. 539, 555–556 (1974).

3. James Jacobs, "The Prisoners' Rights Movement and its Impacts, 1960–80," in Norval Morris and Michael Tonry, eds., *Crime and Justice: An Annual Review of Research*, vol. 2 at 460 (1980).

4. Federal Prison System, "Monday Morning Highlights," U.S. Department of Justice, (January 31, 1983).

5. Quoted from a speech in Jacobs, note 3 *supra* at 453.

6. Atiyeh v. Capps, 449 U.S. 1312, 1315 (1981).

7. Meachum v. Fano, 427 U.S. 215, 225 (1976).

8. *Id.* at 228–229.

9. Rhodes v. Chapman, 452 U.S. 337, 347 (1981).

10. Ramos v. Lamm, 713 F.2d 546 (10th Cir. 1983) (J. Barrett, dissenting).

11. A thorough discussion of these developments, as well as case citations, may be found in the ACLU handbook D. Rudovsky, A. Bronstein & E. Koren, *The Rights of Prisoners* (1983).

12. Pugh v. Locke, 406 F.Supp. 318, 330 (M.D. Ala. 1976).

13. *Id.* at 323.

14. Report of the attorney general on the February 2 and 3, 1980, Riot at the Penitentiary of New Mexico, State of New Mexico (September 1980), prologue.

15. *Id.* at 44.

16. *Corrections Magazine*, June 1983, at 6, quoting 1982 prison census figures from the Bureau of Justice Statistics.

17. 427 U.S. 215 (1976).

18. 433 U.S. 119 (1977).

19. *Id.* at 125.

20. Hutto v. Finney, 437 U.S. 678, 711 (1978) (J. Rehnquist, dissenting).

21. Some of these thoughts on the actions and motivation of the Supreme Court were first articulated in a September, 1981, internal staff discussion paper prepared by Elizabeth Alexander, staff attorney, The National Prison Project of the ACLU Foundation.

22. *See, e.g.,* Procunier v. Martinez, 416 U.S. 396, 414–415, note 14 (1974).

23. 441 U.S. 520 (1979).

24. United States ex rel. Wolfish v. Levi, 439 F.Supp. 114 (S.D.N.Y. 1977).

25. 441 U.S. at 533.

26. 452 U.S. 337 (1981).

27. 452 U.S. at 373–374 note 6.

28. 42 U.S.C. Section 1997.

29. These rights were first enumerated as essential elements of his "citizenship model of corrections" by a distinguished penologist, John Conrad, in his chapter "Where There's Hope There's Life," in *Justice as Fairness* (1981).

30. Report of the Attorney General, note 14 at 2.

PART THREE

CHANGING
CONCEPTS IN
THE STRUGGLE
FOR RIGHTS

PRIVACY

PAUL BENDER

Paul Bender is professor of law at the University of Pennsylvania Law School. He was law clerk to Judge Learned Hand and Justice Felix Frankfurter and has served as an assistant to the solicitor general of the United States. He is active in constitutional litigation and is coauthor of Political and Civil Rights in the United States.

The word "privacy" does not appear in the Constitution. It will be found neither in the original document of 1789, the "Bill of Rights" of 1791, nor in any of the subsequent Amendments that have significantly expanded the rights of Americans.

The Constitution, however, does protect privacy to a substantial extent. Several different kinds of privacy issues are prominent in current constitutional law, in legislative discussions, and in political debates. This is more true now, perhaps, than at any other time in United States history. Moreover, although the present Supreme Court has not been noted for its strong concern for the expansion of individual liberties generally, some aspects of privacy rights constitute an important exception to that rule. Indeed, the Burger Court, unlike any of its predecessors (even the Warren Court that so productively enlarged a broad range of fundamental constitutional rights during the 1950s and 1960s) has fashioned explicit protection for a new constitutional right of privacy that has come to encompass basic marital rights, certain family, procreative, and sexual rights, and (in its most well-known and controversial application) the right of women to be free from government prohibitions upon abortion.

The explanation for this relatively warm reception of some privacy rights within the current Court may lie in the fact that these rights—unlike many of the rights toward which the Burger Court has been less generous—are "middle-class" rights. Privacy rights often hold a strong appeal for those who are relatively affluent and conventional, as well as for those who are economically and socially disadvantaged or who are members of dissident or unpopular groups. Privacy rights may also find adherents among Supreme Court Justices who are not ordinarily thought of as strongly rights-oriented. The late Justice John M. Harlan, for example, an enormously distinguished jurist but one of the most conservative members of the Warren Court, was a strong champion of certain privacy rights.[1] Chief Justice Burger, a proponent of diminished rights in some important areas, has allied himself with the Court majority in its most important abortion-rights decisions. Justice Blackmun (who, like the Chief Justice, was appointed to the Court by President Nixon) has become increasingly sensitive to individual rights concerns during his tenure on the Court: this trend may have begun with his authorship of *Roe v. Wade*,[2] the case that struck down most abortion prohibitions and firmly established the existence of a modern constitutional right to a zone of private behavior that is presumptively free from government regulation.

Privacy rights concern the basic quality of an individual's personal private life—the right to keep the details of that life confidential; the free and untrammeled use and enjoyment of one's intellect, body, and private property; the right of an individual to choose his or her own private (and perhaps unconventional) lifestyle; the right to form, shape, and maintain private associations of one's own choosing; the right, in sum, to a private personal life free from the intrusion of government or the dictates of society. The right of privacy was thus described by Justice Brandeis (another relatively conservative champion of these rights) as "the right to be let alone—the most comprehensive of rights and the right most valued by civilized men."[3] It is not at all surprising that these rights have been absorbed by the Supreme Court into the catalog of the fundamental rights of Americans despite the absence of any wholly explicit constitutional recognition.

As noted above, the right of privacy is really several different (although overlapping) rights. Modern constitutional privacy law has four main branches:

1. With impetus from a law-review article[4] coauthored by Justice Brandeis in 1890 (well before he became a member of the Supreme Court) judicial decisions and legislation during this century have given increasing protection to the right of individuals to be free from intrusions into their privacy by the news media, commercial advertisers, and others, through the publication, without consent or adequate justification, of personal

information, likenesses, names, etc. Some legislative protection has also been given against intrusions such as unsolicited mailings of unwanted material into the home, against nonconsensual house-to-house canvassing, and noisy or disruptive demonstrations or assemblies in residential areas. Since the intrusions covered by these privacy rights are generally individual rather than governmental intrusions, these rights are not generally rights that are directly constitutional in nature (constitutional rights in the United States are ordinarily applicable only as against governmental action). Constitutional rights of free speech, press, and assembly, however, are often set up in *opposition* to these legally created privacy rights, thus calling upon the courts to strike a delicate and often difficult balance between privacy concerns, on the one hand, and constitutionally protected interests in free expression, on the other.

2. The Fourth Amendment protects "[t]he right of the people to be secure in their persons, houses, papers, and effects, against unreasonable searches and seizures." It also requires that search and arrest warrants be based upon "probable cause," and it outlaws the pernicious practice of "general" warrants (one of the leading causes of the American Revolution). The Fifth Amendment supplements these privacy protections by providing that no person "shall be compelled in any criminal case to be a witness against himself." Unlike the judicially and legislatively created privacy rights described in the preceding paragraph, these constitutional provisions protect individual privacy against *governmental* intrusions, primarily by police and other law enforcement officials. These amendments stand as essential barriers against the threat of a police state.

3. The Fourth and Fifth Amendments do not protect against all forms of potentially oppressive governmental surveillance and information gathering. Although no longer limited, as they once were, to *physical* intrusions upon privacy—the Amendments, for example, now limit wiretapping and some other forms of electronic eavesdropping—the Amendments do not ordinarily regulate intrusions that cannot be characterized as formal "searches," "seizures," "arrests," or "interrogations." They give little or no protection, for example, against the maintenance and use of governmental or private data banks containing collections of personal, financial, or political information about individuals. In recent years, however, the Supreme Court has suggested that some constitutional protection may be afforded against governmental gathering and dissemination of private personal information, even when it is not the product of formal searches, seizures, or interrogations. In addition, Congress and

many states have enacted legislation that offers protection to this type of informational privacy against both governmental and private intrusions.

4. Privacy involves the right to engage in private behavior—and to make choices about that behavior—as well as the right to be free from the prying eyes and ears of the government and other individuals. For most of our history, the right to a sphere of private behavior was not separately recognized in U.S. constitutional law. Recently, however, the Supreme Court has used the Fourteenth Amendment's due-process guarantee to establish a new constitutional right that recognizes that there are areas of personal human behavior and decision making that government may regulate only upon a strong showing of society's need to interfere. This is the principle under which the Court's recent abortion rights cases have been decided; it is also responsible for decisions about the rights to marry, to procreate, to use contraceptives both within and without the marriage relationship, and to make basic decisions about family life and the upbringing of one's children.

It is not possible, within the confines of a single essay, to present detailed accounts of these four related privacy concepts.[5] What follows are summaries of the history and content of the leading principles in each area, and how they have fared during the tenure of the Burger Court.

PRIVACY VERSUS FREE EXPRESSION

Common law principles and state legislation sometimes permit individuals to sue book publishers, newspapers, magazines, radio and television stations, commercial advertisers, etc., on the ground that the publication of personal information—or of the plaintiff's name, picture, or likeness—constitutes a wrongful invasion of privacy causing distress, embarrassment, or financial loss. These actions resemble actions for defamation. They are different from defamation suits, however, in that privacy actions often ask damages for the publication of *true* statements, representations, or information, whereas actionable defamation requires that the defendant's statement be false as well as defamatory.

Very few cases involving privacy actions for the publication of truthful information have reached the Supreme Court of the United States. When they have, they have raised enormously difficult issues regarding whether individual privacy concerns can ever justify relief against truthful publications and, if so, under what circumstances such relief is permissible. The Court has not yet resolved many of the basic questions in this area.

The first invasion of privacy v. free expression case to be decided by the Supreme Court arose when the Court had just begun to impose significant constitutional limitations upon defamation laws. (Prior to this time defamation had been considered to be wholly "outside" the First Amendment, so that states were free to give defamation recovery without regard to constitutional limits.) In this 1967 case *(Time, Inc. v. Hill)*[6] the Court appeared to be quite protective of the press when it invades privacy interests. It held that if the publication challenged as an invasion of privacy concerns a matter of public interest, the defendant cannot be required to pay damages unless the publication was made "maliciously." This rule was identical to that which the Court had recently adopted to govern defamation actions based on publications about matters of public interest.[7]

The *Hill* case involved a publication that was false in substantial respects. Plaintiff Hill and his family had been held hostage in their home for nineteen hours by three escaped convicts, two of whom were killed when apprehended by the police. The Hills were released unharmed and had suffered no abuse by the convicts. The incident, however, was front-page news. After the incident, the Hill family moved and attempted to keep completely out of the public eye. A book based on the incident was published a year after the Hills' home was invaded. This fictionalized account, called *The Desperate Hours,* had its victims suffer violence and verbal abuse at the hands of the convicts. Two years later, *The Desperate Hours* was turned into a Broadway play. The dispute involved a review of the play, in which *Life* magazine asserted that the incidents in the play were true, linked them by name with the Hills, and photographed the actors in the Hills' former house while they reenacted some of the play's violent episodes. It appeared that if the Court were willing to give strong protection to the press in this false-light situation, it would likely be at least as protective when the publication of *true* reports was challenged as an invasion of privacy. On the other hand, the *Hill* case involved a publication about a matter that had independently generated considerable public interest. It was not at all clear what attitude the Court would take toward the publication of private information that was not newsworthy in that sense.

Seven years after the *Hill* case was decided by the Supreme Court, the Court cut back substantially on the protection provided for the press in "public interest" defamation cases. The rule requiring a showing of malice in order to obtain recovery was limited to cases where the plaintiff was a public official or a public figure—mere public interest in the subject matter would no longer suffice. At the same time, however, the Court held for the first time that, where private citizens sue for defamation, the First Amendment prohibits recovery unless the plaintiff demonstrates both actual injury and fault on the part of the defendant publisher. The Court also strongly suggested that falsity is a constitutionally necessary element in defamation cases.[8]

This 1974 decision left the constitutional status of invasion-of-privacy actions completely at sea. In view of the Court's emphasis on falsity as an element of recovery, could true statements revealing embarrassing or damaging personal information ever be subject to liability? If the fault and actual injury requirements were to apply to such actions, what would "fault" and "injury" mean in the context of invasion-of-privacy actions? If "newsworthy" private information were to be constitutionally protected, how would that concept be defined (especially in view of the fact that newsworthiness often seems a somewhat self-fulfilling concept— events or information may seem "newsworthy" largely because they are in fact given prominent exposure in the media)?

The Supreme Court has so far given few indications of the answers to these questions. In 1975, in a case arising in Georgia, the Court held that the state had violated the First Amendment in awarding damages to the father of a seventeen-year-old victim of a rape-murder who sued a television station for broadcasting the name of his daughter.[9] It was a crime under Georgia law to publish or broadcast the name of a rape victim. In reversing the damage award, the Supreme Court relied heavily on the fact that, despite the Georgia criminal statute, the victim's name was in fact contained in official court records open to the public. It is not clear what the result would have been if the state had endeavored to keep the victim's name completely confidential. A similar result was reached two years later when an Oklahoma court sought to prohibit the publication of the name and picture of an eleven-year-old boy charged with murder in delinquency proceedings. The Supreme Court held the prohibition unconstitutional because defendant's reporter had learned the name of the boy at the delinquency proceedings (to which the reporter had been admitted in apparent violation of applicable confidentiality rules) and because the picture had been taken in a public place after the hearing.[10]

These cases suggest continued protection for the press in some invasion-of-privacy situations. At the same time, however, the Court has recently made it easier for private citizens to recover from the media for published defamatory statements by narrowly construing the concepts of who is a public official or public figure.[11] The same approach in the privacy area might lead to a relatively narrow concept of "newsworthy" private information that the press would be privileged to publish.

The Court has recently been sensitive to privacy-related concerns in some other areas of alleged commercial or media intrusion. In 1970, for example, it upheld the constitutionality of a federal statute giving U.S. mail recipients the right to have their names removed from a mailing list if they receive unsolicited mail that they deem to be erotically arousing or sexually provocative. Chief Justice Burger's opinion for the Court rejected the argument "that a vendor has a right . . . to send unwanted material into the home of another. . . . The asserted right of a mailer . . . stops at the outer boundary of every person's domain."[12] Municipal restrictions on house-to-house solicitations are another area of Supreme Court ambivalence. Although the Court often invalidates such restrictions because it finds their particular terms unconstitutionally vague or overbroad,[13] it continues to emphasize the legitimacy and substantiality of local efforts to protect the public from undue annoyance through such intrusions.[14] This is an area where the Court seems genuinely torn between two powerful competing considerations of fundamental constitutional dimension.

POLICE INTRUSIONS UPON PRIVACY

This subject is covered in detail elsewhere in this book.[15] A few words are appropriate here, however, because of the close relationship between this aspect of constitutionally protected privacy and the other subjects treated in this essay. In applying the safeguards of the Fourth and Fifth Amendments the Supreme Court has often expressly emphasized the relationship of these Amendments to general privacy interests. For example, when the Court first held in 1967 that police wiretapping constituted a search subject to the provisions of the Fourth Amendment, it did so on the basis that such electronic eavesdropping was violative of "the privacy upon which [the petitioner] justifiably relied."[16] As Justice Thurgood Marshall subsequently observed in 1973, the Fourth and Fifth Amendments "[b]oth involve aspects of a person's right to develop for himself a sphere of personal privacy."[17]

When they originally became part of the Constitution in 1791, the Fourth and Fifth Amendments, like the Bill of Rights generally, applied only to searches, seizures, arrests, and interrogations conducted by agents of the *federal* government;[18] protection from these intrusions by state and local officials depended upon provisions contained in state constitutions and legislation. The adoption of the Fourteenth Amendment in 1868 led to a dramatic change in this constitutional situation. The Fourteenth Amendment for the first time constitutionally prohibited states and localities, as well as the federal government, from depriving individuals of life, liberty, or property without "due process of law."

During the early part of the twentieth century, the Supreme Court began a process of selectively incorporating some of the most fundamental Fourth and Fifth Amendment privacy protections into the due-process concept. As a result, individual privacy began to be protected to some extent against state and local police as a matter of federal constitutional law. This incorporation process was completed during the Warren Court era, when the Court held that all—not just the "core"[19]—of the Bill of Rights protections against police searches, arrests, and coercive interrogations were fully incorporated into the Fourteenth Amendment.[20] The Warren Court also held that the "exclusionary rule"—a constitutionally based evidentiary rule that prohibits the use of unconstitutionally seized evidence to prove guilt in a criminal case—was applicable against the states.[21] The Warren Court further imposed protective interrogation procedures—the so-called *Miranda* warnings—upon federal, state, and local police, and it fashioned an exclusionary rule against the use of statements and confessions taken without the required warnings.[22]

The Burger Court has had a largely negative record in enforcing the constitutional rules governing police when they invade individual privacy through searches, seizures, wiretapping, arrests, and interrogations. On the positive side, the Court has buttressed the constitutional warrant requirement by holding, for the first time, that police must have a warrant to make a felony arrest within a suspect's home[23] (felony arrests had previously been permitted without warrants in the home as well as on the street). The Court has also required warrants for the search of a person's luggage.[24] On the negative side, the Court has, among other things, broadened the power of police to make personal searches and to enter premises after making lawful arrests,[25] loosened the constitutional probable-cause standard that must be met when police obtain a warrant based upon an informant's tip,[26] permitted felony arrests to take place on the street without a warrant even when there was time to secure one,[27] held that warrants are generally not required for the search of automobiles and their contents,[28] made it relatively easy for police to demonstrate voluntary consent for a search made without a warrant,[29] and expanded police power to "stop and frisk" suspects and their possessions in the absence of probable cause.[30] While the Court has not changed the basic elements of the important 1967 Warren Court ruling that electronic surveillance and wiretapping constitute searches subject to Fourth Amendment restrictions,[31] it has made a potentially dangerous exception to this principle by holding that an undercover agent may secretly record a conversation between the agent and an unsuspecting accused.[32] As a whole, the substantive protections against police searches have been seriously eroded in recent years.

The Burger Court's most important inroads into previously established constitutional principles protecting individual privacy against unreasonable police intrusions, however, have come in the area of the *remedies* available for these violations. As noted previously, the Warren Court had found it necessary to adopt an exclusionary rule preventing the prosecution from using unconstitutionally seized evidence to prove guilt. Without such an exclusionary rule, that Court believed, the constitutional limits imposed by the Fourth and Fifth Amendments were often merely a paper tiger. Police are rarely prosecuted for engaging in unconstitutional searches and interrogations (especially when the suspect is convicted) and private damage actions have also generally proved to be an inadequate method of controlling police misbehavior. In the absence of an exclusionary rule police often have little incentive not to engage in unconstitutional investigative techniques, and often have much to gain from such violations. As this is written, the Burger Court has not yet overruled or substantially modified the exclusionary rule as such. Several members of the Court, however, have openly expressed dissatisfaction with the rule, and the Court currently has under consideration a modification of the rule that would make it inapplicable whenever a police officer's violation of the Constitution was committed in "good faith."[33] The Burger Court has already seriously eroded the exclusionary rule's practical impact by strictly limiting its availability in federal habeas corpus proceedings.[34] As a result, implementation of the rule is now largely left to the state courts, some of which have been notoriously insensitive to established constitutional principles in this area. The Court has also closely limited the situations in which individuals have constitutional standing in any court to invoke the exclusionary rule against evidence sought to be used against them.[35]

In recent years the Supreme Court has often appeared to be on the brink of returning to the pre–Warren Court era when police intrusions into individual privacy went largely unregulated by the federal judiciary. Although this has not yet happened, the threat remains, and it is a threat made ominously credible by the fact that the recent Nixon and Reagan appointees to the Court have, by and large, been those most outspoken in their criticism of alleged excessive federal court intrusion into state and local criminal law enforcement processes. In considering the possible effects of a return to a judicial hands-off attitude in this area, it is important to remember that the privacy rights involved are not just those of criminals. Police often arrest, search, wiretap, and interrogate people who are completely innocent. If police feel increased freedom to engage in intrusive investigative behavior without having constitutionally adequate cause to do so, the innocent as well as the guilty will be the victims. Police may, in addition, find themselves able to use these techniques as instruments of oppressive harassment against political dissidents and other unpopular or powerless groups.

INFORMATIONAL PRIVACY

Although the Fourth and Fifth Amendments contain broad and important protections against intrusions upon individual privacy, these constitutional provisions do not nearly satisfy the full range of concern about the ability of individuals to protect themselves from being overheard or spied upon. Nor do they fully protect against the threat that government, private organizations, or individuals may maintain comprehensive dossiers or data banks containing personal information that the individual legitimately wishes to keep private and confidential. The Fourth Amendment, for example, is not an absolute barrier to governmental searches, seizures, or arrests. It merely requires that government officials have probable cause for such activities, and that they obtain proper warrants in certain circumstances. If these requirements are met, the Amendment does not safeguard information thus obtained from retention, disclosure, or use by the government.

Nor does every governmental information-gathering technique amount to a "search" cognizable under the Amendment. Thus, while wiretapping and other nontrespassory forms of electronic eavesdropping are now considered to be Fourth Amendment searches, the Court has nevertheless permitted government to utilize secret or undercover agents and informers who gain access to individual privacy by pretending to be friends, associates, customers, salespersons, maintenance personnel, etc. These undisclosed agents and informants are also permitted to carry and use concealed electronic recording or transmitting devices.[36] In these situations, the Court has appeared to adopt the theory that the subject of the surveillance "consented" to communicate with the informant, even though he or she was unaware both of the agent's true identity or allegiance and of the fact that the agent may have carried a concealed electronic device.

In addition, the Fourth and Fifth Amendments appear to place no obstacle whatever in the way of government agents who wish to compile and maintain information about individuals through presence by agents at public meetings (for the purpose of identifying and maintaining lists of those who attend); through surveillance, eavesdropping, or photography in public places or through comprehensive scrutiny of public or government records and media reports in order to discover personal information.[37] The Fourth and Fifth Amendments, moreover, apply only to *governmental* surveillance; these constitutional protections have no application to private spying or to private disclosure of credit information, private educational or medical records, or the like.

In the last ten years the Supreme Court has, on two occasions, strongly suggested (without, however, formally deciding) that the Constitution may provide protection against comprehensive governmental information-gathering techniques that do not violate the Fourth or Fifth Amendments. In a 1974 case[38] the Court upheld the constitutionality of several provisions of the federal Bank Secrecy Act of 1970, an act which, despite its title, requires banks to maintain records of the identity of their customers, to make microfilm copies of checks, to keep records of other account items, and to report large transactions to the government. Justices Douglas, Brennan, and Marshall dissented in this case on Fourth Amendment grounds. Of primary importance here, however, is Justice Powell's concurring opinion, joined in by Justice Blackmun. These two Justices agreed with the majority that the portions of the act considered by the Court did not violate the Constitution, but they rested this view on the fact that the act's reporting requirements, as limited by the applicable regulations, applied only to transactions of greater than $10,000. They then explicitly noted that an extension of these reporting requirements would pose "substantial and difficult constitutional questions. . . . In their full reach, the reports apparently authorized by the open-ended language of the act touch upon intimate areas of an individual's personal affairs. Financial transactions can reveal much about a person's activities, associations and beliefs. At some point, governmental intrusion upon these areas would implicate legitimate expectations of privacy." When added to the three dissenting votes, this concurrence holds some promise for the future development of important informational-privacy rights.

Another case of this sort was decided by the Court in 1977.[39] A New York statute required the recording, in a centralized government computer file, of the names and addresses of all persons who use doctors' prescriptions to obtain regulated drugs (such as opium, cocaine, methadone, and amphetamines) for which there is both a lawful and an unlawful market. The statute was attacked on its face by doctors who prescribed and patients who used the drugs in question. Although Justice Stevens's opinion for the Court rejected this attack, it did so on the assumption that the administration of the statute (which it held to be "a considered attempt" to deal with an important problem) would not pose an unwarranted danger for privacy interests: "We are not unaware of the threat to privacy implicit in the accumulation of vast amounts of personal information in computerized data banks and other massive government files. . . . The right to collect and use such data for public purposes is typically accompanied by a concomitant statutory or regulatory duty to avoid unwarranted disclosures. . . . We therefore need not, and do not, decide any question which might be presented by the unwarranted disclosure of accumulated private data—whether intentional or unintentional—or by a system that did not contain comparable security provisions."[40]

A disturbing (one is tempted to say outrageous) case which looks in the opposite direction was decided by the Supreme Court in 1976.[41] Police in Louisville, Kentucky, distributed a "flier" to local retailers. This document was captioned "Active Shoplifters" and it contained the names and photographs of persons who had been arrested for—but not necessarily convicted of—shoplifting. Plaintiff, who had been arrested for shoplifting but who had had the charges against him dismissed, objected to the inclusion of his name and picture in the flier. Justice Rehnquist's opinion for the Court (there were three dissents) rejected this suit in language that seemed to ignore the relevance of important informational-privacy rights suggested in other cases. Although the opinion admitted that "the Court has recognized that 'zones of privacy' may . . . impose limits on government power," it said that these limits "deal generally with substantive aspects of the Fourteenth Amendment." Plaintiff's claim, however, "is based, not upon any challenge to the State's ability to restrict his freedom of action in a sphere contended to be 'private,' but instead on a claim that the State may not publicize a record of an official act such as an arrest. None of our substantive privacy decisions hold this or anything like this, and we decline to enlarge them in this manner."

While the constitutional situation thus remains clouded and uncertain, the U.S. Congress has been unusually active during the past decade in seeking to protect individuals' informational privacy interests against both governmental and private intrusions. The federal Privacy Act of 1974[42] was enacted "to promote governmental respect for the privacy of citizens by requiring all departments and agencies of the executive branch and their employees to observe certain constitutional rules in the computerization, collection, management, use and disclosure of personal information about individuals."[43] The act requires federal agencies to publicize the nature of all data banks and information-gathering systems that they maintain; to collect only "relevant," timely, and accurate data; to observe certain information-gathering procedures, such as insuring informed consent; and to make all records concerning individuals available to them so as to allow individuals to correct or delete improper or inaccurate material from those records. The act also prohibits the disclosure of information without the prior written consent of the individual concerned except in specified situations (such as intra-agency disclosure, disclosure to Congress, disclosure pursuant to court order and disclosures required by the Freedom of Information Act) and creates administrative and judicial remedies for violations of the act's provisions. However, certain agency records may be exempted from the coverage of the act, thus impinging upon its effectiveness to some extent. Agencies may thus promulgate rules exempting CIA records, criminal law enforcement files, statistical records, and information derived from confidential sources.

Congress has also been active in several more specific areas that involve private as well as governmental record keeping. The so-called Buckley Amendment to the federal Elementary and Secondary School Act of 1974[44] conditions federal funds for education upon a requirement that schools afford parents the right to inspect official school records relating to their children. These records include academic records, intelligence and psychological test scores, health data, family background information, teacher and counselor ratings, and reports of behavior patterns. Parents may challenge and seek to correct the contents of these records. Student information from school files may not be released without parental consent except to school officials, schools to which the student is applying for enrollment, or certain government agencies. For students over eighteen, the rights otherwise granted to parents are given to the students themselves.

Somewhat similar regulations on consumer credit reports are contained in the federal Fair Credit Reporting Act of 1970.[45] Title III of the Omnibus Crime Control and Safe Streets Act of 1968 contains limits on state, federal, and private wiretapping, eavesdropping, "bugging," and other interceptions of oral and electronic communications.[46] The Federal Law Enforcement Assistance Administration has issued regulations protecting the privacy of certain criminal justice records.[47] The federal Freedom of Information Act[48] excludes from the information required to be made public by that act "personnel and medical files and similar files" and law-enforcement files "the disclosure of which would constitute a clearly unwarranted invasion of personal privacy." The Tax Reform Act of 1976[49] provides, with some exceptions, that tax returns and other personal information submitted to or collected by the Internal Revenue Service may not be revealed to anyone outside the IRS without the individual's authorization. And the federal Right to Financial Privacy Act of 1978[50] imposes limits upon a number of the informational-privacy violations authorized by the 1970 Bank Secrecy Act that had previously been upheld by the Supreme Court. A number of states have enacted legislation similar to, or even broader than, these federal provisions.[51]

In *1984*, George Orwell described a terrifying future society in which an omnipresent government destroys all sense of individual autonomy and personality by comprehensive invasions of informational privacy interests carried on through constant surveillance of and retention of data about almost all aspects of individual private behavior. As 1984 arrives, the technology for such surveillance does indeed exist. Information about almost everything we do (and perhaps about many things we think) can be surreptitiously gathered through a frightening array of undetectable electronic devices; this information can be digested, retained, and marshaled by computers of vast capacity and decreasing size and cost.

Current legislation (and, to some extent, current constitutional doctrine) seeks in principle to impose some limits upon the oppressive use of this technology. Whether such legal limits are meaningfully enforceable by private citizens, however, is an unanswered question. The often secret nature of particular invasions of informational privacy interests makes enforcement of limits through law especially problematic. Moreover, as the potential threat to informational privacy interests increases, the Supreme Court seems less (rather than more) concerned about the development and maintenance of prophylactic and other rules that might contribute to effective enforcement. Nor, as noted above, do we presently have a coherent and firmly established set of constitutional principles protecting informational privacy interests as such. Rather, we are required to depend in large part upon constitutional doctrines developed when current technology was either non-existent or at a very primitive stage of development. Meaningful protection of informational privacy rights at present thus largely depends upon the good faith and vigilance (and perhaps the limited resources) of governmental and private agencies and organizations that otherwise have the full range of modern technology at their disposal. The threat of Orwell's *1984* remains quite real.

SUBSTANTIVE PRIVACY

The three branches of constitutionally related privacy discussed above primarily have to do with an individual's right to be free from intrusions directly linked to the gathering, retention, and publication of *information* about personal life and private activities. In recent years the Supreme Court has, in addition, established for the first time that there are areas of human *conduct* that government may presumptively not regulate or prohibit because of constitutional privacy concerns. These newly constitutionally protected activities are private or personal in the sense that they are, in general, of great importance to the individual's pursuit of happiness —to his or her physical, emotional, or intellectual well-being—while being of little or no legitimate concern to others. This new right of "substantive" privacy promises to become an increasingly important aspect of the fundamental individual rights of Americans.

The history of the new right is an interesting one. As noted previously, there is no direct textual support in the Constitution for the general idea that "private" activities should presumptively be free from governmental regulation or prohibition. The Supreme Court has held that the new substantive-privacy right has its doctrinal source in the Due Process Clause of the Fourteenth Amendment. Although that provision, on its face, appears to guarantee only *procedural* fairness (it provides that individuals shall not be deprived of life, liberty, or property "without due process of law"), the Supreme Court nevertheless began, late in the nineteenth century, to use the Due Process Clause as a guarantee of the *substantive* fairness of regulating legislation. That is, the regulatory content of laws, as well as the procedures through which they were to be enforced, were required to be reasonable—laws were required to be in pursuit of legitimate governmental objectives and to be reasonably and sometimes substantially related to the effectuation of those objectives.

The era of broad-ranging substantive due process was generally a dark period in the history of U.S. constitutional law. During the early part of this century the Supreme Court primarily used the doctrine to strike down a large number of progressive state laws imposing humanitarian and economic regulations upon commercial activities—judgments of unconstitutionality were made regarding industrial safety laws, minimum wage laws, laws regulating maximum hours of employment, and so forth.[52] Among these decisions, however, were several that protected privacy-related concerns. In 1891 the Court held, for example, that federal courts lacked power to order the plaintiff in a tort action to submit to a surgical examination.[53] In 1923 it held that a state could not prohibit the teaching of foreign languages in public or private schools.[54] And in 1925 it held that states could not require children, over their parents' objection, to attend public, rather than private or parochial, elementary schools.[55]

The substantive due-process doctrine was largely rejected by the Supreme Court during the New Deal period of the late 1930s and 1940s; much of the progressive legislation that had earlier been ruled constitutionally "unreasonable" is now in fact a firm part of our social structure. The Justices newly appointed to the Court at that time expressly vowed to reject the then seemingly reactionary idea that courts were free "to hold laws unconstitutional when they believe the legislature has acted unwisely. . . . We have returned to the original constitutional proposition that courts do not substitute their social and economic beliefs for the judgment of legislative bodies, who are elected to pass laws."[56] But the notion of substantive privacy was not altogether abandoned. In 1942, for example, the Supreme Court utilized privacy ideas (in conjunction with other concepts) to strike down an Oklahoma statute that provided for the sexual sterilization of persons convicted three or more times of certain felonies.[57] And in 1944, in upholding a statute prohibiting children from engaging in trade in public places, it recognized that "decisions have respected the private realm of family life which the state cannot enter."[58] It was not clear, however, that the Court could continue significantly to protect such rights without broadly reviving the discredited notion that legislation generally could be struck down for judicially determined "unreasonableness."

The matter came to a head in the famous 1965 case of *Griswold v. Connecticut.*[59] Connecticut had an old and little-used statute that prohibited the use of contraceptives, and another statute that made the aiding or abetting of such an offense a crime. These laws were invoked by the state to prosecute the directors of the Planned Parenthood League of Connecticut when the League sought to open a birth-control clinic in New Haven. Defendants were charged with, and convicted for, aiding and abetting married persons in using contraceptives.

The Supreme Court reversed this conviction by a vote of seven to two. In doing so, Justice Douglas's opinion for the Court restated its resolve not to "sit as a super-legislature to determine the wisdom, need, and propriety of laws that touch economic problems, business affairs, or social conditions." The Connecticut law, however, operated "directly on an intimate relation of husband and wife and their physician's role in one aspect of that relation"; the case concerned "a relationship lying within the zone of privacy." "We deal," said the Court, "with a right of privacy older than the Bill of Rights. . . . Marriage is . . . intimate to the degree of being sacred. It is an association that promotes a way of life . . . a harmony in living . . . a bilateral loyalty."

The *Griswold* case signaled the birth of a substantive constitutional right to privacy. In subsequent cases, the right (sometimes in conjunction with other principles) has been used by the Court to strike down prohibitions upon the distribution of contraceptives to unmarried people, including minors,[60] interferences with the right to marry,[61] a prohibition on the possession of sexual materials in the home,[62] indirect penalties in the right to bear children,[63] and interferences with the right of family members to live together in the same household.[64] On the other hand, the Court has refused to apply the substantive-privacy concept to protect the right of individuals to obtain explicit sexual materials for their own use,[65] the right of unrelated individuals to live in the same household,[66] the right of police officers to be free from hair length and facial hair regulations,[67] and the right of parents to send their children to racially segregated schools.[68] Some of the distinctions made in these cases are difficult to justify. Most inexplicable of all, perhaps, was the Court's 1976 summary affirmance of a decision upholding Virginia's criminal sodomy statute as applied to consensual sexual acts between male homosexuals.[69]

The most important and controversial application of the substantive right of privacy to date has been in the area of abortion. In *Roe v. Wade*,[70] which was decided in 1973, the Supreme Court held (over the dissents of only Justices White and Rehnquist) that this right of privacy "is broad enough to encompass a woman's decision whether or not to terminate her pregnancy." This abortion right, however, "is not unqualified and must be considered against important state interests in regulation." The Court identified two such relevant interests—that in protecting the health of pregnant women and that in protecting "the potentiality of human life." The health interest, the Court concluded, might be promoted by regulations of abortion procedures after the first trimester of pregnancy. The interest in fetal life might constitutionally be vindicated by abortion prohibitions after fetal viability. As a result, state prohibitions upon abortion prior to approximately the last three months of pregnancy (the normal period of fetal viability) were held to be unconstitutional. In subsequent decisions the Court has struck down prohibitions and parental-consent requirements on abortions for minors,[71] spousal consent requirements,[72] and a number of other procedural requirements that seriously interfere with the abortion right.[73] In 1983 the Court reaffirmed both *Roe v. Wade* and the principle that government requires a strong reason to impose procedural regulations on abortion that do not amount to outright prohibitions but that have a "significant impact" on the woman's exercise of her right.[74] Efforts to have Congress propose a constitutional amendment to reverse the abortion decisions have so far failed, although sometimes by close margins.

One glaring exception has appeared to the Supreme Court's protective attitude toward the right to an abortion. This exception well illustrates the Court's dominantly "middle-class" approach to privacy rights and thus provides an appropriate conclusion to this essay. In cases decided in 1977 and 1980[75] the Court held, by five-to-four margins, that state and federal governments were constitutionally entitled to exclude abortions (even medically necessary abortions) from comprehensive governmental programs that provide free medical care to indigents, and that include coverage for childbirth expenses. The Court reasoned that such refusals to fund abortions for the poor did not "impinge on the fundamental right recognized in *Roe*": "It simply does not follow," said Justice Stewart's opinion in one of the 1980 cases, "that a woman's freedom of choice carries with it a constitutional entitlement to the financial resources to avail herself of the full range of protected choices. . . . [A]lthough government may not place obstacles in the path of a woman's exercise of her freedom of choice, it need not remove those not of its own creation. Indigency falls in the latter category. . . . [The refusal to fund abortions] leaves an indigent woman with at least the same range of choice in deciding whether to obtain a[n] . . . abortion as she would have had if [government] had chosen to subsidize no health care costs at all."

Some observers feared (or hoped) that these abortion-funding cases indicated a broad retreat by the Court from the *Roe v. Wade* principle. The Court's decision in 1983 to reaffirm both *Roe* itself and the rule that abortion restrictions—as well as outright prohibitions—are subject to close constitutional scrutiny showed that these fears were not justified. What the funding cases *do* show, however, is that the Court is satisfied, at least at present, to tolerate a situation where constitutional privacy rights are available in theory to everyone, but are in fact available only to the more affluent members of society. This lack of concern for the full availability of rights to the economically and socially disadvantaged has, unfortunately, been a common general theme of the Court's individual-rights decisions during the past fifteen years.

NOTES

1. *See, e.g.,* his powerful dissenting opinion in Poe v. Ullman, 367 U.S. 497 (1961), in which he argued for recognition of the right to be free from governmental prohibitions upon the use of contraceptives. His views were subsequently adopted by the Court in Griswold v. Connecticut, 381 U.S. 479 (1965).

2. 410 U.S. 113 (1973).

3. Brandeis, J., dissenting in Olmstead v. United States, 277 U.S. 438, 478 (1928).

4. Warren and Brandeis, "The Right of Privacy," 4 *Harvard Law Review* 193 (1890).

5. Such detail is contained in numerous books on constitutional law. *See, e.g.,* Dorsen, Bender & Neuborne, *Political and Civil Rights in the United States,* vol. 1 (1976) and supplements, especially chs. 12 (Privacy), 7 (Actions for Defamation and Inva-

sion of Privacy), 2-H (Government Surveillance), and 17 (The Constitutional Litigation Process).

6. 385 U.S. 374.

7. New York Times Co. v. Sullivan, 376 U.S. 254 (1964); *see also* Rosenbloom v. Metromedia, Inc., 403 U.S. 29 (1971).

8. Gertz v. Robert Welch, Inc., 418 U.S. 323 (1974).

9. Cox Broadcasting Corp. v. Cohn, 420 U.S. 469 (1975).

10. Oklahoma Publishing Co. v. District Court, 430 U.S. 308 (1977).

11. *See, e.g.*, Time, Inc. v. Firestone, 424 U.S. 448 (1976); Hutchinson v. Proxmire, 443 U.S. 111 (1979); Wolston v. Reader's Digest Ass'n, Inc., 443 U.S. 157 (1979).

12. Rowan v. Post Office Department, 397 U.S. 728 (1970).

13. *E.g.*, Hynes v. Mayor of Oradell, 425 U.S. 610 (1976). For an important older case *see* Martin v. City of Struthers, 319 U.S. 141 (1943).

14. *E.g.*, Schaumberg v. Citizens for a Better Environment, 444 U.S. 620 (1980).

15. *See Criminal Justice: The Accused, supra* at 203.

16. Katz v. United States, 389 U.S. 347, 353 (1967). *See also* Boyd v. United States, 116 U.S. 616 (1886), emphasizing the privacy aspect of certain Fifth Amendment rights.

17. Couch v. United States, 409 U.S. 322, 349 (1973).

18. Barron v. Baltimore, 7 Pet. 243 (1833).

19. *See* Wolf v. Colorado, 338 U.S. 25 (1949).

20. *See* Malloy v. Hogan, 378 U.S. 1 (1964); Mapp v. Ohio, 367 U.S. 643 (1961). *See generally* Duncan v. Louisiana, 391 U.S. 145 (1968).

21. Mapp v. Ohio, *supra* note 20.

22. Miranda v. Arizona, 384 U.S. 436 (1966).

23. Payton v. New York, 445 U.S. 573 (1980).

24. United States v. Chadwick, 433 U.S. 1 (1977).

25. United States v. Robinson, 414 U.S. 218 (1973); Washington v. Chrisman, 455 U.S. 1 (1982).

26. Illinois v. Gates, 103 S.Ct. 2317 (1983).

27. United States v. Watson, 423 U.S. 411 (1976).

28. *E.g.*, Chambers v. Maroney, 399 U.S. 42 (1970); United States v. Ross, 456 U.S. 798 (1982).

29. Schneckloth v. Bustamonte, 412 U.S. 218 (1973).

30. *E.g.*, Adams v. Williams, 407 U.S. 143 (1972); United States v. Place, 103 S.Ct. 2637 (1983).

31. Katz v. United States, 389 U.S. 347 (1967).

32. United States v. White, 401 U.S. 745 (1971). *See also* United States v. New York Telephone Co., 434 U.S. 159 (1977). Some state courts have been more protective of privacy in this situation. *See, e.g.,* State v. Sarmiento, 397 So. 2d 643 (Fla. 1981).

33. *See* Illinois v. Gates, 103 S.Ct. 2317 (1983). The Court ultimately held that the issue of modifying the exclusionary rule was not properly presented by the record in the Gates case. At the end of its 1982–1983 term, however, the Court granted certiorari in three additional cases that present the good-faith issue.

34. Stone v. Powell, 428 U.S. 465 (1976); Wainright v. Sykes, 433 U.S. 72 (1977).

35. Rakas v. Illinois, 439 U.S. 128 (1978); Rawlings v. Kentucky, 448 U.S. 98 (1980); United States v. Salvucci, 448 U.S. 83 (1980).

36. *See* United States v. White, 401 U.S. 745 (1971); Hoffa v. United States, 385 U.S. 293 (1966); Lewis v. United States, 385 U.S. 206 (1966); Lopez v. United States, 373 U.S. 427 (1963); On Lee v. United States, 343 U.S. 747 (1952). *But see* Osborn v. United States, 385 U.S. 323 (1966).

37. *See* Laird v. Tatum, 408 U.S. 1 (1972).

38. California Bankers Assn. v. Shultz, 416 U.S. 21 (1974).

39. Whalen v. Roe, 429 U.S. 589 (1977).

40. To the same effect is Nixon v. Administrator of General Services, 433 U.S. 425 (1977). Some state courts have been even more sensitive to informational privacy concerns. *See, e.g.,* Burrows v. Superior Court, 529 P.2d 590 (Calif. 1974).

41. Paul v. Davis, 424 U.S. 693 (1976).

42. 5 U.S.C. §552a. The act became effective in 1975.

43. S.Rep. no. 1138, 93d Cong., 2d Sess.

44. 20 U.S.C. §1232g.

45. 15 U.S.C. §§1681 *et seq.*

46. 18 U.S.C. §§2510–2520.

47. 28 C.F.R. 20.

48. 5 U.S.C. §§552(b)(6) and (7).

49. Amending 26 U.S.C. §6103.

50. 12 U.S.C. §§3401 *et seq.*

51. *See generally* T. Hayden & J. Novik, *Your Rights to Privacy* (1980).

52. The most famous of these cases is Lochner v. New York, 198 U.S. 45 (1905).

53. Union Pacific Ry. Co. v. Botsford, 141 U.S. 250 (1891).

54. Meyer v. Nebraska, 262 U.S. 390 (1923).

55. Pierce v. Society of Sisters, 268 U.S. 510 (1925).

56. Ferguson v. Skrupa, 372 U.S. 726, 730 (1963).

57. Skinner v. Oklahoma, 316 U.S. 535 (1942).

58. Prince v. Massachusetts, 321 U.S.A. 158 (1944).

59. 381 U.S. 479 (1965).

60. Eisenstadt v. Baird, 405 U.S. 438 (1972); Carey v. Population Services International, 431 U.S. 678 (1977).

61. Loving v. Virginia, 388 U.S. 1 (1967); *see also* Zablocki v. Redhail, 434 U.S. 374 (1978).

62. Stanley v. Georgia, 394 U.S. 557 (1969).

63. Cleveland Board of Educ. v. LaFleur, 414 U.S. 632 (1974).

64. Moore v. City of East Cleveland, 431 U.S. 494 (1977).

65. *E.g.*, Paris Adult Theatre I v. Slayton, 413 U.S. 49 (1973).

66. Village of Belle Terre v. Boraas, 416 U.S. 1 (1974).

67. Kelley v. Johnson, 425 U.S. 238 (1976).

68. Runyon v. McCrary, 427 U.S. 160 (1976).

69. Doe v. Commonwealth's Attorney, 425 U.S. 901 (1976). *See generally* T. Stoddard et al, *The Rights of Gay People* (1983).

70. 410 U.S. 113 (1973).

71. Planned Parenthood of Central Missouri v. Danforth, 428 U.S. 52 (1976); Bellotti v. Baird, 443 U.S. 622 (1979).

72. Planned Parenthood of Central Missouri v. Danforth, *supra* note 71.

73. *E.g.*, Doe v. Bolton, 410 U.S. 179 (1973).

74. City of Akron v. Akron Center for Reproductive Health, Inc., 103 S.Ct. 2481 (1983).

75. Maher v. Roe, 432 U.S. 464 (1977); Harris v. McRae, 448 U.S. 297 (1980); Williams v. Zbaraz, 448 U.S. 358 (1980).

RELIGIOUS LIBERTY

NORMAN REDLICH

*Norman Redlich is dean and Judge Edward Weinfeld Pro-
fessor of Law at New York University School of Law. He is
the coauthor of a constitutional law casebook and has served
as corporation counsel of New York City.*

The so-called social issues agenda of the Reagan administration has been
directed toward reversing, or at least restricting, Supreme Court decisions
in four areas—abortion, school prayer, government aid to religious
schools, and court-ordered busing. While not all of these areas deal directly, or even indirectly, with the principle of separation of church and
state, it is obvious that a religious constituency fuels the political engine
that drives the social issues agenda forward. The intrusion of a fundamentalist, almost evangelical, element into the political arena has raised serious questions about the proper role of religion in political life, and has
generated new pressures on previously well-established constitutional principles enforcing the First Amendment's command that "Congress shall
make no law respecting an establishment of religion or prohibiting the
free exercise thereof."

It is, of course, true that opposition to Supreme Court decisions in the
areas of religion, abortion, and busing did not begin with the election of
President Reagan; nor are the Court's critics found in any one religious
constituency. The cases that held that prayers, or other religious exercises,
could not be conducted under official public school auspices have been
denounced almost from the day the first school prayer case was decided
in 1962.[1] Catholics, Orthodox Jews, and others who operate religious
schools have long sought to pierce the barrier erected by the Constitution
against government financial support of religion. Theirs is a fight which

started in Colonial times[2] before there were any Catholics or Jews in significant numbers in this country. Opposition to Court-ordered busing cuts across all religious lines and could hardly be said to be primarily religious in origin. And the abortion decision, *Roe v. Wade,*[3] decided in 1973, while opposed bitterly by Catholics and others on religious grounds, has also been criticized by scholars as an improper exercise of judicial power.[4]

If criticism from religious circles existed prior to the Reagan presidency, and if other forces were at work to undo some of these cases, what, then, is the new element which now poses a particularly serious threat to religious liberty? The most obvious answer is that Ronald Reagan directed his campaign and presidency specifically toward this religious constituency. He promised that, if elected, he would seek by legislation, judicial appointment, or constitutional amendment to alter the pattern of the Court's work. Perhaps more importantly, the constituency that Ronald Reagan's election consciously brought to the fore converted most of what were independent issues into questions of religious conviction, so that disagreement meant not just that one differed on matters of social policy, or constitutional law, or the proper role of the Supreme Court. Rather, these legal and constitutional disputes have been transformed into disputes over such fundamental values as one's belief in "family," "morality," or "God." A religious fervor has been infused into the American political and legal discourse and it is threatening some of our most precious and unique constitutional values as reflected in the religion clauses of the First Amendment.

Surprisingly, very few of the constitutional cases on the social issues agenda of the Reagan administration and its allies were decided by the overtly liberal Warren Court. The Burger Court (with six Justices appointed by Presidents Nixon, Ford, and Reagan) has not retreated on the issue of school prayer,[5] and has been responsible for major decisions on abortion,[6] aid to religious schools,[7] and school busing.[8]

Much of the frustration and anger of the more vocal critics of the Court stem from the Court's rather remarkable consistency in adhering to well-charted constitutional principles, despite inevitable shifts in emphasis and varying nuances of interpretation. Dismantling this constitutional structure has been a major goal of the Reagan presidency.

In the area of church-state relations, the political pressures have been most intense, coming not only from evangelical groups like the Moral Majority, but also from a broad spectrum of Americans who sincerely believe that religion should play a greater role in our society and who look to government to support that view. Some believe that religious exercises are desirable in public schools; others seek financial relief from the heavy burden of private religious education for their children. They do not consider these positions as a threat to anyone's religious freedom. Indeed, living in a country with more religious freedom and diversity than any nation on earth, proponents of government aid to religion can easily overlook the crucial link between those freedoms and their constitutional source. As so often occurs with those who propound a religious message (usually their own), opposition to government support is often confused with opposition to religion itself. Sympathizers depict proponents of government aid as being on the side of God and religion, while the opponents are easily characterized as atheistic proponents of secular humanism. In such a political atmosphere, the rational defense of constitutional principles becomes increasingly difficult, and religious freedom and diversity are seriously threatened. Not surprisingly, the constitutional principle which forms the first line of defense is the one specifically designed for times such as these—the principle that church and state are best served by separation rather than by fusion.

The Supreme Court, despite the unpopularity of many of its decisions, has repeatedly reaffirmed its adherence to the concept of separation of church and state, even in its recent opinions upholding one form of tax assistance for private school tuition[9] and approving the hiring of chaplains by legislatures.[10] These recent decisions, however, are cause for concern. Regardless of the limitations expressed by the Court, they will be viewed by many as creating new opportunities for government endorsement of religious beliefs and institutions. In both courtroom and legislature we can expect more pressure on the wall of separation.

THE SCHOOL PRAYER CONTROVERSY

Nowhere has this assault on constitutional principles been more intense than in the controversy over school prayer. In 1962, in *Engel v. Vitale*,[11] the Supreme Court held invalid a so-called nondenominational New York State Regents prayer.[12] The eight-to-one decision, written by Justice Black, did not ban prayers in public schools. Individual children or teachers remain free to pray, as presumably many do for exams, or at the start of the day, or at occasions where individual conscience compels such observance. In this case, and in a similar case involving Bible reading one year later,[13] the Court did hold invalid a state-sponsored religious observance which inevitably stamped the imprimatur of the state in support of religion. Such state support of religion, especially in the public schools, posed all of the dangers that the religion clauses of the Constitution were designed to avoid. Prayers could never be "neutral" among religions. No single prayer could satisfy all religious beliefs, this leading to controversy among religions as to the nature of the prayer to be recited. The selection of any one prayer would throw the power of the state behind a particular set of religious beliefs and behind religion as against nonreligion. Edmond Cahn, a profoundly religious man and a constitutional scholar, pointed out at the time that the so-called "nondenominational" prayer in *Engel v. Vitale* was theologically offensive to many religious faiths.[14] And a government-supported religious exercise is inevitably coercive toward those who, for reasons of personal conviction, elect not to participate.

Thus, *Engel v. Vitale* did not break entirely new ground, although the controversy it generated created the impression that the Court had departed from, rather than followed, long-standing constitutional principles. A series of cases in the 1940s and 1950s had established the principle that the "Establishment of Religion" clause of the First Amendment was intended not merely to prevent the creation of a state religion, as some proponents of state support for religion had argued, but rather to prevent state support for *all* religions as well as any particular religion. These Court decisions, dealing with the use of school facilities for religious instruction,[15] or with the reimbursement to parents for bus transportation to religious schools,[16] had traced the historical origins of the Establishment Clause and concluded that separation of church and state, and not merely neutrality or avoidance of a state religion, was the guiding principle of interpretation of the Establishment Clause. Indeed, the decision of a sharply divided Court in *Everson v. Board of Education,* [17] which upheld government reimbursement for bus transportation to parochial schools, was based on the Court's conclusion that such expenditures were not in support of religion but rather a kind of safety-and-welfare measure designed to help children travel to school without having to run the risk of walking along crowded highways.

Of course, as *Everson* indicated, there could be strong disagreement about whether a government program was an impermissible aid to religion or a general-welfare measure, such as police and fire protection, where the exclusion of religious institutions would itself raise serious problems under the Free Exercise Clause. The bus transportation case demonstrated that the line was not always easy to discern, since the Court agreed on the constitutional principle but divided five-to-four on the application. Similarly, differences could arise as to whether a practice or exercise, such as the singing of Christmas carols or the placing of Christmas trees in a public area, was religious or secular. But a prayer read in school assemblies or in each class at the start of the day was clearly a religious exercise, as was the reading of excerpts from the Bible, or the Lord's Prayer, held unconstitutional in the *Schempp* [18] case, decided one year after *Engel.*

In the prayer cases the Court started to evolve what became known as the three-part test in evaluating whether a government practice violates the Establishment Clause. The practice must have (1) a secular purpose; (2) its principal or primary effect must neither advance nor inhibit religion; and (3) it must not foster an excessive government entanglement with religion. A challenged practice must pass all three tests to be valid. State-sponsored prayer in the public schools flunks all three.

In the more than two decades since the school prayer cases were decided, there has been an almost unbroken string of Court decisions applying the principles of these cases to a wide range of practices in different factual contexts. Clearly, religious practices, such as Nativity scenes,[19] the placing of the Ten Commandments in classrooms,[20] or the placing of a cross or other religious symbol in a public area,[21] have been held to be establishments. The singing of Christmas songs,[22] the objective teaching of religion,[23] the study of the Bible as literature,[24] and the exemption from the reach of Sunday closing laws for those whose religion requires Saturday observance[25] have been held constitutional, and in some instances a desirable accommodation to protect the free-exercise claims of certain minorities. None of these cases has called into question the underlying principles enunciated in the school prayer cases of the early 1960s.

Proponents of state-sponsored school prayer received their first glimmer of judicial hope on July 5, 1983, when the Supreme Court, in *Marsh v. Chambers,* [26] decided that paid legislative chaplains and opening prayers at the start of each session were not violations of the Establishment Clause. Chief Justice Burger's majority opinion, however, was based almost entirely on a historical analysis, emphasizing the fact that these practices were adopted by the very Congress which approved the First

Amendment in 1789. Moreover, there was a reference to the fact that the complaining party was an adult. Justice Brennan's dissent was probably correct, therefore, in observing that the majority's ". . . limited rationale should pose little threat to the overall fate of the Establishment Clause." But the Chief Justice's opinion contains some language which could be seized on by those who seek to narrow or overturn the decisions concerning religious practices in the schools. Although based on history, the opinion did not view the practice simply as a historical exception to Establishment Clause doctrine. Rather, it described the practice as ". . . simply a tolerable acknowledgement of beliefs widely held among the people of this country." Such language, lifted out of the context of the opinion, could be used to argue in favor of public displays of Nativity scenes or other religious symbols, or even prayer.

The current intensive effort to reestablish state-sponsored prayer in the public schools has been spearheaded by religious leaders such as Reverend Jerry Falwell and his so-called Moral Majority and, for the first time, has had the active support of the president of the United States. Previous presidents have either supported, or accepted, the Supreme Court decision. Indeed, our first Roman Catholic president, John F. Kennedy, commented shortly after the *Engel* case that he always thought that the proper setting for prayer was either at home or in church. President Reagan's election in 1980 as a vociferous proponent of returning prayer to the schools has provided a new and strong political impetus for the overturning of the school prayer cases. The president rarely misses an opportunity to criticize the Court and to urge the return of prayer to the public schools. Thus, school prayer has become an intense political issue, with all of the opinion polls appearing to show strong support for the general concept of school prayer, although it is difficult to know whether abstract support for school prayer would be sustained when some of the hard issues of implementation would have to be faced.

The attack on the school prayer decisions has taken several forms, the most direct being an attempt to reverse them by constitutional amendment.[27] As of this writing, no amendment has yet reached a vote in either the House or Senate, although the intensity of the effort to produce such an amendment should not be underestimated. If an amendment were to reach a vote in either House, it is doubtful whether the necessary one-third would stand up to oppose it, despite the personal misgivings of the members about the wisdom of so radical change in our constitutional philosophy.

Fortunately, the supporters of a constitutional amendment differ in their proposed solutions. An amendment which would permit so-called "nondenominational prayer" might have wide public support, but its proponents realize that every organized public prayer, whether sponsored by or permitted by the state, would be subject to litigation, involving the courts in a hopeless inquiry over the meaning of "nondenominational." If, on the other hand, a constitutional amendment were to prescribe a prayer, the debate over the amendment would create a similar controversy, i.e., which prayer to use, but in a forum—Congress—which the legislators would wish to avoid.

In an effort to pass the buck to the future the administration originally proposed an amendment which would simply provide that the Constitution shall not prevent organized public prayer, leaving it to each local or state government, or local school authorities, to prescribe the form of prayer.[28] The administration then modified its proposal by adding a sentence which would bar the federal government or any state from composing an official prayer. Of course, this leaves unanswered the question of whether schoolteachers, principals, elected officials, school boards, or other state and local officials could read or compose prayers.

The administration proposal has spawned the opposition of some opponents of school prayer, like Senator Orrin G. Hatch of Utah, a Mormon and a person sensitive to the rights of religious minorities. He has proposed an amendment which would permit silent devotion, a position which does not satisfy those whose religious convictions require public and vocal expressions of faith. On July 14, 1983, the Senate Judiciary Committee sent both the administration and Hatch proposals to the Senate floor. Senate action on either proposal would spark intensive debate and possibly a filibuster. The congressional debate has already raised the specter of what may be expected in the future if school prayer is legalized. We have already witnessed divisive debate over questions of the form and content of prayer and whether majority sentiment in each community should be able to determine the nature of public prayer. The adoption of a school prayer amendment by the Congress would transfer this debate to the state legislatures and ultimately to school boards and individual schools throughout the country. It is inevitable that the rights of religious minorities, and those who profess no religious faith, will be chipped away in the process.

Apart from mounting this frontal threat, by way of constitutional amendment, the proponents of state-sponsored public prayer have devised other techniques, legislative and judicial, to try to undercut the thrust of the Court's decisions. One type of proposal that has gained broad support, and for which an arguable case can be made for validity, would permit, or require, a period of silence.[29] The legislative proposals vary as to what would occur during this period of silence. Some call for a simple period of silence, some call for meditation, some for prayer, and some for a combination of all of them. A New Mexico law, which allows a moment of silence in the public schools for "contemplation, meditation, or prayer" was held unconstitutional by a United States District Court as a "devotional exercise that had the effect of the advancement of religion."[30] New Jersey's law may be more difficult to challenge successfully since it simply requires principals and teachers to "permit students to observe a one-minute period of silence solely at the discretion of the individual student." This, too, is being challenged by the American Civil Liberties Union.[31]

Regardless of the wording,[32] these laws should be viewed by the courts simply as substitutes for state-supported religion. In light of the legislative history which surrounds the adoption of these statutes, it is virtually impossible to ignore the fact that these laws have little to do with creating a peaceful moment at the start of the day, or permitting a period of inward reflection. Were it not for the controvery over the unconstitutionality of state-sponsored prayer, there would be no pressure for a moment of silence or meditation.

Moreover, unlike such activities as the singing of Christmas carols or ceremonial references to God at school assemblies or graduations, which by the very context in which they occur are most unlikely to be converted into a religious exercise, the moment of silence is almost certain to be used for such a purpose. The adoption of such practices, either by statute or school board resolutions, constitutes an act of public hypocrisy. It is as if our public officials were winking to millions of school children and saying, "We'll show you how to get around the Constitution." It sends a message that a fundamental constitutional value—separation of church and state —can be circumvented by a phony gesture. Nothing could be more damaging to the concept of respect for constitutional rights.

A NEW APPROACH: STUDENT RELIGIOUS CLUBS

Another attempt to reintroduce a form of state-supported prayer in the public schools derives from a misguided reliance on that provision of the First Amendment which guarantees freedom of speech and the free exercise of religion. That school children have a right to pray is unquestioned. And the Court has held that children cannot be compelled to salute the flag or recite the Pledge of Allegiance if such observances violate the student's religious beliefs.[33] Permitting students to be excused, on religious grounds, from an otherwise secular observance is not an establishment of religion. Rather, it is a necessary accommodation by the state to the individual's religious freedom.[34]

There are, moreover, situations where government interference with religious activity on public property would be unconstitutional. For example, if the public is permitted to gather at a park, or at a facility such as the Mall in Washington, D.C., groups of individuals may not be prevented from similarly assembling if their purpose is to join in prayer.[35] The principle is that once the state creates a public forum, it may not deny the use of that forum to religious groups, providing the state does not extend funds for a religious observance, as was the case with a recent visit by the Pope to Philadelphia.[36] Indeed, recently, in *Widmar v. Vincent*,[37] the Supreme Court held that if a state university makes its campus available for meetings by political and social groups, the university could not deny access to student religious groups even if such groups engage in religious worship. Thus, there will be occasions where religious exercises on public property are not only permissible, but are compelled by the Free Exercise Clause of the Constitution.

Some proponents of school prayer have sought to build on these decisions by requiring school officials to set aside time during the day to permit students in the public schools to organize groups for religious purposes, including engaging in prayer. There is a fine, but important, line to be drawn here. Permitting student-initiated prayer clubs to meet during a school's "student-activity" period may not constitute an establishment of religion, and may, indeed, be required as an exercise of the student's rights to free speech and free exercise of religion. But setting aside time during each school day for student-initiated prayer could, depending on the facts of the case, constitute the placing of an imprimatur of the state behind a religious exercise. Federal courts in Texas, New York, and Pennsylvania have found these cases difficult to resolve.[38] Unlike a university campus or a public park, where a wide variety of individuals and groups meet to express divergent views on political, and possibly religious, issues, a public secondary school has few of the characteristics of a public forum. Moreover, the process by which such student meetings or prayer sessions are organized could easily involve the type of official support which the school prayer cases sought to prevent. An example of such official support was cited by the Court in the Lubbock, Texas case,[39] where the policy on religious meetings in schools was part of an official statement setting forth guidelines for religion in the schools, and not part of a policy relating to free speech or student groups generally. It is extremely unlikely that student religious clubs and prayer sessions in public schools spring spontaneously from students without the support of the government.

In an effort to respond to the popular clamor over school prayers, pressure has mounted in Congress to require that public schools, as a condition of receiving federal assistance, permit voluntary prayer by groups of students.[40] These proposals, which have been introduced as legislation and as a constitutional amendment, are appealingly phrased in free-speech "equal access" terms. They require that all public schools that generally permit student groups to meet shall not discriminate against any group on the basis of the religious content of the speech at the meeting. If enacted, these proposals would thus require public secondary schools to do what the *Widmar* case requires of state universities.

Although less damaging than a school prayer amendment, such legislation is both unwise and unnecessary. The courts, sensitive to minority concerns, and not an inevitably political Congress, should decide whether the arrangement worked out by a school constitutes an invalid state-supported religious program or is, instead, a legitimate exercise of the student's right to engage in religious activity on an individual or a group basis. The principles of the *Widmar* case are not of universal applicability even in the state university setting that was involved in that case. There is serious doubt as to whether such organized religious activity in public schools can ever be accomplished without state support. The role played by teachers in such religious clubs raises obvious questions. But these are issues which should be left to the courts. Congress should not mandate for schools a program of support for student-initiated school prayer. Instead, individual cases should determine whether such programs are constitutionally required or permitted.

FINANCIAL SUPPORT FOR
RELIGIOUS SCHOOLS

While school prayers and other religious exercises raise the most highly charged emotional and religious issues, the question of financial assistance to religious schools is, in the long run, probably of greater importance to the cause of sectarian education. Here, the Burger Court has created a body of case law which, thus far, has barred most forms of significant financial assistance to church-related schools.

In 1969, when Chief Justice Burger acceded to his present position, there was great uncertainty as to how the Court would rule on the controversial question of whether states could pay the salaries of teachers of secular subjects in religious schools. Indeed, an opinion by the Court in 1968,[41] upholding a state program for lending secular books to students in religious schools, raised the possibility that the Court might justify government support of religious schools either by drawing a distinction between secular and religious functions of religious schools, or by expanding the notion that the aid was for the benefit of the child rather than for the religious school itself.

In one of this country's major constitutional decisions maintaining the separation of church and state, Chief Justice Burger, in *Lemon v. Kurtzman*,[42] wrote for a near-unanimous Court in striking down two state laws that provided for the payment of salaries for teachers of secular subjects in parochial schools. The doctrines developed in this and later cases emphasize that any program of government assistance to church schools must avoid excessive entanglements of government and religion (including political divisiveness along religious lines) and that the program must have a secular purpose and a primary effect which neither advances nor inhibits religion. Applying these principles the Court has struck down expenditures for instructional materials, maintenance and repair costs, field trip expenses, and therapeutic and remedial services performed on the premises of the religious school.[43]

Other types of government assistance have been upheld: the cost of state-mandated testing and test scoring as part of a system presumably to determine the adequacy of instruction at the religious school;[44] remedial programs conducted off school premises,[45] and construction grants to church-related colleges for facilities devoted exclusively to secular educational purposes.[46] Regardless of one's views about any particular decision of the Court since the *Lemon* case, the effect of the Court's decisions in the past decade has been to cut off any significant direct government financial assistance to religious schools, leaving the contest for public funds to be fought along rather narrow grounds, such as whether remedial programs are conducted on or off school premises, or whether the tests for which reimbursement is sought are prepared by the state or by the teacher. These are fine distinctions, but represent the kinds of lines which courts must draw as they apply broad principles to specific cases.

One form of assistance—the granting of tax benefits[47] to help offset the cost of tuition to religious schools—promises to be the major legal and political testing ground in the years ahead for the issue of government support of sectarian education. In the recent case of *Mueller v. Allen*[48] the Supreme Court upheld a Minnesota plan which granted limited tax deductions to parents for the costs of tuition and other expenses, such as textbooks and transportation, incurred for the education of their children in public or private schools. While reaffirming all prior cases involving government aid to religious schools, including a case striking down a similar New York program,[49] the Court's decision adds a new dimension to the "tuition tax credit" controversy, even though the Minnesota plan was different in several major respects from the programs now being pushed in many states and in Congress.

The *Mueller* case was decided amid strong efforts by the Reagan administration to enact a national tuition tax credit program. The Court's approval has intensified this campaign as well as the pressure for state programs similar to the Minnesota plan. Earlier Supreme Court cases appeared to have ruled out programs where the principal beneficiaries are parents of children attending religious schools and where the financial assistance is in the form of an actual credit against the tax as distinguished from a deduction from taxable income. In a leading case from New York, *Committee for Public Education and Religious Liberty v. Nyquist,*[50] and in a companion case from Pennsylvania,[51] the Court appeared to have concluded that, regardless of labels, if the state uses the tax system to reimburse a taxpayer for a fixed amount of money where the credit is earned primarily by those paying tuition to religious schools, then the primary purpose is to aid religion.

These decisions, however, involved only programs for attendance at private schools in states where the actual effect of the expenditure was to provide benefits almost entirely to those attending religious schools. Moreover, since they involved specified cash benefits to individual taxpayers, the tax savings could easily be calculated and passed along to the private religious school in the form of higher tuition. The possibility was raised, therefore, that if the class of individuals who were benefited could be broadened beyond those attending private schools (the overwhelming majority being religious schools) and if the benefits could be primarily in the form of a deduction from taxable income, rather than a specified dollar credit against the tax, the Supreme Court might distinguish its earlier cases and uphold a tuition tax credit plan.

Rhode Island[52] and Minnesota[53] exploited these possibilities by enacting laws which provided for a deduction from taxable income of up to $500 in some grades and $700 in others. The deductions were available not only to parents of children attending private schools, but also to parents of public school students. Expenses could be deducted for such items as tuition paid by public school children to attend school outside their home district, summer school tuition, tuition for instruction provided for the physically handicapped, and costs of textbooks and transportation. These differences were found decisive by the Court majority in *Mueller* even though it was estimated that anywhere from 84 percent to 96 percent of the families eligible for the tax deductions were sending their children to religious schools. The *Mueller* case was a disappointment to opponents of aid to religious schools, but it is too early to tell whether it will lead to a significant diversion of public funds to private religious education. The Court majority (five to four) set forth certain new constitutional limits which, while permitting the Minnesota plan to stand, may make it difficult for other types of programs to be upheld. And the Minnesota plan itself may be very difficult to duplicate on a national scale.

Of particular importance was the fact that the Minnesota plan created a tax deduction which was available to parents of students in public schools as well as private schools. Moreover, the program was a part of a general policy of tax deductions and not a tax credit of a specified amount. The tax benefits of a deduction to an individual parent are more difficult to calculate and are not so easily passed along to the school.[54]

While the *Mueller* case will encourage the adoption of similar state programs, those aspects of the Minnesota plan that the Court emphasized may render the decision of very limited value to the proponents of tuition tax credits. Congressional proposals for a nationwide program of tuition tax credit differ in several major respects from the program upheld in *Mueller*. The central idea of the Reagan proposal, and those like it, would permit a credit against tax liability of an amount equal to fifty percent of tuition expenses to private schools, subject to statutory maximums ($300 in the bill proposed by the administration in 1983).[55] These proposals have met with strong resistance from supporters of public education, who argue that a national program of tuition tax credits would drain billions of dollars from public education into private (primarily sectarian) schools. Supporters of public education, and defenders of separation of church and state, have found strong allies in those concerned with mounting federal deficits.

To meet the standard set by the Court in *Mueller* a program would, at a minimum, have to be available to children in public as well as private schools. This would sharply escalate the cost by allowing deductions for tuition and other expenses which some states, like Minnesota, may presently charge public school parents. It would also tempt public schools to charge for some expenses which are now free, since a significant part of the cost would be borne by the federal government in the form of the tax deduction. Moreover, there would be some difficult political fallout from the inclusion of public school expenses, since in many states there are constitutional and statutory barriers against any charges for public school students. Thus, a program of federal tax deductions for such expenses would benefit parents unevenly, depending on the laws of their particular state.

The emphasis placed by the Court on the fact that the Minnesota plan involved a deduction and not a specified credit could raise other problems. The proposals in Congress clearly do not meet this test. If they are altered to provide for a tax deduction, the benefits to parents will be unequal, depending on their income tax brackets. Any effort by states and private schools to pick up the exact amount of the deduction by raising tuition to private schools, or by imposing charges for public school expenses in an amount equal to the actual value of the tax deduction, will be challenged on grounds that the program is an impermissible direct benefit to the religious institution.

There is no doubt that the Court has opened the door to government support of religious schools through the tax benefit route. But the programs permitted by the Court may be far more costly than present proposals contemplate being and they may encounter administrative difficulties that could impair their validity, particularly if the tax deduction is converted into a de facto credit.

Nevertheless, pressures will mount for the enactment of programs like those in Minnesota and Rhode Island, and courts will be urged to allow still more deviations from the constitutional standard that was created in the *Nyquist* case and weakened in *Mueller v. Allen.* Interestingly enough, it was a proposal in Virginia, in the early 1780s, to provide public funds for religious education in church schools that inspired James Madison's famous Memorial and Remonstrance against Religious Assessments,[56] promulgated in 1785, an eloquent and prophetic warning against government support of religion. The Remonstrance was the historical antecedent for the Establishment Clause proposed by Madison as the very first protection guaranteed by the Bill of Rights.[57] Two hundred years later the dangers that Madison predicted in starting down the road of financial support for religions are even more apparent. It is useful to recall the following plea by James Madison in opposition to tax support for religious education:

> That the same authority which can force a citizen to contribute three pence only of his property for the support of any one establishment, may force him to conform to any other establishment in all cases whatsoever. . . . Because it will destroy that moderation and harmony which the forbearance of our laws to intermeddle with Religion, has produced among its several sects. Torrents of blood have been spilt in the old world, by vain attempts of the secular arm to extinguish Religious discord, by proscribing all differences in Religious opinions. . . . At least let warning be taken of the first fruits of the threatened innovation. The very appearance of the Bill has transformed that "Christian forbearance, love and charity," which of late mutually prevailed, into animosities and jealousies which may not soon be appeased.

RELIGIOUS PRESSURES IN SCHOOL CURRICULUMS

It is only natural that religious groups should be concerned with the content of education in the public schools. As parents and as citizens who are concerned with the inculcation of certain moral values in the education of their children, members of religious sects have a right to influence curriculum decisions through school board elections, choice of administrators and principals, and through the many avenues by which citizens affect educational decisions in a country where local control of education is a vital tradition. When this influence extends to the point of mandating a religious observance, like a school prayer, Establishment Clause values come into play, as we have observed. When the same pressures seek to impart religious doctrine into school curriculums, the result is at least as troubling as mandated school prayers, but more difficult to control through the judicial mechanism.

Obviously, not every successful effort by religious groups to influence education policy can be viewed as an establishment of religion. To do so would deprive these groups of their First Amendment rights of freedom of speech. Jewish organizations are free to urge that the Holocaust be taught, or that courses on anti-Semitism be offered. On the political level, laws exempting Jews from Sunday closing laws are valid, even though enacted with strong Jewish organizational support. Courts have properly rejected the argument that laws denying public funding for abortions should be held unconstitutional simply because they represent the views of the Catholic Church.[58] Catholics, and others, have the right to seek to enact laws which reflect their moral values about abortion, quite apart from the ultimate validity of those laws.

Religious groups may not, however, impose their purely religious beliefs, as distinct from their moral values, as part of the public school curriculum. Thus, in 1968, in *Epperson v. Arkansas*,[59] the Supreme Court held invalid a state law banning the teaching of evolution in the public schools because the law was based on the conclusion that the subject matter—evolution—was contrary to favored religious beliefs. The most recent effort to influence school curriculums has been the movement to require that "scientific creationism" be taught in the schools in order to balance the teachings of Darwin's theory of evolution. The Arkansas creation-science law was properly held by a District Court to be an unconstitutional establishment of religion after a lengthy trial that demonstrated that the so-called "science" had no scientific basis and was derived from fundamentalist religious teachings.[60]

Litigation, however, is probably of limited value in dealing with the efforts by religious groups to infuse their beliefs into school curriculums. Control over curriculum is traditionally the right of local school board officials who have broad powers to determine its content. In a recent widely heralded case, the Supreme Court struck down an extreme and clumsy effort by a local school board to remove a number of well-recognized books deemed offensive by the local authorities.[61] The Court ruled that the board was creating a "pall of orthodoxy" of belief, but the case may demonstrate less the limits of school board authority than the broad discretion which school board officials may exercise before those limits are reached. The "creation science" movement represents a religious and political force which has the ability to affect classroom teaching in ways that courts cannot reach.

THE BROADER ISSUE: THE ROLE OF RELIGION IN POLITICS

The cases involving school curriculum decisions point up an issue that is difficult to resolve through constitutional litigation and which underlies the resurgence of legislation and litigation in the church-state area. It is the emergence of a strong religious-political force in American life which seeks to impose a conservative religious orthodoxy in such matters as prayer, books in school libraries, motion pictures, sex education in schools, sexual conduct, television programs, etc. There is nothing new in the presence of strong forces advocating such positions in American society. Indeed, the right of individuals to advocate these positions is constitutionally protected. The peculiar threat of the 1980s derives from the linking of these positions with a fundamentalist religious position which equates the conservative position on a wide range of controversial issues with a morality based on religious belief, thereby creating disagreements along religious, rather than political, philosophical, or moral grounds. Followers of the Moral Majority consider themselves part of a religious crusade. Their opponents are no longer the objects of a political disagreement; rather they are nonbelievers.

This development threatens to bring about the very evils which the religion clauses of the Constitution were designed to prevent—the enactment of religious doctrine into law and the fractious division of the country along political-religious lines. A case now before the Supreme Court,[62] involving a Nativity scene erected by the city of Pawtucket, Rhode Island, in front of its City Hall, epitomizes the gravity of the present danger. This obviously religious symbol creates a preference for one religion over others, excludes religious minorities and nonbelievers from the official family of religion, divides a community along religious lines, and demeans the very religion it purports to support by tending to secularize a profoundly religious observance. Two lower federal courts held the construction and display of the crèche unconstitutional. That the United States Justice Department should reach out and, in an amicus brief, urge the Supreme Court to approve this religious establishment demonstrates how far the country's chief law enforcement officials have wandered from their central role of defending constitutional rights.

The situation is aggravated by the fact that another issue—a woman's reproductive freedom—is also dividing the country along religious lines. Clearly, the First Amendment protects the right of religious groups to try to enact laws which reflect their moral position on an issue such as abortion. When such laws restrict a woman's constitutionally protected right to terminate a pregnancy, they can be challenged on that basis. Moreover, there is a difference between a law regulating conduct, which embodies a moral position rooted in religious belief, and a law which directly imposes that belief in the form of religious observances, courses taught in schools, or financial support for religion. Nevertheless, it has to be recognized that the abortion controversy has created religiously based tensions in American political life.

Thus, we find ourselves in an era where the traditional church-state controversies deal with only one part of the broader problem. Some of these tensions are inevitable, particularly in an era when many of our institutions, and our legal structures, are adjusting to the changing role of women in American life. At this time it is particularly important that the constitutional principle of separation of church and state be maintained in those areas of the law where it is directly applicable, such as the teaching of religion, government support of religious observances, or government financial aid to religious institutions. The Reagan administration has sought to fuse a broad coalition of groups into a political force on the basis of strongly held religious beliefs. That coalition, containing diverse groups with varying objectives, could very easily wipe away many of the constitutional protections which have guaranteed religious liberty in this country.

The role of the courts is vital, because if the basic constitutional principles are maintained, it will be far easier to contain the tensions among religious groups that are the inevitable product of an open democratic society. If, on the other hand, those constitutional barriers are pierced, and religion is supported by government, then the tensions cannot be contained and the evils that Madison foresaw will come about.

The events of the past few years have taught us anew a lesson which must never be forgotten by those who would defend the Bill of Rights. While constitutional protections, such as separation of church and state, must be vigorously pursued in the courts, the political arena cannot be ignored. On both the legislative and judicial levels, the wall of separation between church and state is under severe pressure. With some important exceptions, the overall record of the courts has been good. How long the judicial branch can withstand the intense pressure from religiously inspired and politically active groups, enthusiastically led by the president of the United States, is a troubling question to those who value religious freedom and the constitutional principles on which it rests.

NOTES

1. Engel v. Vitale, 370 U.S. 421 (1962).

2. I. Brant, *James Madison the Nationalist 1780–1787*, chap. 22 (1948).

3. 410 U.S. 113 (1973).

4. *See* Ely, "The Wages of Crying Wolf: A Comment on *Roe v. Wade*," 82 Yale *Law Journal* 920 (1973), and the excellent articles in "Symposium, Constitutional Adjudication and Democratic Theory," 56 *New York University Law Review* 259–582 (1981).

5. *See* Supreme Court's summary affirmance of a lower court decision invalidating a Louisiana voluntary prayer law, Karen B. v. Treen, 653 F.2d 897 (5th Cir. 1981), *aff'd mem.*, 455 U.S. 913 (1982).

6. Roe v. Wade, 410 U.S. 113 (1973) and the cases, decided in 1983, holding invalid a series of local laws that sought to restrict a woman's ability to carry out the decision to abort her pregnancy: City of Akron v. Akron Center for Reproductive Health, Inc., 103 S.Ct. 2481 (1983); Planned Parenthood Ass'n of Kansas City, Inc. v. Ashcroft, 103 S.Ct. 2517 (1983); Simopoulos v. Virginia, 103 S.Ct. 2532 (1983).

7. *E.g.*, Lemon v. Kurtzman, 403 U.S. 602 (1971) and Committee for Public Education and Religious Liberty v. Nyquist, 413 U.S. 756 (1973).

8. Swann v. Charlotte-Mecklenburg Board of Education, 402 U.S. 1 (1971); Keyes v. School District No. 1, Denver, Colo., 413 U.S. 189 (1973).

9. Mueller v. Allen, 103 S.Ct. 3062 (1983).

10. Marsh v. Chambers, 103 S.Ct. 3330 (1983).

11. 360 U.S. 421 (1962).

12. The Regents prayer reads as follows: "Almighty God, we acknowledge our dependence upon Thee, and we beg Thy blessings upon us, our teachers and our country."

13. Abington School District v. Schempp, 374 U.S. 203 (1963).

14. Cahn, "On Government and Prayer," *Annual Survey of American Law* (1962), appearing in *Confronting Injustice* 189 (1966).

15. Illinois Ex. Rel. McCollum v. Board of Education, 343 U.S. 203 (1948); *compare* Zorach v. Clauson, 343 U.S. 306 (1951).

16. Everson v. Board of Education, 330 U.S. 1 (1947).

17. *Ibid.*

18. *See* note 13 *supra.*

19. Donnelly v. Lynch, 525 F. Supp. 1150 (D. R.I. 1981), *aff'd*, 691 F. 2d 1029 (1st Cir. 1982).

20. Stone v. Graham, 449 U.S. 39 (1980).

21. American Civil Liberties Union v. Rabun County Chamber of Commerce, 510 F. Supp. 886 (N.D. Ga. 1981), *aff'd*, 678 F. 2d 1379 (11th Cir. 1982).

22. Florey v. Sioux Falls School District, 619 F. 2d 1311 (8th Cir. 1980).

23. Holiday observances "presented objectively as part of a secular program of education" were condoned by Justice Clark in his majority opinion in Schempp, *supra* note 13, 374 U.S. at 225.

24. Wiley v. Franklin, 468 F. Supp. 133 (E.D. Tenn. 1979). *See* further litigation at 474 F. Supp. 133 (E.D. Tenn. 1979) and 497 F. Supp. 390 E.D. Tenn. (1980).

25. *See* Braunfield v. Brown, 366 U.S. 599 at 608 (1961).

26. 103 S.Ct. 3330 (1983).

27. *See generally* hearings on proposed constitutional amendment to permit voluntary prayer, before the Committee of the Judiciary, United States Senate, 97th Cong., 2d Sess., Serial No. J-97-129.

28. The proposed amendment submitted by President Reagan provides: "Nothing in this Constitution shall be construed to prohibit individual or group prayer in public schools or other public institutions. No person shall be required by the United States or by any state to participate in prayer."

29. An excellent summary of the laws in eighteen states dealing with moments of silence or meditation is found in Note, "Daily Moments of Silence in Public Schools," 58 *New York University Law Review* 365 (1983). A constitutional amendment to allow silent meditation has also been proposed.

30. Duffy v. Las Cruces Public Schools, 557 F. Supp. 1013 (D.N.M. 1983). Many scholars have supported the constitutionality of moments of silence. *See* sources cited on Note, "Daily Moments of Silence in Public Schools," note 29 *supra* at 368–369. Cert. denied, *sub. nom,* New Mexico v. Burciaga (D.N.M. 83-9, 11/14/83, ruling below, 10th Cir. 4/8/83 unreported).

31. *See* May v. Cooperman, Civil No. 83-89, slip op. (D.N.J. 1983) (declaring the New Jersey law unconstitutional and issuing a permanent injunction).

32. A moment of silence for the purpose of "Prayer or Meditation" was upheld in Massachusetts in Gaines v. Anderson, 421 F. Supp. 337 (D. Mass. 1976) and a similar law enacted in Tennessee was held invalid in Beck v. McElrath, 548 F. Supp. 1161 (M.D. Tenn. 1982). Alabama's prayer statute, which also permitted teacher-led meditation, was recently struck down. See Jaffree v. Wallace, 705 F.2d 1526 (11th Cir. 1983).

33. West Virginia State Bd. of Education v. Barnette, 319 U.S. 624 (1943); Lipp v. Morris, 579 F.2d 834 (3d Cir. 1974).

34. Church of God v. Amarillo Independent School District, 511 F. Supp. 613 (N.D. Tex. 1981), aff'd, 670 F. 2d 46 (5th Cir. 1982).

35. See O'Hair v. Andrus, 613 F. 2d 931 (D.C. Cir. 1979).

36. Gilfillian v. City of Philadelphia, 637 F. 2d 934 (3d Cir. 1980); apart from the expenditure of funds there was also extensive involvement by the city with Catholic Church officials in promoting the event, such as the sale of tickets.

37. 454 U.S. 261 (1981).

38. Compare Lubbock Civil Liberties Union v. Lubbock Independent School District, 669 F. 2d 1038 (5th Cir. 1981) and Brandon v. Bd. of Education of Guilderland Central School District, 635 F. 2d 971 (2d Cir. 1980) (permitting student groups to meet for religious purposes violated the Establishment Clause and refusing per-mission would not violate children's rights to free speech or free exercise) with contrary holding in Bender v. Williamsport Area School District, no. 82-0692 Civil, decided by Chief Judge Nealon of the Federal Middle District of Pennsylvania on May 12, 1983.

39. Lubbock Civil Liberties Union v. Lubbock Independent School District, note 38 supra.

40. Senator Hatfield of Oregon has introduced legislation, S. 815 in the 98th Congress, similar to an earlier bill offered in the 97th Congress, which provides in part: "It shall be unlawful for a public secondary school receiving federal financial assistance, which generally allows groups of students to meet during noninstructional periods, to discriminate against any meeting of students on the basis of the religious content of the speech at such meeting, if (1) the meeting is voluntary and orderly, and (2) no activity which is in and of itself unlawful is permitted." See vol. 129 Congressio-nal Record no. 32, March 15, 1983, S. 2933. A similar proposal has been introduced as a constitutional amendment. Senator Denton's Bills are not limited to secondary schools. See S.425 and S.815, 98th Cong., 1st Sess.

41. Bd. of Education v. Allen, 392 U.S. 236 (1968).

42. 403 U.S. 602 (1971).

43. Committee for Public Education and Religious Liberty v. Nyquist, 413 U.S. 756 (1973); Meek v. Pittenger, 421 U.S. 349 (1975); Wolman v. Walter, 433 U.S. 229 (1977); Public Funds for Pub. Schools v. Marburger, 358 F. Supp. 29 (D.N.J. 1973), aff'd mem., 417 U.S. 961 (1974).

44. Committee for Public Education and Religious Liberty v. Regan, 444 U.S. 646 (1980).

45. Wolman v. Walter, 433 U.S. 229 (1977).

46. Tilton v. Richardson, 403 U.S. 672 (1971). *See also* Roemer v. Maryland, 426 U.S. 736 (1976).

47. *See* Note, "Laws Respecting an Establishment of Religion: An Inquiry into Tuition Tax Benefits," 58 *New York University Law Review* 207 (1983).

48. 103 S. Ct. 3062 (1983).

49. Committee for Public Education and Religious Liberty v. Nyquist, 413 U.S. 756 (1973).

50. *Ibid.*   .

51. Sloan v. Lemon, 413 U.S. 825 (1973).

52. *See* Rhode Island Federation of Teachers v. Norberg, 630 F. 2d 855 (1st Cir. 1980) (held invalid).

53. For the lower court decision upholding the Minnesota law see Mueller v. Allen, 676 F.2d 1185 (8th Cir. 1982).

54. In an earlier case, the Third Circuit relied on Nyquist in holding invalid a New Jersey law which provided a deduction rather than a credit. The Supreme Court affirmed without opinion. Public Funds for Public Schools v. Byrne, 590 F. 2d 514 (3d Cir. 1979), *aff'd mem.* 442 U.S. 907 (1979).

55. S. 528, 98th Cong., 1st Sess., 129 *Congressional Record* S.1335–38 (Feb. 17, 1983). In November 1983, the Senate rejected the president's proposed tuition tax-credit program. *New York Times* (November 17, 1983), at 1, col. 1.

56. Reprinted in Everson v. Bd. of Education, 330 U.S. 1, 63 (1967) (dissenting opinion of Justice Rutledge).

57. I. Brant, *James Madison, supra* note 2; Cahn "The 'Establishment of Religion' Puzzle," 36 *New York University Law Review* 1274 (1961).

58. Harris v. McRae, 448 U.S. 297 (1980).

59. 393 U.S. 97 (1968).

60. McLean v. Arkansas, 529 F. Supp. 1255 (E.D. Ark. 1982).

61. Board of Education, Island Trees Union Free School District v. Pico, 102 S. Ct. 1799 (1982).

62. Donnelly v. Lynch, note 19 *supra.*

NATIONAL SECURITY

MORTON H. HALPERIN

Morton H. Halperin is director of the Center for National Security Studies and of the ACLU's National Security Project. He is a former White House aide and the author of many books and articles, including Freedom vs. National Security. *He is an adjunct professor at Columbia University.*

The drafters of the American Constitution were well aware of the danger that claims of national security—to use the modern jargon—would be used to erode the liberties that they sought to protect. One of the few protections contained in the original Constitution—as distinguished from the Bill of Rights—guards against unfounded charges of treason being used to imprison those who oppose the policies of the state. Article 2, sec 3, provides: "Treason against the United States, shall consist only in levying war against them, or in adhering to their enemies, giving them aid and comfort." The founders understood that one of the most important ways in which claims of national security could be used to erode civil liberties was to accuse one's opponents of working under the direction or control of a foreign power hostile to the United States.

Episodically in our history we have needed to be reminded forcefully of Madison's warning in a letter to Jefferson late in his life that "perhaps it is a universal truth that the loss of liberty at home is to be charged to provision against danger, real or pretended, from abroad."[1] Particularly in times of war or of perceived threats from abroad, civil liberties have been compromised by actions of the Congress or the president that were upheld by the courts. During World Wars I and II, and the cold war, the president or the Congress took certain action, sometimes approved by the Supreme Court, which suggested that constitutional rights must be suspended before the needs of national defense. Thus, the Court upheld criminal penalties for those who spoke out against the draft during World War I, permitted relocation of Japanese-Americans during World War II, and sustained laws punishing alleged subversives during the cold war.[2]

Nevertheless, the Supreme Court often held firm, refusing to find in "national security" a talisman to sweep away all rights. For example, the Court invalidated President Truman's seizure of the steel mills during the Korean War despite claims that our military forces required uninterrupted steel production.[3] It mitigated some of the harsh anticommunist actions of the McCarthy era.[4] And, later, it struck down a federal statute that barred Communists from working in defense plants.[5] In these cases the Supreme Court did not assume that national security claims were bogus; rather it tried to accommodate them without releasing government from constitutional limitations.

There is no simple rule for determining how to balance national security against individual rights. The starting point, however, must be to take each seriously. If one argues that all national security claims are frivolous, it is easy to conclude that all efforts to expand state power should be resisted. Similarly, if one accepts all claims of national security at face value, then it is a short step to the sacrifice of individual rights. But if one acknowledges the legitimacy of both values, then it is necessary to reconcile the competing interests to enable the government to act consistently in terms of national security while protecting the civil liberties of Americans.

The so-called Graymail statute[6] provides an illustration of how this balancing can work. The national security concern that gave rise to this legislation was the difficulty of conducting criminal prosecutions in espionage cases and in cases concerning government officials charged with violating the rights of citizens. The government was often faced with difficult choices about whether to make public the classified national security information necessary to secure a conviction. Its problem was compounded by the fact that it often had to decide whether to declassify certain information before a court ruled on what information had to be made public.

The civil liberties concern was, of course, to ensure a fair and public trial. At first the government sought to solve the problem by changing the rules of evidence and procedure concerning classified information. When the government realized that this was unacceptable on civil liberties grounds, it agreed to procedures that would enable it to learn at a pretrial hearing how far it would have to go in making information public at trial and then make an educated judgment on whether to proceed with the prosecution. The result was a bill that has substantially increased the government's ability to prosecute cases involving classified information without interfering with a defendant's constitutional rights.[7]

A careful examination of the government's actual national security needs will often yield a means for accomplishing an objective without trampling on individual rights. In the end, however, one must recognize that the pursuit of national security, like all governmental interests, will not be achieved in ways consistent with the country's traditions if the consequence is to rend the Constitution. Unfortunately, there is considerable evidence that this has sometimes occurred.

THE LEGACY OF THE NIXON ERA

As in many other fields, the modern-day concern about the threat to civil liberties justified on national security grounds traces to the Nixon presidency. The most important decision of that period was hailed at the time as a great victory for civil liberties. In retrospect, however, it marks the beginning of an era in which the Supreme Court has often swept aside constitutional protections when the executive branch asserts that national security is at stake.

The case was *United States v. New York Times Co.,*[8] or the Pentagon Papers case, as it is known. The Court's six-to-three decision permitting the *Times* to go forward with publication of the secret history of the American war in Vietnam was hailed as a reaffirmation of the First Amendment. What was more important about the case was what the government tried to do and how the Court responded. Never before in our history had the government asked a court to enjoin a newspaper from publishing information in its possession. Until that time it had been generally assumed that, at least as to prior restraints, the First Amendment meant just what it said—Congress could pass "no law" in violation of the First Amendment. It was thought even clearer that the courts could not grant such an injunction at the request of a president relying on his own authority, that is, without a statute purporting to sanction such a serious step.

One courageous district judge did what the Constitution seemed to demand. He held that the courts simply lacked all authority to prevent a newspaper from publishing information in its possession. But the other lower-court judges who heard aspects of the case, and a majority of the Supreme Court, ruled that the government could enlist judicial aid in supressing publication of information conceded to be important to public debate on a major issue of the day. Acknowledging, at least by implication, the government's right to an injunction in certain circumstances, the courts differed with the government only on the appropriate legal standard and whether it had proved the case.[9]

Justices Potter Stewart and Byron White, who signed the decisive opinion in the Supreme Court, accepted earlier dicta that there was a national security exception to the First Amendment's absolute ban on prior restraint. Their holding foreshadowed a string of Supreme Court decisions that impaired constitutional rights. The opinion appeared to establish a very tough standard, requiring the government to prove that publication would "surely" result in "direct, immediate, and irreparable" harm to the nation.[10] Future cases were to show, however, that the government would allege appropriate facts to meet the prevailing standard, and that the courts would show great deference to such assertions.

This pattern emerged when the Nixon administration returned to the courts to prevent publication of national security information in the possession of a private citizen. It sought to enjoin Victor Marchetti, a former official of the CIA, from publishing a book based on his government experience. The district court and the court of appeals upheld the government's right to censor the book, and the Supreme Court was so little troubled that it declined twice to hear the cases.[11]

At about this time the Watergate revelations led Congress to amend the Freedom of Information Act to provide for judicial review of the government's assertion that information was properly classified.[12] Thus, while the courts, because of national security concerns, were ordering private citizens not to publish information in their possession, they gained the authority, at least in principle, to order the release of information in the control of the executive branch.

A widespread practice of the Nixon era was executive-branch surveillance of lawful political activity. When this was publicized during Watergate, it became politically necessary to impose some rules on the government's conduct of national security surveillance. Executive orders were issued that for the first time specified and limited the authority of intelligence agencies.[13] These regulations had beneficial effects, but they also emboldened the government to assert broad power to conduct surveillance of Americans when national security demanded it.

In considering the degree to which the legacies of the Nixon administration persist and contribute to the endangerment of our rights as we approach 1984, this essay focuses on threats to the Fourth and First amendments.

THE FOURTH AMENDMENT

No claim of the executive branch made in the name of national security is more reminiscent of George Orwell's world of Big Brother than the assertion that there is a national security exception to the warrant and other requirements of the Fourth Amendment.

Successive executive orders issued by Presidents Ford, Carter, and Reagan have asserted the right to conduct warrantless national security surveillances in circumstances where a warrant would be required in a criminal investigation.[14] The claimed authority sweeps away in one sentence the right of a person to be secure in home and person unless the executive has the consent of a magistrate to enter based on a finding of probable cause and unless the constable at the door announces his authority and intention to enter. It asserts that the attorney general may, if he determines that there is probable cause to believe that an American is an "agent of a foreign power" (an undefined term), authorize the FBI to enter one's home or office clandestinely, steal or photograph one's papers, and slip away without notice.

The drafters of the Fourth Amendment would hardly have countenanced the searches conducted by King George if only he had claimed that the rebellious colonialists were French agents. They would have been astonished to learn that the protections of the Fourth Amendment could be vitiated by a simple assertion that the targets were "agents" of a foreign power. Indeed, as we have seen, it was to guard against the temptation to call domestic opponents agents of foreign enemies that the framers wrote stringent limits on treason into the Constitution.

Similarly, those who went to prison for authorizing and conducting the break-in at the office of Daniel Ellsberg's psychiatrist would have been amazed to discover that the only error was Attorney General John Mitchell's failure to find that the alleged purloiner of the Pentagon Papers was an agent of a foreign power.[15] Yet this is what the executive branch has asserted. Using a definition that, if it exists, is too secret to be revealed to the public, any person may be subjected to a secret search without a judicial warrant if the attorney general decides he is an "agent of a foreign power."

Congress is aware of the government's assertion of power but has not acted. The one court that has considered the claim upheld it.[16] How often this power is used to enter our homes secretly we have no way of knowing, since notice is not given and the government's cameras leave no trace on what they copy.

Paradoxically, greater protection now exists against electronic surveillance, which requires a warrant from a judge based on a legislated standard of probable cause. In the past, concern about abuse of the Fourth Amendment focused on wiretapping because the government claimed the right to conduct warrantless electronic surveillance in all national security cases. The Supreme Court rejected this position, ruling that, in cases not involving agents of a foreign power, warrantless electronic surveillance was unconstitutional.[17] After several courts of appeals had upheld warantless surveillance of foreign powers,[18] Congress enacted a statute requiring warrants in virtually all cases of electronic surveillance in the United States.[19] This statute constitutes a reasonable attempt to balance privacy and the protection of national security. Concern remains that the statute might be subject to abuse, but on the whole the fears about warrantless electronic surveillance have abated.

THE FIRST AMENDMENT: PRIOR
RESTRAINT AND CENSORSHIP

Following the Pentagon Papers and Marchetti cases, the Carter administration continued the practice of enlisting the aid of the courts in restraining publication of information in private hands. When it learned that *Progressive* magazine was about to publish an article purporting to describe how to build an H-bomb, the government sought an injunction. Its arguments were a product of the seeds planted in the Pentagon Papers decision. First, the government demonstrated contempt for the high standard of proof apparently established in that case. Although its own affidavits showed that any harm from publication was tenuous, speculative, and remote, its pleadings alleged that the publication would surely result directly in grave damage to the nation. Second, the government sought authority for its injunction in the Atomic Energy Act. While that statute purports to authorize prior restraints, it seems in direct contradiction to the First Amendment's prohibition on congressional abridgement of free speech. Only the publication of the same material on the H-bomb in another magazine prevented the case from reaching the Supreme Court with potentially disastrous results. In any event, the case was a severe setback to the First Amendment prohibition on prior restraint because for weeks *Progressive* was enjoined from publishing an article on a matter of great public importance.[20]

These precedents clearly endanger the capacity of the press to publish and of the public to receive information. It appears that whenever the government is sufficiently upset, it can allege grave and irreparable damage to national security and almost certainly persuade a judge to delay publication until the government has an opportunity to prove its case.

Of equal concern is the extension of the censorship system established under the Carter administration and the extension proposed by President Reagan.

In 1978 the Justice Department brought suit against Frank Snepp, a former CIA official who wrote a book critical of the American evacuation from Vietnam. The government did not allege that Snepp had published classified information, as in the Marchetti case, but merely that he had not submitted his manuscript for review prior to publication.

In its most troublesome national security decision to date, which exhibits disdain for the right to speak and to be informed, the Supreme Court decided the case without the benefit of briefing or oral argument.[21] In a footnote of breathtaking brevity, the Court disposed of the First Amendment issue as follows:

> When Snepp accepted employment with the CIA, he voluntarily signed the agreement that expressly obligated him to submit any proposed publication for prior review. He does not claim that he executed this agreement under duress. Indeed, he voluntarily reaffirmed his obligation when he left the Agency. We agree with the Court of Appeals that Snepp's agreement is an 'entirely appropriate' exercise of the CIA Director's statutory mandate to "protec[t] intelligence sources and methods from unauthorized disclosure. . . . Moreover, this Court's case makes clear that—even in the absence of an express agreement—the CIA could have acted to protect substantial government interests by imposing

> reasonable restrictions on employee activities that in other con-
> texts might be protected by the First Amendment. . . . The
> government has a compelling interest in protecting both the se-
> crecy of information important to our national security and the
> appearance of confidentiality so essential to the effective operation
> of our foreign intelligence services. . . . The agreement that Snepp
> signed is a reasonable means for protecting this vital interest.[22]

Properly fearful of the breadth of the Snepp decision, the Carter administration in its closing days sought to limit government discretion to
censor former officials by establishing criteria specifying when an injunction would be proper. The Reagan administration had no such qualms.
It revoked the Carter restraints and then issued an order vastly expanding
the censorship system.

President Reagan's secrecy order[23] was issued on March 11, 1983—late
on a Friday afternoon, to avoid public attention and debate. The most
radical portion of the new order requires government agencies to establish
procedures to assure that all present and former officials who have access
to special intelligence information, and perhaps all who have access to any
classified information, must agree as a condition of employment to submit
for government review anything they write that is based on their government experience. In November 1983, as federal agencies were preparing
regulations to implement this executive order, Congress delayed its effective date until April 1984.

If the regulations become effective, they will cover every senior official
in the Departments of State and Defense, all members of the National
Security Council staff, many senior White House officials, and all senior
military and foreign service officers. Anything that is written—a book, a
news column, the text of a speech or a TV or radio commentary—must
be submitted even if it obviously does not include classified information.
The government of the day can remove anything that it believes is
classified. Because judicial review is a long and cumbersome process, the
government will ordinarily be able to impose its view of what is classified
since authors will rarely subject themselves to long publication delays
through litigation. If an individual fails to submit a publication for clearance, he or she forfeits all profits from the publication even if the manuscript contains no classified information.

This provision will make it extremely difficult for former officials to
function as a newspaper columnist, radio or TV commentator, or political

figure, since anything they write will be delayed while it is being cleared. (If the new censorship system had been in effect in prior years, even the assessment of the order's impact contained in this essay would be subject to clearance, since it is written by a former official who had special clearances and draws on information acquired in government service.)

The CIA has the only currently functioning censorship system, having reviewed more than eight hundred manuscripts of its former officials. Although the CIA did not have to consult other agencies and was ordinarily dealing with former agents whom it considered friendly, it nevertheless has often required the deletion of material a writer did not believe to be classified, and it has forced protracted negotiations before agreeing to permit other material to be published.

The full impact of the secrecy order can be glimpsed by listing some of those who would have been required to clear their material if this program had been in effect in the past:

• the speeches and writings of Richard Allen, Alexander Haig, and Eugene Rostow

• the political speeches and position papers of candidates such as George Bush, former CIA director

• the memoirs of Henry Kissinger, Zbigniew Brzezinski, and Hamilton Jordan

• columns by Jody Powell, Patricia Darien, and Elmo Zumwalt—with time delays that would make it almost impossible for them to function as journalists

• news articles by Leslie Gelb and Richard Burt

• congressional testimony by Paul Warnke, Melvin Laird, and David Jones—making timely presentation difficult

• lectures by Professors Anthony Lake and Roger Hilsman

• reports to clients by bankers and lawyers such as Brent Scowcroft, Richard Holbrooke, and David Aaron.

If implemented, the Reagan order will drastically alter the conditions of public debate on national security issues and give the government sweeping control over the release of information to the public. Among other things, it will be able to prevent former officials whom it viewed as hostile from publishing their views by arguing that the information they wanted to present was classified. One can conceive of a narrowly drawn regulation that would balance the competing interests properly, but this order completely ignores the public's right to know.

The Reagan administration has also interfered with the free speech of scientists who may come into contact with foreign scientists in the United States or abroad. With no sound basis in the law, it has relied on the Export Control Act to censor unclassified scientific papers and to deter American scientists from discussing unclassified research with foreign colleagues. As of mid-1983 the American scientific community had generally resisted these efforts, but there was a risk that some would succumb because the administration had begun to threaten the termination of research support to those who did not comply.[24]

THE FIRST AMENDMENT RESTRICTIONS ON INFORMATION-GATHERING

In addition to seeking to prevent private citizens from disseminating certain information, the government has expanded its authority to withhold classified information in its own possession. Despite a clear congressional policy that courts be satisfied that information is properly classified before its release is denied under the Freedom of Information Act, judges have regularly deferred to executive-branch assertions even where the government's claims stretched credulity.[25] For example, CIA assertions that it could not reveal details of the Glomar Explorer episode relating to the efforts to raise a Soviet submarine were upheld on the ground that the government's public explanation was merely a cover story without foundation in fact.[26]

The courts have shown equal, if not greater, deference in permitting the government to withhold information that individuals need to pursue damage actions for alleged violations of constitutional rights.[27] Perhaps the most disturbing cases have related to the National Security Agency (NSA). Established by a still secret presidential order, the NSA engages in the interception of communications, including the international cable traffic and overseas telephone conversations of American citizens. In the

1960s, NSA obtained names from the FBI, the CIA, and other agencies, and put them on a watch list for the purpose of intercepting their communications. When individuals with reason to believe that they were targets of this surveillance sued for damages, the courts dismissed the claims after upholding NSA's right to keep secret information relating to the process by which it gathered information and even the fact of whether a particular individual had been overheard.[28] Rulings that defer so broadly to the executive branch place NSA outside the reach of the courts even when clear evidence of constitutional violations exists.

The executive branch has also sought to limit the right of Americans to travel abroad to gather information and to receive foreign visitors, and it has banned or stigmatized foreign publications. The most serious effort to control travel came when the Carter administration sought to confiscate the passport of Philip Agee, a former CIA official, on the ground that his visits to Iran and other countries might harm national security. In disregard of prior Supreme Court decisions and of Congress's expressed intention to restrict the president's power to limit travel on political grounds, the Supreme Court in the Agee case held that the secretary of state could lift an American's passport whenever he concluded that the individual's travel to a foreign country would interfere with the effective conduct of American foreign policy.[29] Unless Congress reverses the case, a potential restraint on travel will hang over Americans in periods of international tension.

Although it has not sought to use the power ceded to the president in the Agee case, the Reagan administration has prevented Americans from traveling to Cuba by invoking provisions of the Trading with the Enemy Act. In the name of curbing the flow of financial resources to Cuba, the administration has sought to prevent Americans from traveling there to decide for themselves whether Cuba threatens American interests.[30]

Although the Congress has generally tried to limit the executive branch's power to curtail the right of Americans to travel abroad, it has accorded the president broad authority to restrict the entry of aliens into the United States at the invitation of Americans seeking their views on matters of public policy. The Reagan administration has relied on the McCarran-Walters Act[31] to deny visas to Japanese who wished to participate in demonstrations at the UN, limit the duration of a visit by a Soviet official, and deny a visa to Mrs. Salvadore Allende, widow of the slain Chilean leader.[32] The administration has also sought to curtail the movement of written materials into the United States by restricting the importation of publications from Cuba[33] and by stigmatizing other materials by labeling them "political propaganda" under the Foreign Agents Registration Act.[34]

Taken together, these actions constitute an assault on the right of Americans to participate intelligently in the political process as well as to obtain information necessary to resist government encroachment on their liberties.

CONCLUSION

Given the "national security" powers claimed by the executive branch and in some instances sanctioned by the courts, a foreign affairs crisis that triggered domestic dissent could lead to a substantial curtailment of civil liberties and free public debate.

Imagine a massive escalation of military involvement in Central American followed by public demonstrations and the organization of groups promoting opposition to American policy. An American government could use the powers discussed in this essay in ways that would seriously threaten civil liberties.

The attorney general might well decide that some of the groups organizing the opposition were "agents of a foreign power" since they would be working with unfriendly political movements in Central America. Although the precise definition of "agent of a foreign power" is secret, it is known that "foreign power" includes foreign political movements that the United States does not recognize as legitimate. If the attorney general were to decide that there was a sufficient link between the American political group and the foreign political movement, he could authorize the FBI to conduct warrantless physical searches of the offices of the organizations and the homes of its leaders. These surreptitious searches would involve the photographing of records, including membership lists, notwithstanding the privacy rights of political groups. Other forms of surveillance might also be authorized, including infiltration with informers. The targeted groups could not know that they were subject to surveillance and hence would be unable to challenge the investigation or the government's use of the information.

Other actions of the government would be visible but very difficult to challenge successfully.

The State Department might seek to prevent Americans from traveling to Central America to meet with opposition figures and to make statements in opposition to American policy. Relying on the Agee decision, the government could lift the passports of those whose travel was found detrimental to the national interest.

If a former government official were planning to write an article critical of the administration's policy, the government might insist that it be subject to prior review and then require the removal of information, relevant to public debate, which it asserted was classified.

If a newspaper gained access to a classified government document describing U.S. military plans for expanded operations in the region, the government might seek an injunction against publication by arguing that the Pentagon Papers standard was met. At best there would be a delay while the court decided the case; at worst the first permanent injunction against publication of politically relevant information would be entered.

Since these actions would be public, they could be challenged in the courts. But given the recent pattern of the Supreme Court to broaden the power of the president and erode constitutional protections in national security cases the likelihood of success would be small.

Prospects in Congress are no better. Experience indicates that there is little or no chance to enact national security legislation that the president or the intelligence agencies oppose. Members of Congress are simply unwilling to take the responsibility for passing such laws.

Accordingly, in the absence of events comparable to Watergate and Vietnam, the only hope for reform is election of a president committed to legislation designed to avoid violations of civil liberties in the name of national security.

Such action is rare but not unprecedented. The Carter administration supported legislation to require warrants for national security electronic surveillance. A committed president would support legislation that specified proper standards for counterintelligence and that would prohibit all warrantless searches. Such a president would also support laws repealing the power to deny passports for political activity and requiring former officials to submit manuscripts for prepublication review.

Even if a president were willing to take these actions, it would be difficult to overcome bureaucratic or congressional opposition without strong public support. This in turn requires public understanding of the great powers now claimed by the president and what their impact on American liberty could be, especially in a foreign affairs crisis.

We must return to the basic principle that guided the founders of this nation. Claims of national security, like all other claims of government power, must be scrutinized with skepticism. Even when they are valid, they must be implemented in ways that protect constitutional rights. Anything less makes a mockery of the assertion that the government is conducting its national security policy in order to maintain an environment in which liberty in America can continue to flourish.

NOTES

1. Letter from James Madison to Thomas Jefferson, May 13, 1798.

2. Schenck v. U.S., 249 U.S. 47 (1919); Korematsu v. U.S., 323 U.S. 214 (1944); Dennis v. U.S., 341 U.S. 494 (1951).

3. Youngstown Sheet and Tube Co. v. Sawyer, 343 U.S. 570 (1952).

4. *E.g.*, Kent v. Dulles, 357 U.S. 116 (1958); DeGregory v. Attorney General, 383 U.S. 825 (1966).

5. U.S. v. Robel, 389 U.S. 258 (1967); *see also* U.S. v. Brown, 381 U.S. 437 (1965).

6. Classified Information Procedures Act, P.L. 94-456 (1980); 94 Stat 2025; 18 U.S.C. App. (1982).

7. For background, see House Reports No. 96-1436 (Conference Report); Senate Report No. 96-822.

8. 403 U.S. 713 (1971).

9. For all the opinions, *see The New York Times Co. v. U.S.: A Documentary History*, vol. I & II (1971).

10. 403 U.S. at 730 (Stewart, J).

11. U.S. v. Marchetti, 466 F.2d 1309 (4th Cir. 1972); Alfred A. Knopf, Inc. v. Colby, 509 F.2d 1362 (4th Cir. 1975), cert. denied 421 U.S. 908 (1975).

12. Public Law 93-502 (1974), 5 U.S.C. § 552 (1976).

13. U.S. Foreign Intelligence Activities, Executive Order 11905 (1976); *see also* Executive Order 12036 (1978); Executive Order 12333 (1981).

14. *Id. See also* Executive Order 12333, § 2.5.

15. U.S. v. Ehrlichman, 376 F. Supp. 29 (D.D.C. 1974), *aff'd* 546 F.2d 1910 (D.C. Cir. 1976), *cert. denied*, 429 U.S. 1120 (1977).

16. U.S. v. Trung Dinh Hung, 629 F.2d 908 (4th Cir. 1980).

17. U.S. v. U.S. District Court, 407 U.S. 297 (1972).

18. U.S. v. Smith, 321 F. Supp. 424 (C.D. Cal. 1971); U.S. v. Clay, 430 F. 2d 165 (5th Cir. 1970); U.S. v. Brown, 484 F.2d 418 (5th Cir. 1973); U.S. v. Butenko, 494 F.2d 593 (3rd Cir. 1974) (en banc).

19. Foreign Intelligence Surveillance Act of 1978; Public Law 95-511 (1978), 50 U.S.C. § 1801 (Supp. V, 1981).

20. U.S. v. Progressive, Inc., 467 F.Supp. 990 (W.D. Wis. 1979).

21. U.S. v. Snepp, 444 U.S. 507 (1980).

22. 444 U.S. at 509 n. 3.

23. NSDD-84 (March 11, 1983).

24. *See generally* A. Adler, "Dangerous Information: A Dangerous Concept," First Principles 1 (July 1982).

25. *See* Shaffer and Halperin, "Exemption 1" in A. Adler and M. Halperin eds., *Litigation Under the Federal FOIA and Privacy Act* (9th ed. 1984).

26. Military Audit Project v. Casey, 656 F.2d 724 (D.C. Cir. 1981).

27. *See, e.g.,* Halkin v. Helms, 690 F.2d 977 (D.C. Dir. 1982).

28. Salisbury v. U.S., 690 F.2d 966 (D.C. Cir. 1982); Jabara v. Webster, 691 F.2d 272 (6th Cir. 1982); Halkin v. Helms, 598 F.2d 1 (D.C. Cir. 1978).

29. Haig v. Agee, 453 U.S. 280 (1981).

30. Wald v. Regan, 708 F.2d 794 (1st Cir. 1983). The Supreme Court has granted review of this decision invalidating the travel ban.

31. 8 U.S.C. § 1182.

32. *Washington Post,* March 4, 1983; The NGO Comm. on Disarmament v. Haig, no. 82-6147 (2nd Cir. June 18, 1982).

33. ACLU, *Free Speech 1984* 22-24 (1983).

34. Block v. Smith, D.C. no. 83-0672 (Complaint filed D.D.C. March 9, 1983).

ARYEH NEIER

Aryeh Neier is vice-chairman of the Americas Watch and the Helsinki Watch, international human rights organizations. He was formerly executive director of the ACLU and is an adjunct professor of law at NYU and Cardozo law schools. His most recent book is Only Judgment.

In July 1983, as the United States launched large-scale naval maneuvers off the coasts of Nicaragua and disclosed publicly that the Central Intelligence Agency would greatly increase its support for the "contras" trying to overthrow the Sandinista government, President Reagan offered this explanation at a new conference:

> [The Sandinistas] made specific promises as to what they would do with regard to freedom of the press and freedom of, well, all the freedoms that we enjoy here in this country. They have violated all those provisions. . . . And what the contras are really seeking, having been members of the Sandinista revolution for the most part, in its effort to bring democracy to Nicaragua, they are trying to restore the original purpose of the revolution.[1]

To anyone aware that the United States provides vast support for governments such as those in Pakistan, Turkey, and El Salvador where freedom of the press and "all the freedoms we enjoy here in this country" are circumscribed more drastically than in Nicaragua, President Reagan's sincerity might seem questionable. Even so, what is remarkable about the president's statement is that he apparently thought that pointing to human rights deficiencies was an appropriate way to justify a measure of military intervention in the affairs of another country. Whether or not it was intended, that is something of a tribute to the growing strength of the idea that nations should be concerned in their foreign policies with the promotion of international human rights, especially as it came from a president who was at pains to repudiate that idea just two and a half years earlier at the outset of his presidency. A review of the brief history of human rights as an international concern may be helpful in suggesting why President Reagan, at least ostensibly, reversed field, and in understanding the implications of his reversal.

What is known as international human rights is built around two ideas: first, that citizens should be protected by international law and international norms against violations of their rights by their own governments; second, that governments should take into account violations of citizens' rights by other governments in shaping their policies toward those governments. Both ideas are relatively new and gained significant acceptance only in the era following World War II and, to a significant extent, because of the experience of World War II.

The United Nations Charter, adopted in 1945, just a few months after the conclusion of the war, embodies both ideas. It establishes an international norm by providing that:

> [T]he United Nations shall promote universal respect for, and observance of, human rights and fundamental freedoms for all without distinction as to race, sex, language, or religion.[2]

It also imposes an obligation on member governments to promote human rights in their dealings with other governments by providing that

> All Members pledge themselves to take joint and separate action in cooperation with the Organization for the achievement of the purposes set forth in Article 55.[3]

Subsequently, a considerable number of international agreements have committed governments to respect the rights of their own citizens. These include the Universal Declaration of Human Rights (1948); the Convention on the Prevention and Punishment of the Crime of Genocide (1948); the Protocol Relating to the Status of Refugees (1951); the Standard Minimum Rules for the Treatment of Prisoners (1955); the International Covenant on Economic, Social and Cultural Rights (1966); the International Covenant on Civil and Political Rights (1966); the European Convention on Human Rights (1953); the American Convention on Human

Rights (1969); the International Convention on the Elimination of all Forms of Racial Discrimination (1965); and the Helsinki Accords (1975). Among them, these agreements spell out, often in considerable detail, virtually all the rights that Americans enjoy under the United States Constitution. In a few instances, the rights protected internationally conflict with American ideas about rights, as in the case of the prohibition on "dissemination of ideas based on racial superiority" in the Convention on Racial Discrimination.[4] In many more instances, the rights protected internationally go beyond those that can be read into the United States Constitution, as in the case of the asserted "right of everyone to . . . a decent living for themselves and their families" in the Covenant on Economic, Social and Cultural Rights.[5]

The United States is a party to only a few of the international agreements on rights. Most countries of the world, however, including countries that fall far short of the United States in actually respecting the rights of their own citizens, have committed themselves to be bound by these agreements. Though it obviously diminishes the significance of these agreements greatly for some governments that actually implement them not to say that they are bound by them, and for other countries that say they are bound by them not to implement them, the international agreements on rights retain a residual importance. This has more to do with the fact that they are international than with their precise language or legal status. Their importance lies principally in serving as part of the apparatus that has legitimized the idea that the way a government treats its own citizens matters internationally. Though such abuses are still as widely practiced as ever, it is now internationally accepted that governments that murder, kidnap, or torture their citizens, or imprison or exile them for their views, are transgressing international legal norms. Indeed, by now that idea is so well accepted that it is hard to imagine the clock ever being turned back to reflect the contrary view that was prevalent until the latter part of World War II and the adoption of the U.N. Charter.

The failure of the United States to commit itself to be bound by most international agreements on rights obviously makes those agreements of little use in protecting Americans against infringement of their rights by their own government. With the prominent exception of the use of international-law principles in attempting to secure political asylum for refugees (discussed in the essay by Steven Shapiro and Wade Henderson in this volume), probably the best use that can be made of international agreements is to persuade courts to look to them for guidance in interpreting U.S. constitutional guarantees of rights. For example, in applying the Eighth Amendment to the United States Constitution in a prison case, courts might be urged to look to the United Nations Standard Minimum Rules for the Treatment of Prisoners in determining whether a practice is cruel and unusual by international standards. By itself, an unratified agreement such as the Standard Minimum Rules is unlikely to be disposi- tive. Conceivably, however, in combination with other factors, attention to international standards could affect the outcome of litigation. There is only scant precedent that can be cited to demonstrate the usefulness of this approach,[6] but that may be primarily due to the infrequency with which American lawyers have tried to persuade courts to use international agreements in this way.

Another value of unratified international agreements in domestic litiga- tion in the United States is that these are part of what is considered "customary international law." The United States Supreme Court has held that

> where there is no treaty, and no controlling executive or legislative act or judicial decision, resort must be had to the customs and usages of civilized nations; and, as evidence of these, to the works of jurists and commentators, who by years of labor, research and experience, have made themselves peculiarly well acquainted with the subjects of which they treat. Such works are resorted to by judicial tribunals, not for the speculations of their authors con- cerning what the law ought to be, but for trustworthy evidence of what the law really is.[7]

The opportunities to apply customary international law to promote human rights through domestic litigation in the United States are rare, but an appropriate instance arose in 1979. A Paraguayan visiting the United States, Dolly Filartiga, learned that another Paraguayan, Americo Pena, was also in the United States. Ms. Filartiga knew Pena as the Inspector General of Police in Asunción and as the man who had kid- napped and tortured to death her brother Joelito, apparently in reprisal for the political activities and beliefs of Dr. Joel Filartiga, father of Dolly and Joelito. The Filartigas sued Pena under a law adopted as part of the Judiciary Act of 1789, the Alien Tort Statute, which provides: "The district courts shall have original jurisdiction of any civil action by an alien for a tort only, committed in violation of the law of nations or a treaty of the United States."[8]

In *Filartiga v. Pena*[9] a United States Court of Appeals found that the prohibition against torture in several international agreements had become part of customary international law and that "official torture is now prohibited by the law of nations."[10] Accordingly, the Filartiga family was sustained in its effort to sue Pena in a federal district court in New York for torture that took place in Paraguay.

Though *Filartiga v. Pena* stirred considerable excitement among some advocates of international human rights, it is not at all clear that there will be much chance to build on this precedent. The human rights practices of other governments may be susceptible to influence through the management of United States foreign policy but, except in the most unusual circumstances, this would seem to be a matter that must be pursued through the executive branch of the federal government and through Congress, not through the judiciary.

In the early 1970s, Congress began to enact laws placing human rights conditions on United States dealings with other countries. In part an outgrowth of revulsion against some practices of the government of South Vietnam (a principal author of such legislation, Rep. Tom Harkin of Iowa, had been the discoverer of the "tiger cages" in Vietnam), and in part a reaction to the violent abuses of human rights that marked the military coup in Chile in 1973, most of these laws established conditions regulating United States economic or military assistance to other countries.

One of the most important laws enacted in the 1970s was the addition of Section 502B to the Foreign Assistance Act of 1961. Its language and its history are typical of laws regulating United States foreign policy so as to promote human rights in other countries.

In 1974, the U.S. Senate debated proposals variously made by Senators Kennedy, Abourezk, and Cranston to link military aid to human rights. These proposals led to the enactment that year of the original version of Section 502B, which provided that it was the sense of Congress that, "except in extraordinary circumstances, the President shall substantially reduce or terminate security assistance to any government which engages in a consistent pattern of gross violations of internationally recognized human rights."[11] In 1976, under the leadership of Rep. Donald Fraser and freshman Rep. Stephen Solarz, the language of 502B was amended by Congress to require an absolute cutoff in military aid to governments engaging in gross abuses of rights. This was vetoed by President Ford, however, and a new, watered-down version was adopted by Congress, and then signed into law by Ford, permitting military aid under circumstances specified in the law itself and requiring a joint resolution of Congress to end military aid to a given country. By 1978, however, with President Jimmy Carter in the White House, who could be counted on not to veto tougher legislation, Congress adopted the version of 502B in the form that prevails today.[12] As in the case of the earlier version of the legislation, the essential language bars "security assistance . . . for any country the government of which engages in a consistent pattern of gross violations of internationally recognized rights." Also, as in earlier versions, the legislation contains an exception for "extraordinary circumstances." However, in circumstances in which an administration is intent on maintaining aid to a government that is grossly violating rights, rather than imposing the onus on Congress to end aid by a joint resolution, the 1978 law requires that military aid must stop "unless the President certifies in writing to the Speaker of the House of Representatives and the chairman of the Committee on Foreign Relations of the Senate that extraordinary circumstances exist warranting provision of such assistance."

The reference in the legislation to "internationally recognized human rights" indicates the significance for United States domestic law of various international agreements on human rights. Even though the United States has not ratified most of those agreements and has not formally incorporated them into domestic law, the rights protected by those agreements are "internationally recognized." Accordingly, United States laws regulating the conduct of foreign policy require that even though the United States has not agreed to be bound by various international norms, its dealings with other countries must be regulated in accordance with their adherence to those norms.

Section 502B contains its own enumeration of "internationally recognized human rights," specifying that the term "includes [freedom from] torture or cruel, inhuman, or degrading treatment or punishment, prolonged detention without charges and trial, causing the disappearance of persons by the abduction and clandestine detention of those persons, and other flagrant denials of the right to life, liberty, or the security of persons." The same enumeration appears in Section 116 of the Foreign Assistance Act,[13] which prohibits economic assistance "unless such assistance will directly benefit the needy people" to any country which "engages in a consistent pattern of gross violations of internationally recognized human rights." Similarly, such an enumeration appears in Section 701 of the International Financial Institutions Act,[14] which requires United States representatives in international lending institutions to oppose loans to gross violators of human rights.

Other legislation simply uses the term "internationally recognized human rights" without defining it. The best-known example is Section 728 of the International Security and Development Cooperation Act of 1981,[15] the law requiring that the president certify that the government of El Salvador is meeting certain conditions if it is to continue to receive United States military assistance. Under the law, one of the conditions that the president must certify is "that the Government of El Salvador is making a concerted and significant effort to comply with internationally recognized human rights." Another provision of this law makes military assistance depend on presidential certification that El Salvador is bringing "an end to the indiscriminate torture and murder of Salvadoran citizens" by the security forces.[16] This is not intended as a complete definition of "internationally recognized human rights," however. That term has acquired a broader significance that is derived from what have come to be considered the essential provisions of the various international agreements on human rights concluded since World War II.

The requirement for certification of El Salvador is an example of what has come to be known as "country specific" legislation. That is, Congress has enacted a series of laws that regulate U.S. relations with named countries in accordance with the way those countries perform with respect to particular human rights problems. In the case of Argentina, those conditions include accounting for the "disappeared" and releasing or bringing to trial prisoners held without charges;[17] in the case of Chile, bringing to justice those indicated by a United States grand jury for the murders of Orlando Letelier and Ronni Moffitt in Washington, D.C. in 1976;[18] in the case of Nicaragua, the free movement within the country of the Inter-American Commission on Human Rights and a "framework for Democratic elections";[19] in the case of Pakistan, "the expeditious restoration of full civil liberties and representative government;"[20] and so on. In addition, a few laws apply to several countries, most notably the Jackson-Vanik Amendment adopted in 1976 that restricts U.S. trade relations with "non–market economy" (i.e., Communist) countries in accordance with their policies on emigration.[21]

Aside from the general laws restricting U.S. military or economic assistance to countries that violate human rights and the country-specific laws, the other important legislation in this field establishes the post of assistant secretary of state for human rights and humanitarian affairs,[22] and requires that the Department of State submit to Congress annually "a full and complete report regarding the status of internationally recognized human rights . . . in countries that receive assistance . . . and in all other countries which are members of the United Nations."[23]

Though most of the laws imposing human rights conditions on United States foreign policy were enacted, in some form or another, prior to the election of Jimmy Carter as president, public opinion came to associate them with the Carter administration. One reason was that the Carter administration was the first that was required by law to appoint an assistant secretary of state to head the State Department's Bureau of Human Rights, and the first that was required by law to publish what has since become an annual report on the human rights practices of other countries.[24] In practice, the Carter administration was far from consistent in its actual implementation of the laws requiring it to condition relations with other countries on their domestic human rights practices, but its public posture was to identify itself with the promotion of human rights.

When the Carter presidency ended at the moment of—and in considerable part, because of—the hostage crisis in Iran, its human rights policy came under fire from the succeeding administration for helping to create that crisis. The reasoning went like this: by criticizing the regime of the Shah of Iran on human rights grounds (such criticism had been, at most, very mild) the Carter administration destabilized his government. This led to the establishment of the Khomeini regime. The Khomeini regime seized the hostages. *Ergo*, the Carter administration's human rights policy helped bring about the seizure of the American hostages. Comparable reductionism characterized the statements of the incoming administration about the overthrow of the Somoza regime in Nicaragua and its replacement by the Sandinistas. Writing in *Commentary* in the month that President Reagan took office, January 1981, Jeane Kirkpatrick, the new President's choice to serve as ambassador to the United Nations, put it this way:

> What did the Carter Administration do in Nicaragua? *It brought down the Somoza regime. . . .*
>
> First, it declared "open season" on the Somoza regime. When in the spring of 1977 the State Department announced that shipments of U.S. arms would be halted for human rights violations, and followed this with announcement in June and October that economic aid would be withheld, it not only deprived the Somoza regime of needed economic and military support but served notice

that the regime no longer enjoyed the approval of the United States and could no longer count on its protection. . . .

Second, the Carter administration's policies inhibited the Somoza regime in dealing with its opponents while they were weak enough to be dealt with. Fearful of U.S. reproaches and reprisals, Somoza fluctuated between repression and indulgence in his response to FSLN violence. The rules of the Carter human rights policy made it impossible for Somoza to resist his opponents effectively.

Third, by its "mediation" efforts and its initiatives in the Organization of American States (OAS), the Carter Administration encouraged the internationalization of the opposition. Further, it demoralized Somoza and his supporters by insisting that Somoza's continuation in power was the principal obstacle to a viable, centrist democratic government.[25]

Missing, of course, is any acknowledgement that the Carter administration's policies on military aid and economic aid to the Somoza regime were dictated by United States laws banning such assistance to governments engaged in a consistent pattern of gross violations of internationally recognized human rights. Also absent from Kirkpatrick's analysis was any attempt to resolve the contradiction between her assertion, on the one hand, that the Carter administration ended military and economic aid by 1977 and, on the other hand, that the administration inhibited the Somoza regime in dealing with its opponents for the two years thereafter until it fell in July 1979 for fear of United States reproaches and reprisals. What was important about Kirkpatrick's analysis, however, was that it blamed the Carter administration's human rights policy for the triumph of a Marxist revolution in Central America.

Kirkpatrick's attack on the Carter administration's human rights policy was characteristic of several such statements by prominent members of the incoming Reagan administration. Indeed, this attack appeared for a while to challenge the very idea that the United States should make promotion of human rights a factor in its foreign policy. The nomination by President Reagan of Ernest Lefever to serve as assistant secretary of state for human rights was particularly important because Lefever was principally known as an advocate of the view that it is inappropriate for United States foreign policy to be concerned with the human rights practices of other countries and for favoring the repeal of all U.S. legislation concerned with those practices.

The designation of Lefever turned out, however, to be a great error from the standpoint of those eager to abandon concern for international human rights. Because his views were considered so extreme, proponents of human rights as a foreign policy concern were able to mount an effective campaign against him, leading to a Senate Foreign Relations Committee vote in June 1981 rejecting the nomination by a margin of thirteen to four. In the face of that vote, the nomination was withdrawn.

Senate rejection of a presidential nominee is very unusual. As of this writing (mid–1983), Lefever is the only Reagan nominee to be rejected; no Carter or Ford nominees were rejected; and it is necessary to go back to the rejection more than a decade earlier of Clement Haynsworth and Harold Carswell, President Nixon's nominees to the U.S. Supreme Court, to discover any parallel to the Lefever episode. What happened to Lefever seemed to indicate that there was considerable sentiment in the country for making the human rights practices of other governments a foreign policy concern. At the same time, the episode greatly strengthened the political influence of human rights proponents.

The Lefever rejection precipitated the adoption by the Reagan administration of a new approach to human rights, signaled publicly by a State Department policy paper that was approved by Secretary of State Alexander Haig in November 1981. It said:

> *Human rights is at the core of our foreign policy* because it is central to what America is and stands for. "Human rights" is not something we tack on to our foreign policy, but is its very purpose: the defense and promotion of freedom in the world. This is *not* merely a rhetorical point: *We will never maintain wide public support for our foreign policy unless we can relate it to American ideals and to the defense of freedom.* Congressional belief that we have no consistent human rights policy threatens to disrupt important foreign policy initiatives. Human rights has been one of the main avenues for domestic attack on the Administration's foreign policy.[26]

This statement was important because it marked the end of the attempt to repudiate the very idea that human rights should be promoted through United States foreign policy. On the other hand, it did not inaugurate a period of harmony between proponents of human rights and the Reagan administration. Rather, it shifted the battle. Instead of arguing about whether it is appropriate for one country to promote human rights in another country, they began to argue about the facts: Who is doing the killing in El Salvador or Guatemala? How many people are being killed? Is Nicaragua a totalitarian state? Is Turkey practicing torture? And so on.

The most heated battles over facts involved El Salvador, in part because of the law requiring certification every 180 days that certain human rights conditions are being met if United States military assistance to that country is to continue.[27] At this writing, the Reagan administration has certified compliance with those conditions on four occasions. Critics in Congress and in the leading voluntary organizations dedicated to promoting human rights internationally contend that none of these certifications is warranted. Accordingly, the two sides present different versions of the facts in El Salvador to justify their different positions.

The Reagan administration's pronouncements on Nicaragua most dramatically illustrate its change of approach. At the outset, concern with human rights was blamed by Kirkpatrick and other leading members of the administration for bringing down the Somoza regime, which was friendly to the United States. Yet, less than three years later, the Reagan administration was justifying its efforts to bring down the Sandinista regime by professing concern for human rights. The constants here, of course, are hostility to the Sandinistas and a longing for the restoration of United States hegemony over Central America. What changed was the administration's assessment of the public acceptability of various rationales for policy.

A cynic might contend that the shift in approach by the Reagan administration represents no progress. Indeed, with respect to El Salvador, as with respect to Nicaragua, it is only rhetoric that has changed. In the case of El Salvador it has made no difference for the Reagan administration to profess concern for human rights but then to paint a much rosier picture of the human rights situation in that country than is seen by just about anyone else. Yet such a cynical appraisal may take too narrow a view.

For a cause as young as the effort to promote human rights through United States foreign policy, it matters greatly that an administration that was outspokenly antagonistic to it has come to endorse it, even if insincerely. Moreover, there are limits to the ability of any administration to engage in disputes over facts. In the case of the Reagan administration, that is evident in considering its actions with respect to Argentina and Chile.

Certification of compliance with human rights conditions is also a prerequisite for military assistance to these countries.[28] Despite the widely held belief that the Reagan administration is eager to certify both Argentina and Chile, at this writing (in mid–1983) neither has been certified by the Reagan administration. Having created credibility problems for itself in the Congress and in the U.S. public by its repeated certifications of El Salvador, the Reagan administration apparently has decided that those problems would be exacerbated by also certifying Argentina and Chile. Preventing a guerrilla triumph in El Salvador is of central significance to the Reagan administration. Accordingly, it appears willing to go to great lengths to present a favorable view of human rights developments there in order to keep military assistance flowing to the government of El Salvador. But this cannot be done every place at the same time, and the noncertification of Argentina and Chile seems to reflect this.

Ironically, the Reagan administration—which came into office expressing vehement opposition to efforts to promote human rights through United States foreign policy—has done more than any previous administration to promote human rights as a cause. At the outset, its very hostility gave the human rights cause a visibility that it lacked previously. Then, the Reagan administration's shift in which it announced that "human rights is at the core of our foreign policy" served to legitimate the cause, all the more so because this represented a reversal by those who had previously espoused an opposite view. Finally, the disputes over facts that the Reagan administration engages in with members of Congress and with voluntary organizations that promote human rights ensure continuing public attention. By their nature, such disputes are far more newsworthy than general exhortations to promote human rights which characterized many public statements by proponents of this cause in an earlier era.

Though it has (albeit unintentionally) promoted human rights as a cause, or as a movement, the Reagan administration can hardly be said to have promoted the substance of human rights. Yet in strengthening the movement, the administration has increased the pressure on itself to promote human rights. Even more significant, it has made it likely that future administrations will also face increased pressures from this movement. Indeed, the Reagan administration is even responsible for stimulating the growth of a human rights movement in other countries where its battles with its human rights critics within the United States have attracted considerable interest.

The interest generated in Western Europe by controversies over human rights between the Reagan administration and its critics within the United States has become a factor in the development of international hostility toward the policies the Reagan administration has pursued in Central America. Previously, as when the Eisenhower administration overthrew the Arbenz government in Guatemala in 1954, or when the Johnson administration sent twenty-five thousand troops to the Dominican Republic in 1965, Western Europeans paid little attention to efforts by the United States to maintain control of the region. Today, in large measure because of controversies over the state of human rights in El Salvador, Guatemala, and Nicaragua, Western Europeans—many of whom might have had difficulty even differentiating these countries until recently—put pressure on their own governments to modify United States policy. Accordingly, the Reagan administration finds itself having to weigh the consequences for its relationships with its allies in Western Europe of the policies it pursues in Central America.

Considering that regimes that systematically abuse human rights currently hold power not only in most of Central America but also in most of Asia, much of Africa, all of Eastern Europe and all of the southern cone of Latin America, it would be folly to suggest that the ideas of the international human rights movement have yet made much of a difference in practice. Victims of human rights violations continue to be as severely abused as ever, and there is not much basis for optimism in the near term. Nor is it probable, for that matter, that the replacement of the Reagan administration by an administration more committed to even-handed efforts to promote human rights would quickly produce any discernible decline in the worldwide quantity of human rights abuses. In the short run, such an administration would do well if it could rehabilitate the image of the United States by dissociating us from the most brutally repressive regimes. Significant impact on the human rights situation in other countries, however, will require sustained effort over a long period.

The most that can be said for what has been accomplished by the human rights movement is that it is increasingly necessary for the nations of the world to profess their acceptance of the twin ideas of the movement —that rights should be protected according to international standards and that governments should be concerned in their foreign policies with abuses of rights by other governments. That is no small achievement for a movement that is barely four decades old and that confronts so monumental a task on a global scale. Maintaining and building upon the momentum that the movement acquired in its struggle against the Reagan administration is necessary for more to be achieved.

NOTES

1. "Transcript of President's News Conference on Foreign and Domestic Matters," *New York Times*, July 22, 1983.

2. Article 55.

3. Article 56.

4. Article 4(a).

5. Article 7(a)(ii).

6. An example of a prison case in which a court did take guidance from the Standard Minimum Rules is Lareau v. Manson, 507 F. Supp. 1177, 1187n. 9 (D. Conn. 1980), *aff'd in rel. part* 651 F.2d 96 (2d Cir. 1981).

7. The Paquete Habana, 175 U.S. 677, 700 (1900).

8. 28 U.S.C. S 1350.

9. 630 F.2d 876 (2nd Cir. 1980).

10. *Id.* at 884.

11. PL 93-559, Sec. 46.

12. §502B, 22 U.S.C. §2304 (Supp. II 1978).

13. 22 U.S.C. §2151 note (Supp. II 1978).

14. 22 U.S.C. §262d (Supp. II 1978).

15. PL 97-113.

16. *Id.*

17. *Id.*, §725(c).

18. *Id.*, §726(b).

19. *Id.*, §724(b).

20. Foreign Assistance Act of 1961, §620E.

21. Trade Act of 1974, §409.

22. Foreign Assistance Act of 1961, §624(f).

23. *Id.*, §116(d).

24. The compilation of the first volume of country reports was undertaken in 1976, the last year of the Ford administration. However, in compliance with the law, it was published in February 1977, two weeks after the Carter administration took office.

25. Jeane Kirkpatrick, "U.S. Security & Latin America," *Commentary* vol. 71, no. 1 at 36 (January 1981).

26. Memorandum for the Secretary From the Deputy Secretary, October 27, 1981, "The Appointment of Elliott Abrams to Human Rights Bureau and Reinvigoration of Human Rights Policy." Excerpts were published in the *New York Times*, November 5, 1981.

27. *See* note 15 *supra.*

28. International Security and Development Cooperation Act of 1981, PL 97-113, §725, and §726.

AN HISTORICAL PERSPECTIVE ON CRISES IN CIVIL LIBERTIES

STANLEY N. KATZ

Stanley N. Katz is Class of 1921 Bicentennial Professor of the History of American Law and Liberty at Princeton University, and a specialist in American legal and constitutional history. He is the coeditor of the Oliver Wendell Holmes Devise History of the United States Supreme Court.

Is it true that our rights are endangered? Are our rights more at risk now than at other points in American history? By whom are our rights endangered? Are there new kinds of risks? What are our rights?

These are some of the sorts of questions the historian must pose in evaluating the status of civil liberties over the past fifteen years. They do not admit of easy answers, nor can they be answered absolutely, since for the historian the story of the past is the study of change over time.

Readers of the preceeding essays in this volume will therefore note some dissonance here: civil libertarians tend to be absolutists and historians tend to be relativists. I hope to show, however, that the difference is really only one of perspective and context. The character of civil liberties crises has changed throughout American history, and even over the course of this century. The range of constitutionally protected freedoms has expanded rapidly, and the meaning of traditional freedoms has altered as society has changed over time. Our rights *are* endangered, but in ways that must be understood in historical perspective. It will help if we start at the beginning.

In the beginning was the American Revolution, and it was in the revolutionary era that basic attitudes were formed with respect to the relations of the individual and the state. The Revolution was, of course, a struggle of states for independence from a despotic imperial government, but the threat to liberty was perceived as being based upon the persecution of individuals: "give me liberty or give me death"; "live free or die."

Colonial Americans conceived of themselves as republicans; that is, they believed that the state was nothing more than the sum of its citizens. The people themselves were sovereign. It is hard to recapture the extent to which this notion of popular sovereignty was genuinely a revolutionary idea in the eighteenth century, but it surely was. One has to imagine the long religious and secular tradition emerging out of the Middle Ages in which both legitimacy and power flowed from above, from outside of society—from God and the monarch—to see how difficult it was to imagine legitimacy flowing from below, from the people themselves. For the republican, that is to say, the state is merely an artifact, serving only to effectuate those purposes specifically assigned to it by the sovereign people. No longer is the state an expression of royal or divine will, serving purposes that are defined historically and arbitrarily by the sovereign ruler.

The American Revolution was thus a genuine upheaval in political theory: it created the modern republican notion of the state and of government. There are two basic aspects of the new conception. On the one hand, the state is ultimately responsible to the will of the majority. On the other hand, the power of the state is strictly limited, no matter what the will of the majority, according to the nonmajoritarian precepts of a constitutional structure. Modern constitutionalism thus specifies that the constitution is framework law which designates the powers and responsibilities of the state, and sets limits beyond which the government may not go. It is clear why such a system appealed to a generation that perceived itself to be literally enslaved to a despotic foreign and arbitrary state.

Constitutionalism was the basic contribution of the Framers, although of course they were also centralizers, reacting against the inefficiency of the Articles of Confederation government and attempting to create a state powerful enough to insure the prosperity and survival of the new nation. Those Americans who opposed the 1787 Constitution, the so-called Anti-Federalists, had two objections to the form of the proposed state: it was too centralized and it was too powerful. The very concept of federalism (the division of power between the national government and the governments of the several states) was intended to answer the first objection; there was nothing the Anti-Federalists could do politically to change the basic structure of the new government, although they created an underlying suspicion of centralized power, which forms a dominant subtheme of American politics to this day. To the second objection, however, the dominant Federalist party was forced to make a practical response—the Bill of Rights. The essence of the Bill of Rights is the specification of limitations on the power of the national government with respect to the claims of state governments and individuals.

In forging the initial amendments in the Constitution, the First Congress created the environment out of which civil libertarianism would grow. In its earliest form, "civil liberties" was synonymous with republicanism, or the sense that the state, no matter how well constructed, could not be trusted to respect individual freedom. The purpose of republican politics was to permit individual citizens freely to express themselves. The people were intended to cultivate private virtue, which republicans defined as the instinct to prefer the welfare of the whole to individual aggrandizement. In a republican state, therefore, everything depended upon the encouragement of the individual's freedom to do good and the limitation of the state to the effectuation of the common good.

> The fundamental goal of the American Revolution had been a government of laws and not of men: freedom in the eighteenth-century sense of the security of every individual in his property and rights. From the beginning, nearly everyone agreed that liberty depended on consent, but few had ever thought that liberty could be secure in states in which the people or their most immediate representatives were given full control. Few had imagined that republican ideals entailed a democratic government in anything approaching the modern usage of that phrase.[1]

It was a demanding (and in the end unrealistic) program, and what has survived is the constitutional structure originally intended to realize eighteenth-century republicanism.

While the basic form of the constitutional system was thus established in the late eighteenth century, the actual conduct of government would fundamentally influence the system. Of the new practices, perhaps the most important was the establishment of judicial review, or the power of the federal Supreme Court to determine the constitutionality of executive and legislative behavior. Judicial review was probably not contemplated by the Framers, and as practiced by the Marshall Court it served to legitimate the pretensions of the central government, but it also created the basic mechanism by which governmental incursions on constitutionally protected liberties could be brought under the inspection of the federal judiciary. Throughout most of American history, constitutional litigation has been the primary resort of those who seek to protect and expand civil liberties, especially in those times of popular conflict when democracy itself seems at odds with liberty. Litigation is a peculiarly American political technique, but as we shall see, it has built-in limitations.

It is perhaps unnecessary to comment that the eighteenth-century sense of the range of human freedom, as recapitulated in the Bill of Rights, was highly restrictive by modern standards. The generation of the Framers retained a medieval notion of social hierarchy according to which rights could appropriately be proportionate to status. Although the revolutionaries employed universalistic language, they viewed the world through myopic social lenses. "All men" may have been created "equal" in some ideal world, but not in the United States of 1776–1787. The term "slavery" is nowhere specifically mentioned in the Constitution, but the institution of slavery is implicitly protected at several points in the document. The original Constitution was designed to preserve the liberty only of those who were conceived to be legitimate members of the political community—for the most part, property-owning white males.

This was one reason why it was necessary to fight a Civil War. The war not only ratified the principle of federalism (rejecting the notion that the nation was really a confederation of states), but it also gave birth to the notion that the political community comprehended *all* Americans. The Reconstruction Amendments thus rejected the institution of chattel slavery, guaranteed equal protection of the laws to all Americans, and confirmed the right of all citizens to participate in the electoral process. The Thirteenth, Fourteenth and Fifteenth Amendments (1865, 1868, 1870) made equality a constitutional value for the first time.

The post–Civil War Constitution therefore carried dramatically new political implications. As I have already suggested, the 1787 Constitution was based upon republican rather than democratic premises. It presumed a polity of the virtuous in a society which associated political virtue with male, property-holding heads of families. The post-1870 Constitution, on the other hand, was based upon liberal democratic premises. It presumed a polity of independent individuals freely competing in the political marketplace. Equality was now a protected value, primarily as an opportunity to participate more or less freely in the society and to enjoy the products of one's labors. Equality of opportunity was the entitlement of a *laissez-faire* society; equality of results was not at issue. From this point of view, the Supreme Court of the late nineteenth century was not reversing the results of the Civil War. Rather, it was fleshing out the constitutional implications of the struggle in terms that were consistent with general social attitudes of the time. Civil liberty in the heyday of liberalism was primarily the freedom to participate and compete. Government was openly accepted as a partner in the enterprise of developing the economic nation, although by the last quarter of the century many Americans had become sensitized to the political dangers of large concentrations of power, whether public or private.

The dawning of the twentieth century brought with it a new political consciousness, out of which arose a distinctively modern civil liberties movement. Historians speak of this period as the Progressive Era, and mean by that an age in which a greatly expanded political community became committed to distributional justice and sophisticated about the implications of governmental power. It was not a movement against government, although it drew on the sensitivity of the republican tradition to the continuing potential for governmental abuse of individual freedom; indeed, the Progressives were eager to employ governmental power in behalf of the commonweal. Both at the state and national levels, they supported the use of executive and legislative power to protect the less powerful in society (especially women and children), to conserve the environment, and in general to broaden the participation of Americans in the tangible benefits of an increasingly wealthy and powerful society. Equality took on a new meaning as demographic heterogeneity transformed the texture of American society and as cultural diversity became the norm rather than the exception. For all of this, the post–Civil War constitutional structure seemed to serve well, when suffused with democratic values.

The first twentieth century crisis of civil liberties coincided with the coming of the First World War. The story is familiar enough. The United States, under the guidance of one of the greatest of the liberal democratic presidents, Woodrow Wilson, entered into a war ostensibly dedicated to making the world safe for democracy. Waging a modern war required, however, a massive coordination of government and the private sector to mobilize the human and material resources of the nation for the European conflict. The effort required conformity of a sort which does not come naturally to Americans, but which the otherwise liberal Wilson was prepared to coerce. Patriotism was demanded, and the federal government (with the ready consent of the Congress) stood ready to force compliance with its wishes. Freedom of thought and of political action were at issue, and the new public policy of political conformity struck at both traditional American republican instincts and newer pluralistic tendencies. State power, exercised in behalf of majority political preferences, overwhelmed individual dissent—the classic form of modern civil libertarian crisis.

It was in the context of World War I repression that the National Civil Liberties Bureau (precursor of the American Civil Liberties Union) emerged out of the peace-oriented American Union Against Militarism. Its original (and long-term) leader, Roger Baldwin, was a typical Progressive: a social worker of well-to-do origin, a Harvard man who worked on probation reform, a convert to the peace movement. As Paul Murphy has pointed out, Baldwin and the Progressive civil libertarians viewed political oppression as only one of several threats to individual freedom in America:

> . . . the road ahead had to involve not only breaking federal power but breaking the stranglehold of private power on millions of vulnerable Americans as well. They hoped to be able to make it more difficult for private power to use informal controls to suppress those "have-nots" in American society who had to be able to manage their own destiny if they were ever to achieve any improvement of their economic or political condition.[2]

On the practical and political level, the newly emerged civil liberties movement was a failure. Wartime repression by the federal government continued unabated; the Supreme Court refused to strike down antilibertarian Wilson programs; A. Mitchell Palmer and the Justice Department carried out their disastrously effective campaign against foreigners and radicals in the years immediately after the war.

On a less tangible level, however, Baldwin and his associates succeeded in planting the seeds of a civil libertarian philosophy in the nation: they abstracted and dramatized civil liberties as an issue. Even progovernment decisions of the Supreme Court, especially when accompanied by the eloquent dissents of Justices Holmes and Brandeis, sensitized portions of the population to the idea that the defense of individual political freedom was an issue in itself. This was particularly true at a time when the demands of war and the requirements of a new industrial order were rapidly increasing the scope of federal government and solidifying its ties with big business. The individual thus seemed threatened both by government and by private corporatism, at least until the economic boom of the mid-1920s spread so much wealth and optimism throughout the society that most Americans forgot the anxiety for freedom that had begun to generate social stress at the beginning of the century.

The euphoria of the Jazz Age did not last long. The 1930s and 1940s brought with them some of the most rapid and profound social change since the Civil War, as war followed hard upon depression. The New Deal transformed the American polity: the interventionist tendencies of the Progressive Era were sharpened as Franklin D. Roosevelt, openly attempting to set national social and economic policy, coaxed from a frightened Congress the delegated power necessary to provide federal executive direction for many of the ordinary tasks of American life. In retrospect, government intervention was not nearly so profound as the rhetoric of the period (both pro and con) suggested, but there is no mistaking the fact that the New Deal succeeded in legitimizing "big" government and constituted the entering wedge of the welfare state.

But, at just the time when the efficacy of New Deal nostrums was challenged by the persistence of economic disorder, another war for democracy emerged to energize the economy, intensify democratic political theory, and heal most of the open wounds in the body politic. Like World War I, the new war necessitated an enormous expansion of federal government power, and temporarily unified the forces of public and private corporatism. The specter of foreign fascism served to unify most of the population in support of war policy (to an extent that far surpassed consent to Wilson's war). The peace movement did not survive Pearl Harbor. Further, government repression of dissent seemed to most Americans justifiable, even when it extended to the forcible relocation of large numbers of American citizens of Japanese extraction on the West Coast. Things changed rapidly after the war. International libertarianism was the spirit of the war years, and it found a fitting culmination in the creation of the United Nations and the promulgation of the UN Charter. Many of the social effects of the war were themselves democratizing: the economy recovered triumphantly, and wealth was spread more widely; massive black migration from the South to the sites of northern war industry, and large-scale black participation in the military effort, contributed to the process of deregionalizing the national race problem; the armed forces were desegregated in 1948; the GI Bill sent more Americans to college than had ever previously received higher education. The domestic prospects for liberty and democracy were bright in the late 1940s.

But once again the end of wartime and commitment and unity seemed to lead inexorably to a civil liberties crisis. The Manicheanism of cold war conflict coincided with a characteristic peacetime reactionary surge to produce McCarthyism, the second twentieth-century civil liberties crisis. Conformity to stereotypical patterns of Americanism once again led to public and private repression of dissent and deviance, this time exacerbated by the entry of the United States into the ideologically charged Korean War. In many respects, McCarthyism reproduced the structure of the Wilsonian civil liberties crisis. Individuals were persecuted for their political beliefs and actions, and xenophobia reappeared. The difference was one of scale, for in the late 1940s and early 1950s practically the entire federal bureaucracy was implicated in repression, and the private sector cooperated more fully. Fear for individual rights was thus much more generally spread throughout the society, and rightly so, for the threat was genuine. Ironically, however, at the same time that political rights were endangered, litigation and legislation began to provide dissenters and minority groups with more equal access to political and economic opportunity.

By the mid-1950s truly important social change began to gain momentum in the United States. The source was unexpected and ironic—the Warren Court. Beginning with the *Brown v. Board of Education* decisions in 1954 and 1955, the Court employed its creative (some would say legislative) power to bring to life the latent potential of the Reconstruction Amendments to the Constitution. The Warren Court rendered equality a functional constitutional value. In so doing, it gave hope to political minorities of all kinds that they could achieve in the courts what they could never have achieved at the polls. From the time of the Greensboro sit-ins in 1960, blacks and white civil libertarians had a new and realistic agenda as the Supreme Court sketched out a map of fresh legal and constitutional possibilities.

In a sense, the 1960s began as the legitimation of the most idealistic aspects of the New Deal. New political leadership emerged, new groups entered the political process, while government at all levels committed itself to Progressive goals and availed itself of modern interventionist techniques. Law became a radical, nearly revolutionary force, and youthful idealism set a seemingly practicable agenda for the entire society: "we shall overcome" was an order, not a prayer. Lyndon Johnson's Great Society, made possible in part by the sacrifice of Martin Luther King and the Kennedy brothers, was the supreme effort to legislate what the Court had led liberals to believe might be achievable in America. The United States could provide food and freedom for all.

Or so it seemed until 1965, when it became clear that the Great Society could not produce both guns and butter, and that the Great Society warriors were no more sympathetic to foreign-policy dissent than the Wilsonians. Idealism turned to disillusionment, Gandhian political action to domestic violence; imperialism reappeared as the keynote to American public policy. These tensions and contradictions produced the election of Richard M. Nixon, and a government commitment to withdraw from the objectives of Johnson's Great Society. The Nixon administration did not in fact reduce the size or pretensions of national government, but it certainly did reorient the thrust of federal programs. Most threatening, from a civil liberties point of view, Nixon was able to replace four members of the Warren Court. These events, along with the Johnson-initiated persecution of draft resisters and war opponents, created the third civil liberties crisis of the century.

This crisis now appears quite different from what it seemed to be at the time. It now appears probable that the Great Society attempted too much too quickly, and that Johnson's New Deal enthusiasm outran his political base. It also seems likely that the prospects for progressive constitutional change were overestimated—that constitutional litigation could not continue to reshape the values and behavior of the society as it had so stunningly in the 1960s. The nation was not prepared for continuation of egalitarianism, at least not at the rate of the previous decade.

Watergate and the events leading to Nixon's resignation in 1974 thus represent the culmination of the civil liberties crisis that began (in the fashion of all modern civil liberties crises) with government repression of dissent during the Vietnam War. The Nixon election was more a reaction to disorder, dissent, and domestic uncertainty than a statement of ideological conservatism. The message of 1972, in particular, was that the country was tired of social experimentation and impatient with individual eccentricity. The administration responded with a centralization of national power and a disregard for legal and constitutional limitations on the federal government, initiating the series of events which ultimately led to the revelations of the Watergate scandal. It was only with the congressional investigations of Watergate that Americans became aware of just how endangered their rights had been, and yet the post-1974 response has been one of satisfaction that "the system" worked well enough to prevent governmental tyranny and to change the administration in an orderly fashion. The more important point would be to notice how close we came to precisely the sort of abuse of central political power our Revolutionary forebears feared. The crisis of the late 1960s and early 1970s shifted from the "normal" pathology of governmental victimization of individual dissenters to a generalized attempt by the federal government to enforce centrally defined norms of behavior.

This most recent crisis was thus perceptibly different from earlier ones, not least in its resolution by the near-impeachment of the president. We must not congratulate ourselves that constitutional mechanisms resolved the crisis; neither should we forget that the larger context of civil liberties had expanded dramatically by 1974. The Constitution had been significantly extended by the Warren Court, so that more people could be afforded a wider range of rights than at any previous time in American history. In part, this continues to be the case because the Supreme Court (despite four Nixon appointments and one by Reagan) has not succeeded in rolling back the substantive innovations of the Warren Court. Several of the preceding essays (note especially Days and Rudovsky) acknowledge as much, and Paul Bender contends that the new constitutional law of privacy is largely a creation of Burger Court decisions. There have been ominous hints that the Court may do away with the Fourth Amendment exclusionary rule or radically limit affirmative action or abortion rights, but so far the Court has stood reasonably firm.

The third civil liberties crisis of the twentieth century coincided with a crucial turning point in American history, the emergence of what Lester Thurow has called the "zero sum" society. Ever since the announcement of the closing of the frontier in 1890, Americans have been at least sporadically aware of the significance and precariousness of our natural resources. It was this sensitivity which propelled the conservation movement of the Progressive Era and which stimulated several New Deal programs. But the coming of the atomic age, the emergence of modern environmentalism, and such traumatic political events as the oil embargo of 1974 compelled a much more widespread acceptance of the finiteness of American resources and, by extension, of the immediate limitations on national power.

The realization of the finiteness of resources was political as well as economic. Just as in the material world, it became apparent that if the sum total of resources was fixed one person's political gain was another's loss. The Great Society (and Earl Warren's constitutional politics) were predicated on the assumption that the infinite was achievable; by the first Nixon administration the thought seemed naive and refutable. The consequences for civil rights were profound, and for three reasons.

First, by the mid-1960s it seemed possible that the Warren Court revolution had gone about as far as it could logically (or at least easily) go. The Court had taken the revolutionary step of constitutionalizing equality, and the Court and the Congress (by 1965) had gone a long way toward erecting barriers to legalized, formal inequality. Constitutional law could be, we learned, an effective antidote to legal discrimination—but it began to appear that litigation was not nearly so effective in combating the private, informal and less visible forms of inequality.

Second, as Martin Luther King realized toward the end of his life, Supreme Court decisions and district court orders cannot by themselves house the homeless, employ the jobless, or put food on the tables of the underfed members of society. Economic equality (or at least the mitigation of economic-class distinctions) is necessary to human dignity, and to the enjoyment of formal rights.

Third, in the context of Warren Court decisions, the prohibition of discrimination and other forms of unconstitutional behavior is reasonably clear-cut, but the construction of politically feasible remedies is not. The de facto segregation of northern public schools can be declared a violation of the Constitution, but what is to be done about it? The solutions have not proved to be as straightforward as those for de jure segregation in southern communities. Or take the case of racial (or gender) discrimination in employment. Even if courts determine what constitutes proof of such constitutional violation, how do they remedy the problem?

And here, of course, is where the zero sum revolution works directly against the extension of civil liberties, for in employment or schooling (or most other constitutionally contested areas), one person's remedy seems very much like another person's deprivation. If there are an infinite number of jobs, or places in medical school, or whatever, then affirmative action works no harm in the long run. In the context of limited social resources, however, affirmative action is understandably threatening to established social groups. So it is the combination of these three factors that creates the modern problem for civil liberties: the need for new conceptual strategies; the nexus between civil and economic rights; and the difficulty of creating socially and politically acceptable remedial techniques.

The sources of current civil libertarian unease are not entirely clear, although the essays in this volume clarify the wide range of problems which manifestly exists. Perhaps the point that the historian can most usefully make is that the ideological character of the Reagan administration has obvious historical roots. Contemporary Reaganism is not far from the liberal populism of Jimmy Carter, with its emphasis on individualism and on the decentralization of power. It is in fact a deliberate and clever throwback to revolutionary American republicanism, stressing individual virtue, warning of the potential corruption and despotism of powerful government, and specifying dispersal of power as the antidote to governmental threats to individual liberty. Reaganism is conservative (in the modern sense) insofar as it uses the classical liberalism inherent in republican rhetoric to prefer established social groups and to fend off change, but we must recognize that part of its appeal (to blue collar workers, for instance) is that it strikes a deeply responsive chord in the American political psyche.

For civil libertarians, the problem is how to respond to libertarianism (our new name for classical liberalism). The authors of this volume are insistent (notice particularly John Shattuck and Sylvia Law) upon the notion that the most important current threat to civil liberties is executive (and, secondarily, legislative) and that our response must be political. They point out the deliberate refusal of the administration to enforce civil rights law and its attempts (through the Department of Justice and the solicitor general) to redefine the meaning of traditional civil rights law. They criticize the attempts of conservative legislators to restrict the jurisdiction of federal courts and to legislate fundamentalist morality. These are all deliberate efforts to coerce individual behavior and to limit the power of the courts to intervene in favor of liberal freedoms, but at the same time many of these antiliberal crusades are waged in the name of a differently defined individual freedom. They appeal to those Americans who have themselves felt coerced by the New Deal and the Great Society. One of the things that Reaganism tells us is that government intervention in the name of liberty can be antilibertarian, and that if we want to justify such interventionism we shall have to go beyond the traditional (and politically ambiguous) language of civil libertarianism. Classical republicanism, like classical liberalism, cuts both ways.

From a historical perspective, the civil libertarian faith that we can articulate, litigate, and legislate a clearly agreed-upon slate of civil liberties norms is no longer plausible. Part of the reason for this dilemma is that Roger Baldwin and his successors succeeded in their task. We are to some extent victims of a revolution of rising civil rights expectations. One result of the incorporation of the Bill of Rights into the Fourteenth Amendment and the dramatic intrusion of egalitarianism by the Warren Court is that the range of actual and potential civil rights has expanded exponentially. We have also (as Sylvia Law urges) begun to understand the link between civil justice and economic justice, and in so doing have reached the realization that litigation can have only a marginal utility in achieving socioeconomic equality. And, of course, having reached this point we have necessarily destroyed the "traditional" (that is, New Deal) civil liberties coalition in politics. Groups that could agree on generalized protections for individual rights diverge sharply on socioeconomic agendas.

We can continue, as the ACLU has always done, to collaborate in litigation and lobbying on behalf of newly traditional legal norms of civil liberty. Constitutional expansion is not at an end, and in any case, eternal vigilance is indeed the price of freedom. But we cannot, without a new conceptualization of civil liberties, effectuate the broader program suggested by the post-1960 expansion of republican thought. How to do that within the practical realities of liberal politics is the challenge to the next generation of civil libertarians.

NOTES

1. Lance Banning, *The Jeffersonian Persuasion* 89 (1978).
2. Paul Murphy, *World War I and the Origin of Civil Liberties in the United States* 265 (1979).

INDEX

ABOUT THE EDITOR

Norman Dorsen is president of the American Civil Liberties Union and Stokes Professor of Law at New York University Law School, where he also is codirector of the Arthur Garfield Hays Civil Liberties Program. An honors graduate of Harvard Law School, he served as an assistant to Joseph Welch during the Army-McCarthy Hearings and as law clerk to Supreme Court Justice John Marshall Harlan. Professor Dorsen has argued many constitutional cases in the Supreme Court and is the author or editor of *Frontiers of Civil Liberties* (Pantheon, 1968), *The Rights of Americans* (Pantheon, 1971), *Disorder in the Court* (Pantheon, 1973), and the two-volume work *Political and Civil Rights in the United States* (Little, Brown, 1976 and 1979). He served as president of the Society of American Law Teachers from 1973 to 1975.